LIEUTENANT-GENERAL SIR G. M. HARPER, K.C.B., D.S O.

THE HISTORY OF THE FIFTY FIRST (HIGHLAND) DIVISION

1914 – 1918

By
MAJOR F. W. BEWSHER D.S.O., M.C.

PUBLISHED BY
THE NAVAL & MILITARY PRESS

Dedicated

TO THE YOUTH OF SCOTLAND,

In the hope that this record of the courage, skill, and endurance of a Highland Division may strengthen their purpose, when their time comes, to uphold in no lesser degree the great traditions of their forebears.

FOREWORD.

IF it were possible for the General who for three years commanded all the British Divisions in France, and was served with equal gallantry, devotion, and success by each, to admit a predilection for any of them, my affection would naturally turn to the Division that drew so many of its recruits from the same part of Scotland where my boyhood was spent and my own people lived. Those who read the pages of this book will find therein a tale of patient endeavour and glorious achievement of which I claim a good right to be as proud as any of my fellow-countrymen. The 51st Division does not need to boast of its prowess or its record. It can point to the story of its deeds, plainly and simply told, and leave the world to judge.

HAIG
OF BEMERSYDE,
F.M.

8th August 1920.

PREFACE.

In compiling the 'History of the 51st (Highland) Division' I have been beset by various difficulties, which have contributed towards the long delay in its publication.

In the first place, it has been written in circumstances in which military duties have afforded little leisure for continuous effort; secondly, the work has been carried out in many places, most of them highly unsuitable for research, such as the desert of Sinai, native villages and the deserts of Lower Egypt, Jerusalem, Bir Salem, and at sea.

Not only had the difficulty of transporting from station to station the large mass of available material to be overcome, but also the conditions of life in huts and under canvas in an eastern climate are seldom conducive to clear and consecutive thinking.

Further, the material available has been unequal. Up to the conclusion of the battle of Arras, no completed narratives of the operations carried out by the Division were compiled. To this point, therefore, the only resources were the bald and rather incomplete entries in the official war diaries and personal diaries, which threw little light on the operations in their broader aspects.

From the third battle of Ypres onwards a detailed account of all engagements was published by Divisional Headquarters shortly after the conclusion of each operation. These have rendered the compiling of the 'History' from this point considerably less laborious, and have allowed it to be carried out in greater and more accurate detail.

It has been necessary, owing to the increased and increasing cost of production, to keep the size of this book within certain bounds, and to reduce as far as possible the number of maps. On this account there has been no alternative but to restrict the detail in which actions are described. It is regretted that in consequence much material which officers and men of the Division and their relatives have submitted, often at my request, has been necessarily omitted.

It was only thus that the book could be kept sufficiently reduced in size to prevent its price prohibiting the circulation desired.

The 'History' is now presented with every consciousness on the part of the author that full justice has not been done to its great subject. Indeed, it is doubtful if full justice can be done to the part played by the British Army in the Great War until a generation not intimately involved in it has arisen and has come to regard the burdens sustained for over four years by the British soldier in the true perspective.

My thanks are due to all those who have assisted me in the compilation of this work by the loan of diaries, maps, documents, &c., and in particular to Lieut.-General Sir G. M. Harper, K.C.B., D.S.O.; Major-General R. Bannatine-Allason, C.B.; Brigadier-General L. Oldfield, C.B., C.M.G., D.S.O.; and Colonel Ian Stewart, C.M.G., D.S.O.

General Bannatine-Allason kindly wrote for me the first chapter, and spared himself no pains in assisting to procure for me information concerning the early days of the Division in France. Had it not been for him and Colonel Ian Stewart, information would have been so scanty that it is doubtful if the earlier chapters could have been written.

To Captain A. Scott, D.S.O., M.C., 7th Argyll and Sutherland Highlanders, late staff-captain 154th Infantry Brigade, I am particularly indebted. Captain Scott has kindly relieved me of the labour of reading through the proofs and of completing the final arrangements for the publication of this book, a labour which residence in the Near East would have made it difficult for me to perform.

Lastly, I am indebted to Mr James Blackwood, in no small degree, for taking upon himself, while I have been abroad, much of the burden of the preparation of this book for the Press, which would normally have fallen upon the author.

F. W. B.

HEADQUARTERS, 3RD (LAHORE) DIVISION,
   BIR SALEM, PALESTINE.

CONTENTS.

CHAP.		PAGE
I.	MOBILISATION	1
II.	ARRIVAL IN FRANCE—FESTUBERT . . .	10
III.	THE PERIOD OF APPRENTICESHIP . . .	28
IV.	TRAINING AND REORGANISATION—THE LABYRINTH	51
V.	THE BATTLE OF THE SOMME—HIGH WOOD .	73
VI.	ARMENTIÈRES AND HEBUTERNE . . .	87
VII.	THE BATTLE OF THE ANCRE—BEAUMONT HAMEL	100
VIII.	COURCELETTE	127
IX.	THE BATTLE OF ARRAS	138
X.	THE BATTLE OF ARRAS (*Contd.*)—ROEUX AND THE CHEMICAL WORKS	160
XI.	THE THIRD BATTLE OF YPRES . . .	192
XII.	POELCAPPELLE	216
XIII.	THE BATTLE OF CAMBRAI	233
XIV.	THE GERMAN OFFENSIVE	263
XV.	THE GERMAN OFFENSIVE (*Contd.*)—THE BATTLE OF THE LYS	296
XVI.	WITH THE FRENCH IN CHAMPAGNE . .	321
XVII.	THE CAPTURE OF GREENLAND HILL . .	356
XVIII.	THE OPERATIONS TOWARDS VALENCIENNES .	372
XIX.	CONCLUSION	408

VCs

Sgt W. Gosling RFA HTTRB ?/?/??
Pte G.I. McIntosh 1/6 Gordons 31/7/17 120?
Sgt A. Edwards 1/6 Seaforth H ?/?/?? ?
L.Cpl R. ?? 1/5 Seaforth 20/?/?
Sgt J. Meikle 1/4 Seaforth H 20/7/18
Lt W.D. ?? ?? ?? ?? 25/?/18

ILLUSTRATIONS.

PORTRAITS.

LIEUTENANT - GENERAL SIR G. M. HARPER, K.C.B., D.S.O.	*Frontispiece*
MAJOR-GENERAL R. BANNATINE-ALLASON, C.B.	*Facing p.* 46
T/MAJOR-GENERAL G. T. C. CARTER-CAMPBELL, C.B., D.S.O.	,, 274

MAPS.

I. ATTACK NEAR FESTUBERT, 15TH JUNE 1915.	,,	18
II. HIGH WOOD, JULY 1916	,,	74
III. BEAUMONT HAMEL, 13TH NOVEMBER 1916	,,	114
IV. CAPTURE OF VIMY RIDGE, 9TH APRIL 1917	,,	150
V. THE CHEMICAL WORKS, ROEUX	,,	162

ILLUSTRATIONS

VI. THIRD BATTLE OF YPRES: ADVANCE TO THE STEENBEEK, 31ST JULY 1917 . . . . . *Facing p.* 200

VII. POELCAPPELLE, 20TH SEPTEMBER 1917 ,, 222

VIII. THE BATTLE OF CAMBRAI: POSITION AT 7 P.M., 21ST NOVEMBER 1917 . ,, 252

IX. THE GERMAN OFFENSIVE: DISPOSITION OF 51ST (HIGHLAND) DIVISION, MORNING, 21ST MARCH 1918 . ,, 274

X. THE GERMAN OFFENSIVE: POSITIONS OF 51ST (HIGHLAND) DIVISION, 24-26TH MARCH 1918 . . ,, 292

XI. THE GERMAN OFFENSIVE. (THE BATTLE OF THE RIVER LAWE): DISPOSITIONS OF 51ST (HIGHLAND) DIVISION, DAWN, 12TH APRIL 1918 . ,, 310

XII. THE COUNTER-ATTACK IN CHAMPAGNE: THE ADVANCE ON 27TH AND 28TH JULY 1918 . . . . ,, 330

XIII. THE FINAL ADVANCE: DISPOSITIONS OF 51ST (HIGHLAND) DIVISION, 5 P.M., 28TH OCTOBER 1918 . ,, 402

The History of the 51st (Highland) Division.

CHAPTER I.

MOBILISATION.

(By Major-General R. BANNATINE-ALLASON, C.B.)

THE Highland Division arrived at its War Station, Bedford, about 15th August 1914, and was billeted in and near that town. The farthest off unit was the 1st Highland Brigade R.F.A., which was at St Neots. The billeting had been previously arranged, with a view, as far as possible, to training facilities.

The units were, many of them, considerably below strength, and, generally speaking, horses and transport (locally acquired in Scotland) inferior in quality, though many animals actually went overseas and did good work.

The Division moved under General Colin Mackenzie, but he was almost immediately transferred to command a New Army Division, and Major-General Bannatine-Allason took over about the 24th August. The Division, having been scattered over the north of Scotland, would and did naturally benefit by concentration, and the work of Divisional and other staffs immediately began to make itself felt. The movement to Bedford was extremely well managed, and gave a foretaste of the good staff work which was to follow.

The country round Bedford can only be called a moderate training-ground for the larger units. The absence of ranges, the particularly obnoxious clay soil, and generally small enclosures were obstacles to overcome. Ranges were at once commenced; but two sites, which were under water in winter, required a lot of pumping to make them serviceable. As a matter of fact, the Division was never really abreast with the necessary musketry training, though, owing to the excellent work of the Divisional sappers, particularly of their Adjutant, Captain Wedd, and to the really strenuous efforts of the units themselves, it is possible, even probable, that the Division left for France with average "Territorial" efficiency in this respect. Shortage of ammunition was, of course, common to all.

It may be guessed that the arrival in the peaceful city of Bedford of 20,000 Highlanders would occasion some sensation, if not misgivings, in minds of the local authorities and townspeople. Be that as it may, it must be recorded that the best feeling soon became pronounced between the troops and the inhabitants; and, as will be shown later, the Highland Division left Bedford with the blessing of the "City Fathers."

Very naturally some at least of the people benefited considerably by the invasion, but, generally speaking, the Division was treated with the greatest kindness, and the survivors of those times will ever be grateful for the generosity and helpfulness accorded. It may be invidious to mention names, but when it is said that the "Chief Citizen," then Mr Browning, set the example, the great majority of the people very naturally followed suit. The Entertainment Committee—chairman, Mr Henry Tebbs, with its secretary, Mr Machin, himself a born organiser—was a boon to every man. To them, assisted by hundreds of ladies and gentlemen, was due the New Year's dinner (appropriate to Scotsmen), the Highland games, and innumerable concerts and other entertainments which materially helped to enliven the few spare moments of a strenuous existence. The clergy of all denominations gave over their churches; schools were given up for hospitals; V.A.D. women vied with each other in helping in the field ambulances. Each field ambulance was opened out for training purposes as well as for care of the sick.

A Mrs Thomson was the first V.A.D. worker, and took charge at once of our reception hospital with much success. The G.O.C. was glad to be able to help to obtain some recognition of her good work.

The police, both town and county, were ever sympathetic; and Major Stevens, Chief Constable of Bedfordshire, laid himself out to smooth out rough ground—in fact, he was a sort of voluntary chief A.P.M. and police adviser to the G.O.C.

The Division kept New Year's "nicht," much to the amusement of the people. Dinners were given at most messes, reels were danced in the market square at midnight, in which, it was said, the Chief Constable assisted. Then "Auld Lang Syne" was sung, and the men of various units played to their billets by their pipers. The whole proceeding was most orderly, and witnessed by many of the leading townspeople in evening dress, while the men were under complete control by the A.P.M.

A swimming-bath—with hot and cold water—was started for the men of the Division, the ground being given by the Midland Railway. The bath was opened with much ceremony, and the little daughter of the Town Clerk (Mr Stimson) gallantly took the first "header" into the tepid water. She was presented at the time with a box of chocolates, but later with a gold watch with a suitable inscription from the Highland Division, which may serve in after life to remind her of her connection with that now rather celebrated fighting unit.

There were, of course, some amusing incidents connected with our stay at Bedford. On one occasion some one wrote to the papers complaining of the behaviour of certain training divisions. His Majesty inquired, through his private secretary, about the Highland Division. The G.O.C. was able to reply, after consultations with the local authorities, that there was far less crime in Bedford than in ordinary times of peace. On this his Majesty was pleased to congratulate the Highlanders on their exemplary behaviour.

To show the sort of feeling existing in the town many stories might be told. But the following rather pathetic one is an example of the many acts of kindness, some anonymous, that actually occurred. During the severe epidemic of measles the G.O.C. was visiting one of the hospitals, and seeing a poor man inside the gates and sentries, asked what business brought him there. The man replied, "I am a working man, but I saw in the papers that the hospitals wanted fruit, so I bring a few oranges twice a week."

It is quite natural that imaginary evils were invented by outsiders, and the work of the staff unnecessarily increased. But at that time, the beginning of the war, every one wanted to do something, sometimes for personal advertisement, sometimes to obtain congenial occupation. Two instances may be quoted. Some one, it doesn't matter who, discovered that the water supply of the town came from the river, and that the health of the troops must suffer from some imaginary germ. It was useless for the G.O.C., the Mayor, the Medical Officers of Health, and others to protest that the people of Bedford had drunk the same water for years, and its many thousand inhabitants were robust and healthy. The correspondence went on for weeks, much useless scribbling resulted, and much valuable time wasted. But the troops drank the water.

Again, there was a serious outbreak of measles among the men. Everything possible under the circumstances was done by the Divisional medical officers and local authorities. But people wrote to the papers, with the best intentions, that the men were being killed almost deliberately, and the result was a good deal of confusion, some useless correspondence, and, again, much valuable time wasted. However, great credit is due to the Divisional medical officers, their assistants, and the V.A.D. ladies, for grappling with the epidemic during the bad months of November and December. The disease worked itself out by the end of January, and by the end of February the Division was practically sound again.

It is an interesting fact that the epidemic was far more deadly in the case of men from the extreme north and the islands. This is shown by the following table, and bears out the opinion of the medical officers as to the probable incidence of the disease in units from different localities.

Taking the southern boundaries of Banff, Inverness, and Argyll, and including the western islands, Scotland is roughly divided into two fairly equal areas. Calling the northern area A, and the southern B, we find that

A supplied 5,200 : Cases of Measles, 477 : Deaths, 59.
B ,, 13,000 : ,, ,, 52 : ,, 6.

The percentage of deaths from measles worked out to 10·8 per cent of the cases, as seven deaths were from scarlet fever and one from diphtheria.

It will be easily understood that the rapid preparation for war of a Territorial Division presents numerous difficulties. It was originally laid down that Territorial troops would require, and have, six months to complete training. Even with a very complete elementary training this is not an over-estimation, assuming that equipment is up to date and complete. But when it is stated that most of the equipment, guns, rifles, technical stores, &c., were quite out of date, besides being ridiculously inadequate, some, at least, of the difficulties are obvious. One of the first troubles was the removal of most of the permanent staff. Only those who know the importance of these instructors can realise what it meant. They were, however, required elsewhere on more important duties, and had to go. Later, the regular adjutants of infantry were taken, also a great blow, but some eventually came back. Such difficulties were, of course, common to all Territorial Divisions. The Highland Division was not singular, but it had, and was able to keep, some very excellent staff officers, both Divisional and Brigade, who did splendid work. Here it may be recorded, and it is due to the General Staff, War Office, and other high formations to say, that so far from interfering with training, we received every assistance, and any reference to that body met with prompt and sympathetic attention. So with the Q.M.G.'s department, and it is obvious that some of those in high places realised the wisdom of trusting the man on the spot, and have therefore earned our gratitude.

The War Office issued a special " syllabus " for training, necessarily modified as experience was gained, and a good deal was left to local commanders ; but, as a matter of fact, it was in most cases necessary to begin with the " goose-step." The " barrack " discipline was excellent, but the field discipline left much to be desired. It was some time before some C.O.'s even could be made to understand that an order in the field did not admit of heated argument before execution ; and the rank and file had to learn that training was not a recreation to stop when they got tired. But all this gradually wore off, and in less than three months units began to assume a workmanlike and even serviceable appearance on parade.

What has been said applies to all units more or less, but while technical units, such as ambulances, transport companies, signal company, and engineers came on very fast, the artillery moved slowly in the direction of preparedness for war. They had ancient " pieces," poor and ill-fitting harness, while only in a few cases was any knowledge of " horse management " evident. Thus, care of horses, riding and driving, had to be instilled from the beginning. Added to this, the horses of all mounted units, and the vehicles of transport, had been commandeered in a great hurry on mobilisation, and were consequently rather a handicap. New vehicles came necessarily very slowly, but with drastic castings and the ever-ready assistance of the Remount Department, the horse question rapidly improved. It is interesting here to record, in connection with remounting, that a hundred polo ponies were sent to England as a present from the " Zemindars " of Madras. They were not looked on with favour by other units; but the G.O.C., with considerable experience of such animals, gladly accepted the offer of them by the Director of Remounts, with the result that the company commanders and staffs of the Highland Division went to France better mounted than any other.

There were two notable exceptions regarding " horse management." One was the Highland Mountain Brigade, which came down with a splendid lot of pack ponies, and made a very creditable turn-out from the first. The other was one of the transport companies, which showed considerable knowledge and good work in respect of its animals. It must, however, be common knowledge that the Highlands is not the best place from which to obtain, in a hurry, four or five thousand good army horses, nor are Highlanders, as a rule, " horsey " people. But in spite of all this the improvement was wonderful, the interest taken in their animals was most creditable to the various units, and the Division was fortunate in digging out a lot of very useful transport officers.

So training went on in its various branches, units gradually completing in personnel, and by December Divisional exercises were attempted. Inspections by the

Commander of the Central Force, and later by his Majesty the King, gave a useful fillip to the proceedings, and if there was one thing more than another which made successful training possible under adverse circumstances, it was the grand spirit of all ranks, and the determination of all to " play the game "—a spirit common to all Territorial units of the kingdom. No praise can be too great for the regimental officers and men.

Towards the end of 1914 certain units were taken from Territorial Divisions to complete the field army, and the first " bomb-shell " came when a field ambulance and a field company were called for. The 1/1 Highland Field Ambulance and the 1/2 Highland Field Company were sent. Then three battalions of infantry were ordered to France. There was not much to choose between the various battalions, so the chief consideration was given to numerical strength. One battalion was selected from each brigade, and 4th Seaforths, 6th Gordons, and 7th Argylls went off. In the same way, shortly afterwards, 4th Camerons, 4th Gordons, and 9th Argylls were sent. To replace these the 2nd line battalions were sent from Scotland, but it was obvious that they would not be ready to accompany the Division abroad. The 2nd line medical and engineer units, however, came on very quickly, and soon took the place of their front line. The mobile veterinary section—a very well-run unit—was also depleted, and replaced by degrees.

The next and last act of depletion was the ordering of the Mountain Artillery Brigade to the East to take part in the Gallipoli expedition. Two batteries only were sent, and the third kept as a training unit for mountain artillery —the only one at home. The health of Lieut.-Colonel Robertson was doubtful, and the G.O.C. decided to retain him, and he was afterwards given the billet of organising and commanding the Divisional Ammunition Column. He was, as a sort of comment to the G.O.C.'s decision, the only Colonel who served with the Division from start to finish.

The winter of 1914-15 was a wet one, and the state of the country round Bedford was all against training. Horse lines and the few hutments were a sea of mud, and movement off the roads for wheeled vehicles was difficult, in some cases impossible. However, such operations as were possible under these conditions were very useful, judged by later experience.

Towards the end of March 1915 it became known for certain that Territorial Divisions would go overseas as complete units, though the exact order of movement was undecided. There had been continual changes in the staff, both Divisional and Brigade. Fortunately, the G.S.O. 1, then Major Moir, Royal Scots, was retained, and to him, both in that capacity and as, later, A.Q.M.G., the Division generally and the G.O.C. in particular is deeply indebted. Several Brigadiers were changed, while commanders of battalions, &c., were also weeded out, chiefly for age. Thus, before leaving for France, the C.R.E., A.D.M.S., A.D.V.S., A.Q.M.G., and various other commanders, were replaced, of whom Colonel Cook of 6th Argylls was nominated as Base Commandant in France.

At last the order came to prepare for embarkation, and there was much to do. To begin with, the Division was six battalions short. So to complete it a whole Lancashire brigade was sent under command of Brigadier-General Hibbert, and two battalions of the Black Watch (6th and 7th), which regiment was not included in the Highland Divisional organisation.

The Lancashire brigade was a very fine one, but, of course, quite unknown to the G.O.C. and staff, and there was little time to get to know them. It is unnecessary to say, however, that they were received with open arms, and still less necessary to say they "played the game," and at once became an integral and very useful part of the Division.

The Black Watch battalions were splendid in physique and appearance on parade, and though they had not been trained with other troops, they very soon proved their value, and vied with the other units in adding to their brilliant regimental records.

So, after about twelve days of the ceaseless work of final equipment, completion in stores, clothing, animals, and every sort of war-like implement, eventually the Division commenced entraining for France with, perhaps, some misgivings as to thorough training, but none whatever as to the determination to uphold the honour of the land of its birth!

In looking back on those last days at Bedford, one can hardly understand how the final touches were given to a unit so incomplete in nearly everything. It seems nothing short of a miracle that Territorial Divisions generally were completely equipped in the short space of ten or eleven days. And it may not be out of place to record the obligations such units are under to the ordnance, remount, and other departments, for the ceaseless work, with depleted staffs, which was necessary, and which was so successfully accomplished. Nor will it be out of place to pay a final tribute to the good people of Bedford, who certainly evinced a quite unexpected sincerity in the " send-off " of the " invaders." Shortly before leaving, the G.O.C. sent the usual short letter of thanks to the Town Council, through the Mayor, for the assistance, general kindness, and consideration accorded during the Division's stay in the town. The following letter was received in reply :—

Bushmead, The Embankment,
Bedford, 29th April 1915.

Major-General Allason.

Dear Sir,—Please accept on behalf of the Town and myself our many and sincere thanks for your kind letter of yesterday.

The people of this Borough will never forget the visit of the Highland Division, and the desire of all concerned to cause as little inconvenience as possible, leaving alone the material benefits that have accrued to the inhabitants generally through your visit.

I need hardly say how much we shall miss you. The friendships formed during the last nine months will last for many years to come.

We shall watch for news of the Division as if they were our own people.

I will have your letter read at the next Council meeting.

May God grant you all a safe return to the friends you leave behind.—Yours very truly,

(Signed)   Harry Browning.

CHAPTER II.

ARRIVAL IN FRANCE—FESTUBERT.

On 13th April 1915 telephone instructions were received from the War Office that the 1/1 Highland Division was at once to be prepared for service overseas. The following day information was received that the battalions which had already been sent overseas would be replaced by the 6th and 7th Black Watch, and by four Lancashire battalions—the 1/4 Battalion King's Own Royal Lancashire Regiment, 1/8 Battalion the King's Liverpool Regiment, 1/4 the Loyal North Lancashire Regiment, and the 2/5 Battalion Lancashire Fusiliers.

By 18th April these battalions had all joined the Division. On 29th April orders were received that the Division would entrain to Southampton and Folkestone for Havre and Boulogne during the next few days.

By 5th May the journey had been completed without any unusual incidents, and the Division was concentrated in billets in the area Busnes, Robecq, and Lillers, and formed part of the Indian Corps (Sir James Willcocks) of the First Army (Sir Douglas Haig).

As soon as the Division had completed its concentration in the First Army area, General Sir Douglas Haig paid it his first of many visits. The assistance which the Division received from Sir Douglas Haig and the First Army Headquarters Staff while finding its legs during its first days in France was invaluable.

At this period the general situation on the Western Front was as follows: The second battle of Ypres, prepared by the first discharge of asphyxiating gases, had begun on 22nd April, and was to continue with great intensity for over a month.

ARRIVAL IN FRANCE—FESTUBERT

During the early part of this period the French were preparing an attack to be launched on 9th May between Arras and the right of the British lines. The First British Army, having been ordered to support this operation by an attack, had issued instructions directing the IVth Corps against the German position in the neighbourhood of Richebourg (south-west of Fromelles), and the Ist and Indian Corps against the German trenches between Givenchy and Neuve Chapelle. These attacks as planned were accordingly delivered on 8th, 9th, and 10th May 1915. They, however, met with little success. It was therefore decided that the First Army should concentrate on the southern point of attack, and renew the operations on 12th May. This attack was subsequently postponed until the 15th owing to low visibility.

In the attack on the 15th the Indian Corps, owing to the strength of the enemy's defences in the neighbourhood of Richebourg l'Avoue, again failed to make progress. The 2nd Division of the Ist Corps, however, captured the enemy's first and support lines. On the following day, the 7th Division on the right of the 2nd Division successfully captured several second lines of enemy trenches, and these two Divisions continued the advance on the day after as far as the Le Quinque Rue-Bethune road.

On 19th May the 2nd Division was relieved on this front by the 51st Division.[1]

On the 25th, the object of these operations having been attained, orders were given for Divisions in the line to act defensively and consolidate the ground won.

These operations were attended by serious casualties, but, to quote Sir John French's despatch, they assisted in securing the brilliant successes attained by the French forces on the right, not only by holding the enemy on this front, but by drawing off a part of the German reinforcements which were coming up to support their forces east of Arras. In this battle of Festubert the enemy was driven from a strongly-fortified position, and ground was won on a front of four miles to an average depth of 600 yards.

---

[1] On 11th May 1915 the 1/1 Highland Division was renamed the 51st (Highland) Division, the Infantry Brigades being numbered, 152nd (Seaforth and Camerons), 153rd (Gordon Battalions), 154th (Lancashire Battalions).

From the above summary it will be seen that the 51st Division was initiated to the ways of war in the midst of a great battle. On 9th May it remained in reserve to the Indian Corps, and was held in readiness to move at short notice until 11th May. By this date it had become clear that the progress of the Indian Corps had not been such as to render the employment of its reserve at all probable.

On 14th May the 51st Division, less two brigades R.F.A. temporarily attached to the Lahore and 49th Division, moved to the area Caestre, Borre, Merris, Meteren, and came into G.H.Q. reserve.[1]

On 18th May the Division moved into the area La Gorgue-Vieille Chapelle. On the night 19-20th May the 152nd Infantry Battalion began the relief of the 2nd Division (General Horne), south of Neuve Chapelle, and on 20-21st the 153rd Infantry Brigade relieved a Canadian brigade in the Richebourg sector.

The Highland Division during its first tour of duty in the line was thus employed in the particularly trying operation of consolidating a newly-won position. Few operations call for more resource and more tactical skill on the part of junior officers and N.C.O.'s, or for more detailed planning and arrangement on the part of commanders and staffs. Order has immediately to be evolved from chaos. Covered approaches are non-existent, and must be constructed before movement during daylight becomes possible; sniping with rifles and, in some cases, field-guns is constant; the protection afforded by barbed-wire entanglements is wanting; arrangements for sanitation and cooking have not been planned. In fact, the amount of work required to make the position defensible and habitable appears overwhelming.

To make confusion worse confounded, officers, runners, reliefs, ration parties, &c., as long as movement is restricted to the hours of darkness, find the greatest difficulty in acquiring a working knowledge of the geography of the defences.

Moreover the Germans, in those days of short advances, were quick at recovering from the confusion in their artillery

[1] Shortly after this move Lieut.-Colonel A. J. G. Moir, who had mobilised as G.S.O. 1 to the Division, returned to the Division as A.A. and Q.M.G.

arrangements created by a successful attack. They were therefore always liable to bombard a newly-captured position heavily before the men had time to construct sufficient field-works to protect themselves from shell splinters.

In the case of the front taken over by the Division on this occasion, the normal difficulties were accentuated by the fact that digging-in was only possible to a depth of from two to three feet. Everywhere in the Flanders mud, below that level water is encountered. It is therefore necessary to erect above ground double rows of traversed breastworks, between which the men must live and have their being.

The difficulty of consolidation in this mud country requires to have been experienced to be fully appreciated.

The work of maintaining breastworks, when completed, in a state of repair is considerable, as they cannot withstand a bombardment by artillery or trench-mortars. In consequence sections of the trenches are frequently levelled to the ground, and have to be reconstructed. The labour of maintaining them when once erected is, however, a small problem when compared with the difficulty of erecting them *de novo* during active operations.

In the first place, owing to the flatness and absence of cover from view, which is characteristic of Flanders, the work of construction is in the initial stages almost entirely confined to night work. As breastworks will only stand if their sides are graded at the proper slope, darkness makes this work infinitely more difficult. Moreover, breastworks during their construction and before they have reached their full thickness can be demolished by light field-guns, and be seriously damaged even by machine-gun fire. Of these two facts the enemy used to take full advantage. He also knew well that much of the work had to be done by men standing in the open on his side of the breastworks, and so made considerable use of machine-guns to inflict casualties on working parties thus engaged.

There are other serious drawbacks to garrisoning breastwork trenches. Deep dug-outs cannot be mined in the clay in the normal way, again on account of water. Concrete shelters, which take a considerable time to erect, are therefore the only alternative form of shell-proof cover. Even these have a marked tendency to fill with water.

There was a good example of a concrete dug-out in the right sector at Armentières in September 1916. Some simple-minded soldier, finding that it was gradually filling with water, made a hole through the concrete floor to let the water out. In consequence the dug-out filled with water up to the level of the ground surface in a few hours, driving its occupants out. A battalion medical officer subsequently visiting the trenches came across this dug-out, and thinking it was a storage tank for water, tested the water and caused a notice-board to be placed on it, saying, "For ablution purposes only; not fit for drinking."

Breastwork parapets, even when they are not subjected to bombardment, require constant attention. They have in particular a disconcerting habit of settling down and losing height, particularly after rain. In consequence it sometimes happens that by the gradual subsidence of the parapet men may unwittingly expose themselves to enemy snipers in places where a day or two previously they were completely hidden from view.

Apart from the amount of labour the upkeep of breastworks requires, there are other reasons which make them unpleasant to live in on an active front. During a bombardment, for instance, when a shell hits the trench, men are constantly being buried in a heap of sandbags and earth. They have then to be dug out immediately to save them from suffocation. In these circumstances the rescue parties often have to work while the bombardment continues, and with enemy snipers and machine-gunners ready to engage them whenever they expose themselves in the breach.

German machine-gunners were also expert at firing a series of bursts into a particular portion of breastwork until it became non-bullet-proof. They would then continue firing bursts at irregular intervals at the same spot, with the result that the bullets penetrated the parapet and came through into the trench. Casualties were often caused in this manner.

The Highland Division, thus having arrived in France with its training only partially completed, was called upon to undertake a difficult and unpleasant task—namely, the holding and consolidation of a newly-captured position in Flanders. Moreover, the circumstances were such that the

ARRIVAL IN FRANCE—FESTUBERT

Division could not carry out a period of attachment in the line to an experienced Division for instruction.

Thus no opportunity was vouchsafed to officers and men of being " put wise " before the full responsibility of holding a captured position was thrust upon them. The significance of this statement is that troops on the first occasion that they enter the battle zone are liable to be " gobrowed " by their new circumstances. They require, as it were, a chaperon to assist them to assess things at their true value, and teach them what not to fear but to respect, and what they may disregard.

Discussing this question, a Brigadier-General once related how when he first arrived in France as a company commander he saw a " woolly bear " burst over a wood in which his company was lying in mass. He turned and galloped back to the wood *ventre à terre* in a frenzied state of mind, certain that he would find numbers of his men dead and dying. He was amazed to find that, on the contrary, not a single man had been touched. A veteran would, of course, have regarded the woolly bear in its true light—as a vulgar and ostentatious beast that usually burst too high and seldom took any effect on the ground.

In the other direction one remembers the novice who, during his period of initiation, cut up a duck-board (a most impious act in itself) in a forward sap and kindled a smoking bonfire on which to boil a mess-tin of water, and his indignant astonishment at the shower of rifle grenades which he unwittingly but naturally provoked.

Indeed, the debutante Division entering its first theatre of battle may well be excused a certain amount of shyness concerning its behaviour, however well prompted it may have been before it left home.

General Davies, commanding the 8th Division, however, gave the 51st every possible assistance, even lending them his own instructors to help to complete their training. His assistance proved most valuable.

On 26th May Divisional Headquarters was shelled out of Lacouture. This bombardment was attributed to an article which had appeared in the press, and which disclosed the location of units about Lacouture, including Divisional Headquarters and a Canadian 60-pounder battery. The Germans appear to have taken full advantage of this information, as both the Divisional Headquarters and the 60-pounder battery were heavily shelled. Several of the Divisional Headquarter signal section were killed or wounded, and General Bannatine-Allason had a narrow escape, the wind screen of his car being shattered. After this episode it was noticed that the censorship of articles appearing in the press became more rigorous.

On taking over the line, the clearing of the battlefield had to be undertaken in addition to the work of consolidation. The bodies of men who had been killed in the recent operations lay thick throughout the whole area. Even the wounded had not all been brought in. The men were thus quickly introduced to war in its worst aspects, in a manner which clearly revealed to them the power of modern destructive weapons. Officers and men still speak of the depressing effect which the spectacle of so many dead had on them. This feeling was augmented by the unpleasant duty of searching for the bodies in the polluted atmosphere and burying them, which had to be undertaken during their first few days in the line.

The whole countryside was further littered with arms, equipment, clothing, tools, and ammunition. Considerable exertions were therefore required to save even a portion of the serviceable stores which had been left on the ground during the preceding operations.

On 30th May the Division was transferred to the IVth Corps, being relieved by the Indian Corps. The following day the 153rd Infantry Brigade relieved the Canadians between Festubert and Le Quinque Rue. This sector was subsequently divided, the 152nd Infantry Brigade taking over the line on the left.

On 7th June orders were issued from the IVth Corps to attack the enemy's positions about Rue d'Ouvert and Chapelle St Roch and farther south on the morning of the 11th, with the object of gaining ground towards Violaines. Later this attack was postponed until the 15th. On the 12th the operation order for this attack was issued. The objective of the IVth Corps was "the German positions from Chapelle St Roch along the Rue d'Ouvert to L12.

"The Canadian Division was to attack on the right and form a defensive flank; the 7th Division was allotted the Chapelle St Roch and the southern end of the Rue d'Ouvert as its objective; and the 51st Division the extreme end.

"The actual objective given to the 51st Division were the houses at L11, L12, L13, and K7. At the last-named they were to join hands with the 7th Division.

"The 154th Infantry Brigade were detailed for the attack, their right being directed on the south-west corner of the German salient—that is, a point about 150 yards east by south of L8. The left of this attack was to be directed through L9."

One section of the 1/1 Highland Field Company, R.E., and "C" Company of the 5th Seaforth Highlanders, were ordered to assemble in the D line towards the left flank, in readiness to construct and occupy a fire-trench between M6 and L12 after that point had been gained.

One section 2/2 Highland Field Company, R.E., with two platoons of the 154th Infantry Brigade, were ordered to assemble in B line near the right flank. Their purpose was "to protect the right flank of the attack and to construct a *point d'appui* on a suitable site between L8 and L10."

It was arranged that sufficient infantry bombing parties should be detailed from the bombers of the Division to carry out various tasks, according to the progress made by the assaulting infantry.

In these days the bomb commonly used was the Bethune bomb. These were made of cast-iron, and were exploded by means of time-fuses fixed into detonators, with patent lighters attached to the fuse. They were but clumsy and dangerous weapons when compared with the modern Mills bomb.

Bombing and its tactics was then an art which could only be acquired by a course of specialist training, which, with the facilities that then existed, lasted a considerable time.

The result was that the output of bombers was small, and it was therefore considered necessary, if full value was to be obtained from them, to amalgamate all the bombers of each brigade into brigade grenadier companies.

On this occasion all three brigade grenadier companies detailed bombing squads to take part in the operations.

The artillery available for this attack was, both as regards the number of guns and the amount of ammunition, insignificant in the light of more recent experience. The Divisional artillery, it is true, had been reinforced by a group of French 75's. The 15-pounders, with which the Divisional artillery was armed, had, however, such faulty ammunition and so little of it that effective co-operation with the infantry was, according to modern standards, out of the question. The artillery programme included wire-cutting, a two days' continuous bombardment, and a final intensive bombardment. The first bombardment was to continue up to the moment of the infantry assault. At 6 P.M., the hour of the assault, the guns firing on the enemy's front line were to lift on to the line L9-L10. At 6.15 P.M. there was a further lift on to the Rue d'Orient.

The general plan can be summed up as being an attempt to straighten out a re-entrant in our line by pinching off a salient in the enemy's.

The artillery began wire-cutting on 13th June, the deliberate bombardment beginning on the 14th. On the 15th it continued, becoming intensive between 5.30 P.M. and 6 P.M. Mountain-guns and trench-mortars also joined in the bombardment.

At 6 P.M., 15th June, the attack was launched by the 4th Loyal North Lancashires and the 6th Scottish Rifles[1] of the 154th Brigade.

The attack was at first successful; the west end of the German salient was carried, and the attack pushed on to the main German line near the Rue d'Ouvert, and for a time the third German trench line was occupied and held. Three companies of the 4th King's Own Royal Lancaster Regiment were accordingly sent forward to reinforce the Scottish Rifles.

Meanwhile "C" Company of the 5th Seaforth Highlanders had advanced to the attack at 6.45 P.M.

The action of this company of the 5th Seaforth Highlanders is amply described by the following extracts from a letter written by a platoon sergeant who took part in the attack :—

---

[1] The 6th Scottish Rifles had replaced the 2/5 Lancashire Regiment, a second-line battalion, which was withdrawn from the Division to complete its training.

MAP I.—ATTACK NEAR FESTUBERT, 15TH JUNE 1915.

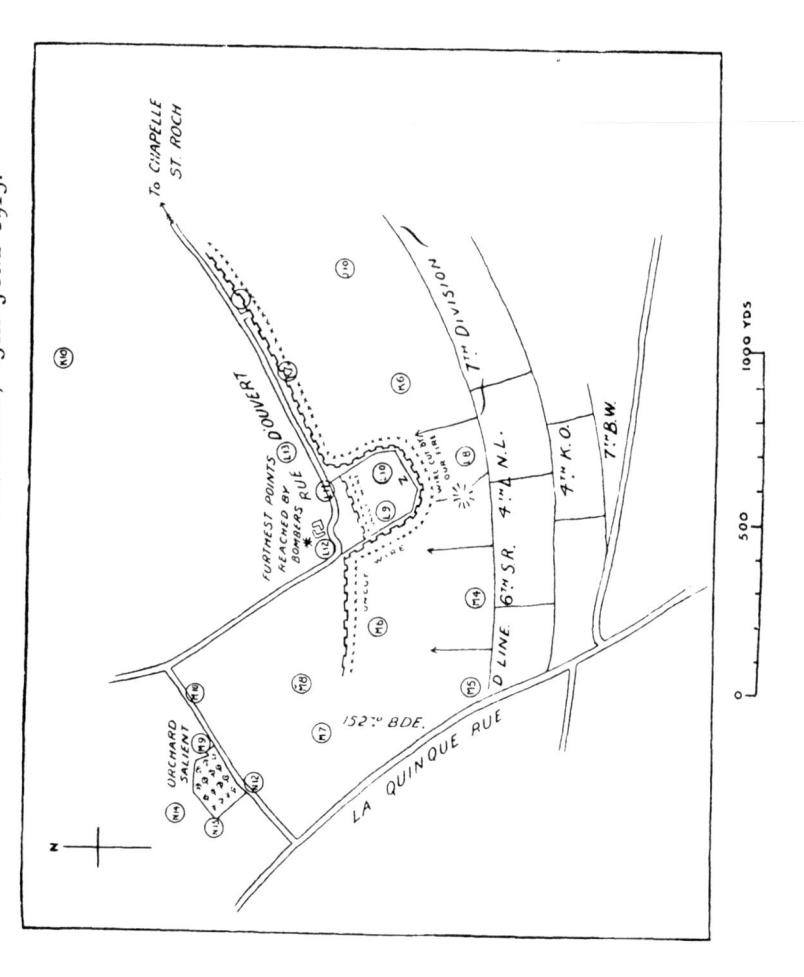

ARRIVAL IN FRANCE—FESTUBERT

"On the night of the 14th we went into the front line, the 6th Seaforth Highlanders having eased away to the left of the Divisional sector towards the Orchard, to make room for our company.

"Communications from reserve trenches to front line were very bad; movement had mostly to be carried out in the open under direct German observation. Daylight movement had therefore to be restricted as much as possible.

"On the 15th we had a most uncomfortable day. The Boche rose early, having apparently known our plans. In fact, some of them were heard to call across No Man's Land, 'Come along, Jocks; we are waiting for you.' And undoubtedly they were. From early morning we were subjected to continual shell-fire, causing many casualties to us. As the afternoon drew on the Boche became still more lively, but we still had great hopes. These, however, became fainter as each occasional look over the top showed the German wire unbroken.

"At 5 o'clock we began to make our final preparations. The adjutant and C.O. arrived and took up a point of vantage in the trench where a view of the 6th Scottish Rifles could be got during their advance. It was only by this means that the C.O. could judge as to the failure or success of the Scottish Rifles.

"Thus we awaited our further orders. From this time onwards an occasional bark from a field-gun could be heard, and a small shrapnel burst could be seen over the German lines.

"At last the hour had come for the 6th Scottish Rifles. Over they went. Then the Germans showed to advantage the quantity and quality of their munitions. Machine-guns swept over the parapets and tore them to pieces; the 154th Infantry Brigade were seen to be advancing gloriously in front of the most colossal artillery and machine-gun fire — their ranks thinned considerably before they were many yards from their own trenches. But on they went and entered the German front line, where they were lost to view.

"Our time had now come. Nothing for it but to go over. The order was passed along, 'Get ready.' At 6.45 P.M. the order came 'Advance!' The place was a perfect hell. Just one solid sheet of bullets. Over we went. Many were hit on the top of the parapet; before a distance of thirty yards was traversed all the officers of our company were hit, as well as the brigade bombing officer (Lieutenants Mowatt and Dunnet killed, Captains Robertson, Ritson, and Lieutenant Fraser-Campbell wounded). On we went; but men were falling in all directions, and by the time we were within reach of the German wire, not more than fifteen of the company were still on the move. The outlook was hopeless, the wire was an insurmountable obstacle, and the few who remained had to take cover in the nearest shell-hole until darkness allowed us to make our own lines again—a sad dejected remnant of a company."

So much for the subsidiary attack of the 5th Seaforths.

The attack of the 7th Division on the right of the 154th Infantry Brigade had failed to develop substantially, and no progress was made. Farther back the 1st Canadian Brigade captured the German front line trenches.

Night thus fell with the 154th Infantry Brigade having penetrated the German positions on a narrow front, but with both its flanks " in the air." The situation, however, remained too obscure to enable the salient thus made in the German lines to be utilised for developing flank attacks against the German front and support line trenches.

The nature of the country, as has been pointed out above, made it impossible for the men to dig themselves in, and they were thus dependent for protection on the slender breastworks that they had been enabled to improvise during the night amongst the débris of the German trenches. In this exposed position they were counter-attacked in the early hours of the morning. Engaged with bombs and machine-gun fire, both from their front and flanks, they were unable to hold their position, and were finally forced back to their original front line trenches. They had suffered considerable casualties, the 1/4 Loyal North Lancashires alone having lost 19 killed, 255 wounded, and 145 missing, amongst them 5 officers being killed and 8 wounded.

During the night the remnants of the 5th Seaforth Highlanders and the sappers who accompanied them crawled back from the shell-holes or long grass in which they had been lying to our own trenches. In a similar way the

ARRIVAL IN FRANCE—FESTUBERT

Canadians, also unable to hold their exposed position on the German trenches, had returned to their own lines.

The failure of the attack was thus complete. Great credit is, however, due to the 154th Infantry Brigade for their advance in the face of heavy artillery and close-range rifle and machine-gun fire. There is little doubt but that, had the operations on their flanks been successful, they would have had every prospect of holding their gains. " C " Company of the 5th Seaforths did all that could have been expected of them in circumstances in which success, as it turned out, was out of the question.

General Ross, commanding 152nd Infantry Brigade, says of them in his report of the operations : " I am glad to say that both officers and men behaved very well indeed, and all went into the attack with the full intention of getting through. The company had been somewhat shaken during bombardment, as they had had several casualties from shell-fire, mainly from our own shells, and the German shells had fallen amongst them more steadily than usual. The casualties are not known yet exactly, but are heavy, being over a hundred in one company."

Results were undoubtedly discouraging in the first attack carried out by troops of the Highland Division, but it is doubtful if, in the circumstances, any troops could have done better.

They had within a few days of arriving in France played a principal part in the deepest tragedy that attacking infantry can assist in—the tragedy of uncut wire.

After a gallant advance across No Man's Land, through which nothing but their determination to close with the enemy could have carried them, the survivors had been suddenly halted by an intact entanglement covered at close range by rifles and machine-guns.

In cases such as this the whole impetus of the attack collapses, skill and initiation are no longer of avail, the brain can no longer help the body. Some men plunge into the entanglement, tearing at it with their wire-cutters, and lacerating their flesh on the barbs until they fall.

Others double up and down the belt looking for a gap through which they may make their way. Odd heroes may find such a gap, and, if they live to reach the German trenches, leap into them, subsequently to be posted as missing. Their story is never told.

Others, with a disregard for death born of despair, may stand for a moment or two and return the enemy's fire until they are shot down.

Only those survive to answer the roll who either fall wounded and have strength subsequently to regain their own lines under cover of darkness, or who with quick perception see that the obstacle is impenetrable, and instantly seek cover in which they may be hid until nightfall.

Uncut wire might be written as the epitaph on the grave of many a British infantryman, and equally well in later days, when air reconnaissance was perfected, on the grave of many a commander's reputation.

During the following night the 6th Scottish Rifles, the 4th Loyal North Lancashires, and the 4th King's Own Royal Lancashire Regiment were withdrawn, and were replaced by the 8th Liverpools and the 7th Black Watch. The latter had been sent up from the 153rd Infantry Brigade to take over the reserve trenches.

On the morning of the 16th orders were received from the IVth Corps to renew the attack at 4.45 P.M. after an artillery bombardment. The 5th and 7th Gordons from the 153rd Brigade were therefore temporarily attached to the 154th Brigade to replace the battalions which had been withdrawn.

The attack met with no more success than its predecessor. The 8th Liverpools, supported by the 7th Black Watch, carried out the advance. It was, however, impeded from the start by a heavy bombardment opened on our trenches by the enemy. The 8th Liverpools managed to get forward in small parties, and passed the west end of the German salient. The troops on their right flanks were, however, unable to make progress, and about 8 P.M. the Liverpools were forced back to our trenches.

It had been intended that, if the 154th Brigade was successful, the 152nd Brigade should continue the attack. These orders were therefore cancelled, and during the night the 5th and 7th Gordon Highlanders replaced the 7th Black Watch and 8th Liverpools.

In view of the failure of the first attack, it is doubtful

if the second, which at best could only be hastily improvised, had any prospect of success. However, at 5 P.M., 17th June, further orders were received by the Divisional commander to renew the attack on the German salient at 3 A.M. on the night 17-18th after a short intense artillery preparation.

At 2.30 A.M., to the relief of all concerned, this attack was postponed and subsequently cancelled.

The failure of these attacks can be attributed to the inadequacy of the artillery preparation. Subsequent battles proved that the number of guns and the allotment of ammunition per gun required is far in excess of those allotted to the Division for the battle of Festubert, if infantry are to have a reasonable chance of success in attacking organised resistance, protected by strong wire entanglements.

In addition to the inadequacy in the number of guns, the 15-pounders again proved themselves highly unsatisfactory. As evidence of the unreliability of their ammunition, it is worth recording that Captain Duncan of the 8th Argyll and Sutherland Highlanders had an eye knocked out by a shrapnel bullet half a mile behind the British front line.

On the day after the launching of the first attack, the following message had been received from Lieut.-General Sir James Rawlinson: "The Corps commander wishes you to convey his appreciation to the troops of the 51st Division for their gallant conduct of yesterday and to-day, particularly to the assaulting battalions—*viz.*, the 6th Scottish Rifles, the 4th Loyal North Lancashire Regiment, and the 8th King's Liverpool Regiment."

On the nights 18-19th and 19-20th June the 7th Division took over the right sector, leaving only the 153rd Brigade in the line.

On the 24th orders were received for the 51st Division to rejoin the Indian Corps, and to take over the line from the Lahore Division south of Laventie. On the 27th June, this relief having been completed, the G.O.C. took over command of the new sector.

All ranks experienced a sense of relief on leaving the Festubert area. Not only on account of the serious casualties suffered by many units during the attacks and the retaliation provoked by them, but also for other reasons, it was rightly regarded as an unpleasant sector.

Communications had been almost non-existent, so that movement by day was very restricted. The trenches, where they existed, were very open, and sniping was rife. The ill-famed " Orchard," which it was hoped might be consolidated and incorporated into the defences, had an evil reputation. Breastworks were no sooner erected there by night than they were knocked down by day. The Germans were, in fact, so opposed to the consolidation of the Orchard that they introduced trench-mortars to check it.

The large calibre trench-mortars, or " Yon Minnie Wafers," as the Jocks styled them, do not so much damage breastworks as remove them. They frequently leave in a place where breastworks once stood nothing but a deep crater, with two feet of water in it. In this case the result was that, in spite of a vast amount of work carried out on the consolidation, the sector was still far from completed when the Division was relieved.

In those days there was little with which to reply to trench-mortars. Appeals to the artillery for retaliatory shoots would seldom be answered, owing to the restrictions placed on the use of ammunition on account of its scarcity. Mountain-guns, manned by the R.G.A., were, however, employed, and also a form of trench howitzer; but these were inferior weapons when compared with the formidable mortars of the Germans.

The Laventie front was in character similar to the Festubert front. When the Division took over the line, the defences consisted of little more than a single line of breastworks. Behind this, some 200 to 400 yards in rear, lay a series of detached supporting posts at intervals of from 300 to 500 yards. A reserve line composed of similar posts lay 1000 to 1500 yards in rear of the supporting posts.

The enemy was occupying the lower slopes of the Aubers Ridge, from which he overlooked all the country in which the British defences were situated.

Each sector has, as a rule, its particular " unhealthy spot." In the Laventie sector Red Lamp Corner occupied this rôle.

The front line ended in a butt-end, some 100 yards from

ARRIVAL IN FRANCE—FESTUBERT

the German line at Red Lamp Corner (Point B on the diagram); 300 yards west of Red Lamp Corner the front line started from another butt-end (Point C). These two butt-ends were connected by a fire-stepped communication trench (C—E). See diagram.

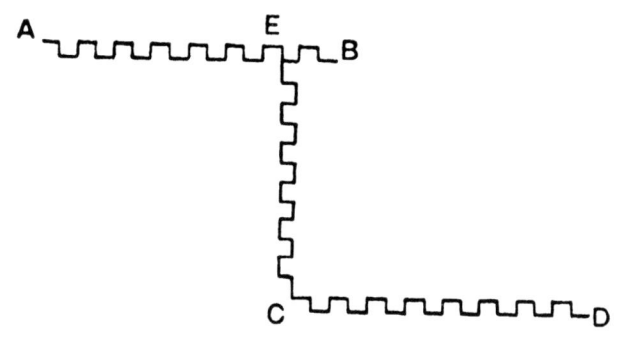

```
A ⊔⊔⊔⊔⊔E⊔⊔B
              |
              |
              |
              |
              |
              |
            C ⊔⊔⊔⊔⊔⊔⊔⊔ D
```

The corner took its name from a red lamp which was lit at dusk and placed at B to prevent the troops garrisoning CD from shooting into those garrisoning AB in the dark. The trench from E to C was continuously subjected to close-range rifle and machine-gun fire in direct enfilade, and both it and the corner itself were places to be avoided.

In these days the red lamp was a necessary precaution, as a form of activity which came later to be known as "wind fights" frequently occurred. A post would see or imagine it saw an enemy patrol, which it took to be a prelude to an attack. It in consequence opened rapid fire. This fire was taken up by posts on its right and left. Subsequently the alarm travelled for several miles, and rapid fire was opened all along the line. The fight, often occasioned by Private X., just out from home, mistaking a pollarded willow for a German, involved an enormous expenditure of ammunition, in which the shooting was not always under complete control.

It will be easily understood that, without the red lamp, CD might have made things very unpleasant for AB in these circumstances.

This sector presented many difficulties. The defences that had been constructed were so limited that the troops in the line were far too congested. They were therefore liable to suffer undue casualties in the event of bombardment. Moreover, the supporting posts being isolated sections of trenches clearly visible, particularly in air photographs, were in consequence liable to attract a considerable volume of artillery fire. Further, communicating trenches, as usual, were quite inadequate to meet the requirements of the garrison.

General Bannatine-Allason therefore at once decided that the whole scheme of defence must be recast and largely augmented. Accordingly work was begun on a continuous support line, and on increasing the number of communication trenches. In fact, a considerable effort was demanded from the ranks to render the sector reasonably defensible.

When the Division was relieved in July much progress had been made, General Willcocks expressing himself to the Divisional commander as very satisfied with the great improvements that had been effected in the defences.

In this period the Division learnt many lessons in trench craft.

On taking over the line enemy sniping was continuous. The hostile snipers were masters of the situation, and inflicted serious casualties. However, every effort was made to check the enemy's activities in this respect, with excellent results. Towards the end of the Division's tour in this sector, the Highlanders were at least on equal terms, if not superior to the enemy as snipers. In some cases telescopic rifles were bought by private enterprise. The men who were entrusted with these rifles were carefully selected from amongst the gamekeepers and stalkers in the infantry, and on several days they were able to register good bags.

On 1st July the Division saw the first British mine exploded. At 3 A.M. two rounds were fired by the artillery as a signal; a moment later the mine exploded. The artillery and machine-guns then opened on the enemy's trenches for fifteen minutes. The German retaliation was slight. When day broke it was reported that about fifty yards of the German parapet was blown in. Later the Germans were seen with stretchers on and about the crater. The blow, therefore, appeared to have been successful. After daybreak, however, the enemy snipers killed several of our men who exposed themselves in trying to see the results of the explosion.

ARRIVAL IN FRANCE—FESTUBERT

As in the last sector, work in the defences was considerably hampered by the enemy's artillery and trench-mortars, which were constantly levelling the British trenches. As usual, appeals for artillery retaliation could seldom be met, owing to the paucity of ammunition. It became most discouraging to the men to see their breastworks being damaged and destroyed in this manner, their labours of the previous night often being undone in a few minutes, without it being possible to fire a round in retaliation. In this sector life in the trenches was made more uncertain than ever by the introduction of the rifle grenade by the Germans.

In the early part of July, Colonel Ian Stewart, D.S.O., Scottish Rifles, who had joined the Division as G.S.O. 1 in June, formulated a scheme of training every man in the use of the bomb. Bombing, before this innovation, had been regarded as the duty of specialists. The new scheme was that every man should be trained to be able to light and throw a bomb in the case of an emergency. At the same time the brigade grenadier companies were put through a longer and more thorough course of instruction than had been the case in the past. The introduction of this scheme marked a big advance in the practice of bombing.

On 20th July orders were received that the Division was to join the Xth Corps under the command of General Morland, in the area of the newly-formed Third Army. The Xth Corps was then to consist of the 5th Regular Division, the 51st Territorial Division, and the 18th Service Division. Accordingly during the nights 22-23rd and 23-24th July the Division was relieved in the line by the Lahore and 8th Divisions.

On the 26th, 27th, 28th, and 29th of July the Division proceeded by train to the Neuilly area east of Amiens.

CHAPTER III.

THE PERIOD OF APPRENTICESHIP.

It was some ten weeks since the Division had heard its first shot fired. Up to the present it had, indeed, experienced war. It had, however, been employed throughout either in actual battle or in consolidating a battle front in particularly trying circumstances. It had, therefore, had little time or opportunity to collect its thoughts and profit by its experiences.

During the next few months it was given the opportunity it required, and it will be seen that these months were profitably employed by all ranks.

This period may be called the Division's apprenticeship to war.

In this connection it must not be forgotten that, in spite of its late successes, there was a time when the Highland Division was what can best be described as "green." That this was the case is no reflection on the spirit which animated the men or the manner in which the troops had been trained by their commanders. Under the conditions of modern warfare it could not have been otherwise.

Lord French writes of the newly-arrived Territorial Divisions: "At first certainly they were crude and untrained, but every day they improved under instruction, and developed great intelligence under a thorough and practical exposition of the objects to be aimed at."

The manner in which the Division "trained on" and developed from apprentices into skilled tradesmen was most creditable, both to the men and to those responsible for their education in the ways of war.

One difficulty that must always exist with inexperienced

THE PERIOD OF APPRENTICESHIP 29

troops, particularly non-regular troops, is the question of discipline. To maintain discipline in the circumstances of peace does not present a tithe of the difficulties which are encountered in times of war. The ill effects of the lack of discipline in peace conditions are evident to all. War, on the other hand, produces fresh and unexpected circumstances, in which experience alone can teach how efficiency is dependent on rigorous adherence to discipline, often in apparently trivial matters. This was felt by the Highland Division, in common with many others, in numerous ways.

In a Division in which the officers and men of the various companies and battalions are recruited from the same villages or towns, and are known to one another intimately in civil life, the enforcement of the rigid discipline demanded by war will always be a difficult matter, until experience has shown the necessity for it.

Officers and N.C.O.'s have first to appreciate the degree to which they must exercise command over their men, if the military machine is to stand the test. They must also learn that the efficiency of the troops under their command is dependent on the manner in which they supervise the daily life and actions of their men, and on the amount of forethought they exercise on their behalf.

Owing to inexperience, delay in reliefs, entailing much fatigue to the men, the miscarrying of working parties, entailing the loss of valuable time, were in the early stages frequent. Further, in spite of continual warnings, men light-heartedly ignored the enemy, and were constantly being killed by enemy snipers through wilful exposure. There were cases of men asphyxiating themselves in their dug-outs with the fumes of their own coke fires through want of the necessary precautions.

The diaries of senior officers contain frequent references to instances in which they found the enemy working in daylight in full view, unmolested, through want of initiative on the part of local commanders. Occasions were not unknown when troops in the line evinced what has since become known as " wind."

However, the Division recognised from the first that it had much to learn, and an organised effort was made to help the men to profit by experience in the shortest possible time. To this effort the men responded admirably.

Junior officers and N.C.O.'s gradually acquired the necessary habit of true command over their men. The men were quick and ready to discover that the better disciplined a unit is, the more efficient it is, the less it suffers from the actions of the enemy and the conditions of war. They learnt, too, that the best-disciplined battalion is the most comfortable and the most contented.

As Lord French writes : " Each unit learned by degrees its own relative place and position in the great Divisional machine. Enthusiasm was raised in the idea engendered in all ranks that they formed part of a great engine of war, furnished by their own country and immediate neighbourhood."

In the early stages of its apprenticeship the Division first took part in a series of unsuccessful attacks. Subsequently it passed many weeks in areas in which trench-mortaring and mining—the two forms of trench warfare most trying to men's nerves—were considerably in evidence. Nevertheless, in spite of their inexperience and of this unfortunate beginning, the men at all times remained in good heart and retained a high standard of morale.

By August 1915 the Division had so successfully overcome its earlier difficulties that it was selected to instruct the 18th Division, newly arrived from England, in trench warfare. Subsequently the 22nd Division, 32nd Division, and afterwards the 36th Division, were also attached to the Highland Division for tours of instruction in the line.

Throughout this period the rivalry between the Territorial and New Army Divisions was acute. The men had a strong impression, further accentuated by the fact that the Division did not take part in the battle of Loos, that since they were a Territorial Division, the higher command would never employ them as a complete Division in a major operation. In this belief, after General Harper had taken over command of the Division, they began to call themselves Harper's Duds, asserting that the Divisional sign, H.D., was formed from the initial letters of these two words.

On 27th July 1915, orders were issued by the Xth Corps for the 51st Division to take over the lines from near Becourt to the river Ancre near Hamel, relieving the 22nd Division of the XIth French Corps.

On the night 30-31st the 152nd Brigade took over the

THE PERIOD OF APPRENTICESHIP 31

left sector from the 116th French Regiment. On the following night the right sector was taken over by the 154th Infantry Brigade, who relieved the 22nd French Territorial Regiment, and by the 153rd Brigade, who took over a portion of the right sector from the 44th French Brigade.

The Divisional artillery, with six batteries of the 18th Division attached for instruction, moved into the line in relief of the French artillery on the nights 2-3rd, 3-4th, 4-5th August.

The taking over from the French, both from a military and from a social point of view, was satisfactory in every way. The details of the handing over were complete, and the arrangements made by the French commands and staffs excellent.

It was a considerable relief to all to find trenches cut deep in the chalk or loam, in place of the hated breastworks. The French system was also extensive, and contained numerous communication trenches and trench shelters. There was not, in consequence, the same exposed feeling which was attached to the Festubert and Laventie trenches.

The French troops were Bretons. Their great traditions as fighters produced immediately a bond of sympathy between them and the Highlanders. The Highland dress and the pipes evoked great interest and admiration in the French soldiers and in the inhabitants of the neighbouring villages, which lost nothing from the fact that the Highland Division was the first British Division to serve in that part of the country.

During the relief the French officers and men did their utmost to help our troops. Their hospitality was unbounded. Indeed, the excellent manner in which the French officers messed, even in the line, was the cause of considerable surprise to the British officers.

When the relief of the French troops was complete and they were marching away to take their place in the line in Champagne, the pipers and drummers of various units accompanied them for several miles of their first day's march. The Bretons, having themselves pipes of a kind, were delighted, and the manner in which they refreshed the pipers during the march clearly showed their gratitude.

Willie Lawrie, the famous pipe-major of the 8th Argyll and Sutherland Highlanders, composed a pipe tune in honour of this event, known as the "Pipers of Bouzincourt," and another called "The 8th Argyll and Sutherland Highlanders farewell to the 116th De Ligne."

A copy of the tune was sent to Lieut.-Colonel V. Arnoux, commanding the 116th, from whom the following reply was received:—

11e CORPS D'ARMÉE, 22ND DIVISION,
43RD BRIGADE.

AU BIVOUAC,
le 10 *Novembre* 1915.

Le Lieut.-Colonel ARNOUX, Commandant le 116th Regiment d'Infanterie à Monsieur le Lieut.-Colonel DOUGLAS BAIRD, Commandant le 1/8 Argyllshire Highlanders.

No. 1 Objet au sujet d'une marche militaire.

MON CHER CAMARADE,—J'ai l'honneur de vous accuser reception de la marche pour cornemutes composée par le corne-musier major de votre bataillon, et jouée par vos cornemutes et tambours le matin de la relève du 116th de Ligne dans le secteur de Thiepval Authuile.

Au nom de tous mes officiers et soldats je vous prie d'agréer mes vifs remerciements. Tous ont gardé au 116th le meilleurs souvenirs de cette marche dont le rhythme et l'harmonie melancolique evoquaient les mélodies du pays natal.

Je l'ai confiée à mon chef de musique qui s'occupe de vous composer une marche appropriée à notre musique sur la thème de la vôtre.

Cette harmonie de nos deux marches militaires sera un souvenir et un gage de plus de la bonne amitié qui unit nos deux regiments et nos deux armées dans la même ardeur vers la victoire commune.

Veuillez agréer, mon cher Camarade, l'expression de mes souvenirs les meilleurs et les plus devoués.

V. ARNOUX.

General Baumgarten, commanding the XIth French Corps d'Armée, remained in command until 5th August, when General Bannatine-Allason took over from him,

THE PERIOD OF APPRENTICESHIP

with his headquarters at Senlis. General Baumgarten subsequently called on General Bannatine-Allason to express his delight with the manner in which the taking over had been carried out without any hitch in spite of the difficulties which arose from the difference of language.

The new sector proved to be both interesting and instructive. Many problems arose while the Division held this portion of the line which required solution, and which, as it turned out, were all solved satisfactorily.

The front was looked upon by the French as a quiet one, with the exception of a section of the line adjacent to the Albert-Bapaume road known as the Ilot. This ground had been captured by the French in a brilliant advance, and on this account, though of little tactical importance, continued to be held. Subsequently, after the Division had been relieved in this portion of the line, the troops were withdrawn from it. There can have been few places on the Western front where the distance separating the Allied and the German lines was less, as in the Ilot the breadth of the No Man's Land was in some places no more than ten yards. The opposing trenches were thus well within bombing range, and the locality was a running sore to both sides.

The sector did not remain a quiet one for long, and throughout the Division's occupation of it every effort was required to prevent the enemy from gaining the upper hand.

The most acute problem was the enemy's activity in mining. When the sector was taken over from the French, the situation in this respect was anything but good. No British tunnelling companies being available, French engineers remained in charge of mining operations. This was an unsatisfactory arrangement, and the work of countermining made little progress, while the efforts of the enemy were fully maintained.

On the 22nd August the 179th Tunnelling Company, R.E., arrived in the area and relieved the French engineers. It had by this time become evident that a very considerable effort would be necessary to check the enemy's mining if it was to continue possible to hold the existing front-line trenches. The 179th Tunnelling Company had only a strength of 300 men with which to take over from the

500 men which the French had employed in the sector. It was therefore decided to reinforce the tunnellers by attaching to them infantry who in civil life had been skilled miners.

Sixty miners from each infantry brigade were accordingly added to the tunnellers. The efforts of the tunnelling company thus reinforced, by dint of working continuous shifts day and night, proved equal to the task, with the result that superiority as regards the mining situation ultimately passed to the British.

It was, however, only after a severe struggle that this result was obtained. The discharging of mines and of camouflets—small discharges used for blowing in the opponent's galleries—were almost of daily occurrence.

Mine warfare played so large a part in the trench warfare of 1915, 1916, and 1917, and so affected the daily life of the soldier in the trenches, that a description of what it means to those engaged in it may not be out of place.

In the first instance, success in mine warfare is dependent on the tunnelling company. By their efforts it is determined whether our troops are to be blown up by the enemy, or whether it is the enemy who is to meet this fate. To secure protection for the troops listening galleries have to be driven at various points along the front, so that the enemy's galleries can be located by sound, and the element of surprise can then be eliminated. The tunnellers who listen in these galleries are equipped with instruments by which the enemy can be heard working. If he is close, he can be heard by the ear alone. In chalk, a good medium for the carrying of sound, he can be heard working, without the aid of instruments, many feet away. If he is heard still using picks or shovels, it is known that he has not driven his gallery as far as he intends, and that there is therefore no immediate prospect of his blowing. If, on the other hand, he is heard tamping—*i.e.*, packing in his explosive—it is known that his work is nearly completed, and that his mine will in a few hours be ready for exploding. In the latter case two alternatives are available, either of which may be adopted to protect the troops from the effect of his blowing. First, if we have a gallery sufficiently close to his, we may blow a small mine or camouflet,

THE PERIOD OF APPRENTICESHIP

designed either to destroy his gallery or so to disintegrate the soil by the explosion as to make further tunnelling impossible. If a camouflet is impracticable, the only other alternative is to evacuate the area which it is estimated will be affected by the explosion.

In some cases the tunnelling company were able to destroy his galleries by camouflets when they were actually being worked, and thus bury the tunnellers and their spoiling parties. On these occasions the tunnelling company were always highly elated, as they took a professional pride in scoring off their real opponents the tunnellers, and considered this a far finer achievement than blowing up a trench full of mere infantrymen.

The Germans also adopted the same tactics, and continuous warfare between the tunnellers of both sides raged underground. Though the tunnellers, when once in their galleries, were free from the attentions of snipers, trench-mortars, and shells, yet their own form of warfare was hazardous and dangerous enough. When the galleries of the opposing sides were close, it was never known whether a gallery had not been located and might not at any moment be blown in, all the men working in it being crushed or suffocated.

On occasions a British and German gallery would meet, and hand-to-hand fights with picks and crowbars underground would ensue, which had to be fought out in darkness in the narrow tunnels.

The danger from natural gases, with all the attendant difficulties of rescuing men overcome by the fumes, was constant. Falls of earth and chalk, possibly due to some heavy explosion above ground, might also occur, which might bury the worker or cut him off from the exit of the gallery.

It must be remembered that the tunnellers were not highly trained soldiers in their early manhood, but professional miners, often men of middle age, who had in many cases come to France straight from the pits at home. They were, indeed, a splendid breed of men, and the infantry owed much to them. There is little question but that they were far superior to the German tunneller. The latter was often a cunning worker, but the British tunneller could always be relied on to beat him for pace. It may also be added that the tunnelling companies all contained an appreciable number of Scottish miners.

Mine warfare affects the infantry in several ways. First, it necessitates their finding an enormous number of carrying parties to assist in getting rid of the spoil, as the excavated earth or chalk is called. The infantryman never liked this work, as, among other things, it made his clothing, particularly his kilt, extremely dirty. It also appeared unending. However, he was reasonably contented with it if he had the satisfaction of occasionally seeing the German trenches and dug-outs hoisted into the air.

The question of finding working parties is, however, a minor consideration for the infantry when compared with the possible effects of the explosion of a German mine. This usually occurred either as darkness fell or during the night. Though warning might have been given by the tunnellers that a mine was to be expected, yet the explosion always appeared to come as a surprise. To a man standing up in the vicinity of an explosion the first sensation was a feeling that he had been struck on the soles of the feet by a heavy beam. This was immediately followed by the opening up of the earth and the issuing forth of a belch of flame, capped with a great rolling cloud of smoke and followed instantaneously by a deep muffled roar.

Huge fragments of earth and chalk, some weighing a ton or more, with wire entanglements, trench-boards, dug-out timbers—all were hurled many feet into the air. There followed a sensible pause, and then for some seconds the falling débris would come pouring down. This in turn was followed by a mist of dust which continued to float in the air for many minutes.

If the explosion had occurred under an occupied portion of the trench, the men in the area which was transferred into the crater were either immediately buried or else hurled many feet into the air in the sheet of flame and smoke, often to descend back into the crater crushed, bruised, burnt, and almost invariably dead. Others in the immediate vicinity of the explosion were crushed in their shelters or buried in the trenches by the collapse of their sides. Men further away, in their turn, were in danger of being killed or mutilated by the falling débris of stones and chalk which whirled down from a great

THE PERIOD OF APPRENTICESHIP 37

height into the trenches. The result was a scene of horrible desolation. Nothing remained intact. Trenches with their garrisons were obliterated. The positions where posts had once been could only be determined by rifles or limbs projecting through the upturned earth. At times, the heaving of the earth showed where some buried man, still alive, was struggling to extricate himself. The whole air was fetid with the sickly stench of high explosive.

Mine warfare was, indeed, the most trying ordeal to which troops holding trenches were exposed.

Next to mining, the most nerve-racking form of trench warfare was provided by the trench-mortar. Towards the latter end of August the enemy began to make a considerable use of these weapons. In consequence the trenches were frequently severely damaged, and many casualties were sustained. The British trench-mortars were in these days only in their early experimental stages; moreover, difficulty always existed in obtaining sufficient ammunition for them to be of any real service.

The enemy, on the other hand, appears to have had an unlimited supply of ammunition for mortars of a considerably heavier calibre and longer range than ours. At this time his commonest types were those that discharged the "oil can" or "rum jar" and the aerial torpedo. The "oil can" was little more than a tin canister about nine inches in diameter, filled with high explosive, and fitted with a time fuze. In those days it was fired from a smooth-bored wooden mortar, and in consequence turned over and over in its flight, and was therefore not particularly accurate. The explosion was, however, terrific, devastating to wire or trenches, and most trying to the nerves of any one who had to live in an area in which they habitually burst.

The aerial torpedoes had a fixed propeller which kept them from turning over in the air, and were in consequence a more accurate projectile. Their effects were if anything worse than those of the "oil can."

The Division had attached to it one 1½-inch mortar battery and a 4-inch mortar battery for which ammunition was available only in small quantities. On 2nd September, a 2-inch trench-mortar battery arrived, though its ammunition did not join it till 7th October.

The 2-inch trench-mortar fired a bomb exactly similar in shape to the hammer used in Highland games in "throwing the hammer." For this reason it was known to the troops as "Donald Dinnie." It was also known as the "Plum Pudding" or "Football." It was on this account that an English brigade-major was once heard to confess that he had always thought "Donald Dinnie" was Scots for plum pudding.

The "Donald Dinnie" was an excellent projectile when it burst in the right place. Sometimes, however, it did not burst at all, while at others it burst within a few feet of the mortar. Again, the mortar frequently misfired. Trench-mortaring was rather a game of chance in those days, with the odds slightly against the man firing the mortar.

In the early days of the "Donald Dinnie" its long iron handle, with a diameter of two inches, was firmly fixed to the bomb. On occasions this handle was blown tremendous distances by the explosion, and more than once fell in the British trenches, causing casualties to the garrison.

There was thus no adequate weapon with which to counter the German trench-mortars. He was therefore able to do considerable damage to our trenches and troops, more or less, with impunity.

It was in consequence necessary to institute a system of artillery retaliation, by which a certain number of rounds were fired back at the enemy by howitzers for every trench-mortar round he fired. Howitzers of various calibres up to 6-inch as well as the field-guns took part in these retaliatory shoots, according to the ammunition supply. As this became more liberal, this system tended to check the enemy's trench-mortar activity, particularly when, by careful observation, the positions of his trench-mortar emplacements were located, and the retaliation was brought to bear actually on the offending mortars.

The enemy could, however, bombard certain sections of trenches so systematically that he was able to obliterate them. This was particularly the case opposite La Boisselle and in an area known as the Salient. The latter received so much attention as to become untenable, and on 1st December it was evacuated, a retrenchment being dug and occupied behind it.

During these trench-mortar bombardments, it had been

THE PERIOD OF APPRENTICESHIP

discovered that the French shelters, having only three or four feet of cover, were not shell-proof. They were, in fact, death-traps, as they gave the men a false sense of security. In consequence, during a bombardment men would crowd into them to take cover, and should a trench-mortar bomb then strike one of them, it was blown in and all its occupants were killed.

On 21st October it was therefore decided to provide fresh dug-out accommodation for the whole garrison. The tunnelling company, as has been explained, was strained to its utmost to keep pace with the mining situation. The construction of the dug-outs was therefore entrusted to the 8th Royal Scots, who had joined the Division as the Divisional Pioneer Battalion on 25th August 1915. Fresh calls were made on the infantry for skilled miners, who were attached to the 8th Royal Scots. Work was carried on day and night, and the greatest exertions were made to provide the Division with shell-proof shelters with the minimum of delay.

These dug-outs were designed to give 10 to 12 feet of head cover. Charges of 60 lb. and 100 lb. of gun-cotton were exploded on the roofs of dug-outs of this depth, and the shock of the explosion was successfully resisted.[1]

Attempts were made to construct dug-outs by digging deep pits and then roofing them in with layers of material calculated to burst shells; but this was found to take more time than was required to construct a dug-out by tunnelling.

While the mining and the construction of dug-outs was being carried on as intensively as possible, an enormous amount of spoil (excavated earth and chalk) was accumulated. The disposal of this spoil became a very serious problem. Chalk cannot be scattered broadcast except at a distance from the shaft-heads, as its presence would disclose to the enemy that work was in progress and draw shell-fire. The accumulation of spoil was thus very difficult to dispose of, and frequently the trenches became almost impassable owing to the heaps of sandbags full of chalk stacked against their sides waiting to be emptied. The usual method of disposing of this spoil was to dump

---

[1] With the later and more delayed fuzes it was necessary to have thirty feet of head cover to be secure against bursts of 5·9-in. or 8-in. shells.

it into disused trenches and shell-holes. These, however, were soon filled, and it became evident that elaborate arrangements must be made beforehand for dealing with the spoil whenever operations entailing excavations on a large scale are planned, otherwise vast accumulations will be formed.

In this sector it was therefore necessary to establish a carefully-organised system of spoiling parties to keep pace with the output of the tunnellers and pioneers. It was only thus that it could be ensured that the intensive mining and dug-out construction would not be checked owing to delays in dealing with the excavated earth.

Large numbers of men had thus to be found daily for this work, with the result that there was little labour available for the ordinary duties of trench maintenance. As long as the weather remained fine, difficulty was not experienced on this account. Subsequently, however, when the weather changed, the whole Division was taxed to its utmost to keep the trenches in a condition which rendered them passable to troops.

This was particularly difficult in the sector between La Boisselle and Thiepval. Here above the chalk was a deep overlay of clay. Thus, when towards the end of the year there was a heavy fall of rain and subsequently of snow, the country in this area became water-logged, and in consequence the sides of the trenches were continually collapsing. This was partly due to the fact that the trenches constructed by the French were cut with perpendicular sides. Trenches of this pattern stood well enough in fine weather or where cut in chalk, but when cut in clay could not withstand the additional pressure which the weight of absorbed rain-water brought into play. The result was that throughout this portion of the sector the sides of the trenches fell in, and they became merely shapeless ditches knee- or waist-deep in mud and water. Water and mud, too, flowed down the stairs of the dug-outs unless dams were carefully made, while the "Bairnsfather" type of shelter collapsed on to its occupants at least once with fatal results.

The nature of the soil was such that revetment was of little avail. Even machine-gun pits revetted with close-lagged timbers—that is to say, with their walls supported

THE PERIOD OF APPRENTICESHIP

by a continuous lining of thick planking—caved in. The result was that the struggle with the elements almost took precedence over the struggle with the enemy. The carrying out of reliefs became a question of many hours, and entailed great exhaustion to the troops. The labour required for trench maintenance was far in excess of the resources of the Division. Attempts were made to dig out the trenches with their sides at a slope of 6/1, which would enable them to stand in spite of the incessant pressure on their sides due to the absorbed water. The soil was, however, of such a nature that digging in its sodden state imposed an immense physical strain on the men. Not only was the weight of the mud on the shovel considerable, but the mud adhered to the face of the shovel and could not be flung clear of the trench. In consequence, the men often had to hoist the shovel with its load out of the trench, leaving the earth to be scraped from the shovel by a man working above ground.

In spite of the increasing labours of the men, as long as the wet weather continued it was only possible to keep the trenches sufficiently open to enable troops to pass along them with difficulty. In some cases, notably in Campbell Avenue, even this was not possible, and the trench became temporarily unfit for use. Subsequently the frost came, and the labours of trench maintenance, to the delight of all, suddenly ceased. The sides of the trenches stood as though they had been carved out of wood. Officers and men began to take a fresh outlook on life. For the first time for many days they went dry-shod, and began to forget the unpleasant feeling of a mud-sodden kilt chafing the back of the knees, and of muddy water oozing between the toes at every step.

But this short-lived return to dry trenches only accentuated the miseries of the inevitable thaw, for the last state became worse than the first. Not only did the clay trenches on which so much labour had been expended collapse *en bloc*, but the action of the frost on the chalk made it crumble. In consequence the chalk trenches collapsed universally. The entire trench area became a ruin. The situation was such that strong measures alone could deal with it. The mining could not be discontinued, as this would involve too serious a risk. All other work was, however, stopped, and the 8th Royal Scots and the Reserve Brigade were all employed on restoring order out of this most appalling chaos. Even with this amount of labour available, as long as wet weather with short intermittent periods of frost alternated, more earth and chalk fell into the trenches day by day than could be cleared out in a day by the available working parties.

Apart from the mining operations, the construction of dug-outs, and the creation of entanglements, little new work was carried out in this sector. The French had already begun a system of defence in depth. This was worked upon and improved. The only important new work undertaken was the construction of the corps reserve lines, known as the Bouzincourt Switch, which ran from Martinsart to Bouzincourt and across the river Ancre to Albert.

In this reserve line there were constructed what are believed to be the first concrete " pill-boxes " made either by the Allies or the Germans on the Western Front. These were formed of walls of reinforced concrete five feet thick, with loopholes through which machine-guns could fire.

After the British lines had been driven back by the great German offensive in March 1918, these pill-boxes were situated in or about No Man's Land, and were on several occasions struck by direct hits. They were, however, undamaged, and, it is hoped, played the part with success for which they were intended.

During the period in which the Division was in this sector, great progress towards efficiency was made by the Divisional artillery. By the time they had arrived in France mobile warfare was for the time being in abeyance. This was a distinct advantage to Territorial gunners, as the conditions of service in peace time afforded them few opportunities for training for warfare of movement. They had, however, devoted a considerable amount of study to technical gunnery. Consequently, they had less ground to make up than would have been the case if they had been engaged in a war of movement.

Their training at home had, however, been carried out under difficult conditions, and when they arrived they still required considerable training as units. This was mostly carried out in the line, as from the time of its arrival in France the artillery was practically continuously

THE PERIOD OF APPRENTICESHIP

in action until early in 1916. In spite of this they made great progress. An artillery brigade commander describes them as follows : " By the end of their first year they were good ; by the end of their second year they were better; and by the end of their third year they were first-class field artillery,—very mobile, very quick, and full of initiative."

On the 31st August the 15-pounders were replaced by 18-pounders, to the great relief of all concerned. The 15-pounders had always suffered from a very restricted supply of ammunition. What ammunition they had was so erratic as to be a positive danger to our own troops. The gunners also had not had the opportunities at home of becoming complete masters of their weapons. The result was that the artillery, working in these adverse circumstances, did not at first enjoy the confidence of the infantry. However, their work in this sector went far towards inspiring in the infantry full confidence in their gunners.

Preparations for the battle of Loos brought to the Division for the first time a fairly liberal supply of ammunition. This was to be employed for the purpose of wire-cutting and bombardment as a feint to the big attack farther north.

On 23rd September 600 rounds (18-pounder) were issued, and on 25th September a further 1200 rounds, an unheard-of amount in those days.

The use of the artillery became less rigid than had been the case during the first few months at the front. On 8th November an 18-pounder gun was run up during the night to Coniston Street, about 800 yards behind the front line. From this position, as soon as there was sufficient light, thirty-six rounds were fired at an enemy sap, on which work was in progress, at a range of 1200 yards.

On 15th December experiments were made in wire-cutting with 4·5 howitzers. One howitzer fired at a range of 800 yards with percussion shrapnel and was most successful, a lane being cut right through the belt of wire.

The following extract from the Divisional war diary for 28th August may be quoted as a typical instance of the enterprise shown by the Division as regards the use of artillery during this period :—

"The repair of the parapets damaged by our mines of the 28th had been constantly hindered by enemy rifle grenades, large trench-mortar bombs, and aerial torpedoes. The last two sorts of bombs, having a very large charge, had reduced the front and support line trenches opposite La Boisselle (where most of our mine shafts are) to such an extent that passage along them had been dangerous. Only one 1½-inch mortar battery was available to reply, as the 4-inch battery had no ammunition. Sanction was obtained for the expenditure of 5-inch and 6-inch howitzer and 18-pounder ammunition to keep down the enemy's fire, and enable a day working party to work on the demolished trenches. Work was continued all day with only eight casualties."

On 28th November 1915 three 18-pounder batteries of the Lowland Brigade were brought into action, bringing the Divisional artillery up to establishment.

An advance was also made in this sector in machine gunnery. Eight machine-gun emplacements were made, fitted with traversing mountings for indirect fire. These mountings were designed by Captain S. J. L. Hardie, machine-gun officer of the 152nd Brigade, and made by the Divisional Supply Column.

By this means aimed indirect fire was brought to bear by day or night on localities known to be constantly used by the enemy.

In this period few events occurred which call for detailed description. The explosion of mines was of frequent occurrence, and in several cases the trenches sustained damage and losses were incurred. On the 12th and 20th August the French tunnellers were successful in destroying sections of the enemy's trenches with mines, but on the latter date the mine also did considerable damage to the British trenches.

In September preparations for the battle of Loos began. The Third Army was not involved in this attack. Efforts were, however, made to lead the enemy to anticipate an offensive in this sector, so as to make him unwilling to transfer reserves from this front to the scene of the actual operations.

Accordingly on 21st September work was begun on preparing the sector for attack. Sap-heads and forming-up

THE PERIOD OF APPRENTICESHIP 45

places were constructed, while the artillery carried out wire-cutting and bombardment.

On 25th September the combined British and French attack was launched at Loos. On the 26th preparations for attack were discontinued in the Divisional sector. On the 27th the allowance of ammunition was reduced to the minimum requirements necessary for retaliation.

During the sojourn of the Division in this part of France bombardments of villages in the back areas occurred fairly frequently — Henencourt (Corps Headquarters), Aveluy, Authuille, Albert, and Martinsart all receiving attention.

The enemy was particularly lucky with one heavy shell which he fired into Authuille on 29th November. It burst close to a working party of the 5th Seaforths, who had just fallen in to draw tools from a dump, and wounded 26 of them, including 2 officers.

On 18th September Martinsart was bombed by a hostile aeroplane, in those days a most unusual occurrence.

On Christmas Day a curious exchange of compliments took place with the enemy. On Christmas Eve he sang carols; this was at once stopped by the Divisional artillery. He then came out of his trenches to fraternise; this was also stopped by the Divisional artillery. He retaliated by shelling Albert; the Division on the right immediately shelled Courcelette. The enemy then shelled Aveluy; the gunners replied by shelling Pozières. The enemy had the last word, for he then shelled Martinsart, where he hit a horse, a mule, and a limber loaded with grenades, which fortunately did not burst.

While the Division was in this sector various other New Army Divisions, as has been mentioned, were attached to it for periods of instruction in the line. The men did not fail to make the most of the fact that they had been selected as instructors for the rival organisation, the New Armies, and it was a matter of great satisfaction to them to find that they had been chosen for the work.

On 2nd August the Divisional artillery had taken over from the French, and taken into the line six batteries of the 18th Division, who were attached for instruction. The artillery were particularly jealous of the 18-pounders with which their pupils were armed, while they were still equipped with the obsolete 15-pounder. The same night the 53rd

Infantry Brigade Group, 18th Division, also moved into the line to begin a period of attachment to the 51st Division for instruction in trench warfare. Other units of the 18th Division followed, and carried out similar periods of instruction in the line.

On conclusion of this attachment, when the 18th Division took over a section of the line from the 51st, Major-General F. I. Maxse, commanding the 18th Division, wrote the following appreciative letter to General Bannatine-Allason : " I must write you a line to say how grateful my Division is for the great assistance we have received from yours. General Ross has done more to help us than I have experienced from any other G.O.C. He not only left officers behind to put us up to local tips on his sector, but he told off his best snipers to put our snipers on to the Huns, which they successfully did. My people all swear by the 51st Division. May we long soldier together."

General Maxse became a great friend of the 51st Division, particularly when, in 1917, the Division carried out two most successful operations under his command as Corps commander in the third battle of Ypres.

In September the 65th Infantry Brigade Group and a brigade of artillery of the 22nd Division carried out its period of instruction in trench warfare attached to the 51st. Later in the same month officers of the 36th (Ulster) Division were similarly attached. In December the 32nd Division was instructed in the same manner, and finally relieved the 51st in this sector.

On 24th September 1915 General Bannatine-Allason gave up command of the Highland Division. He had for some time been in indifferent health. The strain of the past four months, in which he had commanded the Division during its first experiences of war, had been severe, and the General therefore felt that he could not either with justice to himself or to his Division continue in so responsible a position until his health was sufficiently recovered.

He therefore returned to England, and was given command of the 61st (2nd Line South Midland) Territorial Division. During the period of his command of the 2nd Line Highland Division, the General despatched over 15,000 men and over 3000 horses to the front. Most of

Major-General R. Bannatine-Allason, C.B.

THE PERIOD OF APPRENTICESHIP 47

these men were sent as reinforcements to the 51st Division, so that he still materially contributed towards the successes of the Division. From this fact, and from the fact that under his command the Division was first initiated into the ways of war, General Bannatine-Allason is still known in the Highlands as the "nurse" of the 51st Division.

General Bannatine-Allason was succeeded by Major-General G. M. Harper, C.B., D.S.O., who was promoted from the command of the 17th Brigade, 6th Division, to the command of the Highland Division.

General Harper, during his period of command, inspired all ranks with such confidence that it is difficult to express the high regard in which he was held by the Division.

The success and consequent reputation gained by the Highland Division can be attributed to the happy combination of the particular qualities of the commander and his troops, and to the brilliant manner in which the directing genius of the former was seconded by the genius for fighting of the latter.

No better selection of a commander could have been made for the Division, and no Division could have better suited the particular qualities possessed by the new commander. Experience has since proved that General Harper understood the ways and means of defeating the German in a manner which was probably unequalled, and certainly never surpassed on the Western Front. Further, he possessed such gifts as an instructor as enabled him to train his Division in these ways and means in a manner which set a standard to the British armies in France.

On their part, under General Harper's command, the Highlanders proved that they possessed qualities which enabled them to respond to training in a degree which few other troops could equal.

The result was that General Harper, having formulated principles applicable to every phase of attack and defence, was able to imbue his whole Division in their training with these principles. In consequence, during active operations, officers and N.C.O.'s could be relied on to lead their men intelligently in any circumstances in accordance with tactical methods in which they had already been exercised in their training.

The relief of the Division by the 32nd Division began

on 23rd December, and was completed by 2nd January 1916. After the relief, the Division moved to the Flesselles area, coming under orders of the Ist Corps. Their time in the line, beginning as it had done on 30th July 1915, had been long and arduous. The men were in consequence beginning to show signs of becoming stale. Though there had been no infantry action beyond a few encounters between patrols and a small bombing raid carried out by the 154th Infantry Brigade on 2nd January 1916, yet the conditions had been far from pleasant.

Great strides had been made by the enemy in trench weapons, the range, calibre, and accuracy of his trench-mortars, and the numbers in which they were employed, having considerably increased. His rifle grenades had also been improved, and were used with increasing frequency. The mining situation, as has already been pointed out, had at one time been serious, though it never led to the same serious infantry fighting which occurred later in the Labyrinth. The want of shell-proof cover had been considerably felt; the burden of work imposed on the Division when the trenches collapsed had been almost insupportable. The general conditions of trench life during this period are admirably summed up in Sir Douglas Haig's despatch, dated 29th May 1916, as follows :—

" Although the struggle in a general sense has not been intense, it has been everywhere continuous. . . .

" The maintenance and repair of our defences alone, especially in winter, entails constant heavy work. Bad weather and the enemy combine to flood and destroy trenches, dug-outs, and communications ; all such damages must be repaired promptly under fire, and almost certainly by night.

" Artillery and snipers are practically never silent, patrols are out in front of the lines every night, and heavy bombardments by the artillery of one or both sides take place daily in various parts of the line. Below ground there is continual mining and counter-mining, which, by the ever-present threat of sudden explosion and the uncertainty as to where and when it will take place, causes perhaps a more constant strain than any other form of warfare. . . . In short, a steady and continuous fight has gone on day and night above ground and below it."

THE PERIOD OF APPRENTICESHIP

It will be appreciated from the above that, though many of the days under review were described in the official communiqués as "quiet days on the Western Front," the quietude was not always apparent to those who lived within the range of the enemy's activities.

The absence of depression amongst the men in these adverse circumstances was, however, constantly remarked on, and throughout the Division remained in good spirits.

Colonel Ian Stewart reports an incident which bears witness to the imperturbability of the men even in the Ilot, the storm centre of the mining activity. Colonel Stewart was crawling round the front line with General Ross, in such close contact to the enemy that they dare speak only in whispers for fear of provoking a shower of rifle- or hand-grenades. As they came round a sandbagged traverse they found a Jock sitting on his firestep, smoking the inevitable cigarette and reading 'Pearson's Magazine,' quite oblivious to his proximity to the enemy.

Colonel Stewart, shortly after arriving back at Divisional Headquarters, received a telephone message from General Ross informing him that he was just going up to the line to investigate a mine which had been exploded almost in the exact spot where the Jock had been reading 'Pearson's.' The fate of the said Jock was not recorded.

The Division had profited considerably by their prolonged tour in the same sector, and had completed its education in trench warfare in a most thorough manner. The men had learnt trench-craft, that art which enables them to keep the enemy constantly on the alert and at the same time to protect themselves by their wits from avoidable casualties and discomforts.

They had also had time to acquire that sixth sense which a short spell of the war gave to all the fighting troops, of working, walking, and fighting in the dark. They had become good snipers, and experienced trench workers. They had learnt valuable lessons regarding such questions as the influence of the nature of the soil on trench construction, the organisation of working parties, the disposal of mine spoil, &c.

In fact, the Division was most fortunately placed. After

a long experience of close contact with the enemy, it was now to be given a period in which time would be available to collect and crystallise its thoughts on the problems of defence and to be trained by General Harper in the principles of the attack.

CHAPTER IV.

TRAINING AND REORGANISATION—THE LABYRINTH.

THE Division was now out of the line for the first time under General Harper's command, and the latter lost no time in instructing officers and men in a form of attack which at the time was employed by no other Division.

Past experience, emphasised by the battle of Loos, had made it evident that to hold captured ground against the inevitable counter-attack, the attackers have not only to compete with the enemy actually manning the assaulted trenches. They must, in addition, dispose themselves at the end of the advance in a manner which enables them to resist the counter-attacks which will inevitably be delivered by the enemy's reserves. In the past, the objectives of the attack had not been sufficiently clearly defined, with the result that the forward movement frequently came to an end with some bodies of troops far in advance of others, and all in a state of disorganisation. The foremost troops were thus left exposed, holding insufficiently consolidated salients, and disposed in a manner which prevented command being adequately exercised over them. The result was that the enemy was able to employ his fresh reserves against the tired and disorganised troops holding these salients. His counter-attacks, organised so as to be delivered both frontally and from the flanks, were in consequence frequently successful.

It thus followed that Divisions which in the early phases of an attack had carried out a brilliant advance, were subsequently in the later stages often overwhelmed and severely cut up.

It had, further, been the custom in the past for the same body of troops to be ordered to fight its way through a succession of trench lines or defended localities. Thus, as the action progressed, the attack became weaker and more disorganised through casualties, and so increasingly lost its driving power. At the same time, when the forward movement came to a standstill, no organised bodies of troops were left suitably disposed to hold the ground gained.

The plan of attack adopted by the 51st Division was designed to eradicate both these sources of failure. It was realised that if counter-attacks were to be defeated, the advance must be made in a series of clearly-defined bounds. Each bound was to be made good before the operations for the capture of the next began.

Further, the idea was to employ a fresh body of troops for each bound. Thus, when the troops detailed for a particular bound had reached their objective, they remained on it, and disposed themselves in the most suitable manner to hold the ground they had gained against counter-attacks. A fresh body of troops then passed through them and made good the next bound, consolidating in their turn the ground gained.

This form of attack became the sealed pattern for all attacks carried out by the Highland Division, and was largely responsible for the many outstanding successes of the Division.

Gradually as the war progressed and the Division achieved one success after another, its value became apparent, and it eventually became the stereotyped form of attack in the majority of the Divisions in France.

During this period, apart from the training of units under their own commanders, Divisional schools of instruction were formed to give individual training to officers and N.C.O.'s. A Divisional grenade school was formed, at which 13 officers and 260 other ranks were put through a course every week. At this course instruction was given in the Mills bomb, which had now replaced the former types of improvised bomb.

A Divisional school for infantry was also opened at Villers-Bocage under Lieut.-Colonel D. Baird, commanding the 8th Argyll and Sutherland Highlanders. At this school 20 officers and 40 N.C.O.'s attended a series of fourteen-day courses. The object of this school was to increase the powers of command of the senior officers and N.C.O.'s, and to improve their knowledge of tactics.

A show-ground was also laid out, where the best methods to be adopted in trench warfare could be demonstrated. Here also types of trenches suitable to the varying natures and conditions of ground were constructed for purposes of instruction.

On 8th February the course of training was interrupted by the move of the Division to the Daours area, with a view to taking over from the 30th Division, on the sector on the north bank of the Somme. The orders for this relief were, however, cancelled on the 18th February, and the Division moved back to the Flesselles area.

During this period the composition of the Division underwent considerable alteration. The three Lancashire battalions left the Division on 3rd January 1916 to join the 55th (West Lancashire) Division.

The 6th Scottish Rifles joined the 33rd Division. They were met again later by many of their former comrades of the Highland Division in High Wood in July and August 1916.

These four battalions were replaced by the 4th and 5th Black Watch, the 4th Seaforths and 4th Camerons. Brigadier-General C. E. Stewart, Black Watch, was placed in command of this brigade, and it retained the title 154th Infantry Brigade.

In February 1916 further changes took place; the 4th and 5th Black Watch were posted to General Headquarters, and the 4th Camerons to the Base. These three battalions were replaced in the 154th Infantry Brigade by the 9th Royal Scots, the 4th Gordon Highlanders, and the 7th Argyll and Sutherland Highlanders.

All the battalions in the reconstituted 154th Infantry Brigade had landed in France some months before the remainder of the Division, being posted to various regular brigades as an additional battalion.

Thus, as regards the infantry, the original composition of the Highland Division was restored, with the exception of the 4th Cameron Highlanders, the 6th Gordon Highlanders, and the 9th Argyll and Sutherland Highlanders.

During the same month changes were also made as regards the organisation of machine-guns. The infantry battalions had joined the Expeditionary Force each equipped with two machine-guns under the command of the battalion machine-gun officer. In July 1915 the battalion machine-gun section was increased by an additional two guns.

In January 1916 a machine-gun company of sixteen guns was affiliated to each brigade. These companies were formed by the amalgamation of the four battalion machine-gun sections in each brigade, Captains Hardie, Calder, and Board commanding the companies of the 152nd, 153rd, and 154th Infantry Brigades respectively.

In the early part of 1916 the trench-mortar situation was greatly improved. Three 2-inch trench-mortar batteries were formed by the Divisional artillery. These mortars fired the 60-pound bomb already described known as the "Donald Dinnie." They were still considerably inferior to the German trench-mortars in range, but they constituted a considerable advance on all previous experiments. Their chief faults lay in their liability to misfire, and in their frequent inaccuracy, due to the boxes containing the component parts not being water-tight.

When the "Donald Dinnie" did burst on its target, the effect was gratifying. The retaliation they almost invariably drew from the enemy was the best evidence of their efficacy, and made the duty of serving the mortars an extremely hazardous one.

In May 1916 a light trench-mortar battery, consisting of four Stokes mortars, was formed for each brigade. The Stokes gun proved the most satisfactory British light trench-mortar invented, and remained the weapon of the light trench-mortar batteries throughout the war.

On 1st March 1916 orders were received for the Division to march northwards and take over from the 23rd French Division of the XIIme Corps d'Armée in a sector north of Arras, now known to history as the Labyrinth. This move was due to the necessity for the British to take over more line from the French. The object was to free as many French Divisions as possible for the defence of Verdun, against which the German was delivering his great attack.

Preliminary reconnaissances of the new line by senior commanders and their staffs began on 3rd March. The first troops moved off to the new area on 6th March. During the march, the Division staged in the Beauval-Candas area and the Frevent area. Finally, Divisional headquarters opened on 12th March at Duisans, General Harper taking over command of the line at 8 A.M. on that date.

The march to the new area is chiefly memorable to those who took part in it from the fact that much of it was carried out in a blinding snowstorm, with all its attendant discomforts.

The cold was intense, and was severely felt by parties proceeding to carry out preliminary reconnaissances in motor lorries and by the troops as they arrived each night in new billets.

The Division, after its six weeks period of rest and training, was at the top of its form, and presented a most soldierly appearance. It had profited considerably from its training, in spite of the fact that it had been handicapped by spells of bad weather.

This was the last period of rest of more than ten days' duration which the Division was to have until the following January.

The new sector extended roughly from the ruined village of Roclincourt on the right to the ruined village of Neuville St Vaast (exclusive) on the left. The front line trenches were some thousand yards east of these two villages.

This country had been the scene of tremendous fighting when the French had advanced along the Lorette ridge and attacked the Vimy heights in conjunction with the British operations at Loos.

Here the French had made considerable progress, much of it yard by yard, after bitter fighting. Their gains, however, had not all been held. The fighting had been of so desperate and stubborn a nature that French and Germans had repeatedly dug themselves in in close proximity to each other. As a result, the whole sector consisted of an unintelligible maze of trenches, aptly called by the French the Labyrinth.

The country in rear of the lines contained many villages now well known to the Highland Division—the ruins of Ecurie, Anzin, Marœuil, Bray, Ecoivres, Mont St Eloi. This area can almost be called the spiritual home of the

Highland Division in France, since it occupied it for three months in 1916, five months in 1917 during the battle of Arras, and returned there in May 1918. From May onwards it remained in that part of the world, with the exception of a brief interlude in Champagne, and from it began its victorious advance which culminated with the Armistice.

In this sector the whole countryside was overlooked by the enemy in an astonishing degree. He occupied the famous feature known as the Vimy Ridge, of which the highest point just north of Thelus reached the height of 135 metres. His foremost trenches were on the outlying spurs of the Ridge, while the trenches taken over from the French were in the low-lying ground at the foot of these spurs.

The enemy thus possessed all the advantages of close observation over our lines; while, in addition, from the upper slopes of the Ridge, he obtained a magnificent panoramic view of the whole of the areas in rear of the British trench systems. On a clear day he could see from Thelus as far westwards as the road running from Habarcq to the Hermaville-Arras road.

Moreover, south of the Scarpe, Observatory Ridge stared down at Roclincourt and Ecurie.

The French, to neutralise his facilities for observation, had constructed communication trenches of what seemed interminable length. These ran from Anzin, Marœuil, and Mont St Eloi to the fire trenches, none of these villages being within two miles of the front line. The labour of walking along these trenches, all cut on a very winding pattern, was severe. It, however, fortunately transpired that the French in constructing trenches of this length had either flattered the enemy's vigilance, or that his vigilance had subsequently diminished, as it proved unnecessary to walk inside the trenches, certainly for the first three-quarters of a mile.

The enemy did, however, keep a sharp look-out for movement on the roads within range of his artillery. He had, shortly before the Division arrived, killed a French regimental commander who took the liberty of riding on horseback along the Arras-Bethune road.

These long communication trenches were admirably dug by the French Territorials, who had constructed them,

TRAINING AND REORGANISATION

and were still standing and in daily use when the Division returned to this sector in February of the following year.

In the British lines the defended village of Ecurie, about 100 metres above sea-level, afforded a good view of Thelus and of the enemy's defences at a distance of from 400 to 500 yards behind his front line. Observation of his front-line trenches could in most places only be obtained from observation posts in the forward area.

The relief of the French 23rd and 24th Divisions of the XIIme Corps d'Armée was completed by 14th March. It was carried out during a blizzard of great severity, which continued for forty-eight hours. During this period the troops could do no more than remain where they had been placed by their guides, or misplaced as the case might be. During the relief and, in fact, until the blizzard abated, officers and men had only a hazy idea as to where they actually were. Similarly commanders were ignorant of the position of their troops. All three infantry brigades were in the line—the 154th Brigade on the right in the vicinity of Roclincourt, the 152nd in the centre, and the 153rd on the left.

When the weather cleared, it was found that the Division had taken over from the French an unintelligible tangle of trenches dug in what can only be described as a vast cemetery, in which the earth in many places barely covered the dead.

The sector was also honeycombed with mines from end to end, the enemy apparently being complete masters of the mining situation. In fact, his supremacy in mining had become so complete that, immediately prior to the relief, the French had drawn up a scheme for evacuating the front line except for lightly-held outposts. The plan they had intended to adopt was to recast the scheme of defence and construct amidst the existing network of derelict trenches a new support and reserve line. The scheme had been completed, and was on the point of being put into execution when the Highland Division took over the sector. The Divisional commander decided to continue with this policy. The construction of the new scheme of defences necessitated a vast amount of work, and was only fairly complete three months later when the Division left the sector.

This alteration in the siting of the trenches demanded the construction of an enormous number of dug-outs. It soon became evident that without these the daily casualty list must be heavy. Not only was the artillery activity considerable, but the German had also concentrated in this sector every type of trench-mortar which had been evolved, and was extremely free in his use of them.

The mining was of a more savage nature than had been the case in La Boisselle, and in many instances resulted in serious infantry fighting. The mines were, as a rule, blown by the enemy with two objects. If the breadth of No Man's Land was not considerable, they were frequently blown with a view to destroying our trenches with their garrisons. If, however, the breadth of No Man's Land was great, or his system of defensive galleries were good, he would blow his mines in No Man's Land with a view to occupying them as a line of observation and snipers' posts. By the frequent blowing of this type of mine, he was able to cover his front with a screen of craters which denied the British observation of his front line, and created for him a chain of commanding mounds along our front.

In some cases, if the crater formed by a mine explosion was some distance from the British front line, no infantry action would follow. If, however, a mine was blown under a British trench, it was usually accompanied by an enemy raid, which was planned to enter our trenches during the confusion caused by the mine and surprise the surviving garrison. If, on the other hand, it was blown in No Man's Land close to the British front line, it was necessary at all costs to prevent the enemy from occupying it. Thus in the two last cases heavy infantry fighting often occurred. In the latter case, the object of these actions was to prevent the enemy from establishing himself on the crater. If he did so the position was serious, for the crater became a permanent menace to the security of our lines. Where the ground might have been flat, a large hollow mound had now arisen. If the enemy established himself on the British side of the mound (*i.e.*, the near lip, as it was called), he might construct sniping-posts which would dominate the trenches. Should he only establish himself on the far lip, he still was able, by working around the lip of the

TRAINING AND REORGANISATION

crater towards the flank, to shoot down into our trenches in enfilade.

It was suggested that the Germans, by some peculiar method of tamping (*i.e.*, packing the explosive in the chamber), used to blow his craters with the far lip higher than the near lip. Thus, if he only established himself on the far lip, the near lip, being lower, did not obscure his view to the front; conversely the view from the near lip, if occupied by the British, was obscured to the front by the higher far lip. Whether his craters were formed in this manner from accident (*i.e.*, the lie of the ground) or from design is not clear. The fact remained that an examination of many craters in the Neuville St Vaast area proved this to be the case.

These crater fights often developed into considerable minor operations involving many casualties. They almost always took place in the dark, and were an unpleasant ordeal for all concerned.

The crater, still smoking from its base like a miniature volcano; the stench of the fumes; the whiteness of the freshly-turned chalk standing out in the darkness, produced a setting which intensified the normal horrors of battle.

When the German blew a mine he, of course, knew the hour and the place at which the explosion would occur. He knew also from the depth of his gallery and from the amount of explosive used how close to the spot his assaulting troops might assemble without fear from the falling débris. He was also able to assemble dumps of loophole plates, prepared and portable obstacles, bombs, &c., close to the scene of operations. The troops might or might not have been warned that a mine was to be expected in a certain area.

In these circumstances he therefore started with the odds considerably in his favour; and yet, as will be seen, as far as the Highland Division was concerned, he seldom met with the success he anticipated.

His plan was to form up his consolidating party as close to the place where the crater was to be blown as was safe. He then blew the mine, and simultaneously opened a barrage of artillery, trench-mortars, and rifle grenades, &c., on the two flanks and on the British side of the crater.

He thus hoped to deny to our troops access to it. Under cover of this barrage he then rushed his assaulting parties up to the crater, and attempted to consolidate posts both on the near and far lips.

Immediately, therefore, that a mine was blown, parties had to be organised to rush to the crater and seize at least the near lip. These parties had, of course, no previous knowledge as to the time at which the mine was to be exploded. They were also liable to be temporarily disorganised in the general confusion caused by the explosion. Thus, as a rule, when the crater fighting began, the enemy was already on the near lip before our parties were fairly on the scene.

A closely-contested fight would then ensue with bombs, Lewis guns, and rifles, and would continue until the enemy had been ejected at all events from the near lip. Posts would then be established on it, and a sap would be dug connecting the posts to the foremost British trench.

In these encounters casualties were frequently heavy, as the parties had often to pass through a heavy barrage, followed by their bomb carriers. The latter were employed in large numbers, as in this form of warfare several hundred bombs were often thrown in one night.

On first taking over, the mining situation was obscure. The French tunnellers had been withdrawn, leaving only old French Territorials to man the listening galleries. These veterans considered this duty *très dangereux*, as indeed it was.

In consequence, the period was marked by a constant state of anxiety as to what portions of the line were safe from the possibility of being blown up at any moment.

However, on the arrival of the British tunnelling companies, which were again largely reinforced by the coal miners in the Division, accurate information was soon obtained as regards the enemy's underground activity. The defensive galleries were first perfected, so that timely warning could be given of any mine that he was likely to explode. By this means camouflets could be used to hinder his progress. Subsequently it became possible to take the offensive, and mines were blown to destroy his crater positions and trenches.

Later, when heavy calls were made upon the German

troops to sustain the fighting on the Somme, they were compelled to relax their efforts in this sector, with the result that the British tunnellers established a marked superiority over them.

As soon as the aforementioned blizzard had cleared and commanders could find out the disposition of the men, it became evident that the ground in the forward area was far too thickly held. Orders were in consequence issued for the line to be thinned immediately. Small sectors of disused trenches were dug out to accommodate the surplus men temporarily while a more detailed scheme of defence could be formulated.

The advisability of this measure was soon proved, as from 24th March mines were continually being exploded under or in close proximity to the front line. A typical case occurred on 26th March, when at 2.30 A.M. the enemy fired two mines simultaneously, one on the left of the 152nd Brigade, the other on the right of the 153rd.

These explosions were followed by a heavy bombardment of our front and support trenches with shrapnel, all types of trench-mortar bombs, and rifle and machine-gun fire. A party of about eight Germans then advanced towards the crater in the 153rd Brigade area, but were driven back by two officers and a party of grenadiers. Our losses were severe: 4 officers (1 killed, 2 wounded, and 1 missing) and 74 other ranks (14 killed, 24 wounded, and 36 missing). In addition, there were 24 other ranks suffering from shock. Of these, one company of the 6th Argyll and Sutherland Highlanders lost 2nd Lieutenant M'Neil and 4 men killed, 5 wounded, and 15 missing. The missing were those unfortunate men who were buried by the falling earth. Of these two craters, the one on the right proved to be seventy yards in length.

On 31st March another mine was fired by the Germans on the front of the 153rd Brigade, with the loss of 1 officer wounded, 6 other ranks killed and 3 wounded. The explosion of this mine was also followed by an intense bombardment by weapons of all natures. A party of Germans then entered a sap. Of these one approached a Jock who had survived the explosion, and pointing his rifle at him, said, "Hands up, Englishman!" The infuriated Jock threw a Mills bomb at the German, having failed to remove the safety-pin, and shouted, "Scotsman, you —— bastard." The bomb struck the German full on the forehead and felled him. He was captured, and subsequently died in the casualty clearing station from a fractured skull.

The 6th Argyll and Sutherland Highlanders were particularly unfortunate as regards mines, and by the 10th April had already experienced six mines on their fronts.

On 28th April four mines were exploded in front of the 6th Seaforth Highlanders and 8th Argyll and Sutherland Highlanders. The resultant casualties to these two battalions were 6 officers wounded at duty, 12 other ranks killed, 75 wounded, and 30 missing, believed buried. The explosions of these mines were followed by a forty-five minutes' intense bombardment. The Divisional artillery, however, opened a barrage on the enemy's lines opposite the newly-formed craters with such rapidity that he was unable to employ his infantry. Throughout the whole period the manner in which the artillery supported the infantry in this form of warfare was admirable, and gave the latter great encouragement.

The explosion of mines became of such frequent occurrence that the troops became very expert in rapidly seizing and consolidating craters. Dumps were made at frequent intervals along the front containing all the materials required for consolidation. In a short time the troops could be relied on to establish themselves on the near lip, however unexpectedly a crater might be blown. This was largely due to the gallantry and initiative of the junior officers, on whose skill and leading success in these enterprises was dependent.

Demonstrations were given in consolidation, and a platoon for each front-line battalion was ear-marked for the consolidation of any mine crater which might be blown on the battalion's front.

A natural concomitant to mining was sniping. The lip of a crater affords an excellent post from which to snipe, particularly when, as was the case in this sector, the ground sloped from the German position towards the British. The trenches on this sector were also particularly open.

After the enemy positions in this sector had been captured by the Division in April 1917, an examination was made of the German crater posts. It was astonishing to

TRAINING AND REORGANISATION

see to what an extent he could look down into the British trenches. It was realised at the time that men walking along the trenches were often under observation, and, indeed, the casualties from sniping proved that this was so. It was not, however, appreciated till later to what a degree men in the trenches, particularly the communication trenches, were visible to the Germans. In some places even the duck-boards at the bottom of the trenches were in enemy view.

The result of this situation was that at first the enemy made a considerable bag by sniping; Colonel Campbell, commanding the 4th Seaforth Highlanders, was killed by a sniper the day after the Division had taken over the line. Within a fortnight his successor was killed in a similar way.

However, the Highland Division, with a number of stalkers and gillies in its ranks, had probably the best material the country produced from which to make snipers. After a short period devoted to organisation and training, the snipers of the Division soon obtained a superiority over the enemy. It, however, always remained a sector in which the greatest care had to be exercised in looking over the parapet or in moving amongst the saps and forward boyaux. Enemy snipers were continually shattering periscopes with rifle shots.

In the Labyrinth the Division made its first organised raids. These raids consisted in heavily barraging a certain area, then at a given moment the barrage lifted off certain portions of this area and allowed the assaulting infantry to enter it. The barrage remained down on three sides of the area to protect the attackers who entered it from the fourth side from interference from without while they were destroying the Germans within. This form of barrage, originally first employed by the Germans, was known as the Box Barrage.

The two most successful raids which took place during this period were those carried out by Lieutenant E. A. Mackintosh of the 5th Seaforth Highlanders (since killed in action), and Captain Herd of the 6th Black Watch. The former was in consequence awarded the Military Cross, and the latter the D.S.O.

Raids subsequently became of such frequent occurrence

that want of space forbids description of them all. Certain raids have, however, been selected for description, which will be dealt with later.

These raids in particular brought to light certain facts concerning German trench construction. The German trenches did not resemble the small ditch-like trenches commonly seen at schools of instruction and training grounds. They can better be compared to the marker's gallery in a rifle range. They were ten to eleven feet deep, with the sides for the most part revetted with planks. To get into them was not easy; to get out of them still less easy; while evacuating the wounded from them was a matter of very considerable difficulty. In fact, in the case of Mackintosh's raid, it is doubtful if his wounded could have been brought back to our lines at all had not a sally-port through which the more severely wounded were carried been discovered.

On 21st May the enemy became extremely active. The Divisional artillery were heavily bombarded during the afternoon and evening with lachrymatory shells, as also were the communication trenches. At the same time the trenches of the 25th Division on the left of the Highland Division, and of the 47th Division, were intensely bombarded. Marœuil, Anzin, and Mont St Eloi were also shelled during the night, as well as several villages in rear of the 25th and 47th Divisional areas. At Marœuil an 8-inch shell burst in the 152nd Brigade headquarter office within a few seconds of the clerks having left it for the cellar, completely wrecking it, and killing the staff captain's two horses, which were tethered outside it.

This bombardment culminated in a successful hostile attack, the enemy, with apparently little difficulty, attaining his object and establishing himself firmly on the western slopes of the Vimy Ridge.

The cause of his success was due to the fact that he succeeded in secretly concentrating a large force of artillery with which to support his attack. He then subjected all the trenches involved to a bombardment of an intensity which in those days was considered unparalleled. The garrisons of the trenches attacked were almost completely without the protection of shell-proof dug-outs, and the defenders were thus for the most part killed or wounded

TRAINING AND REORGANISATION

by the bombardment before the infantry attack was launched.

At this juncture the Divisional sector was considerably increased; in fact, the Division took over the whole front of the XVIIth Corps. This extension was caused by the necessity of withdrawing troops from this part of the line preparatory to the Somme battle.

The 152nd Brigade was withdrawn on 23rd May, the 153rd and 154th Brigades extending their brigade sectors so as to include the area previously held by the 152nd. On the nights 1-2nd June and 2-3rd the 152nd Brigade moved northwards and relieved troops of the 25th Division in the Neuville St Vaast sector.

To conceal from the enemy the fact that the whole Corps front was held by the Highland Division alone, the kilt was no longer worn by the troops in the line, khaki trousers being issued instead.

The situation in the new sector taken over by the 152nd Brigade was a curious one. The extreme left of the enemy's attack on the Vimy Ridge rested on the left boundary of the new sector. Thus on the brigade left boundary in the front and support lines the British and the Germans occupied the same trenches, sandbag bombing-stops alone separating them. In some cases the British held communication trenches while the Germans occupied the trench into which the communication trench led, bombing-blocks again separating the two forces.

Across these blocks lively exchanges of bombs and rifle grenades spasmodically occurred. The distance separating the opposing sides was, however, so small that artillery and trench-mortars could be used by neither owing to the danger of short rounds inflicting casualties on friends as well as foes.

In these circumstances the left flank in the front and support lines was very unprotected and presented to the enemy a "raw edge." It was an uncomfortable situation, as there appeared to be every prospect of the enemy's developing his initial success by a flank attack delivered southwards from the area into which he had penetrated.

The feeling of apprehension on this score was accentuated by the fact that if he supported this attack with a similar concentration of artillery, the absence of shell-proof dug-outs in the Neuville St Vaast sector would ensure for him success. In these circumstances the artillery would have had an easy task, as this sector was completely overlooked by a high crater called Broadmarsh, from which the Germans obtained magnificent observation of the whole Divisional left front. Broadmarsh crater was an awe-inspiring feature that appeared to follow one with its eyes wherever one went. It was like a volcano that might erupt at any moment, and played a prominent part in every minor enterprise which took place in its vicinity.

In these adverse circumstances it became clear that the only way a hostile attack against the Neuville St Vaast sector could be defeated was by employing to the full every day's grace which the enemy gave.

A defensive flank was therefore sited and its construction begun, so as to round off the defences where the troops were in closest contact to the enemy and present to him a continuous front rather than an edge. The digging of a reserve line was also put in hand, and the construction of a large number of shell-proof dug-outs begun.

In actual fact the enemy made no further attacks, but he maintained a continuous activity with artillery and trench-mortars. Later, after the Somme battle had begun, the calls made on the German troops compelled him to relax his efforts considerably. The feeling of tension was thus appreciably lessened, though the sector could at no time be described as a quiet one.

During this period of anxiety the situation was made still more difficult by a snap of bitterly cold weather in June, which had followed a period of violent rain-storms. The result was that a number of cases of trench-feet occurred in midsummer, when all materials and stores used for the prevention of this complaint had been handed in as no longer required.

The weather, combined with the constant work on trench construction and the continual mine explosions and bombardments, proved very wearing to the men. At this period, with all three brigades employed in holding the line, the men were in the trench area for twenty-one days and at rest only for seven every month. The result was that, when the Division was ordered to the Somme, they had, owing to the constant strain, become thoroughly tired

TRAINING AND REORGANISATION

and stale. Indeed, in the Labyrinth and Neuville St Vaast sectors, trench warfare, as far as the Highland Division was concerned, reached its zenith of intensity. A great effort was required from all ranks, first to reduce the superiority which the enemy had established, later to reduce the balance so that the superiority gradually passed to the British. There was no feature in trench warfare in which, during the period immediately following the relief of the French, the enemy did not hold the advantage. The mining situation, the sniping, the absence of dug-outs, all produced acute problems which demanded immediate solution if disaster were to be avoided.

His observation of our lines in this sector was probably unparalleled in the British zone. He employed in large numbers rifle grenades and trench-mortars of every calibre with astonishing accuracy. Finally, he added to the troops an additional embarrassment by his capture of the Vimy Ridge.

The enemy, the 2nd Guards Reserve Division, proved themselves throughout worthy opponents, ready and eager to profit by any weakness displayed opposite to them. This Division is remembered for an act of courtesy of a kind seldom associated with the German people.

A certain Private Robertson of the 5th Seaforth Highlanders was captured in a saphead after having made a gallant attempt to defend himself, in spite of a fractured skull. The following day a number of undetonated rifle grenades were fired into the British lines stating in English that the gallant soldier Private Robertson, Seaforth Highlanders, had died of his wounds and had been buried with full military honours in the cemetery at Rouvroy.

In spite of the strength of the opposition the men showed excellent spirit throughout, having carried out many good raids, and having repulsed with losses numerous hostile raids, nor was a square yard of ground lost.

On Saturday, 24th June, an intense bombardment started at some distance to the south, and lasted throughout the day and night. This was the opening of the preliminary bombardment of the great Somme offensive. It continued incessantly until 1st July, when the attack was launched Rumours of every kind began to circulate round the trenches, and much speculation arose as to whether and when the Division would be given an opportunity of taking part in the battle.

During this period the artillery carried out periodical bombardments of the enemy's trenches, with the idea of making him think that an attack in this sector was imminent. In this they seem to have been successful, for each night the Germans fired intermittent short hurricane bombardments on the front and support and communication trenches, presumably with a view to preventing the assembly of attacking troops. These bombardments were extremely heavy while they lasted; but, thanks to the large number of dug-outs which had by this time been completed, they inflicted little loss on the trench garrisons.

On 27th June arrangements were begun for the attachment of the 60th (2nd Line London Territorial) Division to the Highland Division for a period of instruction in the line. The news of the arrival of the 60th Division was welcomed by all ranks, as it was looked on as a sure indication that the Division would be relieved and would move to the Somme battle.

It had been arranged that as soon as the 60th Division were ready to take over the line, the Highland Division should be moved to the back areas for a period of much-needed rest and training before proceeding southwards.

Possibly, with its later experiences of battle fighting the Division might not have been so anxious to hurry off to take part in a great attack. In these days, however, apart from the battle of Festubert, it had not been employed in an offensive. Officers and men were therefore anxious that the Division should be given an opportunity of operating in an attack as a complete unit.

The 60th Division began their attachment on 30th June. This was carried out first by individual officers and N.C.O.'s, then by sections, by platoons, by companies, and finally by battalions. On 13th July the brigades of the 60th Division began taking over from the brigades of the Highland Division. On 14th July General Bulfin, G.O.C. 60th Division, assumed command of the sector.

This system of instruction meant that there were reliefs of some kind being carried out every night. These were

TRAINING AND REORGANISATION

greatly hampered by the sudden intense bombardments to which the enemy subjected the British trenches. In consequence, casualties were frequently heavy. In one brigade sector alone over sixty casualties were sustained during a single night.

As a parting gift to the Germans on the last day the Division was in the line, the 5th Gordon Highlanders raided the enemy's trenches, bombed his dug-outs, and killed several of the garrison.

On 14th July the Division moved by motor lorry to the Doullens-Lucheux-Baudricourt area. The popular supposition amongst the troops was that they were bound for a rest area. On the 15th the move was continued by march south to the area Bernaville-Candas-Hem.

All doubts were dispelled on the 20th, for the Division then entrained at Candas and detrained at Mericourt. While passing through Amiens, it was interesting to pass several trains going westwards, packed with battle-soiled soldiers, all in the very best of spirits. They were a Division coming out of the Somme battle to rest and refit. Many of them wore captured German pickelhaubers. Apart from the raggedness of their appearance and their stubbly beards, they looked at the top of their form. One always felt that it was spectacles such as these which gave the war correspondent that erroneous theory to which he adhered so fixedly throughout the war, that soldiers like " going over the top," and do so full of jests and wreathed in smiles.

From Mericourt the Division marched to the Ribemont-Meaulte area, parties being sent in advance to reconnoitre the line.

On 21st July orders were received that the Highland Division would relieve the 33rd Division in the line northeast of Fricourt during the coming night.

Just prior to the arrival of the Division on the Somme, two officers joined it who, second only to General Harper, were most responsible for the high standard of efficiency which it attained. These were Brigadier-General L. Oldfield, D.S.O., R.A., and Brigadier-General H. Pelham Burn, D.S.O., Gordon Highlanders. The former was appointed C.R.A. in place of Brigadier-General M. J. MacCarthy,

C.M.G., who left to take up a new appointment. The latter assumed command of the 152nd Infantry Brigade in place of Brigadier-General W. C. Ross, C.B., who took up an appointment at home, and later commanded a brigade in Salonika.

General Ross's departure from the 152nd Infantry Brigade caused the deepest regret to all ranks. He had been intimately known in peace time to many of the officers, N.C.O.'s, and men whom he now commanded in war. He was secretary of the Territorial Force Association for his county, and he had commanded his brigade since November 1914. General Ross had a personality which won for him the friendship of all who came in contact with him. The Highland soldier had become one of his first interests, and he possessed a great knowledge and understanding of him. Further, no one could fail to admire his natural courage. General Bannatine-Allason has described him as spending many hours, both by day and night, in crawling round the most exposed saps and dangerous places in his sector. General Ross spent so much of his time amongst his men that he was a familiar figure to them all, while he knew numbers of them by name, and in many cases knew also their parents, families, homes, and employers.

General Oldfield was not only a scientific gunner of the first order, but also rapidly developed a commanding knowledge of infantry tactics.

This knowledge enabled him, in conjunction with General Harper, to draw up the artillery plans for attack and defence, so that in all operations the infantry were directly supported by the maximum energy of his artillery covering them. The successes of the Division were in no small measure due to the effective manner in which the two arms co-operated.

General Oldfield was continually moving towards artillery perfection. He set a very high standard to his officers, to which they admirably responded. In the later stages of the war, his energy as a commander had resulted in the Divisional artillery having reached a high degree of efficiency. They could improvise a barrage in a shortness of time which surprised many artillery commanders from other Divisions. They had, further, become extremely mobile, and were possessed of extraordinary initiative. Later chapters in this book will show how General Oldfield's officers not only handled their guns with great skill, but also, as a result of his teaching, were able in emergencies to take command of disorganised detachments of men and fight equally skilfully as infantry officers. During General Oldfield's command, all infantry commanders had complete confidence both in the artillery and in the artillery arrangements.

General Burn was at the time of his appointment the youngest Brigadier in the British Army, being thirty-four years of age. Later in the war there were several younger, but prior to the Somme fighting the day of the young Brigadier had hardly come.

He is perhaps best described by a Jock, who said, in speaking of him, "They a' have their fads, and his fad is effeeciency."

General Burn had abundant experience of warfare in the front line. He had served as Adjutant, Staff-Captain, and Brigade-Major, and had commanded three separate battalions.

It can safely be asserted that he spent every moment of the day, and much of the night, in thinking how he could increase the efficiency of his command and how he could do damage to the enemy.

His vast experience enabled him to grasp details which actually were far-reaching in effect, but which to a man of less experience might have appeared trivial or have passed unnoticed.

In every direction, even in the smallest points, he accepted only one standard—namely, the highest; nothing less was tolerated. He spared himself no pains to attain this standard. Holding these principles as strongly as he did, it is natural that he found it frequently necessary to check officers and N.C.O.'s. They, however, bore him no ill-will for this, and officers were frequently heard to say, "You can't argue with P.B. when he strafes, because he's always right."

To those who served with General Burn he will always stand out as a man who possessed in full the essential qualities of the perfect soldier.

While the Division was in this sector the 6th Argyll and Sutherland Highlanders left the 152nd Brigade, being posted to the 5th Division as pioneer battalion, their place being taken by the 6th Gordon Highlanders, who had landed in France in 1914, and had seen considerable service with the 7th Division.

CHAPTER V.

THE BATTLE OF THE SOMME—HIGH WOOD.

THE Division entered the area of the Somme battle under bad auspices. It undoubtedly required a rest before it could be expected to reproduce its true form. On the 21st of July it received orders to take over the line on the same evening. On the 22nd it received orders to carry out an attack. Moreover, this attack, for which the Division was given less than twenty-four hours to prepare, was to be delivered from the point of a salient. There was, in fact, a general impression throughout the Division when they left the Somme area that their efforts had not been attended by a reasonable chance of success.

As far as the Highland Division is concerned, the tactical feature with which this phase of the Somme operations is primarily associated is High Wood. This wood, the highest point in Picardy, is perched on the summit of a large upland flanking the road, which, passing between the two Bazentins, leads from Contalmaison to Longueval.

Between the two Bazentins is the road junction where the road through the Mametz valley strikes the Contalmaison-Longueval road.

During previous operations, in which the 7th Dragoon Guards and the Deccan Horse had participated, the whole of High Wood had been captured. The enemy had, however, regained a footing in it. When the Division arrived in this area the German line ran through Guillemont, through Delville Wood north-east of Longueval, through High Wood, but on the reverse slope of this aforementioned upland, north of Bazentin-le-Petit, and between Contalmaison and Pozières.

The enemy did not, however, hold sufficient of High

Wood to secure observation of the country south-west of it, with which the Division was primarily concerned.

Of this section of the front the portion taken over by the Division at one time or another during its tour at duty in the line ran from a point about half-way between Longueval and High Wood to Bazentin-le-Petit exclusive.

The Divisional area was traversed throughout its length by the road which ran from Becourt-Becordel-Fricourt, south of Mametz Wood-Bazentin, and on to Longueval.

The Mametz Valley, through which this road ran, was familiarly called the Happy Valley. The valley, with the possible exception of the Chemical Works at Roeux, has probably stamped itself more on men's minds than any other topographical feature with which the Division came in contact. In Happy Valley was situated the headquarters of the brigade in the line, and of the supporting brigade itself. In addition, the advanced dressing station and many batteries were also located in it.

Running as it did towards the apex of a salient the enemy could concentrate a tremendous weight of artillery against it. Thus, when he was bombarding it with his maximum intensity, shells used to arrive from the direction of Leuze Wood in the right rear, and from Gueudecourt and Courcelette frontally, and from behind Pozières on the left.

This valley was the only line of communication through which every relief, every round of ammunition, and every ration had to pass on their way to the line, not only for the Highland Division but for several neighbouring Divisions.

Portions of the valley were under observation from balloons, while throughout its whole length the clouds of dust raised by the continual stream of wheeled traffic disclosed to the enemy any considerable movement that was taking place in it.

The enemy shelled Happy Valley mercilessly day and night, an intense barrage of high explosive, air bursts and gas shells being placed completely across it at irregular intervals, and moved backwards and forwards, up and down it.

For the most part the only protection the residents in the valley had against shell-fire were slits cut in the ground

Map II.—High Wood, July 1916.

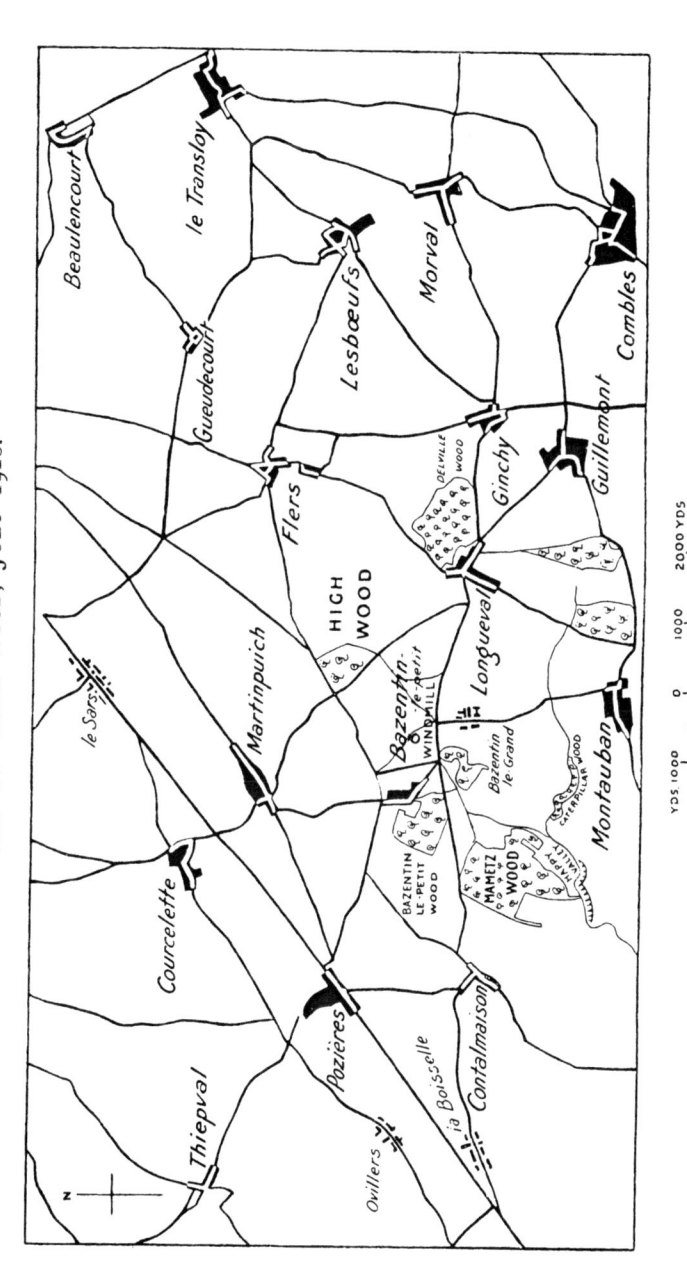

covered with waterproof sheets or corrugated iron. By degrees, however, more and more German dug-outs were discovered, until shell-proof accommodation was ultimately found for almost all.

The valley was traversed day and night by a constant stream of traffic. The infantry used overland tracks well clear of the road, and marched in platoon or section groups. All wheeled traffic was, however, restricted to the single road, so that periods of great congestion often occurred.

When the German barrage opened, men, animals, and motor vehicles broke into their best speed. Great columns of white dust, due to the intensity of the summer heat, rose up, choked everything, and made seeing a matter of difficulty. Guns and limbers moved at a stretch gallop, lorries bounded from shell-hole to shell-hole, and every effort was concentrated on getting out of the zone involved in the barrage with as little delay as possible.

The heavily-burdened infantryman on his way to and from the line, however, carried too much on his back to make him think of doubling. He used to plod along at his regulation three miles an hour, trusting that his luck would take him through.

It was no uncommon sight to see direct hits scored on gun-teams, limbers, and groups of infantry. When the barrage ceased and it was possible to take stock of the result, appalling scenes were often disclosed. Teams with their riders lying in a heap, ammunition dumps on fire, riderless and driverless horses and waggons bolting in all directions, and coming down in the midst of old wire entanglements, were daily spectacles in the Happy Valley.

At each pause in the barrage all haste was made to complete the work of succouring the wounded and collecting the dead, and filling in the latest shell-holes in the road before it reopened.

In this valley the conduct of the Royal Army Medical Corps was superb. Other troops could at least make some effort to make their way out of the danger zone as fast as possible, but the bearers of the field ambulances and the regimental stretcher-bearers could not. They slowly pushed their wheeled stretchers from the Crucifix at Bazentin to the dressing station, heedless of the shell-fire and their own security, and careful only to evacuate the wounded with the minimum of discomfort to them.

Similarly ambulance car-drivers could not join in the helter-skelter for security on the road to Fricourt. Day and night they plied slowly along the damaged road with their burden of wounded, returning again and again through the valley as soon as their cars had been cleared.

Had the Germans in those days been in possession of the instantaneous fuze which bursts its shell before it has had time to bury itself in the earth and thus lose much of its missile effect, this road could have been made almost impassable. Happy Valley, with its dust and its flies and its stench of half-buried animals and men, will remain to all who knew it an ineffaceable memory.

The trench lines taken over by the Division consisted of odd, narrow, and shallow trenches which had gradually evolved from the connecting of posts in which troops had dug themselves in during previous engagements.

By means of saps running into High Wood from the trench dug along its southern and western edge, a footing was held in the wood. Between High Wood and Delville Wood the British trenches were hidden from the Germans opposite them and *vice versa* by the crest line of the upland.

To the left of the wood the trench lines, which were not continuously connected up, curved in a south-westerly direction towards Bazentin-le-Petit, leaving the wood as the apex of an acute salient. In this section of the front the trenches seemed to fulfil no tactical requirements. There was no depth to the defensive system; the trenches were little more than knee-deep, and were choked with dead. Work on a single communication trench—High Alley, running from the Crucifix at Bazentin to High Wood —had been begun. The Germans held a strong redoubt in the eastern corner of High Wood. In this corner the contours were such that there was a depression in the ground similar in shape to a saucer. The Germans had fortified this saucer, and garrisoned it with machine-guns, mostly sited so as to fire to a flank. They could thus, by firing eastwards from this redoubt, rake No Man's Land in direct enfilade. By firing westwards, they could place an enfilade barrage of low trajectory bullets which swept the rides through the wood. This redoubt was surmounted

BATTLE OF THE SOMME—HIGH WOOD

by wire entanglements, the tops of the pickets being just visible when looked at frontally and from our foremost saps.

Passing through the north-east corner of the wood was a strong switch line, which ran from Flers through High Wood towards Martinpuich. This was a well-dug, heavily-traversed trench protected by wire, but during this period had no completed dug-outs in it. Air photos, however, showed where work on the shafts of several dug-outs had been begun.

The whole of this area had been the scene of repeated encounters, as the ground amply testified. In the undergrowth of the wood, and in the standing corn which covered the whole area, lay the dead of many different regiments.

The result was that, owing to the scorching summer weather, the troops in the line lived in an atmosphere of pollution and in a positive torment of bluebottle flies. In one sap in particular, as one moved along it the flies rose in such clouds that their buzzing sounded as the noise of a threshing-machine. In this sap the sentries could only tolerate the conditions by standing with their handkerchiefs tied over their mouths and nostrils.

By 3 A.M. on 22nd July, the 154th Infantry Brigade had completed the relief of the 33rd Division. The 13th Brigade of the 5th Division were on their right, and the 57th Brigade of the 19th Division on their left.

Of the 154th Brigade two battalions held the line, the remaining two being in support and reserve in Bazentin-le-Grand Wood and Bazentin le Grand.

The Divisional artillery were in position in the open, the personnel for the most part living under tarpaulin shelters. Some batteries were in the Mametz Valley, while others were on the high ground south of Bazentin-le-Grand. It is difficult to determine who were most to be sympathised with—the gunners who lived alongside their guns, or the drivers who had to pass two or three times a day through the Happy Valley with ammunition. The batteries in positions in the valley itself probably lived in circumstances which could not have been more hazardous and unpleasant.

The 153rd Brigade in support occupied the area about the south-east corner of Mametz Wood and Caterpillar

Wood. The 152nd Brigade in reserve bivouacked between Fricourt Wood and Mametz Wood.

At dawn on the 23rd the Happy Valley barrage, about which the Division had received no information, opened with great intensity. The 153rd and 152nd Brigades were seriously involved in it, and suffered considerable casualties. The 152nd Brigade was immediately fallen-in and marched westwards towards Fricourt, ultimately moving to bivouac in the vicinity of Becourt-Becordel. The 153rd Brigade extended its area so as to diminish the number of casualties.

It was later discovered that numerous shell-proof dug-outs existed in and about Mametz and Fricourt Woods. Apparently no organised reconnaissances of this area had been made, for had this been the case, and had the location of these dug-outs been made known to the Division on its arrival in the area, many unnecessary casualties would have been avoided.

The day on which the relief was concluded, 22nd July, the Division received orders to carry out an attack during the coming night. The objectives given were the north-east and north-west edges of High Wood and the switch trench from the north-east of High Wood to a point five hundred yards north-west of it.

The 154th Brigade was detailed to carry out this operation. As a preliminary the redoubt at the eastern corner of High Wood was to be seized at 10 P.M. in conjunction with the left brigade, 5th Division. The main attack on the German switch line was timed to take place at 1.30 P.M.

The troops engaged in this attack had little or no knowledge of the enemy's dispositions. They had barely completed the relief by dawn on the previous night. During the day movement was restricted and patrolling impossible. Thus when the attack was launched at 10 P.M., circumstances had afforded the attackers no opportunity of studying the ground, or of forming any detailed plan of action. Added to this the wood was such that the trees prevented a shrapnel barrage from being effective. Further, the "going" within the wood, owing to shell-holes, brambles, dense undergrowth, and wire entanglements, was extremely bad —so bad, in fact, that even many weeks after its capture, to walk from one end of the wood to the other was a laborious process demanding considerable physical effort.

BATTLE OF THE SOMME—HIGH WOOD

The attack was therefore delivered with an ineffective barrage with which the men were unable to keep up. The result was that the enemy had little inducement to take cover. He was thus able with his machine-guns and riflemen, whom he posted at night in the woods in advance of his trench lines, to defeat the attack completely and inflict heavy losses on the 4th Gordon Highlanders, and the 9th Royal Scots.

At 1.30 A.M. the main attack was delivered, but it met with no better fate. The volume of fire, particularly from the machine-guns in the redoubt, was so intense that no progress could be made. The men had advanced to the attack with great gallantry, but the cross-fire opposed to them rendered success impossible. Morning found them back in their original line, but seriously depleted in numbers.

The day was spent in improving the trenches and in connecting by a trench the southern edge of High Wood with the Windmill north of Bazentin-le-Grand. Both the troops in the line and the brigade in support were heavily shelled during the day, lachrymatory shells and 5·9 howitzers being used profusely.

During the night work was continued on the trench joining High Wood and the Windmill, and in High Alley. By the end of the night the latter was negotiable for traffic to within sixty yards of the wood. The following day the former of these two trenches was heavily and accurately bombarded.

At 7.30 P.M., 24th July, the enemy launched a surprise attack against High Wood and against the left company of the 154th Brigade. For some time the situation was obscure, but by 10 P.M. the artillery had been asked to slacken. It subsequently transpired that our line remained intact, and that the German attackers were falling back.

During the attack the enemy again barraged the new trench mentioned above extremely heavily. He also bombarded High Wood and set it on fire.

By 11.30 P.M. the situation was completely in hand, and work in the trenches was resumed.

Meanwhile orders had been received that the 154th Brigade was to relieve the left battalion of the 5th Division, and thus extend its front towards Longueval. This relief was completed by 6 A.M., and gave the brigade a frontage of some 2500 yards to hold.

On 25th July the enemy bombarded Mametz Valley and Fricourt Wood in a most savage fashion with guns of all calibres. This bombardment opened at noon, and continued until 6 P.M. It was the worst experience of shell-fire which the residents in Happy Valley encountered during the Division's sojourn in the Somme area. Much material damage and many casualties resulted.

At 9.20 P.M. the 4th Seaforth Highlanders delivered another attack against the German redoubt. It, however, met a worse fate than its predecessor. An intense machine-gun fire was opened on the British trenches at the moment when the attackers were mounting the parapet. The troops suffered such losses from this fire that the attack never materialised.

This operation roused the enemy considerably, and he shelled the forward area throughout the night. In this bombardment he used a considerable number of shells containing phosgene gas. This was one of the earliest occasions on which this form of gas was used. It was particularly insidious, as at first it did not cause any inconvenience, and its smell was not offensive, being similar to that of sweet apples.

Meanwhile the brigade in support had been kept fully occupied. The intense heat created a great demand for water for the first-line troops. The water supply in the forward area was, however, non-existent, so that a dump of petrol tins of water had to be formed in the Happy Valley. From this dump all the water used in the forward area was carried by the supporting brigade. Similarly, with no light railways in repair, every round of S.A.A. bombs, trench-mortar ammunition, Very lights, barbed wire, screw pickets, &c., had to be carried forward by man power. The result was that practically every man in the supporting brigade made at least one journey daily from the dumps at the south-east corner of Mametz Wood to the forward dumps in rear of High Wood. The labour thus entailed, coupled with the fact that the supporting brigade lived in a heavily-shelled area with insufficient dug-out accommodation, meant that the troops had lost much of their fighting efficiency before they went into the line. In the circumstances there was, however, no alternative.

On the 26th July the 153rd Brigade relieved the 154th Brigade, and the 152nd Brigade moved forward to the support position. This relief was considerably interrupted by a further lavish use of phosgene by the Germans.

The work of consolidating and digging more trenches south and south-west of the wood was continued, as until touch in the front line could be obtained on the left, that flank was in the air.

On the 27th the forward area and the supporting brigade (152nd) in Mametz Valley were heavily shelled all night. This shelling was intense, it being estimated that two shells per minute burst in the area close to brigade headquarters alone throughout the night; 77 mm. gas shells were primarily used, but 5·9's were also from time to time employed freely. As a result of this bombardment the 8th Argyll and Sutherland Highlanders alone sustained eighty gas casualties.

During the following day the 153rd Brigade co-operated in an attack on Longueval by rifle and machine-gun and Stokes mortar fire. They, however, took no part in the infantry action.

During the night 27-28th July, connection in the front line was established about 200 yards north-east of the Bazentin Windmill by the 6th Black Watch with the 29th Division. For the first time in this sector a continuous line of defence was presented to the enemy.

The 153rd Infantry Brigade had carried out a number of patrols. They had already had three days in which to reconnoitre the enemy's position and study the lie of the land when they received orders to attack the enemy's line from halfway between Delville and High Woods to the western edge of High Wood.

Patrols had located the enemy as occupying various positions, and these were subjected to bombardments during the forty-eight hours previous to the attack. At this stage in the war the shooting of the heavy howitzers had not reached that pitch of accuracy to which it afterwards attained. Nor was the liaison between the infantry and the Corps artillery as close as it became later. These causes and faulty observation made the shooting somewhat

F

erratic at a place where very exact shooting was necessary. To these bombardments the enemy usually replied by shelling the Mametz Valley and the infantry in the line.

The attack was launched at 6.10 P.M., and to the east of the wood proceeded some distance. However, on topping the rise in the middle of No Man's Land, the troops came under a very severe machine-gun fire, in which the accursed redoubt on the eastern corner of the wood, as usual, played a prominent part.

In the wood itself the advance was again checked by enfilade machine-gun fire, and the result of the action was much the same as it had been in the case of the 154th Brigade.

The net gains were, however, an advance of 200 yards on the right and centre, and of 70 yards in the wood. The men maintained themselves in their new positions in the wood for some time. Finally, however, owing to the intensity of the enemy's bombardment, they withdrew to their original positions.

The right and centre consolidated their new position in posts, and held their gains.

Orders were meanwhile issued for the attack to be resumed at 9.45 P.M. These orders were, however, not received at Divisional headquarters in sufficient time to enable them to be transmitted to the attacking companies before the attack was due to start. No further action therefore took place.

The 31st July was remarkable for a violent bombardment of the country between Bazentin-le-Grand and Mametz Wood, which was practically continuous throughout the day.

On 1st August, the 152nd Infantry Brigade relieved the 153rd, and the 154th Brigade moved forward to the support brigade area. It had now become quite clear that no good purpose could be served by ordering the Division to carry out any further local attacks. There was no reason to suppose that such attacks would meet with any more success than their predecessors. The 152nd Infantry Brigade was therefore instructed to adopt a vigorous policy of peaceful penetration. By that is meant that the policy was to be the acquisition of more ground by digging and

BATTLE OF THE SOMME—HIGH WOOD

by minor operations, without the delivery of any set piece attack involving a large number of troops.

Orders were thus issued for as much ground as possible to be gained in High Wood by sapping forward. Progress was also to be made between High Wood and the Divisional right boundary, by digging-in posts in advance of the existing front line during the night, and ultimately connecting them up into continuous trenches.

The actual labour of digging in the wood was considerable, as beneath the soil there lay a tangled mass of thick roots, in many cases too stout to be severed by a spade. The work, therefore, was slow and arduous, axes and billhooks having to be employed as well as picks and shovels. The enemy, however, paid little attention to the working parties.

On the right it was considered likely that, as there was no cover, the enemy would interfere considerably with digging operations. An apparatus was therefore employed, known as the Bartlett Forcing Jack. The Bartlett Jack was designed to drive iron pipes loaded with tin canisters of ammonal (containing two lb. of ammonal per foot run) through the ground at a depth of from four to five feet. When a sufficient length of pipe had been driven into the ground in the required direction, the charge was exploded. The explosion blew a fissure in the ground which served as a trench. In this instance the labour of carrying the pipes and ammonal up to the line, and of working the task, proved incommensurate with the results obtained. This was particularly so when it became evident that considerable liberties could be taken by working parties without interference from the Boche.

On the night 3-4th August General Burn decided to employ a considerable working party and boldly " jump " a trench some 200 yards in front of the existing front line. That is to say, instead of sapping forwards and digging " T " heads at the ends of the saps for the posts to occupy, and finally connecting the " T " heads together so as to form a continuous trench, a continuous fire trench was dug in the first instance during the night, and occupied by a garrison at dawn. Subsequently communication trenches were cut to connect this trench with the support line, Seaforth Trench.

The Germans thus on 4th August woke to find that the whole of the Divisional front line, exclusive of the wood, had advanced some 200 yards towards them.

When the Division was relieved on 7th August, more than half High Wood was in our hands and consolidated. The redoubt in the eastern corner was, however, as formidable as ever. To the right of the wood the line had been advanced some 300 yards, while to the left the position had been so consolidated that there was no gap in the lines, and the flank was properly secured.

In addition, High Alley, 1000 yards in length, had been cleared out and made into a first-class communication trench by the 8th Royal Scots. Further east they had also dug a completely new communication trench called Thistle Alley. The digging of these trenches was a considerable task, as the soil for the most part consisted of chalk containing countless large flints or gravel, so that every spadeful had to be loosened by the pick before it could be thrown out of the trench.

On 7th August the 152nd Brigade was relieved by the 100th Brigade, 33rd Division. Owing to the intensity of the enemy's shelling of the valley at night, it was decided for the first time to carry out the relief in daylight. In spite of some apprehension caused by three German aeroplanes flying low over the lines while the relief was in progress, the experiment proved highly successful. The 152nd Brigade, in fact, did not sustain a single casualty during the operation.

On 8th August the Division remained in bivouacs near Meaulte, in glorious weather. In the evening the "Balmorals," the Divisional troupe, using the tail-board of a lorry as a stage, gave a performance in the open air, which was attended by practically the entire infantry of the Division. It is doubtful if, in the whole of their highly successful career, any performance given by the "Balmorals" was more appreciated than this one.

The Division had passed from sixteen days of continuous and unsatisfactory strife to an unexpected haven of rest, set in the midst of corn-lands during harvesttime.

It was a real refreshment for the men to sit in the cool

of a delightful summer evening and listen to "Stanley" and "Gertie," both of whom rose to the occasion admirably.

So ended the first offensive operations in which the Division had been employed as a whole unit. The results had been disappointing and dispiriting to all. Over 3500 casualties, including more than 150 officers, had been sustained in two fruitless attempts to carry a German position which remained intact, in spite of many attacks by a succession of Divisions, until 15th September. The Germans had shown that High Wood could not be taken hurriedly by a direct frontal attack.

Three months later General Harper was able to show that the much stronger position of Beaumont Hamel could be stormed frontally after careful preparations and with adequate artillery support.

High Wood was finally overcome by a mine, which shattered the redoubt, and by tanks, which on this occasion were employed for the first time in the Great War.

The mine referred to above was suggested by General Pelham Burn on the morning of 5th August as being the least costly means of subduing the redoubt. His suggestion was at once adopted. Tunnelling officers reported at brigade headquarters the same evening, the actual mining operations beginning on the following morning.

It was most satisfactory to those engaged in High Wood to visit it after the German withdrawal in the Somme area, and see in place of the saucer in which the German redoubt was situated a vast crater. Many graves were in it and round it, and arms, equipment, and ammunition lay scattered about it. In fact, it had all the appearance of having admirably served its purpose.

On the 9th August the Division, less the artillery, which remained in the line, entrained at Edgehill and Mericourt, and was moved to the area Longpré-Pont Remy. The following day it again entrained, and began to move into the Blaringham area.

High Wood now stands in the centre of a vast cemetery. There is barely a portion of ground of the size of a tennis court in all that countryside which does not contain the graves of one or more British soldiers. In the wood itself stand memorials erected to the memory of the fallen of many Divisions which were shattered there. The Highland Division was not by any means the only Division which failed to capture a natural fortress situated at the apex of a salient.

CHAPTER VI.

ARMENTIÈRES AND HEBUTERNE.

ON 15th and 16th August the 153rd and 154th Brigades relieved the 1st New Zealand Division in the line. The new front extended from Chapelle d'Armentières on the right to the river Lys on the left. The 152nd Brigade in reserve was billeted in Armentières. Divisional headquarters opened at 98 Rue Sadi Carnot.

By 19th August the Divisional artillery had arrived from the Somme, and completed the relief of the New Zealand artillery.

The tour of duty in the Armentières sector was remarkable for its tranquillity. The weather was excellent, the breastwork trenches reasonably comfortable, and the enemy's activity slight. The town of Armentières itself provided many excellent billets for the troops in reserve, and for all three brigade headquarters. The batteries were also for the most part comfortable, some of them being in the unique position of occupying houses for quarters, with their guns in the gardens and conservatories.

Armentières was indeed fairly described by the Jocks as *bon*. In these days it was still occupied by civilian inhabitants in large numbers. There were in consequence plenty of the beloved "estaminets," as they were usually called, and numerous shops. The latter all appeared to keep the same articles in stock—"vin blonk," "oofs"—either to be consumed on the premises or taken home; chips and those wonderful post-cards on which patriotic designs were embroidered in alarmingly coloured silks, and on which were superscribed such mottoes as "To my dear sweetheart," "To my darling wife."

The officers were equally well catered for, considering

that Armentières was within range of the lightest field-guns. There were a few naturally expensive and equally naturally indifferent tea-shops. There were one or two restaurants where dinner could be obtained, in which the French cooking afforded a relief from the normal efforts of the company's mess cook. And there was the famous Lucienne's.

Lucienne lived at a corner house in the Rue Sadi Carnot, and had assisted in the management of a restaurant there since the early days of the war. The majority of the neighbouring houses, including the large church some fifty yards from the restaurant, had at one time or another been struck by shells. Most of Lucienne's windows had been broken during these bombardments. She, however, still possessed the most buoyant spirits. She had ready wits, and in any form of badinage usually had the last word. She, in fact, resembled a character from a light opera rather than a player in the real drama of war. After the German offensive in April 1918 she was driven out of Armentières, but remained undaunted ; and subsequently, after the tide had turned, opened a similar establishment in Amiens. The officers of the Division had to thank Lucienne's courage for many a pleasant evening spent in Armentières.

The sector, in fact, acted as a tonic to the Division, and with its quiet trenches, wonderful weather, and good billets soon effaced all the bitter memories of the Somme and the weariness of the Labyrinth.

The enemy's activity, such as it was, was directed chiefly against the town and the suburbs of Houplines, both places being intermittently shelled, particularly the latter. At times the bombardments were severe, Divisional headquarters being ultimately shelled out of their house in Rue Sadi Carnot, and being in consequence moved to Steenwerk.

On 14th September the Division sustained a considerable loss in the death of Brigadier-General C. E. Stewart, C.M.G., commanding the 154th Infantry Brigade. General Stewart and his intelligence officer were walking through Houplines when a chance shell burst within a few feet of them, killing them both. It was a case of the cruellest bad luck, as this was the only shell which fell in that vicinity during the day. General Stewart had commanded the 154th Brigade since its reconstitution as a Highland brigade. His troops were considerably attached to him, and his loss was much felt by them.

On 17th September, Brigadier-General J. G. H. Hamilton, D.S.O., Black Watch, assumed command of the 154th Brigade.

Operations at this sector were for the most part confined on the part of the enemy to a fairly consistent but only moderate activity with the Minnenwerfer. At times, too, he was active with his Grenatenwerfer, known to the troops as the "Pineapples" or "Fishtail." "Yon minnie-wafers" were fortunately clearly visible in the air, and so with a little judgment could be avoided. They had, however, a most devastating effect on breastwork trenches, with the result that, as a rule, more damage was done in a day than could be repaired in twenty-four hours by the troops available. Minnenwerfer sentries were posted who, whenever they saw or heard a "minnie" fired, blew a whistle. The troops in the trenches then at once looked into the air to locate the bomb. As soon as they had judged where it was going to fall, they took the necessary steps not to be there at the time of its arrival. Watching the "minnies" in the air rather resembled waiting for a high catch in the deep field at cricket. If there was no wind it was comparatively easy to judge them. If, however, there was a strong breeze blowing, the wind would catch them and alter their flight considerably. The men, however, soon learnt their idiosyncrasies, and it was a rare occurrence for casualties to be inflicted by them.

The Grenatenwerfer was quite a different proposition. This form of projectile was fired from a machine of about the same size and weight as a typewriter, and in consequence it could be moved with ease from place to place after every few rounds. It was thus difficult to locate the position from which it was fired. Further, it was most unusual to be able to see the projectile in the air, so that no steps could be taken to avoid it.

As regards British operations, a discharge of gas from cylinders took place on 31st August. The preparations for this discharge involved a considerable amount of work. The cylinders of gas had to be carried the full length of the communication trenches, each one being supported by two men. The weight of these cylinders was so great that a second pair of men were also required for each cylinder to act as reliefs.

Enormous carrying parties were therefore required to carry the cylinders to the fire-bays in the front line into which they were to be installed by the gas companies. This was always an unpleasant task, as the danger of a bullet or fragment of shell striking a cylinder and causing a leakage of gas in the midst of the carrying party was ever present.

The discharge on this night was followed by a raid half an hour later. The enemy, however, was found to be alert, and he met the raiders with such a heavy machine-gun fire that they were unable to reach the hostile wire.

Subsequently raids became a frequent occurrence. On 15th September four raids were carried out. In each case Bangalore torpedoes—*i.e.*, long tubes of ammonal with a time fuse—were used to destroy the enemy's wire.

These raids were carried out by the 6th Gordon Highlanders, the 6th Seaforth Highlanders, the 7th Gordon Highlanders, and the 7th Black Watch.

Of these, the first and third failed owing to the torpedoes not bursting; the second was an unqualified success, and is described in detail later. The fourth was successful, but only two Germans were found in the trench.

The following night two more raids took place. Of these, one carried out by the 5th Gordon Highlanders was completely successful, and twenty-five Germans are reported to have been killed. The second raid, carried out by the 9th Royal Scots, was also successful, but only one German was found in the trenches. He was killed.

On 22nd September the 6th Gordon Highlanders made a second attempt at the raid which had been unsuccessful on 15th September. However, the enterprise again had to be abandoned, as the torpedo failed to explode and the wire remained uncut.

As raiding became so marked a feature of the war, space forbids that each raid should be described in detail. General Harper was therefore asked to select the raid he considered most suitable for description, and he has chosen that carried out by the 6th Seaforth Highlanders on 15th

September 1916. This raid is therefore now described in detail.

The area selected for the operation was a most prominent salient formed by the German front line. Through the apex of this salient, and running at right angles to the fronts of the opposing forces, ran the Armentières-Lille Railway. Across the base of the salient ran a well-defined entrenchment.

The general plan was as follows: The raiders were divided up into two parties, each consisting of one officer (Lieutenants J. Sainter and D. F. Jenkins), one sergeant, one corporal, and ten privates, with a blocking party each of one N.C.O. and three men.

The scheme was that each party should cut the wire at its own point of entry by means of Bangalore torpedoes, while the wire was to be cut for a point of exit by the 2-inch mortars.

The two parties were to enter the salient from opposite sides and close to its base. They were then to leave their blocking parties to cover their rear, while they both worked forwards to the apex. By meeting at this point it was hoped that the entire garrison of the salient would be accounted for.

The Bangalore torpedoes, both seventy-five feet in length, were to be placed under the wire thirty minutes before zero, Lieutenants Sainter and Jenkins, each with two men, being responsible for placing the torpedoes in position.

The raiding parties were ordered to leave their trenches and form up in No Man's Land about thirty yards away from their torpedoes, ready to rush through the gap in the wire as soon as the explosions took place.

The actual trench area to be raided had been reproduced exactly according to scale in a large pasture close to Armentières. It was thus possible to practice the men continually over the course, so that they acquired a true sense of direction, and of the distances they would have to traverse during the raid.

The parties paraded for the raid with their faces and knees blackened, with their bayonets covered in mud, and with their steel helmets encased in sandbags to which grasses and weeds had been sewn. These precautions were necessary, as the men had to lie out in No Man's Land, where they would be in danger of being observed by a German sentry, so that they could enter the trenches immediately the torpedoes were exploded.

Ropes were also carried, as it was anticipated that there might be some difficulty in getting the prisoners out of the deep breastwork trenches, and it might be necessary to drag them out.

The men wore Dayfield body-shields to protect them from bomb splinters.

The arms carried were as follows: Officers, 1 revolver, 6 bombs, and 1 electric torch; N.C.O.'s, 1 revolver, 10 bombs, and a bludgeon; 4 bayonet men, rifle and bayonet, 6 bombs, electric torch attached to rifle, 30 rounds of ammunition; 8 throwers, 10 bombs and a bludgeon; 8 spare men, a bludgeon, 10 bombs, and a wire-cutter; blocking party, rifles and bayonets, 30 rounds of ammunition, and 10 bombs.

In the first instance the success of the raid was dependent on the gaps being adequately cut in the wire. At the time many persons thought that General Burn's scheme of using torpedoes seventy-five feet long was too ambitious. Certainly when the torpedoes were constructed and were seen for the first time, they looked awkward things with which to have dealings in No Man's Land, being as they were considerably longer than a cricket pitch. When the time arrived the torpedoes were hoisted out of the trenches, and the torpedo parties set off with them. Lieutenant Jenkins had little trouble with his; he reached the selected point in the German entanglement without incident, and placed his torpedo in position. This was difficult work. Here were two parties, each of three men, within 70 yards of the German sentries, forcing a metal tube 3 inches in diameter, 75 feet long, and loaded with ammonal, underneath the German entanglements. Very lights were fired by the enemy continually, illuminating the whole countryside and making the work more hazardous than ever.

It was further impossible to place the torpedoes in position without a certain amount of noise being made, which the German sentries might at any time hear. The whole wire entanglement stood in a mass of rank undergrowth, through which the nose of the torpedo had to be forced. The posts supporting the entanglements were not placed in irregular rows, so that occasionally as the torpedo was pushed forward its movement was brought to a standstill by a wooden post standing directly in its way, and its course had to be altered. The lower strands of wire also scraped along the upper surface of the torpedoes, and made a horrible grating noise.

In spite of these difficulties, Lieutenant Jenkins placed his torpedo in position exactly as arranged, and in sufficient time to return to the trench and to lead his party out to a point about thirty yards from the German wire. The party followed the fuse which connected the torpedo to the firing mechanism in the trench, so as to ensure joining up in the right place.

Lieutenant Sainter, on the other hand, was completely out of luck. His torpedo came apart at several of its joints on three separate occasions, and had to be repaired by him in No Man's Land. Sainter reported that had it not been for the German Very lights, he did not think that he could have managed to repair it. Having finally arrived with it intact at the right place, he had forced it nearly through the German wire when it stuck and could be moved forward no farther. He therefore had to extract it and make a second attempt at a different place. On this occasion he was successful. The operation, however, had taken so long that no time was left for Sainter to return to the trench and lead out his party. The party was therefore ordered to advance, following the fuse as Jenkins' party had done, until they came upon Sainter. This was done, and the party had joined him and was in position just ten minutes before zero.

At zero the two torpedoes were fired almost simultaneously, leaving gaps clear through the German wire 15 feet broad and 25 yards deep. At the same time the barrage opened. Major A. G. Graham, M.C., commanding the 6th Seaforth Highlanders, writes in his account of the operations: "The barrage opened punctually, and can only be described as perfect. All ranks taking part in the raid were unanimous in their praise. The efficacy of the barrage is borne out by the fact that no German machine-gun fired for forty minutes. The casualties caused by the barrage must have been heavy, as both parties report that on entering the trenches parties of the enemy were seen rushing away from the salient into our barrage."

Immediately the torpedoes exploded, the raiders rushed through the gaps in the wire and into the enemy's trenches. The enemy was taken completely by surprise. The first sentry encountered by Sainter's party was bayonetted in the back, while still staring over the parapet in blank amazement at the curious explosion that had just occurred in front of him.

From now onwards all the luck came to Sainter, Jenkins meeting with considerable difficulties. Sainter's men acted exactly as they had done in the practices. They entered the trench at the point intended; there they killed a couple of sentries. They then found a dug-out containing four Germans, which they bombed until all were killed. At the next dug-out two Germans came out, one being immediately shot by Sainter, the other being killed by a bayonet man. Other Germans were killed in the dug-out with bombs. Four Germans were then found hiding in the trench; three of these were killed, the fourth being kept as a prisoner. Later he refused to leave his trench, and was also killed. A lasso had been put round him to assist in hauling him out of the trench. At this he became so terror-stricken that he became incapable of movement, and so had to be despatched. Unfortunately, his remains were left lying in the trench with the rope still around them. The party then searched the point of exit, where they found the wire well cut by the 2-inch mortars, and returned to our lines, having been in the German trenches six and a half minutes.

Lieutenant Jenkins' party entered the German trench according to plan; the first fire-bay they entered contained arms and equipment, but no sentries. There was a dummy parados to this trench made of boards, behind which dug-outs were found. Four of these were bombed until all sounds within them ceased. The party then proceeded another ten yards along the trench, where they encountered an organised German bombing party. A bombing fight lasting some two minutes then ensued, the Germans apparently being all knocked out. Lieutenant Jenkins' party sustained five casualties in this encounter, three men being seriously wounded, and two slightly. Orders were therefore given to retire by the gap at which the trench had been entered. As the retirement was being carried out a second party of Germans attacked. These were heavily bombed; many were killed, the remainder running away. Three Highlanders had, however, caught one of them alive, and hurled him bodily over the parapet, and then jumped after him and pinioned him in a shell-hole. He was finally taken back to the British lines as the solitary prisoner.

On a bugle sounding the two parties began their withdrawal. Sainter's party regained our trenches without having sustained a casualty. Jenkins on his return found that three of his men were missing. He therefore returned to the German trenches three times with Private A. Macdonald, and each time succeeded in bringing in a wounded man.

The Dayfield body-shields were found to have numerous splinters of bombs sticking into them, and undoubtedly saved the raiders from several casualties.

The German trenches were formed of enormous breastworks 12 to 15 feet wide, and were revetted with brushwood. Let into the parapet were numerous concrete dug-outs, each capable of holding from four to six men. The floor of these dug-outs was level with the bottom of the trench. The effect of a Mills bomb inside these confined spaces was devastating, and there is no doubt that every German inside them was killed. One of the Jocks was asked how he had dealt with these dug-outs. He replied, "Och, we just boomed yon stone boxes until they stopped their blether, and then went to the next one."

The barrage for this raid was worked out to the minutest detail. All weapons were employed, the following amounts of ammunition being used: 2-inch mortars, 228 rounds; Stokes guns, 981 rounds; Vickers guns, 29,500 rounds; 18-pounders, 1200 rounds; 4·5 howitzers, 100 rounds; and several hundred rounds of rifle grenades.

Every weapon had a particular task given to it. These tasks were arranged (*a*) so that no fire could be opened by the Germans which might be brought to bear on men crossing No Man's Land; (*b*) so that no troops could run away from the area being raided to the rear; (*c*) so that no troops could counter-attack the area raided over the open either from the rear or flanks ; (d) so that no movement could take place in the German trenches within about 800 yards of the raid. Every trench junction and every known trench and mortar position on a front of 1500 yards was steadily bombarded throughout the operation.

The results were beyond all expectations. No Germans were able to reinforce the salient, so that the raiders could deal with its garrison without fear of interruption. The Germans who broke from the salient and fled to the rear ran into a barrage of 18-pounders, 4·5 howitzers, Stokes guns, and 2-inch mortars. Not a single round was fired by the enemy occupying the trenches on the flanks of the salient.

The barrage thus cut off the troops in the area raided from any support which their neighbours might have given them, and enabled the raiders to despatch them just as had been planned.

Many of the Germans on the opening of the barrage had left their arms in the trenches and run into the dugouts. When the raiders arrived and began bombing a panic seems to have set in. The Boches ran about in terror on seeing the Jocks with their blackened faces and knees and with grasses in their helmets, holding up their hands, crying, "Kamerad Kaffirs, Kamerad Kaffirs!" They had apparently mistaken the Jocks for some species of native troops. This impression and the sight of the ropes reduced many of them to such a condition that they were even too terrified to be carried off as prisoners, and refused to move. In consequence many had to be despatched who might otherwise have been taken back to our lines alive.

The one prisoner captured turned out to be a good one. He volunteered much information about the German position, the positions of headquarters, routes to the trenches, hours of relief, hours and places at which ration and working parties assembled. A series of violent bombardments were accordingly arranged based on the information he had given.

During the remainder of the night the area was occasionally subjected to short intense bursts of artillery and trench-mortar fire for the benefit of any Germans who might be inspecting the damage in the salient.

As a result of their gallant conduct on this raid Lieutenants Sainter and Jenkins were awarded the Military Cross, and four men the Military Medal.

During the remainder of the Division's sojourn in the Armentières area, the only other noteworthy operations that took place were outbreaks of the most excessive trench-mortar activity on the part of the Jocks.

Organised bombardments of the enemy's lines were repeatedly taking place, with the result that whole sections of the breastworks were obliterated. Whenever rain occurred and his breastworks became sodden they were heavily bombarded, so as to give them the necessary incentive to collapse and bury the Germans in them.

On one occasion over 1200 rounds of Stokes mortar bombs were fired in a single day by one light trench-mortar battery. It soon transpired that these bombardments produced very little retaliation from the enemy. It was therefore felt that we were in a position really to bully him and make his life a burden to him. The bombardments therefore became more frequent than ever, and he was unmercifully harassed day after day to the great delight of the troops.

It was not a sector in which the Germans were much exposed to view. There was, however, a barricade across a road near Prémesques, where both men and waggons tended to congregate. This barricade could be seen from an O.P. at Square Farm on the extreme right of the sector. An electric bell was therefore rigged up in the gun-pit, with a bell-push in the O.P. A gun was then kept permanently laid on the barricade. Every time the observer saw a reasonable bag of people and waggons collected round the barricade he rang the bell and the gunners fired. This sport, however, became too popular, with the result that, after a day or two, no Boche would show himself anywhere in the vicinity of the barricade.

The holding of the Armentières sector will always be regarded as the most pleasant period of trench life which the Division passed through.

On 12th September 1916 the first Divisional Horse Show was held. It proved an unqualified success, and stimulated a great interest in the condition of horses, harness, and vehicles throughout the Division. To the delight of the Jocks, the officers' jumping competition was won by General Harper on Charlie, a big bay horse well known to many members of the Division.

In the Armentières sector, the 152nd Infantry Brigade received a large parcel of picture post-cards, displaying types of Russian soldiers, from the 152nd Vladicaucasian Regiment, with the following message printed on them :—

"21 *May* 1916.

" Friends ! The birthday of your king is also a holiday for us. Long live our alliance of the fight with the lie and may the victory triumph the ingression of low force. From your comrade, a soldier of the Vladicaucasian Regiment."

General Pelham Burn retaliated by sending the Vladicaucasians half a dozen haggises, a case of whisky, and a tin of oatcakes.

On 25th September the Division was relieved in the line by Frank's Force, and moved to the area Bailleul, Meteren, Estaires. On the 30th the Division entrained again for the south at Bailleul and Merville, Doullens and Candas being the destination.

On 1st October the Division proceeded by march route to the area Bus-les-Artois, Bois du Warnimont, Authie, Vauchelles, Thievres, and came under the orders of the XIIIth Corps.

On 4th October the 152nd Infantry Brigade relieved the 6th Brigade, 2nd Division, in the sector east of Hebuterne from John Copse on the right to Sixteen Poplars Road on the left. The Divisional artillery came into the line on 6th October.

The next ten days were devoted to preparations for an attack on Puisieux. The scheme was that the Division should attack on a one-brigade front, all three brigades being employed on the leap-frog principle. The attack was to be carried to a considerable depth, Puisieux being the first objective. Those who were to take part in this attack had strong misgivings as to the likelihood of its success. The natural fortress of Serre, which had been enormously strengthened with every modern artifice, lay on the flank of this attack on the summit of a crest. Thus if the operations against Serre failed, the whole Divisional attack would be compromised. Urgent representations were made on this score, and finally the attack in its original form was abandoned. Meanwhile the whole German trench system had been reproduced by means of tracing tapes, and practice of the attack had been well advanced.

In this sector the trenches had been named after characters in French history, the pronunciation of whose names tried the Jocks very high. Jean Bart they could manage, though they assumed that the trench was named after some female celebrity. Du Guesclin and Vercingetorix in particular were, however, a sore trial to them. "What's the sense in giving a trench a name like that?" said one of them, referring to Vercingetorix. "I suppose," replied his platoon commander, " you would like it called Sauchiehall Street or Auchtermuchty Avenue." "Aye," said the Jock, "anything that a decent body can pronounce." There were probably only three French place-names which the Jock really appreciated; they were Auchonvillers, Villers Plouich, and Martinpuich.

On 17th October the 153rd Brigade, which was then in the line, was relieved by the 92nd Brigade of the 31st Division, and the 152nd Brigade relieved the 189th Brigade of the 63rd Division in the Beaumont Hamel sector. The remainder of the Division moved to the Lealvillers-Forceville-Varennes area.

On 20th October the 153rd Brigade came into the line on the right of the 152nd Brigade and took over part of the front. Systematic and deliberate preparations were then made for the capture of the village of Beaumont Hamel and the ridge beyond it.

CHAPTER VII.

THE BATTLE OF THE ANCRE—BEAUMONT HAMEL

THE village of Beaumont Hamel and the surrounding country was admirably adapted by nature for defence. The village lay on low ground at the meeting-point of several of the rolling uplands which are the characteristic feature of Picardy. The slopes of these uplands were gradual, and so provided large areas on their reverse side which were entirely free from observation from the ground. Further, they were intersected by numerous sunken roads, which provided every facility for the construction of dug-outs, where reserves could be concealed and protected from bombardment.

The chief centres of resistance lay in the village itself and in the now celebrated "Y" Ravine. The village, which the guide-books tell us was famous for its manufacture of powder-puffs, contained vast caves and cellars capable of containing many hundreds of men, in addition to the countless concealed dug-outs with which the German invariably strengthened all ruined buildings occupied by him.

The "Y" Ravine, so called on account of the resemblance of its shape to the letter Y, was a deep ravine with almost precipitous sides. It lay with its two arms pointing like antennæ towards the British lines, some 300-500 yards south of the village.

It ran from the Station Road, a road entirely screened from observation which led from the village to the river Ancre, to the Front Line. It was honeycombed with dug-outs, and was crossed by numerous trenches. Its garrison could thus be reinforced either from the Station Road or from any of the neighbouring trenches.

BATTLE OF THE ANCRE—BEAUMONT HAMEL

It was therefore a place of tremendous strength, and obviously one which would be extremely difficult to clear of the enemy.

From the centre of Beaumont Hamel there ran in a north-easterly direction the Waggon Road, deeply sunken, riddled with dug-outs, and protected at its southern end by a large chalk-pit of most forbidding appearance.

The German position to be attacked by the Highland Division was traversed by two valleys running east and west, one being the " Y " Ravine and the other containing the old Beaumont Road, which traversed the village and met Station Road and Waggon Road at the chalk-pit mentioned above.

These two valleys were linked together by a highly-organised system of defence. The Germans had occupied the same trenches since the early days of the War. With their characteristic efficiency they had laboured to render their position as nearly impregnable as human energy and ingenuity made possible. Their trenches were at a great depth, and were lavishly provided with dug-outs. Of these, some contained two underground stories; all of them had several entrances, one in particular having eleven. The trenches were also connected from front to rear by numerous tunnels, so that reinforcements could be sent forward along underground passages proof against any bombardments.

In addition, the whole position was heavily and skilfully protected by strong wire entanglements throughout.

In fact Beaumont Hamel, after the disastrous attack on it on 1st July 1916, had come to be regarded, by British and Germans alike, as almost impregnable.

So much was this the case that the original plans for this coming attack assumed that the Beaumont Hamel position could not be taken frontally, and contemplated engaging it only in front and turning it from both flanks.

In preparing for the attack the destruction of the wire entanglements was one of the first considerations. In many places, owing to the undulations of the ground, this presented considerable difficulty, as direct observation could not be obtained.

Even with the wire cut the attack could only be considered a difficult operation. The enemy was afforded such protection from his dug-outs that success was likely to be dependent on the attacking troops keeping close on the heels of the barrage. The artillery could not be expected to do more than drive the enemy to ground.

Following the barrage closely was, moreover, in this case a difficult operation, as in few cases were the trench lines parallel. Thus the keeping of direction was certain to require skilful leading. The elaboration of the trench system also entailed a very careful detailing of objectives to the different bodies of troops, and an exact knowledge of what these objectives were.

Wire-cutting was begun by the artillery and the 2″ trench-mortars on 20th October, and was carried on continuously until the day of attack. Every precaution was taken to ensure that this was successful. Patrols, often accompanied by artillery officers, inspected the wire protecting the enemy front lines every night.

Maps were made daily, in which the portions of the enemy wire which could be observed were shown in one of four colours, a separate colour being used to denote the varying conditions of the wire—*i.e.*, satisfactorily cut, partially cut, damaged, and intact. These maps were submitted daily to Divisional Headquarters, and were passed on to the gunner officers responsible for the wire-cutting.

The results were beyond expectation, and the success of the attack was in no small measure due to the skilful manner in which the artillery destroyed the entanglements. Not only was the wire under observation shot to pieces, but concealed belts of wire, whose existence was only discovered from the study of air photos, were so damaged as to give the infantry a free passage through them. Strands of cut wire lay in heaps resembling hay-cocks throughout the trench area.

The general scheme for the attack was as follows: The Reserve Army, as the Fifth Army was then called, was to attack and establish itself on the line Miraumont-Beauregard Dovecot-Serre. Cavalry were to be held in readiness to exploit their attack in the direction of Achiet-le-Petit and Achiet-le-Grand. The IInd Corps was to attack south of the river Ancre, the Vth Corps north of the river.

The Vth Corps consisted of five Divisions: the 63rd

BATTLE OF THE ANCRE—BEAUMONT HAMEL

Division on the right, the 51st Highland Division and the 2nd Division in the centre, and the 3rd Division on the left, with the 37th Division in reserve.

The 51st Division was to capture Beaumont Hamel and push forward between the converging flanks of the 63rd and 2nd Divisions as far as Frankfurt Trench between Glory and Leave Avenues. The 63rd and 2nd Divisions were then to continue the attack, and join their inner flanks east of the 51st Division, thus pinching the latter out of the front line of attack.

General Harper was urged to attack with his three infantry brigades in line. He did not, however, consider that an attack launched in such strength and unsupported by a complete unit of reserve was justified. He therefore decided to attack with two brigades in line. It will be seen that the success of the attack and the length of time the Division was able to continue in the line after the attack bears ample testimony to the accuracy of General Harper's judgment in this respect.

The 153rd Brigade was detailed to attack on the right, the 152nd Brigade on the left, with the 154th Brigade in reserve.

Two distinct objectives for the attack were selected. The first, the Green line, included the Station Road and the village of Beaumont Hamel. The second objective, the Yellow line, was the portion of Frankfurt Trench mentioned above. A further objective east of the Yellow line was given to the 63rd and 2nd Divisions.

In the attack on the Green line, three intermediate objectives were selected, known as the Pink line (the German front line), the Blue line (the German second line), the Purple line (the German third line).

Each of these lines had a separate wave detailed for its capture composed of units from the following battalions :—

> Front line : 7th Gordon Highlanders, 6th Black Watch, 5th Seaforth Highlanders, 8th Argyll and Sutherland Highlanders.
> Blue line : 7th Gordon Highlanders, 6th Black Watch, 5th Seaforth Highlanders, 8th Argyll and Sutherland Highlanders.

Purple line : 7th Gordon Highlanders, 6th Black Watch, 5th Seaforth Highlanders, 8th Argyll and Sutherland Highlanders.

Green line : 7th Gordon Highlanders, 6th Black Watch, 6th Seaforth Highlanders (in two waves).

The bulk of the machine-guns of the Division were massed in Trench 86 near the Bowery, a small rise in the shape of a tumulus just east of Auchonvillers. From this position an intense barrage was to be fired, moving forward from the German third line through the Green line and across the western slopes of the high ground east of Beaumont Hamel. This barrage was designed to prevent the enemy from using long-range machine-gun fire against the attacking waves, and to hamper the movement of his reserves. In both these respects it proved effective.

This was the first occasion on which the Division had employed machine-guns to fire an overhead barrage during the attack. The men were accordingly specially warned that the enormous volume of bullets passing over their heads would sound as if they were only a few inches above the crowns of their steel helmets, whereas in reality there would be a margin of safety of many feet. This warning proved to be a sound precaution when the barrage was first to be experienced, since the bullets seemed unpleasantly close and might have otherwise created despondency and alarm.

The trench-mortar batteries were also fully occupied, and were continually employed in wire-cutting and assisting the raids and trench bombardments.

The attack was originally planned for 24th October, but owing to the weather a succession of postponements took place. The first postponement was until 30th October; on 25th October a further postponement of forty-eight hours was ordered. On 29th October the date of the attack was changed to 5th November. Later, it was again postponed to 9th November, and again to 10th November. On 7th November information was wired that the attack was indefinitely postponed. On 10th November it was ordered to take place on 13th November. On 11th November the hour for zero—that is, the hour at which the infantry advance begins—was selected as 5.45 A.M.

BATTLE OF THE ANCRE—BEAUMONT HAMEL

The weather, which was responsible for these postponements, could not well have been worse. The country had become water-logged owing to excessive downpours of rain. Continual mists and the absence of wind prevented the rain from being absorbed in the atmosphere. The ground thus remained sodden, the roads were reduced to a pulp, and tracks and paths became lost in oozing mud of the consistency of porridge.

In fact, the state of the ground had become so bad that a small raid which took place on 11th November failed because the raiding party found it a physical impossibility to keep up with a very slow-moving barrage. Not an officer or a man could move a yard at the double.

The results of this spell of bad weather were such that for a period not more than four lorries daily per Division were allowed on the roads, for fear that the foundations of the road would disappear permanently into the abyss of mud beneath them. The inconvenience caused to " Q " by this unavoidable restriction was immense, but the ingenuity of the quartermaster's staff, as usual, overcame the difficulty with marked success.

The repeated postponements, though very trying to the men's nerves, proved in reality a blessing. The plan was that the attack should be preceded by a four days' bombardment, including a lavish use of gas shells. The result was that in many cases the first and, in some cases, the second day's bombardment had been fired before the postponement took place. They, therefore, had to be repeated when a fresh date for the attack had been selected. In consequence, the German positions were continually being subjected to a bombardment of intense violence. The enemy thus received a far larger ration of shells than would have been the case if the attack had taken place on the date selected in the first instance. Moreover, these bombardments not only assailed the Germans frontally from batteries in positions west of Beaumont Hamel, but also in enfilade from positions south of Beaumont.

In the period of preparation for the battle a considerable amount of labour was required to keep the trenches fit for traffic. In the low-lying land which separated the various chalk downs, the soil was a red loam. In consequence, whenever it rained, the sides of the trenches fell in great flakes like miniature avalanches. The water was also very slow to soak into the ground. Thus large sections of communication trenches became knee-deep and even waist-deep in liquid mud. When it is remembered that all munitions, rations, water, tools, &c., required for the battle had to be carried on the backs of men through these trenches to the forward dumps, it will be appreciated what a burden of discomfort and toil the conditions due to the weather imposed on the troops.

A considerable amount of work had also to be done on the construction and extension of dug-outs for reserve troops and headquarters. The successive postponements, however, enabled this work to be satisfactorily completed, and in consequence the casualties sustained in our own trenches during the battle were negligible. In one portion of the area a chalk cliff some forty feet in height lent itself admirably to tunnelling operations. Enough head-cover was provided without the necessity of making chambers to dug-outs at the foot of a long flight of stairs. Full use was made of this feature, and many dug-outs were hewn in it, as well as a large vault capable of holding a company, secure from the heaviest artillery.

This feature lay at the foot of the reverse slope of a large chalk upland, and was thus entirely hidden from enemy view. Looked at from the reserve British lines, it appeared as a great white scar on the landscape, and was an obvious centre of activity. It had in consequence been christened the "White City." It ran northwards for some considerable distance, and was put to similar uses by neighbouring brigades on the left of the Division.

An attempt was made to blow an assembly trench for the troops detailed for the attack on the Green line by means of tubes of ammonal buried in a shallow trench cut through the surface of the soil. The ammonal was discharged successfully, but the results were disappointing. The disintegrations in the soil caused by the explosion, coupled with the rain, produced conditions of mud that rendered the trench which the explosion had created impassable.

During the fortnight preceding the attack patrolling and raiding were carried out with great activity, both with a view to gauging the strength of the resistance likely to be encountered and to inspect and damage the enemy's wire. This activity disclosed the fact that the German was employing knife-rests [1] made either of heavy timber or of iron, to fill the gaps caused by our artillery and trench-mortars in his entanglements.

Knife-rests are not easily damaged by shrapnel sufficiently to give the infantry a free passage through them. Efforts were therefore made to locate the places where they were in use, and to destroy them with 4·5 howitzers.

The fire of enfilade machine and Lewis guns was then employed to prevent fresh knife-rests being put in position to replace those which had been damaged. Twenty thousand rounds of S.A.A. were frequently fired in a single night for this purpose.

At the end of October it was realised that these knife-rests were being employed by the enemy in most formidable numbers, and were becoming a serious proposition.

A number of Bangalore torpedoes were therefore made and carried up to the trenches. Raiding parties then carried these torpedoes into No Man's Land with them, and blew gaps in the rows of knife-rests. On 1st November a particularly good raid of this nature was carried out. Lieutenants Booth and Carnie of the 6th Gordon Highlanders with a party of men placed four torpedoes under the enemy knife-rests. These were exploded, and after a short interval the officers led the party through the gap caused by the explosions. They then exploded four more torpedoes under the next double rows of knife-rests. The party returned without a casualty, and reported that still a third row of knife-rests existed beyond the last one they had damaged.

Raiding parties had also been employed to enter the enemy's trenches to gain identifications—that is, to return with evidence as to what units were holding the line in front of the Division.[2]

[1] Knife-rests are portable wire entanglements. The framework is shaped like a knife-rest, numerous strands of barbed wire being stretched from end to end of it. It is carried up to the trenches folded up so as to make it easily portable. At night they are taken into No Man's Land, opened out, and placed in position and pegged to the ground.

[2] Obtaining identifications was a matter of extreme importance, as it enabled G.H.Q. to estimate the number of German Divisions holding the line, and the number in reserve available to be moved from one portion of the front to another.

On 26th October both the 6th Black Watch and the 7th Gordon Highlanders of the 153rd Brigade entered the enemy's front line, the latter capturing a prisoner of the 62nd Regiment. On the same night the 7th Argyll and Sutherland Highlanders of the 154th Brigade made a similar attempt, but could not find a passage through the enemy's wire. In the raid of the 7th Gordon Highlanders, Lance-Sergeant Morrison killed four Germans and disarmed a fifth, who was taken prisoner. At this point Sergeant Morrison had expended all his ammunition and bombs, and was faced by two more Germans with fixed bayonets. Appreciating the situation, Private Louis Thomson rushed past Sergeant Morrison and killed the first German with his entrenching tool. He then picked up the fallen German's rifle and with it killed the second. For this exploit both Sergeant Morrison and Private Thomson were awarded the Military Medal.

On 29th October a patrol of the 154th Brigade entered the enemy's front line and proceeded to his second line, which they found protected by an impassable belt of knife-rests. This patrol encountered none of the enemy. The absence of the Boche on this occasion proved rather disconcerting. In consequence, the 4th Gordon Highlanders and the 9th Royal Scots carried out further raids. In each case they found the enemy holding the trenches in strength, and were unable to effect an entrance. This was partly due to the fact that the ground was so sodden that the troops found it a physical impossibility to keep up with the barrage.

A further raid attempted on 4th November by the 6th Gordon Highlanders also met with strong resistance, and made no progress. It was therefore almost impossible to form an impression of the strength in which the enemy was holding his line.

On 31st October a deserter entered our lines. He was a miserable creature, described officially as "undersized and of poor physique." He stated on examination that the battalion was holding a front of only 700 yards, and that the rifle strength of the four companies was about 180 each. His statement, if it was accurate, meant that the enemy was holding the position in considerably greater force than was probable. In view of his apparent poverty of intellect, it was considered that his evidence was unreliable. It, however, transpired during the attack that his statements were not exaggerated, and that the enemy was indeed very thick on the ground.

The final preparations for the attack consisted in forming dumps of ammunition, water, rations, &c., sufficiently far forward to enable carrying parties to take forward supplies to the advanced troops after the capture of the enemy's position.

This was a heavy task, as the following figures of supplies which were carried through the water-logged trenches and placed in the brigade dumps testify :—

Small arms ammunition	400,000 rounds.
Mills grenades	23,000
Petrol tins of water	1,600
Rations	4,800
Stokes bombs	7,500
Very light cartridges	8,000

On one night alone one brigade had 34 waggons and 150 men employed in bringing forward material for these dumps.

By the time the attack took place sufficient stores had been accumulated to render it unnecessary for any waggons to be employed in the forward area on the night after the battle. This was a great advantage, as the enemy was always liable during a battle to make a lavish use of high-velocity guns and gas shells to harass our communications.

Some days prior to the day of the battle, the troops in the line witnessed an attack on a fairly large scale delivered against the famous Stuff and Schwaben Redoubts. These were situated just below the crest on the northern slopes of the Thiepval Ridge, of which a magnificent view could be obtained from many places in the Beaumont Hamel sector. The spectacle certainly had an encouraging effect on all who saw it. The barrage appeared excellent, and several waves of infantry could be seen following it apparently without difficulty. Subsequently parties of German prisoners could be seen moving back to the rear.

These two redoubts were notorious for the strength of their defences, and had figured largely in recent communiqués, yet as far as could be judged they were captured behind the barrage exactly according to plan. This attack therefore gave a most practical example of the possibilities of the 18-pounder barrage when closely followed by the attacking infantry.

The assembly of the troops prior to the attack on the 13th was an arduous performance, some of the battalions being billeted in the Forceville area some five miles from the front line.

At 9 P.M. on 12th November the march to the position of assembly began, the last battalions being reported in position at 4.30 A.M. A halt of three-quarters of an hour was made *en route*, between Mailly-Maillet and Auchonvillers, and tea was served to the men from the field-kitchens there.

The length of time required for this march was due to the deplorable state of the roads and communication trenches, and to the weight carried by the men. In addition to battle order equipment, each man carried on him at least two Mills bombs, a pick or a shovel, and two days' preserved rations. Moreover, numbers of aeroplane flares, Very light pistols and cartridges, phosphorus bombs, &c., were distributed throughout the different platoons.

Owing to the mud in the trenches movement was largely carried out over the open. The attention of the enemy was not, however, attracted, and there was little artillery fire before zero.

So many troops had to be assembled that it was necessary for the leading companies to be in position several hours before those that were to be the last to assemble. Further, to ensure that the assembly was completed up to time, orders were issued for the troops to be ready in their appointed positions one hour before zero.

This allowed a good margin in which to make up for any delays which might be caused by gas-shelling or bombardments occurring during the advance to the assembly trenches.

During this period a covering screen of troops, who were not detailed to take part in the first phase of the attack, lay out in No Man's Land to prevent German patrols from approaching our trenches and discovering that assembly for an attack was in progress.

BATTLE OF THE ANCRE—BEAUMONT HAMEL

This period of waiting in assembly trenches for the hour of zero to arrive is one of the most unpleasant ordeals which a soldier has to endure. On this foggy November night the troops arrived with their kilts and hose-tops sodden with water and mud. The duck-boards in the assembly trenches were in many places under water. The fire-steps on which men sat, or the parapets and parados against which they leant huddled together for warmth, were exuding moisture and occasionally land-sliding into the trenches, bringing down in their fall a multitude of telephone wires, over which men stumbled and tripped for the remainder of the night.

Rifles and Lewis guns needed the greatest care to prevent them from becoming clogged with mud and unserviceable. Silence was enforced and smoking forbidden, for fear that the arrival of a large force of men in the front line— a sure indication of an impending attack—might be disclosed to the enemy. Men were forbidden also to use their water-bottles before zero hour, partly because the need for water would become acute later during the battle, and partly on account of the noise which a half-emptied water-bottle is capable of producing, particularly when silence is most desired.

During this anxious and seemingly endless vigil, the morale of even the boldest depreciates. The most unimaginative loon, particularly if it is not his maiden fight, knows that there are many men assembled with him who in an hour or two will see the dawn break for the last time. The stoutest-hearted cannot help reflecting on what his own fate is to be, and on the odds for or against his being hit; if hit, will the wound be a "cushy" one, or will he, in the next few hours, be transformed from an able-bodied soldier into a permanent cripple or a dead man?

These are not pleasant reflections, particularly when the solace of speaking and smoking is denied.

As a rule, when the assembly is complete there is too much congestion for officers and N.C.O.'s to move about amongst their men. Then walking along the trench is like passing to one's seat in the centre of the stalls after the curtain has gone up; in the darkness the floor seems carpeted with feet, and one stumbles along what appears to be a narrow passage with its walls bristling with projecting knees.

The time spent in the assembly trenches hangs heavily. The throats of the men get dry, partly because they are told they must not cough, and partly perhaps for other reasons. In these circumstances men have a peculiar desire to cough, just as a congregation has towards the end of a long and tedious sermon. If one man begins, the rest take it up. The noise thus made appears deafening. To obviate this, petrol tins of water and tea in hot food-containers have been dumped about the assembly positions, so that men may from time to time moisten their mouths and throats. Further, a tot of rum is served to all. Rum played a great part in the war. It produces a marvellous and immediate effect, dispelling depression, creating warmth, and stimulating the morale. Even the staunchest teetotallers will drink rum with avidity in the assembly trenches.

There is a further disquieting thought which occurs during this period, particularly to commanders. Will the enemy discover that our foremost trenches are packed solid with humanity, that almost all our eggs are in one basket? Has that infernal listening machine overheard details of the day and hour carelessly spoken over the telephone, in spite of the many orders on the subject? If he discovers we are here, he will produce what he pleases to call annihilating fire, in which he concentrates his guns and trench-mortars on our assembly position.

When he has been successful in doing this, the results have been indescribable. Each shell that falls into the trench bursts in the midst of a closely-packed group of men. The members of the various headquarters therefore anxiously listen for any signs of an enemy bombardment, and are only relieved of their anxiety when the arrival of zero hour is denoted by the opening of the British barrage.

The reserve troops of the two leading brigades were safely accommodated in deep dug-outs, secure from any bombardment which the enemy might open in reply to the attack.

The 154th Brigade in reserve lay at Mailly-Maillet Wood, out of the range of field howitzers, their headquarters being at the Café Jourdain.

BATTLE OF THE ANCRE—BEAUMONT HAMEL

The signal for zero hour was to be the explosion of a mine. In the attack that had been launched against Beaumont Hamel on the first day of the Somme offensive, a mine had been exploded just short of the enemy's front line. As the attack had failed, the enemy had been left in complete possession of this mine. He had fortified it with dug-outs and made considerable use of it both as an observation-post and as a position for snipers. Arrangements had therefore been made to run out another shaft and lay a fresh charge in chambers constructed below this crater.

At 5.45 A.M. this mine was successfully exploded, and the artillery opened an intense bombardment of the German position. At this time dawn had only just begun to show signs of breaking. The darkness was further accentuated by a fog, similar to a typical London November fog, which did not lift throughout the day. This fog was a definite asset to the attack, as, though it made the maintenance of direction more difficult, it concealed the movements of the attackers, and prevented the enemy gunners from seeing the artillery signals fired by their infantry. The result was that the hostile artillery barrage on the British front line and in No Man's Land was ragged, and did not open with any intensity until 6.15 A.M. In consequence, the losses from hostile artillery fire in the assembly trenches and while the troops were crossing No Man's Land were negligible.

The infantry had crept close to the barrage before it had lifted, so that when it moved forward they succeeded in entering the trench at most points. Indeed, so close did they get to the bursting shells that many of them reported that they were waiting on the outskirts of the remnants of the enemy's entanglements while the barrage was still down in the Boche front line. The 6th Black Watch pressed forward so close to the barrage that they sustained some casualties from it.

The two right companies of the 7th Gordon Highlanders took the first line without difficulty. They continued keeping close up to the barrage, each successive wave capturing its objective, until they had occupied the Green line according to the programme. These two companies could not have carried out their task in a more exemplary manner. Throughout this advance on the right flank touch was maintained with the left of a Royal Marine Light Infantry battalion of the 63rd Naval Division.

On the rest of the front the attack bore no resemblance to the traditional form of attack as pictured in the illustrated weeklies, or demonstrated by the bayonet-fighting expert. There was no wild charge of Highlanders with flying kilts and glittering bayonets. On the contrary, it was carried out at the rate of an advance of twenty-five yards per minute. As the barrage lifted off a trench, the troops made their way into it as quickly as they could, but a steady double was the most that they could manage. In many cases even that was found impossible.

The men floundered in the dark in mud over their ankles; the weight they carried was enormously augmented by the moisture that their clothing had absorbed and by the mud which glued itself to their kilts and which clung to their boots; the ground was ploughed up into a sea of shell-holes half filled with water; stooks of cut strands of wire and overturned knife-rests lay everywhere. Forward movement of any kind called for considerable physical effort; to charge was out of the question. In some places men even became bogged up to their waists, and were unable to extricate themselves from the morass, until parties of German prisoners could be organised to dig them out.

Let two teams dressed in battle order play football in the dark on a ploughed field in a clay soil after three weeks' steady rain, and the difficulties of the attacking troops might then in some measure be appreciated.

The left of the 7th Gordon Highlanders and the right of the 6th Black Watch were delayed in their advance by machine-guns from the south of the "Y" Ravine. The German garrison on the point of this salient was thus able to man the front trench, and beat off our attack at this point by the volume of their fire. Here the enemy maintained himself for several hours. Being in a position from which they obtained splendid observation both to the north and south, they made communication with the forward troops who had swept on, on either flank extremity, difficult.

A gap had also been caused in the centre of the next

Map III.—Beaumont Hamel, 13th November 1916.

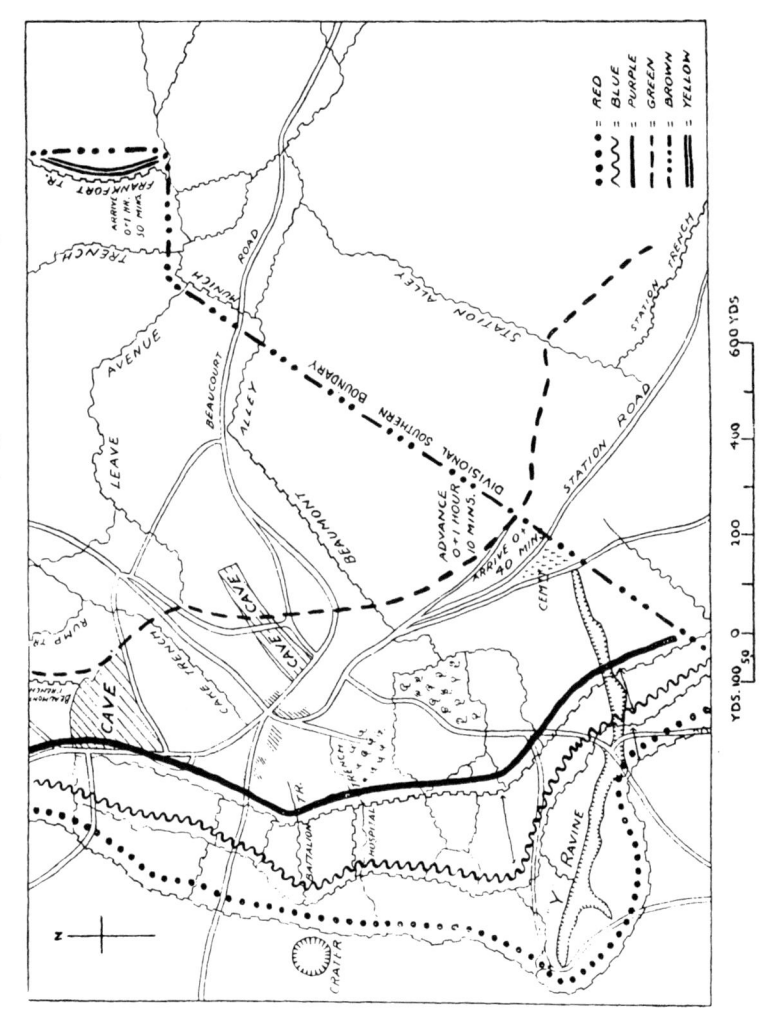

battalion through wire just south of the crater, which had been screened from observation by being uncut.

On the left of the 5th Seaforth Highlanders, the 8th Argyll and Sutherland Highlanders had received a temporary check caused by machine-gun fire on their extreme left, and had suffered heavily. The remainder of the battalion had, however, pressed forward on the flanks, captured the guns, and enabled the advance to be continued to the third German line.

By 7.50 A.M. it was reported that troops of both brigades had reached the third German line, and many prisoners had been taken, but pockets of Germans were still holding out in various points in the first and second lines. These pockets were, no doubt, formed by parties of the enemy who had come up into the front line out of the various underground tunnels.

Casualties had been unduly heavy, as the state of the ground had proved in places so bad that the troops had been unable to keep up with the barrage.

At this hour the position in the village was obscure. The 153rd Infantry Brigade had employed all its reserves in its endeavour to carry the " Y " Ravine, where a party of the enemy, estimated at from three to four hundred strong, was offering a most gallant and successful resistance, all attacks to overcome them being beaten off.

Two companies of the 4th Gordon Highlanders from the Divisional reserve were therefore ordered forward and placed at the disposal of General Campbell. Meanwhile General Burn had ordered forward a company from the reserve battalion (6th Gordon Highlanders) to fill the gap caused in the ranks of the 5th Seaforth Highlanders by uncut wire. This company successfully entered the German second line, but was unable to debouch from it owing to machine-gun fire from the German third line. Two bombing squads from the 6th Gordon Highlanders were therefore sent forward to clear the front. These squads were extremely well handled by their leaders, and by attacking the machine-guns in the third line from the flank succeeded in capturing 2 officers and 51 men. This action enabled the whole of the right battalion to reach the Green line. Two other bombing squads were also ordered forward from the 6th Gordon Highlanders to bomb southwards, so as to clear the left flank of the 6th Black Watch. It was not, however, until dusk that all resistance in this area was successfully overcome.

The 8th Argyll and Sutherland Highlanders were meanwhile consolidating the Green line in touch with the 2nd Division on their left.

At this time little news could be obtained by headquarters of the 153rd Brigade, as all their runners were killed or wounded by Germans still holding out in the trench system. The situation was therefore obscure except at the "Y" Ravine, which was known to be held by the enemy. The two companies 4th Gordon Highlanders were therefore ordered to supply three bombing parties to work inwards towards the "Y" Ravine, one from the north and two from the south.

The 5th Gordon Highlanders, who had followed in support of the leading battalions south of the salient, were fighting with elements of the 6th Black Watch and the 7th Gordon Highlanders for the German second line. In front of the salient parties of men who had been held up had returned to the British front line. These men were collected by Lieut.-Colonel T. M. Booth, D.S.O., commanding 6th Black Watch. He at once sent out patrols to locate exactly where the enemy was holding out, and on the information thus obtained organised a fresh attack against the "Y" Ravine.

Colonel Booth arrived with this party just as Lieutenant Leslie of the 6th Black Watch, by a most gallant action, had gained an entrance at the point of the "Y" Ravine. He was immediately followed by Colonel Booth with forty men and a Lewis gun, and by parties of the 5th and 7th Gordon Highlanders who had been hanging on to the occupants of the "Y" Ravine all the morning.

During all this time a party of about a hundred of the 6th Black Watch and 5th and 7th Gordon Highlanders were in the centre of the "Y" Ravine, where they had been surrounded by Germans who had emerged from dugouts and tunnels and pinned them to their ground by machine-gun fire. As soon as Colonel Booth and Lieutenant Leslie arrived and a bombing action had begun, these men began bombing outwards from their position, and cleared the whole ravine up to the third German line.

BATTLE OF THE ANCRE—BEAUMONT HAMEL

General Campbell then ordered the 4th Gordon Highlanders to advance to the Green line. This operation was carried out without opposition, the 6th Black Watch in the Third German line joining in the advance.

On arrival in the Green line, the 4th Gordon Highlanders learnt that the 7th Gordon Highlanders had not only reached the Green line according to plan, but had continued their advance 250 yards beyond in the direction of the Yellow line. At this point they encountered and captured fifty Germans. In this advanced position they remained for some considerable time, but as no troops came to support them on either flank, they finally withdrew to the Green line. Every runner that had been sent back by these companies to report their position was either killed or wounded in attempting to pass through the German trench system.

Even after the capture of the Green line on the whole Divisional front, isolated pockets of the enemy continued to offer resistance, particularly on the south-western edge of the village. Here a belt of marshy country, just east of the mine crater, had been found impossible to cross owing to the depth of the mud. The result was that the Germans in this area were not put out of action until troops from the reserve had moved round the northern edge of the marsh and attacked them in flank.

At 10.30 A.M. two tanks were sent forward to clear up isolated pockets of the enemy still holding out in the village. This was the first occasion on which the Division had co-operated with tanks. The condition of the ground was, however, such that the tanks only just reached the German front line. By the time they had travelled this distance they had built up great mounds of mud under their bellies, which prevented their further advance.

One of the tank officers, incidentally a Scot, refused, however, to be prevented from joining in the fight. He therefore made some captured Germans carry his Hotchkiss guns and their ammunition up to the Green line, where he joined in the consolidation.

The attack on the Yellow line, apart from the individual effort of the two companies of the 7th Gordon Highlanders, never took place. The fighting had been so severe that, by the time the leading troops reached the Green line, the barrage had been lost irretrievably. Moreover, the troops detailed for the capture of the Yellow line had been considerably involved in the fighting for the Green line, and were too reduced in number for an attack unsupported by an artillery barrage to have any chance of success.

Later in the day orders were given for the 153rd Brigade to renew the attack on the Yellow line; they were, however, subsequently cancelled, as the Corps commander had decided to renew the attack on the following day.

Towards the evening two companies of the 7th Argyll and Sutherland Highlanders were placed at General Burn's disposal. The two companies of the 6th Gordon Highlanders which had not as yet been employed were therefore ordered to march up the Beaumont Road at dusk and occupy and consolidate the Green line.

The night was spent in consolidating and reorganising. At 2.30 A.M. on the night 13-14th orders were issued for the attack on Munich Trench to be resumed at 5.45 A.M., the remaining two companies of the 7th Argyll and Sutherland Highlanders and two companies of the 9th Royal Scots being placed at General Burn's disposal for the purpose.

The headquarters and the remaining two companies of the 9th Royal Scots were placed at the disposal of General Campbell. During the night a telephone message, spoken over a faulty wire, was misunderstood, and the attack was cancelled instead of being postponed. When this error had been discovered, a fresh attack was initiated, in which the 7th Argyll and Sutherland Highlanders carried out a most successful bombing operation up Beaumont Alley and Leave Trench, and occupied Munich Trench. This attack, hastily improvised as it was, was admirably and gallantly executed, and was a complete success. Subsequently, however, the Argylls could not maintain themselves in their exposed position in a trench almost obliterated, and withdrew to Leave Alley.

On the night of the 14th the 2/2 Highland Field Company, R.E., and one company of the 8th Royal Scots dug a new trench 150 yards west of Munich Trench. This trench was named New Munich Trench, and was occupied by a garrison before dawn.

During daylight on the 14th, the 4th Gordon Highlanders

BATTLE OF THE ANCRE—BEAUMONT HAMEL

took over the whole of the Green line on the 153rd Brigade front, the 6th Black Watch returning to Mailly-Maillet Wood. On the 152nd Brigade front the 6th Gordon Highlanders similarly took over the whole of the Green line, the 5th Seaforth Highlanders and the 8th Argyll and Sutherland Highlanders being withdrawn to Mailly-Maillet, and the 6th Seaforth Highlanders to the old British trench area.

At 9.50 P.M. on 14th November, General Burn was ordered to prepare an attack in conjunction with the 2nd Division, the frontage of attack of the 152nd Brigade being that portion of Frankfurt Trench between Leave Avenue and Glory Lane. At 5.30 A.M. orders were received that the attack was to take place at 9 A.M.

The attack was made by two fresh companies of the 7th Argyll and Sutherland Highlanders, who had relieved the troops in New Munich Trench during the night. One company of the 7th Argyll and Sutherland Highlanders was in support.

The 2nd Division formed up with its right on the Waggon Road at least 500 yards in rear of New Munich Trench. The lifts of the artillery barrage of the 51st Division were therefore arranged to suit the major attack by the 2nd Division. It was placed, in the first instance, in Munich Trench, and subsequently lifted on the Frankfurt Trench by bounds of fifty yards. These short bounds in the barrage were arranged so as to allow the 2nd Division time to come up into line.

When the attack was launched, it was found that the enemy was no longer holding Munich Trench, so that it was occupied without difficulty. However, after passing Munich Trench, the attackers ran into our own barrage, and suffered severe losses sufficient to disorganise the whole attack. This unfortunate incident was due to the impetuosity of the men. Their previous training had been to follow a barrage which moved forward by bounds of a hundred yards. No blame, therefore, rests with the artillery, the over-anxiety of the men to gain their objective being the sole cause. Only a few individuals managed to reach Frankfurt Trench.

While this action was in progress, the right of the 2nd Division had lost direction, and had come up in rear of the

7th Argyll and Sutherland Highlanders, reaching Leave Avenue to the west of Munich Trench.

In these circumstances it was decided not to renew the attack without further artillery preparation.

This attack was an unfortunate conclusion to what had otherwise been a successful series of operations. Had the 7th Argyll and Sutherland Highlanders succeeded in capturing Frankfurt Trench, their position " in the air " on a 300 yards front would have been a precarious one, and a source of embarrassment to the artillery when called upon to bombard the remainder of the trench.

To ensure success, it would have been advisable to have made certain that the 2nd Division's line of attack was abreast of the 51st Division's before a further advance against Frankfurt Trench was made. The chances of success would also have been greatly increased if the whole attack had been carried out by a formation under one command.

During the day of the 15th, the 154th Brigade took over the whole battle front from the 152nd and 153rd Brigades.

The 51st Division took no further part in active operations, although it continued to hold New Munich Trench until 17th November, on which date the foremost positions were taken over by the 32nd Division.

The battle of Beaumont Hamel was the foundation-stone on which the reputation of the Highland Division was built. General Harper's leap-frog system of attack had been proved; his attack with two brigades instead of three had been fully justified, and an experience had been gained from which the future training of the Division was evolved.

The whole position up to and including the Green line had been captured with over two thousand prisoners and a vast amount of material in a few hours. Moreover, had the positions of the Divisions on the flanks been less obscure, an advance to the Yellow line could have been undertaken with every prospect of success.

The satisfactory results of these operations may be put down to the following causes :—

First, to the resolution and gallantry of the officers and men. In spite of heavy losses and of the appalling state

BATTLE OF THE ANCRE—BEAUMONT HAMEL

of the ground, they pressed on to their objectives with the greatest determination. In many cases the barrage was irretrievably lost. The resistance of a courageous and cunning enemy, protected by the strongest field defences that experience could devise, had then to be overcome by the superior fighting qualities of the infantry soldier alone. The manner in which he overcame this resistance was in accordance with the highest traditions of the Highland regiments.

The artillery played no small part in this battle. The heavy gunners had demolished the enemy's trenches in an exemplary manner. In the village of Beaumont Hamel there was barely a square yard that was not torn up by shell-fire. The deep dug-outs alone escaped destruction, and even in their case many entrances were blown in. A German battalion headquarters sustained three direct hits, all of which went through the roof. In one case two layers of reinforced concrete and one layer of tree-trunks had been penetrated. In the enemy front line machine-gun emplacements, made of concrete over a metre thick, were in many cases wrecked.

Both the destruction of the wire and the accuracy of the barrage further strengthened the great confidence of the infantry in the Divisional artillery. It was the first occasion on which most of the troops had followed an artillery barrage. Those who were able to keep up with it could not speak too highly of its accuracy.

The decision to have no preliminary bombardment immediately before the attack proved to have been a wise one. Such a bombardment would only have served to warn the enemy of our intention to attack. As it was, the infantry began their advance the moment the artillery opened. They were thus able to assault the front line within a few seconds of the barrage having lifted. The enemy was in consequence to a large extent taken by surprise, and large numbers of them were captured before they had had time to leave their dug-outs.

The enemy had, however, this advantage. It could not be told whether a shaft was the entrance to a dug-out or to a tunnel connecting two lines of trenches. As a result, it was difficult to ensure that any particular trench would remain cleared of Boches. The large traversed dug-outs were also difficult to clear up. A Mills bomb did not seem to have much effect on their occupants. A phosphorus bomb, however, bolted eighty-six Germans in all stages of undress out of a single dug-out.

The machine-gun barrage appeared to have been very effective. The 7th Gordon Highlanders reported a considerable number of German dead between the Green and Yellow lines who are believed to have been caught in this barrage. The machine-gunners who went forward with the attacking waves also executed their tasks admirably.

Vickers guns were in position in the German front line within half an hour of zero. One gun-team had some close-range fighting with revolvers and bombs, and captured seventeen prisoners, not, however, before the section officer had been wounded and a sergeant killed.

Vickers guns were assigned definite rôles in the consolidation and were placed in depth throughout the captured area. Several guns took up advanced positions well east of the Green line.

The light trench-mortar batteries fired in the initial barrage, according to all reports, with considerable accuracy. Subsequently two mortars were placed at the disposal of each battalion commander to be employed to assist the advance when required. In the attack on Frankfurt Trench on the morning of the 15th, four Stokes mortars of the 152nd Trench-Mortar Battery fired in the preliminary bombardment. These mortars carried out their task extremely well in difficult circumstances. They did not leave brigade headquarters until 3 A.M., but by 6 A.M. they were dug into their positions with 20 rounds per gun in the emplacements.

Among the prisoners captured were two battalion commanders with their staffs complete. These were captured by 2nd Lieutenant G. V. Edwards of the 6th Seaforth Highlanders and Lieutenant W. D. Munro of the 8th Argyll and Sutherland Highlanders, both since killed in action. These officers had been detailed to lead their platoons straight to certain points which had been marked as battalion headquarters on a captured map. The result of this plan was that the battalion commanders were rounded up and captured before they had had time to exercise any influence on the battle by the use of their reserves.

BATTLE OF THE ANCRE—BEAUMONT HAMEL 123

The headquarters allotted to Lieutenant Edwards for capture was situated in an enormous cave. Some 300-400 prisoners surrendered to his party in the first instance, but as his platoon was by this time considerably reduced in numbers, he was compelled to hand them over to troops of the Naval Division under the command of a chaplain. It was, however, undoubtedly due to Lieutenant Edwards that these men took no part in the battle.

The leading of these two platoons was admirable. The exact manner in which their instructions were carried out considerably upset the enemy's defensive arrangements.

The captured booty included weapons of all kinds, with the exception of artillery, as well as large magazines of ammunition. In addition, a large canteen containing tinned beef from Monte Video, Norwegian sardines, cigarettes (including Wills' Gold Flake), cigars, and many thousand bottles of excellent soda and of beer fell into the hands of the Jocks and was much appreciated. For many days afterwards the Jocks were to be seen walking out smoking large cigars with evident satisfaction.

Further, a piano, some ladies' dancing slippers, silk stockings, and petticoats were also found, but there was no evidence to show whether they belonged to a German lady or to a local Boche " Gertie."

A light trench-mortar battery officer also captured the whole of the German incoming mail.

The casualties sustained by the Division during the month of November amounted to 123 officers killed, wounded, and missing, and 2355 other ranks. For modern warfare these were not heavy, particularly when compared with the number of prisoners captured during the operations. It must, however, be borne in mind that at the time of the battle the battalions were extremely weak in numbers. The casualties during the action represented 45 per cent of those who took part in the attack.

The results of the capture of Beaumont Hamel were far-reaching. It was undoubtedly the loss of this stronghold and its immediate effects which largely determined the German High Command to evacuate in the following spring the salient formed in their lines during the battle of the Somme.

The artillery arrangements made for this battle introduced for the first time that liaison with the heavy artillery which, as far as the Division was concerned, continued until the end of the war, and was of the greatest value to the infantry. For this the Division is mainly indebted to Brigadier-General R. P. Benson, C.B., C.M.G., commanding the Vth Corps Heavy Artillery.

On 19th November the 152nd Infantry Brigade relieved the 154th Infantry Brigade. The 5th Seaforth Highlanders formed into two composite companies, and the 6th Gordon Highlanders took over the Green line. The 6th Seaforth Highlanders and the 8th Argyll and Sutherland Highlanders, each formed into two composite companies, took over the old British trench system. On completion of this relief the 152nd Brigade came under the orders of the 32nd Division.

This tour of duty was uneventful, the enemy carrying out no infantry action. He was, however, at times fairly active with his artillery, particularly against the village of Beaumont Hamel and the Green line. The weather, however, remained bad, dense fogs continuing day after day, so that the enemy had little chance of locating our positions.

During this tour of duty an immense amount of salvage work was carried out. The whole battlefield was cleared of arms and equipment; old dumps were moved forward so as to be available for use in the consolidation of the Green line. Large parties were also employed in collecting the dead, and loading the bodies on to waggons, so that they might be buried in the British cemeteries at Mailly-Maillet or Auchonvillers. Parties were also employed in burying the numerous skeletons which lay scattered about the old No Man's Land. These were the remains of the troops who had taken part in the unsuccessful attack on Beaumont Hamel on 1st July. The flesh had been devoured from the bones by the rats, which swarmed in thousands, and made their homes in the empty trunks. Six hundred and sixty-nine of these skeletons were buried on the front of the 152nd Brigade alone—an unpleasant task, and one which had a considerable effect on the highly-tried nerves of some of the men.

On 23rd November an operation was arranged by the 32nd Division with the object of relieving 5 officers and

BATTLE OF THE ANCRE—BEAUMONT HAMEL

120 of their men who had been isolated and surrounded in Frankfurt Trench. They had made their position known by attracting the attention of a British aeroplane. Later, several of these men made their way back to our lines at night, and reported that the position of the party was desperate. They had few bombs, and depended for rations on what they could recover from the dead at night. The only water they had to drink was obtained from shell-holes. They, further, had several severely wounded men, who required immediate attention if their lives were to be saved. In support of this operation the 6th Gordon Highlanders were ordered to hold themselves in readiness to move in case the enemy were to counter-attack.

The attack was timed to take place at 3.30 P.M. It, however, failed in its object, the attackers being unable to do more than gain a footing in Munich Trench. In consequence, the isolated party, after a most gallant and prolonged resistance, were compelled by the circumstances to surrender.

On the morning of the 24th the 152nd Brigade was relieved by the 7th Division. A dense fog enabled the relieving troops to march by parties up the old Beaumont Road into their positions, with their company officers still mounted.

Lieut.-General Sir E. A. Fanshawe, K.C.B., commanding the Vth Corps, summed up the part played by the Division in the battle of the Ancre as follows :—

" The 51st Division leaves this Corps to-morrow to take a place in another part of the line, and although this postpones a well-earned rest, it is also a sure sign of the very efficient state of the Division that it should be called upon to do this by the army after its recent splendid fight.

" It is evident from the newspapers that all the world looks upon the capture of Beaumont Hamel as one of the greatest feats of arms in the war, and to those who know the ground and the defences it must ever be a marvellously fine performance.

" I can only hope that the good-bye which the Vth Corps now wish the 51st Division is for a short time, and that the good luck may be for many years to come."

One of the Jocks summed it up more briefly in the

single sentence, " Onyway, they winna ca' us Hairper's Duds noo."

The spirit of the men in this battle is exemplified by a certain Jock who was found lying in a shell-hole in advance of the Green line, with a shattered leg, forty-eight hours after he had been hit. He was asked by the medical officer if no one had come near him, and he replied, " Aye, a German Red Cross man came up to me." " Surely he attended to you," said the M.O. " Attended to me ? " replied the Jock, " I flung a boom at the blighter."

CHAPTER VIII.

COURCELETTE.

IMMEDIATELY after the battle of Beaumont Hamel, Lieut.-Colonel Ian Stewart, D.S.O., left the Division. Colonel Stewart had been chief staff officer to the Division through all those months in which it was learning the art of war, and in which many battalions were for the first time blooded in active operations.

During this period the amount of work which Colonel Stewart carried out, and the careful thought exercised by him on behalf of the Division to lessen the difficulties of all and to raise it to the high standard that it reached, was indeed vast. It was therefore a matter of great satisfaction to the Division to hear that his services had been rewarded by promotion to be Brigadier-General, General Staff of the XIIIth Corps.

It must also have been equally satisfactory to Colonel Stewart that the Division should have proved its worth at Beaumont Hamel before his service with it came to an end.

Lieut.-Colonel J. K. Dick Cunyngham, D.S.O., Gordon Highlanders, succeeded Lieut.-Colonel Ian Stewart as G.S.O. 1. Lieut.-Colonel Dick Cunyngham will always remain to those who came into contact with him the ideal of what a staff officer should be. He had a wide sympathy with the regimental officer, and understood his difficulties thoroughly. He had, moreover, an unruffled temperament, which enabled him to keep a clear head and think quickly and correctly even in the most adverse circumstances. The speed with which he would write a long and intricate operation order in clear and unambiguous language was a definite asset to the whole Division, and largely eliminated that confusion which is so liable to occur during the fluctuations of a modern battle. "Dick," as he was familiarly known, was certainly one of the chief pillars on which the efficiency of the Division rested.

The whole Division was now out of the line, lying in the area Arquèves-Rancheval-Hedauville-Varennes-Forceville-Lealvillers. It was not, however, to be allowed to rest, for on 25th November the 153rd Brigade began its march to Ovillers Huts. The following day the 154th Brigade moved to Aveluy, and the 152nd Brigade to Bouzincourt and Senlis. It was then learnt that the Division was immediately to take over a peculiarly unpleasant sector.

On the 27th the 153rd Brigade relieved the 12th Canadian Brigade, 4th Canadian Division, in the Courcelette sector. This sector extended from the dyke valley just west of Le Sars to the western of the two roads running from Courcelette to Miraumont. The Dyke Valley in particular, and the whole area in general, were painfully open to observation from tree observation-posts in Loupart Wood. This wood was perched on the summit of a commanding upland. There was hardly a square yard in the Divisional sector which was not overlooked from some portion of it.

Moreover, the enemy made the fullest use of his observation. Even single men were frequently sniped by howitzers and field-guns to such an extent that movement in the forward area by day became out of the question.

The ground taken over by the Division had been captured by the Canadians a few days previously. The conditions could not have been worse; the limits of human endurance were all but reached. The whole area had been ploughed up by shell-fire to such an extent that the vegetation had completely disappeared. The rain, which had been the cause of the frequent postponement of the attack on Beaumont Hamel, continued day after day. The whole countryside had in consequence been transformed into unending acres of treacherous and, in some places, dangerous mud. It was no uncommon thing for men to sink up to their waists and for horses to be drowned. By December the mud had become saturated with water to such an extent that it became necessary to issue ropes as trench stores to enable men who had become bogged to be extricated.

Moreover, the earth had become so disintegrated by the shocks of the continuous bursting of shells that trenches could not be cut in it. No sooner had they been dug than the sides fell in and filled them again. The front and support line troops thus lived in shell-hole posts. In a few cases these were connected to one another by what had once been trenches.

The condition in which the men lived in these posts defeats imagination, and needs to have been seen to be appreciated. They could not move by day. Their only seat was the oozing fire-step; if they stood up they gradually sank into the mud; even ration-boxes and duckboards used as platforms soon became submerged. The conditions of sanitation were ghastly, the possibilities of cooking were non-existent, and from dawn till dusk the troops were cut off from communication even with the next post.

Trench feet became an epidemic, frost-bite occurred frequently. In some cases old wounds reopened, as they did in the days of scurvy. In December dysentery appeared. The wastage amongst the troops became serious, and a general air of depression settled down over the Division. In fact, General Harper once confessed that he had never seen a man smile east of Pozières.

One of the great problems of the Courcelette sector was the difficulty of finding one's way to the forward area. All movement being restricted to the hours of darkness, and the whole countryside being a featureless abomination, working parties, runners, reliefs, and ration parties were continually losing their way, and wandering through the mud until they had become exhausted.

To make matters worse, when the Division took over the sector there were no wire entanglements created, so that there was always a reasonable chance of men who were lost wandering into the German lines, as it was difficult to discover when one was in No Man's Land. This, indeed, happened several times, while similarly lost Germans were more than once found wandering in our lines. In fact, prisoners were taken in this manner on six different occasions.

I

The Division, therefore, had many problems to face on its arrival in this area. At first an attempt was made to link up the front line posts, wire them in, and dig communication trenches leading up to them.

The whole area was further littered with the unburied dead and with salvage of every kind.

The troops in the reserve line had in a few cases dug-outs, which had been discovered in Regina Trench—a famous trench captured by the Canadians a few days previously.

The reserve battalions were little better off than those in the line. They were for the most part quartered in disused gun-pits and Bairnsfather villas, proof neither against shell-fire nor the weather.

The artillery were in a similar plight; their gun-pits were constantly flooding, and the movement of wheeled transport became impracticable. All gun ammunition had therefore to be brought to the gun emplacements on pack-saddles, eight rounds only being carried on each horse. Journey after journey with the pack animals had therefore to be made by the gunner-drivers, with the German field-guns doing their best to aggravate the conditions.

The Division took over this sector within a few hours of leaving another battle front. The men had been given little or no opportunity of resting and recuperating after a severe engagement. The result was that their vitality was low, and that their powers of resistance were not at their best. They in consequence suffered considerably more from the adverse conditions than would have been the case with fresher troops.

Every method of constructing trenches was tried, and pumps were employed to keep them dry. The results were, however, always the same. No sooner was a trench dug to a depth of three feet than water began to rise in it and the sides fell in. Trenches had therefore to be given up, and overland tracks took their place. For this purpose duck-boards or wattle tracks were laid, the routes being marked out with tracing-tape or posts and wire until such time as the track was completed.

As regards protection for the troops against the weather, it was evident that if men were to be left lying for many hours exposed to the weather in shell-holes the wastage from sickness would be appalling. A considerable effort was therefore made to provide the battalions both in the line and in brigade reserve with weather-proof accommodation.

For the troops in the line the Divisional engineers designed a highly satisfactory form of shelter, composed of corrugated iron elephant shelters sunk below the level of the parapet of the trench or shell-hole. The material for each shelter could be carried up to the line by ten men, and could be completed in a day and night's work. When completed it accommodated a section post.

Large elephant shelters were made for reserve battalions in the sides of sunken roads, while all troops that could be spared were moved back to the camps in the back areas.

Thus, after three weeks, conditions had been materially improved. During this period, however, there was a snap of sharp frost. For a while this dried up the mud and much improved the situation ; but, as is always the case, the thaw which followed seemed to render the mud, if possible, more all-pervading than had been the case before the frost came.

Meanwhile the "Q" staff had been making every effort to alleviate the sufferings of the men. A gum-boot store had been established at Pozières, with sufficient boots for the whole brigade in the line. There was, however, a continual wastage of these boots, as, though they reached almost up to the hip, many of them were sucked off the men's legs in extricating themselves from the mud. It was found that these thigh boots and the kilt did not make a good combination. The boots had to be worn underneath the kilt, with the result that the top edge of the boot, rubbing against the bare thigh, used to chafe the men and cause septic sores. In consequence, the kilt was for the time being abandoned, and six thousand pairs of trousers were issued to the men.

A soup-kitchen was also established outside brigade headquarters. Here the Divisional master-cook, an old Hussar, used to issue hot soup to working parties and reliefs on their way to and from the trenches. The master-cook was shelled in his kitchen on most days of the week ; but beyond asking for a party to repair it when it had sustained any damage, he made no complaints. His services to the Division on this and, indeed, on many occasions were invaluable.

Efforts were also made to provide the men with hot meals in the line. The portable hot-food containers issued for this purpose proved too heavy a burden for a man to carry over two thousands yards of water, shell-holes, and slippery mud, and they had to be abandoned.

In place of them the men were issued with Tommy Cookers, small tins of solidified alcohol on which they could heat their own food. Tins of meat-and-vegetable rations were on this account made the permanent issue for troops in the line. Each man was thus able to heat for himself a really good and nourishing stew, even if he lived in a shell-hole and had no previous knowledge of cooking. This system proved very satisfactory, and the number of hot meals a man could have during a day was only limited by the number of Tommy Cookers that could be obtained. Ingenious quartermasters therefore discovered means of improvising Tommy Cookers, and making them in large numbers for their battalions. This in itself was a great improvement for the men, and it became no longer necessary to live from dawn to dusk with nothing but cold meat and biscuit to eat and with cold water to drink, as had been the case when the sector was first taken over.

In spite, however, of all the arrangements made, the men did not recover their vitality, and the wastage remained immense. A system of relief was therefore introduced by which battalions held the line for only forty-eight hours each. They were also given twenty-four hours complete rest before going into the line and after coming out. This system had an immediate effect on the health of the men.

Further, on 11th December it was arranged that the whole Divisional front should be held by two battalions, each battalion being on a one company front. These front-line companies were reinforced by two Lewis guns of the remainder of the battalion manned by nucleus crews. As company strengths had by this time fallen to about fifty to sixty men, this meant that the line was extremely lightly held. So much was this the case that a German machine-gunner, who was returning to his emplacement with filled water-bottles and had lost his way, wandered right through our lines, and was captured by some machine-gunners close to brigade headquarters. These machine-gunners were the first British troops he had seen.

Operations in the line, apart from combating the mud and water, were confined to sniping. When the Division first took over the line the Germans showed themselves in a most daring manner. The 153rd Brigade took full advantage of this in their first few days in the line, Colonel Cheape's battalion claiming eleven hits in one day. After this the Germans unfortunately became very much shier, and the bags fell off considerably.

Brigade reliefs in this sector were a sore trial to the men. Apart from the exhaustion caused by the conditions in which they lived, the struggle through the mud from the line to brigade headquarters was in itself a heavy task for a man in battle order.

Added to this, the continual standing in mud and water and the prolonged wearing of gum-boots caused the men's feet to become so swollen and soft that a march of even a few thousand yards became a physical impossibility to many of them. It was therefore necessary to bring motor-buses along the Albert-Bapaume Road to Pozières. Here, as the men straggled in, the loads were made up and driven off to Wolfe Huts, near Ovillers, where the men spent the night.

For many hours after the relief was completed, stragglers would come limping along in ones and twos to the embussing point, coated from head to foot in mud, with a three days' growth of beard on their faces. They were a depressing spectacle. Their exhaustion was in some cases so great that many of them would lie at the roadside in these winter nights wet through, and fall asleep often when another half-mile would have carried them to the buses, to daylight, and to a warm hut. War has certainly lost much of its romance since going into winter quarters went out of fashion.

To the rank and file Courcelette will remain as a nightmare. Though the men in the shell-holes may have been too obsessed by the beastliness of their conditions to appreciate the fact, yet on few occasions can the administrative services of the Division and its commanders have exercised more thought on their behalf. Nothing that could have been done to alleviate their sufferings was left undone; much was done which would not have occurred to a less efficient staff.

Left to himself, the Jock, exhausted as he was, was in danger of sitting down and doing no more than saying, "Isn't this b——y ?" He was right; it was what he called it, and General Harper, who had visited the men in their shell-holes, knew that it was so. But he knew also that so long as the men remained passive it would become still more so. He therefore insisted that the men should either be in complete rest, or should be working their utmost to improve the conditions. On no account was the merely passive and reflective attitude to be adopted.

During this period Colonel A. J. G. Moir, D.S.O., who had come out with the Division, and after leaving it for a short time had returned to it as chief administrative staff officer, and Major J. L. Weston, D.S.O., were responsible for the "Q" services of the Division. The latter had also come out with the Division, and subsequently succeeded Colonel Moir, remaining as A.A. and Q.M.G., 51st Division, until a few months from the armistice.

Colonel Moir seconded General Harper's efforts to keep the Division going in a most effective manner, and it was largely due to his administrative ability that the Jocks ultimately went back to rest with sufficient powers of recuperation left in them to recover their old form after a nineteen days' rest behind the line.

Colonel Moir was, in turn, admirably served by Major Weston, whose unwearying devotion to his Division and unfailing good temper made him an ideal "Q" officer.

Great as was the wastage owing to sickness, casualties owing to enemy action were few. This was owing to the small number of men employed holding the line. The total in killed, wounded, and missing for the months of December and January amounted to 4 officers killed, 15 wounded, and 1 missing; and to the men, 86 killed and 333 wounded.

Amongst the killed was Captain Lauder of the 8th Argyll and Sutherland Highlanders, son of the famous Scottish comedian. He was shot while moving from one front-line post to another in the early morning.

Amongst these casualties, twenty-five were caused by a single 4·2 shell at Tulloch's Corner. This shell burst amongst a working party of the 6th Seaforth Highlanders, killing the officer and 3 men, and wounding 21 other ranks.

On 12th January the Division was relieved by the 2nd Division. Divisional headquarters moved to Marieux, the 152nd Brigade to Beauquesne, the 153rd Brigade to Puchevillers, and the 154th Brigade to Rubempré. The Division then marched to the Buigny-St Maclou area west of Abbeville, arriving there on 16th January, having staged in the Bernaville and St Riquier areas.

At the time that the sector was handed over to the 2nd Division, a vast change had been wrought in it. A system of defence had been put into force which reduced the number of defenders to a minimum. Shelters had been provided for the whole trench garrison. Dug-outs were nearing completion, one in the East Miraumont Road being capable of holding two companies. Overland routes had been marked out, laid, and notice-boarded. Large numbers of elephant shelters had been erected for the reserve battalions, so that men not actually holding the line were able to obtain adequate rest in fair comfort. The whole front had been wired so as to have at least one belt to protect the garrison of the front line from hostile raids. A vast amount of material had been salved and put into use. All dead had been buried except those lying in the actual trench area.

Considering the conditions this is a fine record of work. Though the infantry contributed to it in some degree, it must be said in justice to the Royal Engineers and pioneers that theirs was the lion's share. The efforts which these units made to ameliorate the conditions for the infantry were magnificent. That the sickness and wastage was not greater, and that the whole conditions of life materially and visibly improved, was mainly due to the enterprise, energy, and endurance of the three field companies and the 8th Royal Scots.

The Division was, however, now at its lowest ebb. It had been in the line for a year, including two very trying periods of mine and trench warfare, plus the fighting in July and August on the Somme and the battle of Beaumont Hamel. It was considerably reduced in strength, and had lost heavily in company commanders and N.C.O.'s. A period of at least a month's rest was considered essential in which to train the new drafts and restore the fighting efficiency of the Division. It was therefore with some misgiving that it was learnt that on 30th January the 8th Royal Scots and the 1/1 and 1/2 Highland Field Companies, R.E., had proceeded to Arras to work in the Third Army area. This could have only one meaning.

The rest lasted exactly nineteen days, as on 5th February the Division moved to the Barilly area *en route* to join the Third Army.

The Buigny-St Maclou area was not a good one. Training-grounds were difficult to obtain, while in many villages the billets were indifferent. They consisted for the most part of mud-plaster barns, verging on a state of collapse, and with unpleasantly ventilated walls. Since this was the coldest period experienced in France during the Great War, the men suffered considerably. An intense frost set in, which continued almost without interruption up to the last days of February. On some nights twenty-four degrees of frost were registered. In consequence, both work and recreation were greatly hampered, and it was extremely difficult to provide warmth for the men at nights. Where men were housed in the mud-plaster barns there were numerous cases of frost-bite, the men's knees suffering in particular.

Thus the recollections of the first nineteen days' rest which was vouchsafed to the Division since it first went into action are not as pleasant as might be imagined.

When the march to Arras began, the effects of the frost were felt still more acutely. The march lasted six days, the route lying across a country of hills and valleys, including many steep ascents and descents. The result was that, as in many places the roads were little better than sheets of ice, the transport had the greatest difficulty in carrying out the march. In consequence, field-kitchens and cooks' carts often arrived several hours after the men had reached their billeting area. This was attended by considerable discomfort to the troops, as they were dependent on the kitchens and the cooks' carts for their next hot meal. The cold was also felt considerably more " on trek " than in ordinary circumstances, as the men, since they were changing their billets daily, had no time or opportunity to make their quarters comfortable.

The difficulties of this march reached their climax at St Pol. Water-mains had in many places burst, and flooded the roads with several inches of water, which had frozen into hard ice. In consequence, the steep descent into, and the equally steep ascent out of, the town became barely negotiable. In fact, it was only by employing large numbers of men with drag-ropes and additional teams that the transport could make its way through the town. Blocks occurred in the road which checked the columns, often for considerable periods, and which kept the men shivering in the roads and delayed them from reaching their billets until late in the evening.

Indeed, it was hard to believe during the last three months that one was in what the railway advertisements call " Sunny France." One had lived in fogs which were a match for London, and mists and rain which compared favourably with the Western Highlands, and degrees of frost, wind, and snow which could hardly have been improved upon in Caithness. There were, however, no winter quarters in this war in Gaul. The men lived as hard a life as could well be imagined; and though it would not be true to say they thrived on it, they endured it in an exemplary manner. One requires to have wintered in " Sunny France " in canvas tents, open-work barns, and " Bairnsfather " shacks on perhaps one hot meal a day to appreciate the hardships and discomforts of winter warfare.

CHAPTER IX.

THE BATTLE OF ARRAS.

ON 11th February the Division took over the left sector of the XVIIth Corps front from the 9th Scottish Division, and was disposed as follows: the 152nd Brigade in the line, with brigade headquarters at Marœuil; the 154th Brigade at Ecoivres and Bethonsart, with headquarters at Acq. The 153rd Brigade was at Frévilliers, and was employed entirely in finding Corps working parties.

The sector taken over extended from Bogey Avenue east of Roclincourt to Old Fantome Trench, just west of the Arras-Lille road. The Division had thus returned to familiar ground.

Preparations were at once begun for an attack on a large scale. From now onwards, up to the signing of the armistice, the Division was to be continuously engaged in major operations, with the exception of the few months in which it held the line between the battle of Cambrai in November 1917 and the German offensive in March 1918. As it was once put, for the next two years the Division was in a permanent state of being in a battle, or preparing for a battle, or coming out of a battle.

On this occasion the general plan of the Allied armies comprised a series of offensives on all fronts. The rôle of the British was to attack the enemy troops occupying the salient, into which they had been pressed as a result of the Somme battle, between the rivers Ancre and Scarpe.

Both shoulders of this salient were to be attacked simultaneously, the Fifth Army operating on the Ancre, while the Third Army attacked from the north-west about Arras. Further, to quote from Sir Douglas Haig's despatch: "The front of the attack on the Arras side was to include the

Vimy Ridge, possession of which I considered necessary to secure the left flank of the operations on the south bank of the Scarpe. The capture of this ridge, which was to be carried out by the First Army, also offered other important advantages. It would deprive the enemy of valuable observation, and give us a wide view of the plains stretching from the eastern foot of the ridge to Douai and beyond. Moreover, although it was evident that the enemy might by a timely withdrawal avoid a battle in the awkward salient still held by him between the Ancre and the Scarpe, no such withdrawal from his important Vimy Ridge position was likely."

The rôle of the Highland Division was to capture the southern shoulder of the Vimy Ridge in conjunction with the Canadian Corps on the left and the 34th Division on the right.

It was clear that an attack against a position of such great natural strength and tactical value as the Vimy Ridge would only be successful if the most careful and elaborate preparations were made.

As far as the Highland Division was concerned, these preparations took three forms—the preparation of the British trenches for offensive operations, the preparation of the enemy's trenches for assault, the preparation of the troops for the attack.

As regards the first much work was, as usual, necessary. The thaw, after a long period of intense frost, reduced the trenches to an appalling condition of mud. The overlay of loamy clay which covers the chalk in the Arras sector, when thoroughly wet, is of a bad texture for purposes of digging. It has such adhesive qualities that on many occasions during this period the earth could not be thrown off the shovel. The men working in the trench had to throw their shovels with their load of earth clear out of the trench, as had been the case in the Aveluy sector. Thus, the keeping open of the communication trenches and the opening up of the assembly trenches, which in any case were in a most desperate state of dilapidation, was a heavy task.

As regards the preparation of assembly trenches, it was decided to form up the leading waves in the foremost old French trench. This trench had been evacuated owing to the danger from enemy mines when the Highland Division was holding this sector in 1916.

The trench was reconnoitred throughout its length, and it was found to have fallen in to a depth of about four feet, and to have been completely filled in with entanglements of barbed wire. There was, further, a fairly strong wire entanglement in front of it. The saps connecting this trench to the present front-line trench had all been completely blocked when they joined the existing front line, and had also been wired up throughout their length. A large amount of work was therefore required to clear this trench so that the troops could occupy it for assembly. It was, however, decided to do no work in it beyond removing the barbed wire from it so as not to attract the enemy's attention.

The whole area was found to be very deficient of dug-outs suitable for headquarters. Three new brigade battle headquarters had therefore to be tunnelled as well as some additional battalion battle headquarters and regimental aid posts.

Machine-gun positions had also to be constructed for guns firing in the machine-gun barrage during the attack, and accommodation had to be provided for their crews.

The Divisional area also contained an insufficiency of artillery positions, particularly of forward positions required by the guns firing in the barrage. Considerable preparations had therefore to be made by the artillery.

The system of buried telephone cables was also incomplete. In fact, it was only completed in time for the engagement by concentrating every available man on this work.

As regards the preparations of the enemy's position for the attack, the chief consideration was his wire entanglements, which had been erected in profusion.

Those which were to be encountered in the first phase of the attack, being on the western slopes of the Vimy Ridge, were visible, and could be cut by the artillery with direct observation.

The later stages of the attack were, however, planned to pass over the ridge and reach the plains beyond it. The wire to be encountered in this phase of the attack was, therefore, on the reverse slope of the Vimy Ridge, and could only be seen from the air.

Unfortunately, at this period the German air service established a marked superiority over our reconnaissance machines. In a single period of twenty-four hours, three R.E. 8's (reconnaissance aeroplanes) were crashed within full view of a single brigade headquarters, one of them being hunted right down to the ground, where it overturned, with both its occupants wounded.

At this period the policy of the Higher Command was to wait till a new type of aeroplane was completed, and then definitely and suddenly to take command of the air. This superiority, of which the Germans were successfully deprived, as planned, on the opening of the offensive, was due to the arrival in this part of the line of the " circus "— that is, the squadron commanded by Baron von Richthofen —which included the picked fighting pilots of the German air service. The aeroplanes used by this squadron were painted red, with yellow or pink bellies, and gave to laymen, at any rate, an impression of amazing efficiency.

In consequence of this temporary superiority in the air, the wire-cutting on the reverse slopes of the ridge could seldom be successfully carried out. It was, however, at this period that the now famous 106 or instantaneous fuze arrived in the country. This fuze burst its shell instantaneously when the fuze-cap touched the ground. As a result, the explosion occurred before the shell had time to bury itself in the earth, and its full force was therefore felt above ground. The effect of this shell on wire was devastating, and an accurate shot would blow a gap clean through an ordinary entanglement. So much was the energy of this shell spent on the surface of the earth, that even heavy howitzer shells left craters little bigger than wash-hand basins.

The plan was that no action should be taken which was likely to warn the enemy of an impending attack until as late as possible. Therefore in February and the early part of March wire-cutting was only carried out in conjunction with raids.

As regards the preparation of the troops for the attack, much time had already been spent in teaching the lessons gained at the battle of Beaumont Hamel to the new drafts which had since arrived. General Harper had been continuously developing his theories on the application of tactical principles to the conditions of modern warfare. Possessed of great gifts of imagination and powers of deduction, he was in this respect always in advance of his time. He therefore spared no pains to train the Division in the practice of his theories. He achieved this object to a certain extent by lectures to officers and men, but more particularly by informal discussions. He regularly visited units in the line and out, and seldom left without having discussed some tactical principle, explained his views on it, and impressed all with their soundness. What the General thought to-day the Division thought and practised the following week.

The main principles on which General Harper based the training of his units and planned his attacks at this time may be summarised as follows :—

1. That the objective of all offensive operations must be to envelop the enemy—*i.e.*, hold him in front and attack him in flank.

2. That the fullest use must at all times be made of mechanical weapons—*i.e.*, guns, machine-guns, trench-mortars, &c. The minimum use of infantry; to rely for success on the weight of infantry, either in attack or defence, was to ensure unnecessary casualties.

3. That troops must always be in depth; they must neither attack nor defend in one or two dense lines of men, but in a succession of well-extended lines.

He also made a point of impressing on all that a leader without personality will achieve nothing.

Though the application of these theories may not at this time have reached its full development, the problems connected with them had certainly been considerably discussed before the battle of Arras took place.

The 152nd and 154th Brigades were detailed for the original attack, it being the custom of the Division for the brigades to take part in the initial operations of a new battle in turn. The German trenches on the battle fronts of the two brigades were therefore taped out exactly according to scale in the vicinity of the billeting areas. The men were then continually practised in the attack over the taped-out course. The 18-pounder barrage was represented by men with signalling flags and by the pipers, under the command of an artillery officer. Hostile machine-guns were indicated by the drummers. The attack was practised so often that the men obtained a thorough knowledge of the distances from one objective to the next, of the length of the pauses in the barrage, and the trace of the enemy's trenches.

Various raids which were carried out preparatory to this attack had brought out some valuable lessons concerning the close combat. In these raids it had become clear that the blind leap into a trench was not a sound policy. Not only were the German trenches in many places of a great depth, but they also contained many straight lengths of trench covered by a machine-gun mounted on the top step or a dug-out cut in the side of a traverse. These machine-guns were sited so as to fire straight along the trench as soon as any attacking party had leapt into it.

Considerable pains were therefore taken to train the men not to rush blindly at their objective, but to come up on to the parapet properly extended (" carrying a good head," as the General put it), and shoot down all the garrison of the trench that were visible before they entered it. The men were therefore constantly practised in assaulting reserve trenches near Villers Chatel, in which targets were placed representing the trench garrisons. On reaching this trench each man fired five live rounds at the targets. A good many rounds ricochetted into the adjacent parts of France, but fortunately no damage appears to have been done to the local inhabitants. On the other hand, the men rapidly began to acquire the right instincts for engaging the Germans in close combat.

It was after these raids, to which reference is made later, that General Harper in an increasing degree emphasised in training his troops the necessity for fighting with their wits, and not by a mere display of seeing red and brute courage.

During the period in which the Division held the line prior to the attack few incidents worthy of note occurred. The enemy employed " oil-can " trench-mortars and aerial darts freely, in his usual wooden way of shooting—at the same place, at the same hours daily—without doing much damage.

He had, however, one successful shoot, when snow was on the ground. A machine-gun team living in a concrete dug-out in Bidot Trench lit a fire inside it. In consequence the snow quickly melted from the top of it, and it stared out a squarish black mass in the midst of the snow. The Germans were quick to observe this, and bombed it with "oil-cans." A direct hit was scored, the dug-out collapsed, and the machine-gun team was wiped out. This incident afforded a good example of one of the many precautions that must necessarily be taken if snow is not to disclose occupied portions of the trenches.

Sniping was also prevalent. In the left sector there was a particularly good German sniper. It was his custom to start work just after dawn when the sun was rising behind his back. In the morning mist, to persons facing the sun, observation appeared bad; on the other hand, they themselves were clearly visible when looked at by a person with the sun behind him. The troops facing east were therefore inclined to expose themselves, having a false sense of security. In this manner Lieut.-Colonel W. MacL. Macfarlane, D.S.O., H.L.I., commanding the 5th Seaforth Highlanders, was killed by this sniper. A few days later another officer was killed in the same place, also just after dawn, probably by the same German. Lieut.-Colonel Macfarlane was the third Seaforth commanding officer to be killed in this sector.

When the wire-cutting necessary for certain big raids began, the Germans became very free in the use of their artillery. In fact, in the fortnight preceding the attack, when numbers of men were employed in the trenches both cable-burying and filling dumps, the sector became a most unpleasant one. Many of the communication trenches, badly enfiladed by enemy artillery, were continually bombarded, and movement in the trench area became a hazardous occupation.

During the preparations for the Arras battle, in another part of the front a most important event occurred. Between Soissons and Arras the enemy voluntarily retired. His rearward movement began about 24th February, and extended almost as far north as the village of Thilloy les Mouflaines. News of this retirement reached the Division at about 11 P.M. on 24th February, and orders were at once issued to the 152nd Brigade to patrol their whole front and see if the enemy showed any signs of withdrawing. He was, however, found to be maintaining his usual alertness.

This withdrawal considerably reduced the potentialities of this phase of the spring offensive. Instead of attacking from the Ancre northwards, simultaneously with the advance of the Third Army from the north-west, the Fifth Army had now to follow up the retiring enemy, and to dig itself in in front of the Hindenburg Line to which the enemy had withdrawn.

The Hindenburg Line system, which subsequently became well known to the Highland Division, had been very strongly fortified and sited with great care and skill, so as to deny all advantages of position to any force attacking it.

The enemy had thus already escaped from the great salient which it was hoped to nip off during the forthcoming operations. He was now established in the south of Arras in a position considerably stronger than that which he had vacated.

As regards the sector held by the Division, the only other noteworthy incidents during the period of preparation for the attack were a succession of raids.

These raids were carried out for two purposes : to obtain information concerning the enemy's garrison and defences, and to inflict the maximum amount of damage to his defences in view of the coming operations. The battle of Beaumont Hamel had disclosed how strongly the German could fortify himself in a chalk soil. The trenches which the Division was to attack, supported as they were by the commanding ground of the Vimy Ridge, comprised a most formidable defensive system. It was therefore arranged that raids should be carried out on a large scale on both brigade fronts, so that serious damage could be done to the entanglements and dug-outs, prior to the launching of the offensive.

The first took place on 5th March, the raiding party consisting of 11 officers and 303 other ranks of the 6th Gordon Highlanders. The plan was to assault and capture the German front and support line on a frontage of 485 yards, and to remain in occupation of them for a period sufficient to allow time for the destruction of both the garrison and the dug-outs.

Nine gaps were cut in the German wire on the frontage of attack by the artillery and the 2-inch mortars, the latter firing 1137 rounds during the process.

Gaps were also cut, as a feint, along the whole Divisional front. The raid therefore ensured that a considerable amount of damage would be done to the enemy's defences prior to the big attack.

The raiders were divided into squads of 1 N.C.O. and 8 men, each officer commanding a group of three or more squads. Each squad had a particular section of a particular trench given to it as its objective. Air photographs were carefully studied, and where dug-outs could be located. The squads detailed to deal with them carried either 20 lb. charges of ammonal or phosphorus bombs and tins containing one gallon of petrol. The ammonal was to be used to blow in the dug-out entrances, while the petrol was to be hurled down the stairs, followed by the phosphorus bomb, which caused the dug-out to catch fire. Unless some such measures were taken, in a raid in which the troops could only remain in occupation of the German trenches for a limited time, the Boches could remain secure in their dug-outs until the raiders had departed. The ordinary Mills bomb had little effect in a dug-out containing several chambers, while the men would have little chance of succeeding had they attempted to enter an unknown dug-out and deal with the enemy below ground.

The raid was a complete success, every squad with the exception of four reaching its objective. One officer and 20 other ranks of the 2nd Bavarian Reserve Infantry Regiment were captured, and 66 dead were counted in the enemy trenches apart from those who succumbed in the dug-outs. The total casualties to the 6th Gordon Highlanders were 6 officers and 48 other ranks, of whom many were only lightly wounded.

Eight Stokes bombs, 660 lb. of ammonal, 16 tins of petrol, and 164 phosphorus bombs were thrown down the dug-outs. Many entrances were destroyed, while several were observed to be still burning twelve hours after the raid. The wire was found to be badly damaged, and the trenches much destroyed from the bombardment.

The raid impressed on all ranks that the Bavarian is a

magnificent fighter. Lieut.-Colonel J. Dawson, D.S.O., commanding the 6th Gordon Highlanders, who was responsible for the details of the raid, reported as follows : " A stout resistance was offered in every part of the area, men in the open trench resisting chiefly by bomb-throwing, while the firing of rifles and throwing of bombs took place from every occupied dug-out. Until this was discovered, several casualties were inflicted on men passing dug-out doors. The sound of the explosion of Mills bombs thrown down the stairways had not died away before rifle-firing and bomb-throwing up the staircase was resumed, and silence was not obtained until the mobile charges of ammonal were exploded. Isolated snipers hung on until knocked out, and one machine-gunner, who was ultimately killed and his gun destroyed, was firing from in front of the German second line before our men had withdrawn from that trench. In only one single instance, where five men came voluntarily from a dug-out, were surrenders made, and in most cases pockets held out until all were killed."

The German battalion involved had only come into the line six hours before this raid took place. The fine fight put up by the Bavarians in these circumstances was therefore highly creditable to them. It showed how well the line must have been handed over by the outgoing battalion, and what a sound system of defence existed.

The fullest value was made of this enterprise. A map was prepared from the information given by the raiders, which showed every feature in the sector of German trenches concerned. Further, many lessons were learned as regards trench fighting. It was found that close-range shooting was considerably employed by both sides. The Germans appeared to rely to a large extent on enfilading short lengths of their trenches from loopholes cut in the traverses, and from the entrances to deep dug-outs cut in the sides of the traverses. As these doorways were not visible until the troops were almost abreast of them, they created a difficult situation. The raiders found that this could best be met by remaining outside the trench and shooting or bombing the enemy from above. These tactics proved highly successful.

The raiders were moved by lorry after they had left the trench area to Haute Avesnes, where they were inspected with the rest of the battalion by Sir Douglas Haig and General Allenby.

On 17th March a bold experiment was tried, the same raid being repeated by the 8th Argyll and Sutherland Highlanders. It was hoped by this means to complete the utter destruction of the section of trenches raided, and to lower the Bavarians' *morale* before the great attack. The strength of the party was increased up to 13 officers and 378 other ranks. The time the raiders were to remain in the hostile trenches was also lengthened, so as to enable the work in hand to be thoroughly completed.

The party took over with it 1618 Mills bombs, 87 20-lb. charges of ammonal, 164 phosphorus bombs, and 41 tins of petrol. Of these, 4 ammonal charges, 8 phosphorus bombs, and 2 tins of petrol were allotted to a certain dug-out known to be used as an officers' mess and offices.

This raid was accompanied by an intense bombardment and creeping barrage similar to that of the 6th Gordon Highlanders. The Stokes guns alone fired 2497 rounds.

On this occasion the raiders met with, if anything, severer fighting than had the 6th Gordon Highlanders. The wire had on one flank either been repaired or the party had made a slight error in their direction, so that on this flank the barrage was lost, and the troops had to complete their advance to the trench without its protection.

The raid was, however, successful, most squads reaching their objective and overcoming all resistance encountered. Our casualties amounted to 8 officers and 102 other ranks, of whom, as before, many were only lightly wounded. The casualties appear heavy—and, indeed, were heavy—but it must be borne in mind that in any trench fighting in which bombs are freely used, a number of lightly wounded men is an inevitable result. The enemy, suspecting that another raid might be attempted, had reinforced his trench garrison, and was in considerable strength. In consequence, he suffered serious losses.

The raids were of great value to the battalions which carried them out, as both were destined on "the day" to pass over the same area as they had raided. The enemy's wire and trenches had been reduced to an almost irreparable condition. The men had had a further experience of following the creeping barrage, which had been fired without a fault, and had given him the greatest confidence. The artillery, including the 64th Army Brigade R.F.A. attached to them, had twice fired a barrage over a portion of the front to be covered by them in the battle.

The raiders expressed themselves as delighted with the shrapnel barrage. The men again reported that they were able to wait in the remnants of the enemy's wire entanglements while the barrage was still on his front line.

Moreover, the heavy work of clearing the old French trench, in which the troops for the main attack were to assemble, had also been completed at least on one battalion frontage.

The disadvantage that came from these raids was that the casualties had been fairly heavy, and affected chiefly one company in each battalion. Thus, when the day of attack came, these companies contained an undue proportion of inexperienced reinforcements.

On 31st March the 6th Black Watch raided a small salient in the left brigade front with two parties, together totalling 2 officers and 50 men. Preparatory to this raid, and also as a blind to the two raids described above, much wire had also been cut on this brigade front. In spite of this, one of the parties was unable to effect an entry into the enemy's trenches. The second party was, however, successful, but the trench was found to be only lightly held. Two dug-outs were bombed, six men were killed, and the 2nd Bavarian Reserve Infantry Regiment was identified as still holding the line.

It had now become clear that if the Division was to be opposed in the big attack by these Bavarians, it would meet an enemy who would offer the maximum of resistance. It therefore was a matter of first importance to ensure that the men fully understood that success would depend on the speed with which they reached the enemy parapet after the barrage had left. It may be said that there would be a race for success. While the barrage was on the trench, the Bavarians would be on the dug-out step, and the Highlanders would be waiting from seventy to a hundred yards short of the trench. As the barrage lifted the race began. Would the Bavarian reach his fire-step and open fire on the Highlanders, or would the Highlanders reach the parapet and shoot the Bavarian down before he could man his trenches ?

The men learnt to appreciate this fact, and all developed the fixed determination that they would stick close to the barrage whatever else might happen. The result was that when the day came in the first phase of the battle the issue was never in doubt.

The plan of the attack was as follows : A frontage of just over 3000 yards, gradually increasing up to 4000 yards, was allotted to the Highland Division. The depth to which it was hoped the attack would be carried was 5500 yards. The 152nd Infantry Brigade was to attack on the right, the 154th Brigade on the left ; on the right of the Division the 34th Division carried on the attack, and to the left the Canadian Corps. The Highland Division was the left flank Division both of the XVIIth Corps and of the Third Army.

The attack was divided up into three main objectives, known as : First objective, the Black line ; second objective, the Blue line ; third objective, the Brown line ; while there was a further objective towards which his attempts, if successful, were to be exploited, known as the Green line.

Before reaching the Black line in all parts of the front, three lines, and in some places four lines, of hostile trenches had to be overcome, as well as numerous communication trenches which contained dug-outs.

Between the Black line and the Blue line, as far as the 152nd Brigade was concerned, lay only two lines of trenches, of which one was in close support to the other. In front of the 154th Brigade the country between the Black and Blue lines was intersected by numerous communication trenches, which led into a central redoubt. In addition, a heavily-wired fire trench traversing the whole brigade front passed through this redoubt.

In consequence, on the left there was little chance of a straightforward attack behind the barrage being completely successful, as it could not be accurately foreshadowed where, in the maze of trenches, resistance was most likely to be met.

Between the Blue line and the Black line there were no organised defences, except the communication trenches and

Map IV.—Capture of Vimy Ridge, 9th April 1917.

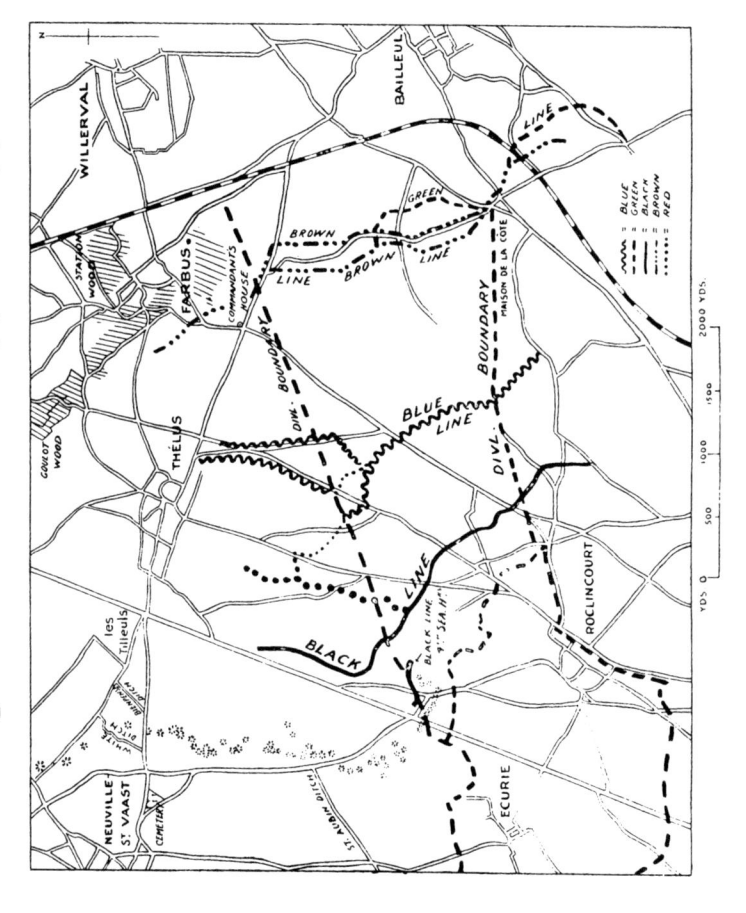

THE BATTLE OF ARRAS

a few sections of fire trench connecting one communication trench with another.

The Brown line itself consisted on the left of two heavily-wired fire trenches containing numerous dug-outs. On the right, however, the work had not been completed, and consisted of a section of unfinished fire trench, with a deep sunken road running behind and parallel to it.

On the whole Divisional front the advance to the Blue line lay over a considerable forward slope; beyond the Blue line it continued over a large plateau, finally dropping down on to the Brown line on the reverse slope beyond the plateau.

Prior to the attack a considerable amount of gas was employed against the enemy. Livens projectors, a form of smoke which discharged a cylinder of gas a considerable distance, were chiefly employed. On one occasion on the Divisional front, Mr Livens, the inventor of these projectors, observed their effect from an aeroplane.

Four-inch Stokes mortars were also extensively used for firing gas bombs. In fact, the enemy was gassed on 4th April, 5th April, and 8th April, over 600 drums of gas being discharged into the trenches.

The bombardment of the enemy's lines began in earnest on 4th April, and from that date wire-cutting by the artillery and 2-inch trench-mortars became intense. The trench-mortar batteries carried out their daily task of wire-cutting with the greatest gallantry, as the Germans developed an intense dislike to them, and retaliated on them heavily with artillery whenever they opened fire.

On more than one occasion the artillery fired rehearsals of the creeping barrage, which, as far as could be observed, were very accurate. These practice barrages disclosed the fact that, as soon as they were opened, the enemy could put down a heavy bombardment of 4·2 and 5·9 howitzers on to our front line in about two minutes.

Some batteries of 9·45 mortars had also been placed in positions from which they could deal with particular centres of resistance on the German lines. It was when in charge of one of these mortars that Sergeant Gosling, R.F.A., won the first Victoria Cross for the Division. A mortar was fired, but the charge was faulty, and though the shell left the gun, it fell only a few feet in front of the emplacement. Sergeant Gosling immediately sprang from the emplacement, drew the shell from the ground, into which it had buried its nose. He then unscrewed the fuze and threw it away before it could detonate the shell. The fuze was set for seventeen seconds, so that by the time Sergeant Gosling had reached the shell and drawn it from the ground, it was a question of only a few seconds before it would explode. The sergeant had, however, the presence of mind to take a fuze-key from his pocket, unscrew the fuze, and thus save the lives of the detachment.

The following day a shell landed in the emplacement and killed the entire detachment, with the exception of Sergeant Gosling, who at the time happened to be elsewhere.

About 1st April a high-velocity gun came into action against Marœuil, with some most unfortunate results. One shell burst amongst a working party of the 6th Black Watch as they were returning their tools at a dump, killing and wounding some twenty of them.

On the evening before the battle a shell from this gun burst in a Nissen hut used as a company officers' mess, and killed two and wounded two officers from one company of the 5th Gordon Highlanders.

During the week before the battle some improvement had taken place in the weather, and the condition of the ground was reasonably good for the time of year.

In spite, however, of the improvement in the weather, the mortality amongst horses, one of the features of the preparations for the Arras battle, continued. Horses dead and dying, not from wounds but from debility, were in these days one of the commonest sights. The horses of the Division were in fairly good condition, and few of them were lost. Those of army brigades of artillery and other units who had been in action on the Somme during the winter were, however, in a pitiable condition. The reduced rations which were then all that was available were insufficient to keep horses in hard work fit, the results being that they were in no condition to resist the effects of cold and mud. It was no uncommon sight to see a horse in harness drop down and die from sheer exhaustion, while the carcases of dead horses lay in numbers on the sides of the roads and tracks.

Assembly began on 7th April, the night being fine with a bright moon. On the right brigade front the relief was carried out without any delay. This proved most fortunate, for at 4 A.M. the enemy put down an intense barrage of 5·9's and 77's on the front of the right battalion. So heavy was the bombardment of the communication trenches that, had this been the night of the final assembly, the rearmost troops would probably have been unable to reach the assembly trenches.

The enemy continued very active with his artillery all the following day, obviously being in a suspicious frame of mind. When, therefore, the hour for the completion of the assembly arrived, our artillery heavily countered all his known battery positions with gas and high explosive, with the result that the troops reached their positions without any interference from his guns. Had the artillery not taken this precaution, he would doubtless have repeated the bombardment of the previous night, and greatly prejudiced the chances of success.

The arrangement of the assembly required careful planning. Seven double waves were to be assembled for the attack; there was, in consequence, little shell-proof cover in which to place the troops detailed for the capture of the later objectives. Moreover, the trenches in the forward area had been subjected to a considerable amount of artillery and trench-mortar fire, and had thus become shallow and open-mouthed, and afforded little cover to their occupants.

At least two double waves had, therefore, to remain in the open for some considerable time before their turn to close up with the barrage arrived, and were in consequence liable to suffer severely from the enemy S.O.S. barrage.

On the right the 6th Gordon Highlanders and 6th Seaforth Highlanders, and on the left the 9th Royal Scots and the 4th Seaforth Highlanders, led the attack. The 8th Argyll and Sutherland Highlanders, the 5th Seaforth Highlanders, the 4th Gordon Highlanders, and the 7th Argyll and Sutherland Highlanders were detailed for the attack on the farther objectives on their respective brigade areas. The 5th Gordon Highlanders from the 153rd Brigade were allotted to the 152nd Brigade as a reserve.

On the extreme left of the attack the 4th Seaforth

Highlanders had a small but difficult operation to perform in the first instance. The Divisional boundary on the left was the Lille Road, which crossed the enemy's trench system at the apex of a prominent salient. The 4th Seaforth Highlanders, opposite the southern shoulder of the salient, had to attack due north, while the direction of attack for the remainder of the Division was due east. The carrying out of this operation had to be so timed that the salient had been dealt with before the succeeding waves could move forward on to the attack on the German second and third lines, otherwise they would have come under enfilade fire from their left flank in the first stages of their advance.

By 4 A.M. on 9th April all troops were assembled. The bombardment had continued through the previous day except during two intervals of half an hour each, which were arranged to enable the Flying Corps to photograph the results of the gun-fire.

It was maintained throughout the night, and at 5.30 A.M. the attack was launched, supported by an intense artillery and machine-gun barrage.

Thus began an action which developed into a true soldiers' battle, in which the Highland infantrymen fought the Bavarian for possession of the field. Perfect as the artillery barrage was, the course of events was such that in numerous instances, in all parts of the battle area, the infantry from one cause or another were unable to keep up with it, and fought out the issue with their own weapons.

On the left the 154th Brigade carried all their objectives as far as the Black line, according to plan, though they were engaged in some stiff fighting. The 4th Seaforth Highlanders carried out their initial operation with complete success, and opened the way for the rest of the advance, as had been arranged.

The 152nd Brigade, however, met with difficulties from the start. The 6th Gordon Highlanders, attacking the trenches they had raided, reached all their objectives behind the barrage. On their left the 6th Seaforth Highlanders experienced some heavy fighting both in the second and third German lines. Indeed, so strong was the resistance encountered by the 6th Seaforth Highlanders that when the 5th Seaforth Highlanders attempted to advance through them to form up under the barrage, they found them still engaged with the enemy. The 5th Seaforth Highlanders had no other alternative than to join in the mêlée and help to clear the ground for their own advance.

The German fought magnificently, and was well supported by his artillery. In front of the 6th Seaforth Highlanders he had evacuated his front line, and was thus able to bombard it without danger to his own troops. In consequence, the 6th Seaforth Highlanders suffered some casualties from shell-fire before they reached their second and third objectives.

The casualties thus sustained caused gaps in the attacking waves, which enabled the enemy to man his machine-guns effectively after the barrage had passed.

Each machine-gun that thus came into action required a separate minor operation on the part of the infantry to subdue it.

The following figures, compiled by General Burn, illustrate the nature of the fighting :—

" The 6th Seaforth Highlanders lost 326 officers and men in capturing the Black line.

" One company of the 5th Seaforth Highlanders detailed to capture the Blue line suffered 90 casualties before reaching the Black line.

" A second company of the 5th Seaforth Highlanders, detailed for the Blue line, had used all its rifle grenades before reaching the Black line.

" Only one officer of the 6th Seaforth Highlanders, detailed for the capture of the Blue line, reached it; the remainder were all either killed or wounded."

It will thus be seen that in the centre success was only achieved by the gallantry and determination of the officers and men engaged.

Two tanks had been allotted to the Division to assist the infantry advance, but they were both out of action before they had reached the leading infantry, and so did not in any way contribute to the success of the attack.

The advance of the 5th Seaforth Highlanders and of the 8th Argyll and Sutherland Highlanders had been considerably interfered with in an unexpected manner. As the troops for the Blue line were crossing the Black line, an enormous explosion occurred. As a result a number of men were buried and several killed in both battalions. It was assumed that the Germans must have intentionally exploded a Minnenwerfer bomb store, as shortly after the explosion six Germans voluntarily emerged from a dug-out. These men were assumed to have been responsible for this disaster, and were immediately killed.

Eight hours and forty-eight minutes after the attack had been launched the 152nd Brigade had captured the whole of the Blue line, and were in touch in it with the 154th Brigade.

On the 154th Brigade front, though the Blue line was captured throughout the front, the fighting had been severe. The 4th Gordon Highlanders had sustained such serious losses in their fight for the Swischen Stellung that, in consequence, their two remaining companies were sent forward to consolidate the Blue line.

Meanwhile the Canadians on the left hand had been completely successful in their advance, and were pushing on exactly according to plan, while the 34th Division on the right was also reported to be holding the Blue line.

The capture of this line had been most materially assisted by the initiative of Captain Saulez of "D" Battery, 64th Brigade R.F.A. He observed from his observation-post a German machine-gun in action at the junction of a communication trench and the Blue line, holding off the infantry advance. He therefore telephoned to his own battery, and turned a section of howitzers from firing on the barrage on to the machine-gun. By this means he put the gun out of action, and enabled the infantry to continue their advance. Captain Saulez' shooting was admirable, and his action undoubtedly saved the infantry from many casualties. Unfortunately, he was himself killed in the later stages of this battle, a shell bursting in a trench shelter in which he was lying.

At 3.15 P.M. the enemy was turned out of a line known as Regiment Weg, which ran in rear of the Blue line opposite the 152nd Brigade front. Meanwhile the 154th Brigade had pushed on towards the Brown line, and were reported to have reached Tommy Trench at 1.40 P.M.

After the capture of the Regiment Weg, the 152nd Brigade were unable to continue their advance, as they were held up by Germans holding Elect Trench, which was situated about half-way between the Blue and Brown lines.

At 6.30 P.M. a message was received that the 154th Brigade had reached the Brown line, and were in touch with the Canadians at Commandant's House. At the same time the 34th Division reported that they were not in the Brown line. Orders were therefore issued for the 152nd Brigade and the 103rd Infantry Brigade of the 34th Division to assault the Brown line under cover of darkness.

The 5th Gordon Highlanders, who had been placed at the disposal of the 152nd Brigade, were detailed for this attack.

It was carried out at 5 A.M., and was a complete success. In conjunction with troops of the 103rd Brigade (34th Division), two companies of the 5th Gordon Highlanders advanced in a double wave, each rank being extended to ten paces. The attack was planned to be in the nature of a surprise, and was therefore not accompanied by an artillery barrage. The whole of the objective was captured. Some thirty dead Germans were found in the position, and fifty or more prisoners were captured in a redoubt known as the Maison de la Côté by the 103rd Brigade.

A curious situation now arose, as the 5th Gordon Highlanders on the Brown line could not get into touch on their left with the 154th Brigade. In fact, they were continuously being fired on with rifles and machine-guns from the Brown line to the north of them.

It subsequently transpired that the officer of the 154th Brigade who had reported that he was holding the Brown line was really in Tommy Trench, several hundred yards west of the Brown line, which was still occupied by the enemy on the 154th Brigade front.

General Hamilton therefore ordered the 7th Argyll and Sutherland Highlanders to initiate bombing attacks against each flank of the Brown line. These and subsequent attacks were, however, all held up by heavy machine-gun fire.

Later the 5th Gordon Highlanders made an attempt to rush a machine-gun post in front of the Brown line, which was located on a small knoll on their left flank urgently required for purposes of observation. By this time, however, snow had fallen, and men moving above ground had become highly visible, with the result that the enterprise failed, two sergeants and an officer being killed.

This battalion had been most unfortunate. It had not only lost four officers of one company at Marœuil, as already described, but it had also two officers killed by a chance shell in Roclincourt on the morning of the 9th. In addition, the company commander who led the night attack on the Brown line was killed, while in this last operation yet another officer was killed.

The 7th Gordon Highlanders were now moved into the forward area, and one company was placed under the orders of the 5th Gordon Highlanders. This company took over from the 103rd Brigade on the night of 10-11th April from the frontage between the Maison de la Côté and the railway.

By this time snow lay thick over the battlefield, with the result that the whole terrain was transformed. Familiar landmarks and tracks had disappeared, and it had become a matter of considerable difficulty for officers and men to recognise their position on the ground. On the night of the 11-12th orders were received that the heavy artillery would cut the wire in front of the Brown line, and that the 154th Brigade would then renew the attack behind a creeping barrage and assisted by a tank.

The 5th Gordon Highlanders and 152nd Machine-Gun Company were ordered to assist this attack by flanking fire. It was also decided to send forward Stokes guns to the front line held by the 5th Gordon Highlanders to bombard the Brown line from a flank. Captain Amos of the 152nd Trench-Mortar Battery therefore went forward to select suitable gun positions, and found that the enemy were no longer holding the Brown line on the immediate left flank of the 5th Gordon Highlanders.

Shortly afterwards, one of the Divisional observers, Corporal Mitchell of the 6th Gordon Highlanders, reported that he had made his way into the Brown line, and that it was unoccupied. He had found the electric light still burning in the dug-outs, packs and equipment neatly stacked, and unopened parcels and unfinished meals lying on the tables. Patrols from the 154th Brigade also returned with similar reports.

THE BATTLE OF ARRAS

The Brown line was then occupied without opposition, and the 9th Royal Scots and the 7th Gordon Highlanders pushed forward towards the railway.

On the night of 11-12th April the 2nd Division relieved the Highland Division in an intense blizzard.

So ended the first phase of the battle of Arras.

The Division had finally reached all its objectives after some Homeric fighting. The losses had been heavy, but not heavier than an attack against so formidable a position held by such expert fighters would lead one to expect. Numbers of the enemy had been killed, and many hundreds taken prisoners. Large captures were also made of machine-guns, trench-mortars, and material and equipment; while on the whole battle front several Bavarian Divisions had been knocked out.

In fact, the blow sustained by the enemy had been so great that after the relief the 2nd Division were able to carry out a substantial advance and occupy the village of Bailleul unopposed.

On 12th April Divisional headquarters opened at Hermaville. The troops were, however, given a bare forty-eight hours in which to rest, clean up, refit, and reorganise before they were again called upon.

CHAPTER X.

THE BATTLE OF ARRAS (*Contd.*)—ROEUX AND THE CHEMICAL WORKS.

ON the night of 15-16th April the Division relieved the 9th Division on the battle front east of Fampoux, with its right resting on the river Scarpe.

The reserve brigade was quartered in Arras, this being the first occasion on which any of the Division had occupied billets in that town. During the next six weeks the Jocks were continually moving into Arras for short periods of rest, and they became much attached to it.

By a curious coincidence all three Scottish Divisions, the 51st, the 9th, and the 15th, were engaged in operations close to Arras, as well as many Scottish battalions from other Divisions, such as the 3rd and 34th. Arras, therefore, became a great social centre. Though considerably damaged, it had many good billets and excellent cellars and caves for use in emergency. The whole town was, however, in the early days of April, in a most insanitary and disgusting condition. Accumulated heaps of months-old refuse and garbage lay everywhere in the courtyards and gardens. In course of time, however, the town was cleaned up by the troops, who would otherwise have been refreshing themselves for their next fight, and became most comfortable.

One felt then and often how unfortunate it was that the infantryman had so frequently to be employed on tasks menial to a fighting man, such as road sweeping, scavenging, or unloading coal trains, when he should have been either resting himself or perfecting himself in the profession of arms. Circumstances, however, compelled these burdens to be thrust on the fighting units. In this

THE BATTLE OF ARRAS

connection one remembers a cavalryman, up to his hocks in mud, sweeping the streets of Acheux one November morning, who, on being asked to what unit he belonged, replied feelingly, " We used to be blinkin' Hussars." But this is a digression.

The trench system taken over was one which will for ever remain fresh in the memory of all who fought there. Its chief characteristics were numerous defiles, which daily had to be traversed, and which were more or less permanently bombarded. These defiles consisted first of the bridges over the river Scarpe, which had to be crossed by all whose business took them into the right sector, and which were within range of machine-guns and rifles. There was also the straight embankment of the Arras-Douai railway, down which the Germans looked from its highest point. This embankment was continually bombarded. There was the road from Athies to Fampoux, and Fampoux itself, and the road from Feuchy to Fampoux, which were shelled almost every hour of the day.

Further, there was the Hyderabad Redoubt, which was a veritable cockshy. This redoubt was an old German headquarters north-west of Fampoux, perched on the crest of an upland. It was shelled so heavily that approach was seldom comfortable; while, having once entered, to make a graceful exit was equally rare.

Lastly, there were the few valleys which afforded shelter for the guns, which were treated to special and intense bombardments of their own several times a day, an abundance of gas being used against them.

The main characteristic of this period was a continual and savage bombardment of the British infantry by the German artillery. To the infantryman this is a most trying and aggravating form of warfare, as though his own guns may be supporting him by giving the German infantry similar treatment, he has no adequate means of ventilating his own feelings towards the enemy, and can but passively endure the bombardment.

The troops in the front line on the right had their backs to the river Scarpe, flowing south-east, only a few hundred yards in rear of them. This river is in itself only some thirty feet in breadth, but flows in the main through swampy marshlands. In advance of the foremost trenches lay the village of Roeux, masked on its western edge by a hanging wood which sloped down towards the river. North-west of Roeux was a small but conspicuous copse standing on high ground, called for some obscure reason Mount Pleasant. Due north of Roeux lay the now famous chemical works—a large factory surrounded by numerous buildings that had been used as workmen's dwellings, offices, &c.

Diagonally across the left of the position ran the Arras-Douai railway, passing through a deep cutting on the summit of a high rise about a thousand yards in rear of the chemical works. This rise was known as Greenland Hill. It was the most prominent feature in the landscape, and overlooked all the neighbouring countryside. It possessed the peculiarity of having its summit, which was actually south of the railway, shown as being north of the railway on the official maps.

On it were a large quarry and two woods, named Hausa and Delbar, which commanded extensive views, observation posts in the tree-tops covering a vast expanse of the surrounding country. The whole feature formed an extensive and lofty plateau, which stretched almost to the Scarpe, the ground falling down to the water's edge in a steep slope. This slope, being covered with trees, afforded the enemy a good covered approach along the banks of the river.

The position as it stood was one which could not be allowed to remain. A successful attack from the Germans would force our troops into the Scarpe. Moreover, there was little room in the confined area between the front line and the river in which to manœuvre troops to resist attack.

On the other hand, if a force moving over Greenland Hill and north of it could strike at Plouvain, the Germans between Plouvain and the chemical works would find it almost impossible to extricate themselves.

Orders were therefore issued for an attack to be prepared with this intention.

In the circumstances, one of the earliest considerations was the gaining of ground by minor enterprises, so as to extend the area in which troops could be assembled for the attack.

MAP V.—THE CHEMICAL WORKS, ROEUX.

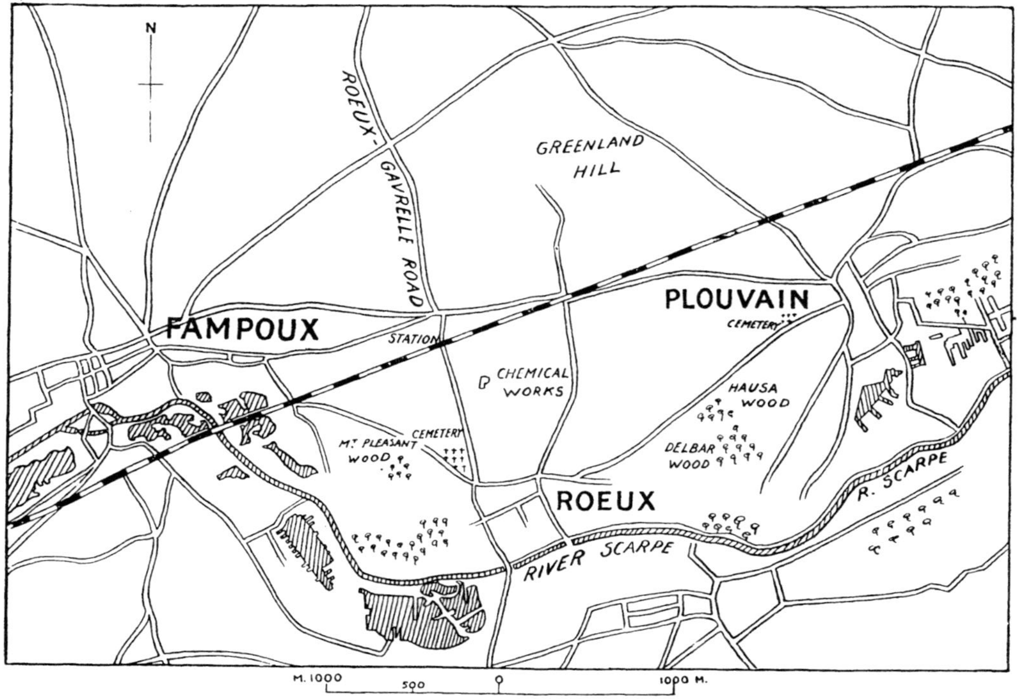

On 18th April the front line was extended southwards by the occupation of a portion of sunken road running parallel with the Scarpe about 300 yards east of it.

At 3 P.M. on the 21st the 9th Royal Scots carried out an operation with a view to extending our hold on this road farther southwards. This attack was at first successful, but subsequently a local counter-attack on the right restored the situation for the enemy. The net result was, however, that one additional post was established 150 yards in advance of the sunken road.

Meanwhile, on the left, where the trenches were well clear of the river, work was carried on in digging new assembly trenches.

As a preparatory measure attempts were made to harass the enemy with discharges of gas. The difficulty of bringing up the necessary apparatus was great owing to the poor communications, and the plan met with little success. On one occasion a sergeant in charge of a train of mules loaded with gas, which came under heavy shell-fire on the railway embankment, noticed that his men were showing some signs of nervousness as the shell splinters came amongst the cylinders. He therefore encouraged them by shouting out in a stentorian voice, "Great God A-michty, ye canna a' be killed." Apparently his words of encouragement comforted the party, as it continued on its way without any further misgivings.

The plan of action for the operation was that the 17th Division should attack south of the Scarpe, and that the 37th Division should continue the attack to the left of the 51st. Objectives were selected as follows:—

The first objective, known as the Black line, was a line running west of the Roeux-Gavrelle Road, excluding the buildings of the chemical works and the village of Roeux.

The second objective, the Blue line, included the western half of the village of Roeux, the chemical works, and the Roeux-Gavrelle Road.

The third objective, the Brown line, took the line of the road running due north from the eastern end of Roeux, and included all the remaining trenches of the German front system.

The fourth objective, the Red line, included Hausa and Delbar Woods and Plouvain Station.

The final objective, the Pink line, included Plouvain.

The 154th Brigade was detailed to attack on the right, the 153rd Brigade on the left.

The 154th Brigade had a particularly difficult operation to perform, as the frontage available for the assembly of their troops was considerably narrower than the frontage to be attacked. The attacking lines had therefore to expand laterally as the advance progressed, so as to cover the whole of the frontage allotted to them.

The number of guns available for the barrage appeared inadequate for an operation of this nature. It was anticipated that, as the enemy was practically without dug-outs to which he could be driven by the approaching barrage, he would have no other alternative but to remain in his shell-holes and fight.

To ensure success, it was therefore considered necessary to provide a barrage sufficiently dense to sweep the whole area to be attacked with shrapnel bullets. However, additional guns could not be spared readily, while attendant circumstances made it imperative that the attack should be carried out without delay.

The attack was launched at 4.45 A.M. on 23rd April, and developed into perhaps the most savage infantry battle that the Division took part in. Attacks continued throughout the day, followed by a succession of determined counter-attacks on the part of the enemy. Both sides sustained serious losses, and many positions changed hands several times in the twenty-four hours.

The main attack was delivered by the 153rd Brigade, the 7th Black Watch being on the right, the 7th Gordon Highlanders on the left. In rear of these two battalions, the 6th Gordon Highlanders, temporarily attached to the 153rd Brigade, were on the right, and the 6th Black Watch on the left. The plan was for the two leading battalions to seize the Black, Blue, and Brown lines, while the 6th Gordon Highlanders passed through to the Red line. The 6th Black Watch were to consolidate a line running due north from the left flank of the 6th Gordon Highlanders in the Red line.

As soon as the infantry moved forward, a heavy machine-gun fire was opened on them, followed in a few minutes by the German artillery barraging the ground in rear of

THE BATTLE OF ARRAS

our assembly trenches. The left of the attack at first proceeded satisfactorily. The 7th Gordon Highlanders repeated their success at Beaumont Hamel. Their left company captured the Black line, according to programme, and killed a number of Germans in it; the second wave passed through them and reached the Blue line, though in very reduced numbers. Only five of this company answered the roll at the end of the operations. The right company of the 7th Gordon Highlanders occupied the Black line, and the left platoon of the second wave entered the Blue line. The remainder of this battalion were held up between the Black and Blue lines, where, incidentally, they captured seventy-six prisoners.

The 7th Black Watch were held by machine-gun fire in front of the Black line, and could not get forward.

On the right the position of the 154th Brigade remained obscure. It is certain that at one time they were well in Roeux Wood and towards Roeux village, as the bodies of Highlanders were found in those places when the Division subsequently occupied Roeux. This brigade also captured the Black line, in spite of considerable opposition, and killed a number of Germans there.

The 4th Seaforth Highlanders carried the chemical works, and they held them on the evening of the 23rd; they were also in the Black line just south of the railway.

It appears, however, that the chemical works were not captured behind the barrage, which had failed to subdue the resistance, as had been anticipated, but were taken by the action of a tank. This tank was a "male," armed with two 6-pounder guns, and was commanded by a sergeant. It arrived on the scene at a time when the attack was held up in front of the Black line, and units had become badly confused. It moved forward to the Black line, and annihilated the enemy in it with point-blank fire from its 6-pounders. It then worked along a communication trench towards the chemical works, strongly held by the enemy, and destroyed its entire garrison.

The tank then advanced through the chemical works, turned up the main road, and round the north-east corner of the village. It next continued along the eastern outskirts of the chemical works, dealing with all the parties of the enemy it encountered.

A machine-gun which still survived amongst the ruins of the chemical works, and which was causing casualties to the advancing troops, was pointed out to the tank. It accordingly engaged the machine-gun, and destroyed it and its crew.

By the aid of this tank a line of shell-holes was occupied by a mixed body of troops, but chiefly 6th Gordon Highlanders, 200 yards east of the chemical works. The tank waited with these men for an hour, and then having little petrol and no ammunition left, withdrew out of action.

The gallant handling of this tank by the sergeant in command of it, and his tactical skill, had enabled the chemical works to be taken, in spite of the barrage having been lost.

Taking advantage of the disorganisation of the enemy caused by the tank, Lieutenant Still, the only surviving officer of the right company of the 7th Gordon Highlanders, went forward with the remainder of the two companies to the Blue line. He captured fifty wounded Germans in a dressing station on the way forward, two trench-mortars between the Black line and the Roeux-Gavrelle Road, and a machine-gun east of the road.

He then proceeded with his party 800 yards east of the Blue line, and almost reached the Brown line. Here he held up with his Lewis guns several attempts to advance made by the enemy. At 9 A.M., having few men left, he withdrew to the vicinity of the Gavrelle Road.

For his gallantry, initiative, and skilful handling of his party during these operations, Lieutenant Still was awarded the Military Cross.

The position then was that at one time our troops were east of the Roeux-Gavrelle Road almost as far south as the junction with the Fampoux-Plouvain Road, that the enemy was in and about the station buildings, that we held the chemical works, that he held the whole of Roeux village and about one-third of Roeux Wood.

During the day the 6th Seaforth Highlanders had been placed at the disposal of the 153rd Brigade, and had moved up into the Black line north of the railway.

Later, Lieut.-Colonel S. Macdonald, commanding the 6th Seaforth Highlanders, received orders that he was to cross the railway, get into touch with the 4th Seaforth

Highlanders east of the chemical works, and consolidate a line from their left to the railway.

Colonel Macdonald then instructed his battalion to cross the railway in two parties, one north of the station and the other south of it. The party detailed to advance north of the station found that the enemy was holding the station buildings, and two officers who went forward to try and locate the 4th Seaforth Highlanders east of the chemical works were captured. They walked right into a strong party of the enemy immediately south of the level crossing. This party of Germans then became engaged with the leading company of the detachment of the 6th Seaforth Highlanders, and sharp skirmishing took place.

The companies which crossed south of the station came under heavy machine-gun fire while crossing the railway, and it soon became evident that the enemy must have retaken the chemical works, and that he was holding them in strength.

The 6th Seaforth Highlanders therefore constructed a trench on the north side of the railway and parallel to it, to form a flank defence to the troops dug in on the eastern side of the Roeux-Gavrelle Road.

It subsequently transpired that, while the position of our troops was as described on page 166, the enemy continually counter-attacked during the day. He concentrated a considerable amount of artillery on the chemical works and on the Black line, and ultimately had by this means so reduced the defenders that they were compelled to fall back. During the withdrawal most of the remaining officers had been hit, and the troops had become disorganised owing to their losses. The result was that the withdrawal of the various posts could not be well co-ordinated, thus some remained in position while others fell back. In this manner a complete section of the 152nd Brigade Machine-Gun Company, left isolated in the chemical works, was surrounded by the enemy and captured.

When it was definitely known that the advance had been held up, orders were issued for the Division to resume the attack in conjunction with the 17th and 37th Divisions at 6 P.M. Orders for this attack were issued to the brigades; but the troops were so closely engaged with the enemy resisting his counter-attacks that their action was restricted to an attempt to keep touch with the advance of the Divisions on the flanks by means of strong patrols.

The hostile counter-attacks, already frequently referred to, began at 9 A.M. The enemy several times attempted to advance over Greenland Hill in extended lines. In each case on this portion of the front his attacks were broken up by artillery and machine-gun fire, and were checked some 500-800 yards east of the Roeux-Gavrelle Road.

At 3 P.M. the enemy, about a battalion in strength, advanced in extended order from Hausa and Delbar Woods towards the railway east of the chemical works. This advance was again stopped by artillery fire, and many of the Germans turned and fled. Later, another force was seen forming up in rear of the Roeux-Plouvain Road, but was again dispersed by the artillery. At dusk the Germans made a further attempt to assemble for attack in the same place, but were similarly dispersed by the artillery.

Seldom have gunners had such targets as were given them during these attacks. Time and time again the German infantry resolutely attempted to advance over the forward glacis of Greenland Hill in full view of the abundant observation posts on the battle front. Not until it was dark could he make his way through the barrage which the artillery and machine and Lewis gunners were able to fire, and regain the chemical works.

During the day reports of enemy counter-attacks reached Divisional headquarters so constantly that a battalion of the 103rd Infantry Brigade was ordered forward as a reserve to the 154th Brigade; similarly a second battalion was placed at the disposal of the 153rd Brigade.

After dark orders were issued for the 103rd Brigade, with the 26th and 27th Battalions Northumberland Fusiliers and the 6th Seaforth Highlanders, to take over the battle front of the 153rd Brigade.

As soon as it had become clear that the enemy was again in possession of the chemical works, the 4th Seaforth Highlanders were ordered to make a further attempt to retake them. This attack was launched during the night, but failed to achieve its object.

Dawn therefore broke to find the Black line south of

the railway, some of the buildings just north of the station and a trench line east of the Gavrelle-Roeux Road north of the station, in our hands. This line was maintained throughout the night, in spite of many attempts made by the enemy to penetrate it.

On 24th April no important actions occurred, both sides being too exhausted to continue the engagement. The enemy's artillery, however, remained very active on the Black line.

On the night 24-25th April the Division was relieved by the 34th Division, with the exception of the 6th Seaforth Highlanders. It was arranged by the Brigadier commanding the 103rd Brigade that the 26th Northumberland Fusiliers, who were holding the line on the 154th Brigade front, should be relieved on that front, and move across to relieve the 6th Seaforth Highlanders. Dawn had, however, broken before the relief of the 6th Seaforth Highlanders had been begun. In consequence, the battalion had to spend another very uncomfortable twenty-four hours in the line.

On the 25th Divisional headquarters moved back to Chelers, the 152nd Brigade to Acq, the 153rd and 154th Brigades to the Tincques-Ligny-St Flochel area. The following day the 152nd Brigade moved to the Ternas area.

So ended a most sanguinary encounter. From most difficultly-situated assembly trenches, an attack had been launched against a position of considerable strength. It had been supported by a weak barrage. Moreover, as the enemy's defences were ill-defined and composed in many places of unlocated shell-holes, the barrage could not have that precision which obtains in a trench to trench attack. From the outset, in most part of the attack, the barrage was lost, and such advances as were carried out were made by unsupported infantry, with the exception of the brilliant action of the tank. The men had advanced against a stout opposition and had suffered heavy casualties, had then been systematically bombarded in shallow trenches and shell-holes, and had been repeatedly counter-attacked.

They, however, maintained a portion of their gains

against all comers, and had appreciably deepened the area held east of the Scarpe.

The artillery had played a large part in the destruction of many hostile counter-attacks, and had afforded our troops great protection against the action of the enemy's infantry. The losses which the gunners had inflicted on the enemy were such that by nightfall he was not in a position to attempt any action on a large scale, and could do no more than reoccupy the chemical works.

In one respect, however, the artillery were at a disadvantage. The enemy had withdrawn his guns so far to the rear that he could do little more with most of his pieces than shell our trenches and foremost battery positions at their extreme range. In consequence, it was difficult to counter his batteries. Efforts were made to push forward heavy howitzers for this purpose, but his observation was so good that he was able to knock many of these out. In one case, a four-gun 9·2 howitzer battery had five guns put out of action in twenty-four hours, a fresh gun which had been sent forward as a replacement meeting the same fate as its predecessors.

Moreover, his guns were so placed that he could concentrate on to the chemical works the artillery, not only of the corps operating against it, but also of the corps on either flank.

The artillery commanders, both field and heavy, did their utmost to check the shelling of the infantry, but they were able to produce little effect.

The Division had been continually in the line since February, had fought for three days in the battle of 9-12th April, and had had only forty-eight hours' rest before again taking over a battle front. In these circumstances the battle of Roeux and the "Comical" works, as the Jocks called it, gave abundant evidence of the magnificent fighting qualities of the troops.

During this battle the Divisional rear headquarters on the St Nicolas-Bailleul road—in which the "A" and "Q" offices and a rear signal office had been established—received a direct hit from a 9-inch high-velocity gun. The signal office was destroyed, several men and horses of the signal company were killed and wounded, and ten motor bicycles were so damaged as to require replacing.

THE BATTLE OF ARRAS

During the month of April 1917 the casualties sustained by the Division were severe. They were as follows :—

	Killed.	Wounded.	Missing.
Officers	66	140	8
Other ranks	828	2972	482

—a total of 214 officers and 4382 other ranks.

Of individual units the following suffered most severely during the month :—

6th Seaforth Highlanders.	16 officers and 508 other ranks
6th Gordon Highlanders.	25 ,, ,, 491 ,, ,,
7th Argyll and Sutherland Highlanders.	22 ,, ,, 499 ,, ,,
4th Gordon Highlanders.	24 ,, ,, 575 ,, ,,

while the 5th Gordon Highlanders lost 9 officers killed and the 7th Black Watch 8.

Amongst the wounded were Major Rowbotham, M.C., 9th Royal Scots; Lieut.-Colonel S. R. M'Clintock, 4th Gordon Highlanders; Lieut.-Colonel J. Dawson, D.S.O., 6th Gordon Highlanders. The latter was severely wounded by a machine-gun bullet while gallantly directing the advance of his leading company. Colonel Dawson's wound kept him out of the field for the remainder of the war, the Division thus losing one of its most brilliant commanding officers.

After the completion of the relief of the Division, the following message was sent to General Harper by Lieut.-General Sir Charles Fergusson, commanding the XVIIth Corps :—

"I wish to express to the Division through you my congratulations on the splendid work which they have done in the recent fighting, especially on Monday, 23rd April.

"Had it not been for the fine fighting spirit of the Division, the result might easily have been disadvantageous to us. I am proud and delighted with the Division, as they may be themselves with the grand fight they put up, and I know when they are rested and reorganised they will be keen to add to their reputation."

The Commander-in-Chief also wired to General Harper as follows : " The fierce fighting of yesterday (23rd April) has carried us another step forward. I congratulate you on the results of it, and on the severe punishment you have inflicted on the enemy."

The Division remained at rest until 10th May in a delightful area. The villages had seldom been occupied by troops, and so did not contain numerous unsightly heaps of empty tins, derelict horse-standings, salvage dumps, &c., which in most rest areas prevented the men from shaking off the more sordid atmosphere of war, even when resting behind the line.

On this occasion the Division lay in a country of pleasant clean villages, nestling amongst orchards in blossom and woods in new leaf. Moreover, the weather was perfect, one cloudless day following another.

The policy adopted during this period was to give the men the maximum of rest and recreation, as it was evident that the Division would shortly be called upon to take further part in active operations.

After the men had cleaned themselves up and all deficiencies in equipment had been made good, training was practically confined to musketry. It was found that in the case of the older men musketry had become a forgotten art, while in the case of the new drafts it was an art which had never been adequately acquired. Long periods of trench warfare, and the undue importance which has been attached to the subsidiary weapons—the bayonet and the bomb—at the training centres had relegated the rifle to a secondary place. A concerted effort was therefore made to revive the prestige of the rifle by giving all ranks an intensive training in its proper uses.

As was the case in most areas at this stage of the war, facilities for musketry were either non-existent, or consisted only of indifferent thirty-yard miniature ranges. However, by working at high pressure, whenever the country suited the purpose, serviceable ranges were soon improvised in every area, and were continuously used from dawn till dusk. Some of them were not quite as safe as those that one had been accustomed to at home; but the Division was lucky, and no one working in the fields was actually shot. On occasions peasants were certainly seen ploughing at the double behind the stop-butts, but they fortunately always managed to avoid the bullets.

THE BATTLE OF ARRAS

By the time orders to move back to the line had been received, every man had been put through a course, and had fired a considerable number of rounds.

The scores made during a brigade competition held during this period show how the musketry of the army had suffered since the early days of the war. The ten best shots were picked from each company, and were given two minutes in which to fire 15 rounds each at a bull's-eye target at 200 yards. The average score made was 16·5 out of a possible 60, and this by picked shots.

On 10th May the Division began to move to the line again, the 152nd Brigade by tactical trains to Arras, and the remaining two brigades by march route.

On the night of 12-13th May, with rather mixed feelings, the 152nd Brigade relieved the whole of the 4th Division in the Roeux chemical-works sector.

It was a difficult relief, as one brigade was taking over the line from two brigades, both of which had been reduced to the strength of about a weak battalion each. The relief was further complicated by the fact that the brigade-major of the outgoing brigade who was to hand over the greater portion of the front was killed on the morning of the relief.

The 4th Division had, however, improved the situation since the Highland Division had left the area on 25th April. They had occupied Roeux as far as the centre of the village; they held the eastern edge of Roeux Cemetery. They were established along a line some 300-500 yards east of the chemical works, and were on the railway about 600 yards east of Roeux station.

The whole battle area was found to be in a ghastly condition. The fighting had been too intense for any attempts to be made to bury the dead. In consequence, the whole area was littered with corpses. Germans in large numbers, men of the 4th, 9th, 34th, and 51st Divisions lay everywhere. Between Fampoux and Roeux Station, the British dead lay in swathes, where they had been cut up in an attempt to exploit the success of 9th April against German machine-gun rearguards. Salvage of every kind lay broadcast over the countryside, while the ground itself, particularly round the chemical works, had been churned by shell-fire into an immense dust-heap.

An air of depression hung over the whole place that it was almost impossible to dispel. As a Jock once put it, " To be in the Comical works made a body windy whether it was shellin' or not."

This was the eve of a great battle, so it may be well to describe the dispositions of the brigade in detail. Instructions had been issued that no further advance was contemplated during the coming tour of duty. The troops, therefore, went into the line with orders to make good what ground they could by patrolling, and to consolidate all gains.

The 5th Seaforth Highlanders took over the right sector and the 8th Argyll and Sutherland Highlanders the left, the railway line being the northern boundary in the front line. As, however, the railway ran obliquely across the front, troops of the 8th Argyll and Sutherland Highlanders in the rear lines were also in position north of it. The 6th Seaforth Highlanders were in support, occupying two lines of trenches from 300-600 yards east of the Scarpe. The 6th Gordon Highlanders were in reserve occupying old German trenches astride the Athies-Fampoux road just west of Fampoux. Brigade headquarters were in an old German 8-inch howitzer position in a sunken road immediately south of the railway at Fampoux.

Orders were given that on no account were troops to occupy the ruined buildings of the chemical works, as these were certain to draw heavy shell-fire.

During this period rumours were frequently circulated that the enemy was about to withdraw to the Queant-Drocourt line, a strong defensive system similar to the Hindenburg line some miles in rear of his existing positions. Orders were therefore issued for patrolling to be actively carried out, so that early information of any such withdrawal would be obtained, and further, that the ground which was made by patrols was to be consolidated.

The first twenty-four hours spent in the sector were sufficient to make it quite evident that the hostile artillery had not decreased since the Division had been relieved towards the end of April. The left battalion trench system, then Roeux village, then the area between battalion and brigade headquarters, and finally the reserve battalion, were all heavily bombarded on the 13th. Brigade head-

THE BATTLE OF ARRAS

quarters, being in deep dug-outs, were well protected against bombardment. The battalion headquarters were, however, not so well situated. Those of the right and support battalions were in elephant shelters cut into a bank just east of the river Scarpe. As these shelters were in an area that drew a considerable amount of shell-fire, and as they were not even proof against a 4·2 howitzer, they were most unsatisfactory domiciles. The left battalion had its headquarters in an old German bomb store in a quarry north of the railway. This bomb store was reasonably shell-proof, but the quarry was a well-marked feature to which the German gunners paid continual attention.

During the day of the 13th the enemy shelled the eastern portion of Roeux ; it was therefore assumed that he had evacuated it. Accordingly at 10 P.M. the whole line south of the railway was advanced to a road running due northwards from the eastern outskirts of Roeux. Positions were then taken up in shell-holes clear of this road. The whole of the village of Roeux also was occupied, six wounded prisoners being captured, one German being killed, and several wounded men of the 4th Division being brought in. As this considerable advance was made without any fighting, the day became known to the Jocks as "The Meatless Day." Vickers guns were sent forward during the night to take up positions in the most forward line of posts or in advance of it. The results of this method of disposing the Vickers guns, as will be seen, proved far-reaching.

During this period the enemy was extremely active with low-flying aeroplanes over the forward area, and it was clear that he was making every effort to locate our defences. At 9.40 A.M. on the 14th there were nine such aeroplanes flying low over our trenches at the same moment. On occasions coloured lights were fired by them, a heavy shelling of the chemical works or some portion of the trench area ensuing. At other times his artillery was directed by observers who were seen to climb into " crows' nests " in the trees of Hausa and Delbar Woods. Machine-guns and shrapnel were frequently employed to discourage this form of activity.

Throughout the 14th the enemy artillery remained active. The opinion had therefore generally been formed that, so far from it being his intention to withdraw, he was preparing for a deliberate attack on our positions. There were, however, still optimists who thought that his excessive shell-fire was accounted for by the fact that the German gunners were emptying their dumps prior to withdrawing. On the night of the 14-15th the sector was decidedly quieter than it had been for some days. The optimists put this down to the fact that the German artillery was busy withdrawing. However, this theory was rudely dispelled, for at dawn on 15th May the bombardment of the brigade area began again with tremendous vehemence, 8's, 5·9's, 4·2's, and 77's all being freely employed. Messages were received from all parts of the brigade front reporting heavy shelling. The 8th Argyll and Sutherland Highlanders reported by runner that they were being violently bombarded with 5·9's, and that all the telephone wires had been cut. The support battalion and the troops at Roeux similarly reported intense shelling. In fact, the only troops who were not involved in this bombardment were those which occupied the foremost line of shell-holes, to which they had advanced unopposed on the night of the 13th. They remained in their position quite secure without a round falling amongst them, and it was evident that they had not as yet been located in their new position.

Officers and men who were in the trench area during this bombardment all reported that the shells, from the sound of their flight through the air, appeared to be fired at the extreme range of the guns. This statement was confirmed by the fact that the corps heavy artillery, though they were continuously in action during the day attempting to counter the enemy's batteries, could not diminish the volume of hostile fire.

It was assumed that this bombardment was preparatory to an attack. The Divisional artillery was therefore employed in shelling the enemy's foremost trench line, which patrols had discovered running just west of Hausa and Delbar Woods, in bombarding the woods and the area between them and Plouvain. It was thus hoped to interfere as much as possible with any attempt the enemy might make to assemble.

At noon the village of Fampoux was heavily bombarded

THE BATTLE OF ARRAS

with gas shells. At this period it was estimated by the artillery that twelve German heavy batteries were firing on the front of the 152nd Brigade.

At 3 P.M. orders were received that two companies of the 152nd Brigade were to relieve two battalions of the 51st Brigade, 17th Division, holding the line immediately north of the railway. In the existing circumstances the situation astride the railway was not satisfactory, as touch had not been found by our foremost troops with the foremost troops north of it. The railway, therefore, constituted a weakness in our defensive system. By the carrying out of the relief ordered the situation would be much improved, as the guarding of the railway, a natural approach leading into the heart of our position, would then be in the hands of one commander.

Two companies of the 6th Seaforth Highlanders were therefore detailed for this duty, and were placed under the command of Lieut.-Colonel R. Campbell, D.S.O., commanding the 8th Argyll and Sutherland Highlanders.

At 7.55 P.M. the shelling was still so severe that all working parties were told to stand by and not to proceed to the trenches. At 9.15 P.M., however, the shelling had ceased. The troops had been heavily and continuously bombarded for fourteen hours by howitzers of all calibres. Moreover, they were entirely without the protection of shell-proof dug-outs. Competent artillery observers estimated that during this bombardment shells were bursting in the brigade area at the rate of one 5·9, two 4·2's, and two 77 mm. shells per minute in every seventy yards of the front. In addition, a number of 8-inch howitzers were freely employed. However, all buildings having been carefully avoided and the front line having been advanced to a position undiscovered by the enemy, the casualties inflicted by the bombardment were not excessive. The three battalions in the forward area were estimated to have lost a total of about 450 men at the time when the bombardment slackened off.

On the other hand, it had undoubtedly been a trying ordeal for the men to endure. General Burn, therefore, decided to relieve the two front-line battalions. Thus the 6th Seaforth Highlanders were ordered not only to relieve the 51st Brigade north of the railway, but also to relieve the 8th Argyll and Sutherland Highlanders as well. On the right the 6th Gordon Highlanders were ordered to relieve the 5th Seaforth Highlanders.

The relief of the 51st Brigade meant the taking over of an additional 1000 yards of front.

This relief as planned was destined never to be completed. The 6th Gordon Highlanders had no sooner received their orders to move than the battalion bivouacs were heavily bombarded with gas shells. This necessitated the men moving off to the bridges over the Scarpe wearing box-respirators. As the ground to be traversed was by nature much broken, and in addition considerably torn up by shell-fire, this movement in the darkness could only be slowly executed. Much delay in the carrying out of this relief was caused at the outset.

At 3.15 P.M., before dawn had broken, an intense bombardment again opened on the whole brigade front. At this hour the relief was in progress, but far from complete; the shell-fire was, however, too intense for it to be continued. The situation at the moment was as follows: Two platoons of the right company of the 6th Gordon Highlanders had entered Roeux, and had relieved one of the 5th Seaforth Highlanders' posts; the remaining two platoons manned a communication trench joining the original front line and the new line consolidated north of the eastern outskirts of Roeux. A second company 6th Gordon Highlanders were moving forward in the area south of the chemical works. This company manned trenches in this vicinity. The third company, which had suffered most severely from the gas-shell bombardment, had only just crossed the Scarpe. It therefore occupied a trench east of the river. The fourth company subsequently occupied trenches in the same vicinity.

Two companies of the 6th Seaforth Highlanders had practically completed the relief of the 51st Brigade, except in a section of the foremost trench about two hundred yards in length immediately north of the railway. The troops on either side of the railway were, therefore, still not in touch with one another, and the railway remained a weak point in the first-line defences. These two companies had both been skilfully disposed in depth by their commanders.

The first bombardment was a prelude to an attack delivered by two successive brigades of a fresh German Division which had recently been transferred from the Russian front. The enemy's plan appears to have been to advance along the bank of the Scarpe and along the railway line, and then to turn inwards and so gain possession of all the country enclosed, as it were, within the jaws of the pincers.

At the moment of attack, no reliefs having been completed, the whole of the 152nd Infantry Brigade was east of the river Scarpe. Moreover, the troops were for the most part occupying positions which were unknown to their commanders, as no information was received in the first stages of the battle as to how far the relief had progressed.

When the attack was launched, the events which occurred on the right are clear. The attack along the river bank made some progress. Some of the enemy certainly reached the western outskirts of Roeux Wood, where they were engaged by a Vickers gun firing to its rear and by bombs thrown by the machine-gunners.

The 5th Seaforth Highlanders in the eastern outskirts of Roeux were attacked frontally, but defeated this attack by rifle and Lewis-gun fire. In the midst of this action they observed the enemy working round their flanks between the village and the river; the right section therefore faced its outer flank and stopped this movement by its fire, while the other neighbouring posts, after having disposed of the frontal attack, also faced half-right and strengthened the defence of this flank. In this manner a large number of Germans were accounted for. The resistance of the 5th Seaforth Highlanders in this corner was so effective that the enemy suddenly evacuated the whole area between Roeux and the river, and this portion of the line remained intact for the rest of the day.

The enemy's effort on his left wing had therefore collapsed. On his right he was, however, more successful. He advanced on either side of the railway, firing Very lights across it so that the attacking forces hidden from each other's view by the embankment could keep in touch with each other. He occupied the foremost trench north of the railway, while south of the railway he continued his advance along the embankment. The area immediately south of the embankment should have been adequately covered by the machine-guns. These were, however, knocked out during the bombardment, and so could not play their part.

To the north of the railway the enemy at once attempted to widen the area of his penetration by a series of heavy bombing attacks against the 6th Seaforth Highlanders, delivered from both flanks.

The first of these attacks was successfully repulsed by Lieutenant Dow and his company, who, however, were compelled to use all their bombs in doing so. They therefore repulsed the second attack by advancing to meet the enemy with rifle and bayonet, these tactics completely discomfiting him. At 10 A.M. the enemy made a third and more determined attack. Lieutenant Dow was forced out of his front-line trench into a communication trench. Here he immediately organised a counter-attack, and led it in person against the enemy. The attack, however, failed, and Lieutenant Dow was mortally wounded. The gallantry and leadership of this officer had successfully limited the enemy's gains to a small footing in a section of the front-line trench.

Farther to the north the second company of the 6th Seaforth Highlanders, under the command of Lieutenant King, had been skilfully disposed by this officer. This company was able to bring flanking fire to bear to support Lieutenant Dow against the enemy's attack, and in addition to defeat more than one frontal attack delivered against itself. Lieutenant King retained all the ground occupied by his company through the action.

The two wings therefore held firm. The enemy had, however, penetrated the front in large numbers along the railway embankment, and immediately south and north of it. Having effected a lodgment in our trenches in this manner, he then delivered a series of flank attacks. By this means he successfully occupied the whole of the chemical works and the trenches immediately west of them, and in addition the buildings north and south of the railway adjacent to the chemical works.

In this position he was pinned. He first attempted to develop an attack southwards from his south-east corner of the chemical works. This attempt was defeated by a company of the 8th Argyll and Sutherland Highlanders, who, seeing the enemy in their rear, left their trenches, charged them, and routed them. This company, which suffered severe casualties, was led by Captain A. Mactaggart. No officer could have shown a finer example to his men. His right hand was shattered by a fragment of a shell early in the attack. Subsequently, owing to a second shell wound, he lost an eye. Nevertheless, he continued to lead and encourage his men until he was mortally wounded, and could continue no farther. Mactaggart's complete disregard for the pain of his wounds and for his own personal danger, and his devotion to duty, may perhaps have been equalled, but can never have been surpassed. Even as he lay mortally wounded with a gaping wound in the abdomen, he continued urging on his men until he lost consciousness.

A second attack of the same nature was stopped by the rifle and Lewis-gun fire of the 5th Seaforth Highlanders and a Vickers gun. Covering fire was then arranged, under which a bombing party advanced, forced the enemy to retire across the open, and captured 1 officer and 20 other ranks.

In the course of these operations the troops, led by the junior officers and N.C.O.'s, had so disposed themselves that the enemy could not develop his advance in any direction except by delivering a frontal attack. Before the enemy had time to bring up fresh troops with which to deliver further attacks, Lieut.-Colonel R. Campbell, D.S.O., commanding 8th Argyll and Sutherland Highlanders, personally organised a counter-attack which restored to us the whole of our line south of the railway.

Colonel Campbell, realising that the Germans had made a deep penetration into our lines, fell in the personnel of his battalion headquarters, and assisted by Captain Pollard, his bombing officer; Lieutenant Worlock, his Lewis-gun officer; Captain A. MacDonald, the adjutant; and Captain Fairlie, his artillery liaison officer, delivered an immediate counter-attack against the Germans north of the railway. This attack was delivered as follows: Captain Pollard, a skilful bomber, drove the enemy from his shell-holes with rifle grenades, while the remainder of the party shot them down as they ran. Colonel Campbell himself killed six Germans with his rifle.

By 6.45 A.M. he had killed or captured all Germans on the north side of the railway. However, about this hour he heard heavy rifle-fire taking place on the south side. He therefore led his party on to the embankment, from which he saw a party of Germans just west of the chemical works being engaged by the 6th Seaforth Highlanders both from their front and from their left flank with rifle-fire.

Colonel Campbell immediately sent his adjutant to tell the 6th Seaforth Highlanders to deliver a frontal attack while he enfiladed the Germans from the embankment. This operation was carried out with complete success. Captain Pollard was, however, killed by a bullet which passed through his heart. Colonel Campbell narrowly escaped a similar fate, a bullet flattening itself against the railway line on which his chest was resting as he fired.

Colonel Campbell then joined the 6th Seaforth Highlanders with his party, advanced through the chemical works with them, and dug himself in just east of them.

Meanwhile Captain Donald Clarke, M.C., of the 6th Gordon Highlanders, had also organised a counter-attack, and with men of the 6th Gordon Highlanders and 5th and 6th Seaforth Highlanders carried out a sweep forward covering the whole of the brigade front south of the chemical works. The advance of this force made great progress except in Roeux village, where it was checked for a time by a heavy enemy barrage. On the rest of the front over which they advanced they reached the foremost British lines. Here Captain Clarke reorganised his troops and disposed them in depth. He found the front line still occupied by its original garrison. These troops had not been shelled either during the actual attack or in the preliminary bombardment, the enemy doubtless not having discovered their position. In the grey of the dawn, they had seen by the assistance of Very lights large numbers of the enemy advancing in small columns to the attack. Vickers and Lewis guns and riflemen opened on them, and fired round after round into them, thus bringing the advance to a complete standstill, and killing large numbers of the enemy. As it became lighter, the enemy repeated his attempts to advance, on this occasion adopting an extended formation. Again these men, who had not been shaken by any previous bombardment, steadily engaged the splendid targets offered them, and annihilated the attacking force. The Vickers guns in particular played tremendous havoc with the enemy, and the policy of pushing them well forward, though often condemned, proved in this case to have been amply justified. No further attacks were delivered against the front of these two companies.

Meanwhile all telephone wires were cut, and information was extremely difficult to obtain. The enemy's barrage had now lifted on to the area between the river Scarpe and brigade headquarters, and numbers of runners were killed in trying to pass through it.

Prisoners and wounded men on their way to the dressing stations had, however, reported that the Germans had captured the chemical works. Arrangements had therefore been made to counter-attack behind a barrage with a view to recapturing the works. The 5th Gordon Highlanders, having been placed at General Burn's disposal, were detailed to carry out this attack.

As soon as this order was issued, Lieutenant J. B. Simpson (5th Seaforth Highlanders), the brigade bombing officer, was ordered to go forward, get in touch with Colonel Campbell, and find out what the situation was. After successfully passing through the German barrage about the river, he found Colonel Campbell with his party dug-in east of the chemical works. Colonel Campbell, however, on hearing that an attack behind a barrage was to be delivered, withdrew his men from the works and informed brigade headquarters of the situation. On Lieutenant Simpson reporting that Colonel Campbell had cleared the chemical works, it was decided to attack north of the railway only with a view to restoring a firm line, particularly astride the embankment east of the chemical works.

The counter-attack of the 5th Gordon Highlanders was to be delivered in conjunction with an attack by the neighbouring Division on the left flank. It was successfully launched, covered by an intense and accurate 18-pounder and Stokes mortar barrage. It was, however, held up by a heavy enemy barrage along the line of the

Roeux-Gavrelle road. This barrage, fortunately, suddenly ceased, and the 5th Gordon Highlanders carried on their advance unsupported by the artillery, the 18-pounder barrage long since having passed on. It appears that they reached their final objective, the old British front line, but were immediately heavily counter-attacked from the left flank, and were forced to withdraw to the original British second line. It subsequently transpired that the reason why the 5th Gordon Highlanders arrived in their objectives with an open flank was due to the fact that the attack to be carried out by troops of the neighbouring Division on the left was cancelled, and that no intimation to this effect was received by General Burn or by his attacking troops.

On the completion of this attack the enemy effort seems to have been spent, and the whole of our original line was left in our hands, except for the foremost trenches immediately astride the railway.

The enemy had suffered unusually heavy losses from rifle, Lewis gun, and machine-gun fire. His columns and waves had been completely broken many times. Eighty-three prisoners remained in our hands, including men from six different battalions and two pioneer companies. The observers of the Corps R.F.C. squadrons reported that they had never before seen German dead and wounded lying as thick as they were in front of our trenches and between the British front line and the chemical works.

The manner in which this attack was resisted and beaten off was due, in the first place, to the fighting spirit, leadership, and initiative displayed by officers and men. It proved that the Divisional commander's efforts to train the Division to fight, not merely with gallantry but also with tactical intelligence, had been successful.

Further, the thorough training in musketry carried out during the last period of rest could not have been more opportune, as the men had undoubtedly gone into the line with a determination to make full use of their rifles if the opportunity occurred.

The Vickers gunners also played a great part in this battle. Not only did they fire on targets such as machine-gunners dream about from their foremost positions, but they also were so disposed as to be able to fire an intense

THE BATTLE OF ARRAS

barrage 500 yards in advance of the British front line. This barrage was fired from half an hour before dark until darkness set in on the evening before the attack, and at intermediate periods throughout the night. It was also fired from the beginning of the attack until there was sufficient light to see whether it was required or otherwise.

The teams of the two Vickers guns farthest forward stood-to all night, occasionally firing Very lights to illumine their front. It was in the glare of one of these lights that the Germans were first observed advancing in artillery formation. The two Vickers guns at once engaged them, and at the same time fired an S.O.S. signal, which was immediately followed by the opening of the whole machine-gun barrage. Before the enemy had time to extend, he was exterminated. Subsequently a succession of waves advanced at the double, only to meet a similar fate. These two guns remained in action all day, dealing with parties of the enemy trying to regain their own lines by running from shell-hole to shell-hole.

Another machine-gun about a hundred yards east of the south end of the chemical works faced its rear, and killed a large number of Germans bolting from the chemical works in the face of Colonel Campbell's counter-attack; while a further gun fought facing its rear in Roeux Woods, and was even there compelled to protect its flanks by bombing. This gun team finally put to flight or killed all the enemy who engaged it. Indeed, infantry could not have been better supported by their machine-gunners.

The Divisional artillery also gave the infantry the support which the latter had now become accustomed to expect. They had been a little slow in opening the barrage on account of all lines having been cut and the difficulty of seeing the S.O.S. signals in the dust and smoke caused by the German bombardment. The barrage fired in support of the 5th Gordon Highlanders' counter-attack, in spite of the fact that it had been hastily improvised, was fired with great precision.

The German artillery could not, however, be checked by the British heavy artillery. Many of his guns were firing from new positions in the open, which had not been previously located. They were also firing from positions as far in rear of their lines as the range of the guns would allow. They were therefore beyond the reach of the bulk of the British counter-battery guns.

The British field-guns in the most advanced positions received considerable attention from the enemy's artillery, and were in particular deluged with gas shells. A number of field-guns were also knocked out by direct hits.

Two anecdotes connected with this battle are worth recording. During the early stages of the German attack a runner arrived at the headquarters of the 6th Gordon Highlanders. Colonel Fraser asked him where he came from.

"Aberdeen," said the runner.

"No, no! Where do you come from now?"

"Yonder," replied the runner, pointing towards the front line.

"Well," said the Colonel, "what's happening there now?"

"Well, a Boche officer comes up to us and he says, 'Surrender!'"

"Well?"

"We told him, 'To hell with surrender.'"

"Where's the officer now?" said the Colonel.

"Yonder."

"What's he doing yonder?"

"Doing?" said the runner; "doing? He's dead."

Some of the tunnelling company, with their infantry assistants, also joined in the fray, and took part in Captain Clarke's counter-attack. On their return from the trenches they met the staff-captain, who hailed them, and said, "Are you the tunnelling company?"

"Tunnelling be damned," a voice replied; "we've been ower the bags."

The casualties to the 152nd Infantry Brigade, with the 5th Gordon Highlanders, amounted to about 900, including 53 officers. In this case most of the wounds were serious. The men had had such slight protection in which to withstand the bombardment that the shell-splinters unfortunately did considerable execution. The medical officers reported that they had never seen so large a percentage of seriously-wounded cases. The spectacle of a steadily-increasing number of men arriving at the dressing stations with shattered limbs was most pitiable, and the medical personnel could hardly keep pace with the number of cases brought in.

The stretcher-bearers went backwards and forwards through the most hellish barrage both on the day before and during the attack in their usual exemplary manner. Many of them were, however, killed, often with the wounded man they were carrying.

On 19th May the following message was issued to the troops by the Divisional Commander :—

" The Divisional Commander wishes to express his sincere appreciation of the resource and bravery shown by all which led to the great defeat of the enemy on the 16th May. He has much pleasure in communicating the following message from the Corps Commander :—

" ' Heartiest congratulations to you all on fine work on 16th and 17th May 1917, and especially on General Burn and 152nd Infantry Brigade, whose tenacity and pluck saved an awkward situation. The Division may well be proud of their latest achievement.' "

General Allenby, commanding the Third Army, wired : " Convey to 51st Highland Division my congratulations on their great gallantry at Roeux and the chemical works."

On the night 16-17th May the 153rd Brigade and the 5th Gordon Highlanders were relieved in the line, the 6th Black Watch taking over the left sub-sector, and the 4th Seaforth Highlanders the right. On the extreme north of the Divisional boundary about fifty men of the 6th Seaforth Highlanders could not be found in the darkness, and were in consequence not relieved until the following night. The command of the front was then divided between the 153rd and 154th Brigades ; the 152nd Brigade moved back to Arras to recuperate and refit. They were not employed again in this sector, the other two brigades remaining permanently in the line until the Division was relieved on 31st May.

From the day following the battle until the date of relief the 153rd and 154th Brigades were severely and constantly bombarded by guns of all calibres up to 8-inch. The enemy was extremely active in the air, and made considerable use of aeroplanes in co-operation with artillery. The Divisional war diary for 24th May runs as follows : " Hostile shelling intermittent but accurate. Enemy aeroplanes for the past week have had an uninterrupted survey of our lines. Between 3 p.m. and 3.30 p.m. an aeroplane registered the right brigade headquarters, scoring several direct hits, and causing considerable casualties."

The following day the right brigade was shelled out of its headquarters, and had to move back to an embankment west of Athies. The activities of these aeroplanes were to a certain extent checked by employing Stokes guns to engage them with air-bursts. It was the first time that the use of Stokes guns as anti-aircraft guns was attempted; and though it was almost impossible to obtain any degree of accuracy, the Stokes bombs certainly had a deterring effect on the enemy's pilots.

In spite of the continual bombardments, with the assistance of the 8th Royal Scots, the field companies, and some tunnellers, the troops in the line made rapid progress in the consolidation of the position. The trenches everywhere were deepened, wire entanglements erected, and the construction of dug-outs begun.

It was during this period that a party of sappers had an interesting adventure. The party, led by Major Bisset, M.C., and Captain Grant of the 404 Field Company, R.E., went forward to destroy a bridge which was shown on air photos to have been constructed across the river Scarpe. This bridge crossed a stretch of the river which flowed due east and west. At this time our line on the north bank was some thousand yards in advance of the line on the south bank. Thus this bridge, though it was well behind our lines on the British bank of the river, was well behind the German lines on the German bank. Any attempt to blow it up was, therefore, certain to be attended by considerable danger.

On arrival at the so-called bridge, it was reconnoitred and found to be nothing more than a tree which had been knocked over by a shell, and which, lying across the surface of the water, had formed a dam and collected a mass of floating débris. It had thus the appearance of a broad wooden bridge on the air photographs.

Major Bisset decided that as the tree was in a position in which it could be utilised as a bridge, it was advisable to destroy it. A sergeant accordingly waded into the river, and was standing with water up to his neck fixing

THE BATTLE OF ARRAS

the charge to the tree, when a German sentry walked out along the tree-trunk towards the centre of the river. When his feet were a few inches from the sergeant's head, he stopped, unaware that he was covered by the revolvers of the two officers. After a pause, apparently suspecting nothing, he moved away. The tree was then successfully blown up without incident. The adventures of this party were, however, not yet over. On their return through the British lines they were mistaken for a German patrol, and were engaged with close-range rifle-fire. Fortunately no one was hit, but the whole party was compelled to take refuge in shell-holes. The trench party then proceeded to bomb them. The bombs produced such a torrent of unmistakably Scottish oaths that it ceased at once—not, however, before a Mills bomb had pitched between Major Bisset and Captain Grant as they lay in the same shell-hole.

On the arrival of this bomb both officers feverishly searched for it in the dark, in the hope that they might be able to throw it away before it burst. When it was found, they discovered to their great relief that in the excitement of the moment the man who had thrown the bomb had forgotten to extract the safety-pin, and that therefore it was fortunately innocuous.

The R.E. made considerable use of pontoons in this area, not so much for bridging purposes as for navigation. They were used for conveying ammunition up the river Scarpe to battery positions in the Scarpe valley, and wounded were conveyed down the river in them on their return journey.

It was interesting to watch them manipulate the rapids which had been formed where the large brick railway bridge just south of Athies had been blown into the river by the Germans. There was always a large crowd of Jocks at these rapids, who gave loud and conflicting advice to the sappers as they were navigating them. The jest in this part of the world, of which the Jocks never tired, was to ask one of the mariners on a passing pontoon to bring him back a parrot.

The pontoon ferry service from Fampoux *viâ* Athies to Blangy was maintained under great difficulties owing to the shell-fire, the numerous obstacles in the water, and to other causes. All difficulties were however overcome, and it was finally extended as far as the railway bridge, east of Fampoux. In one night over two hundred seriously-wounded men were evacuated from the foremost area in pontoons. This system relieved the heavily over-taxed roads, and considerably lessened the difficulties of communication.

After the German attack, the Division played a considerable part in the clearing of the battlefield in this area. The dead lay so thick on the countryside that drastic measures were necessary to deal with the situation.

Accordingly a hundred men from a labour battalion were placed at the disposal of Lieutenant Brown of the 8th Royal Scots, and formed into a Divisional burial party.

This party was constantly working in heavily-shelled areas, as it had become essential that the positions occupied by reserve and supporting battalions should be cleared.

Altogether Lieutenant Brown and his men buried over 3000 dead between 9th April and 31st May, not, however, without having suffered some casualties themselves.

When active operations were not in progress, the troops in rest were well situated in Arras, and rather more comfortable than usual. A certain number of shops existed, against the few remaining windows of which the nose could be glued. There were almost sufficient estaminets to cope with the demand for them. Numerous Divisional troupes were performing in the vicinity, and a large number of bands were available. There was therefore plenty of relaxation to be obtained close at hand.

In this sector the massed pipe band of the Division, consisting of over a hundred pipers and ninety odd drummers, played on several occasions. On one of these occasions a distinguished General came to hear the massed bands, and at the conclusion of the performance horrified the drum-major in charge of the parade by congratulating him on the " most inspiring noise " produced by the pipers.

The " Balmorals " also gave many performances, often to distinguished audiences, in a marquee behind Divisional headquarters at St Nicolas. Frequent discussions arose as to whether the " Balmorals " gave a better performance than their rivals from the 56th Division, the " Bow Bells." There were, however, few persons who did not admit that our " Gertie " was second to none.

THE BATTLE OF ARRAS

In spite of Roeux and the chemical works, the Jocks carried away many pleasant recollections of Arras.

On 31st May the 9th Division began to relieve the brigade in the line. On 2nd June the relief was completed, and two days later the 51st began its northward march to prepare for the third battle of Ypres.

CHAPTER XI.

THE THIRD BATTLE OF YPRES.

ON 7th June the Division arrived in the neighbourhood of Eperleques, near St Omer, the 152nd, 153rd, 154th Brigades being allotted the Tilques, Houlle, and Nordausque areas respectively. This district was a properly constituted training area, administered by the headquarters of the Second Army, in which troops were allowed full liberty of manœuvre, and in which there were no restrictions as regards the digging of practice trenches, &c. Moreover, it contained first-class classification ranges up to 600 yards in length, with all the necessary appliances. This was the first occasion on which the Division had occupied an area in which adequate arrangements for training existed.

Musketry was vigorously continued, and competitions were organised, which showed that the shooting had considerably improved, as, indeed, it was bound to do where facilities for practice were available.

In addition, the tactical training of the Division advanced another stage. It had frequently been exercised in the attack behind the barrage, and in the consolidation of a captured position, and could be relied upon to perform these two tasks well. The Divisional commander, therefore, next concentrated on training the platoons how to overcome local resistance by the aid of their own fire power.

Each platoon was taught that, if it came under the fire of a machine-gun or a pocket of riflemen, it was useless to lie halted in the zone of the hostile fire, and that by engaging the point of resistance frontally by one or more sections the remainder under cover of their fire could work round to the flank and overcome it.

In the light of subsequent events, it turned out that no form of training could have been more appropriate, as the salient feature of the third battle of Ypres proved to be the concrete pill-box, impervious to the field-artillery barrage, which in many cases could only be subdued by the individual action of the platoons opposed to it.

The successful manner in which, as will be seen, the Division overcame the pill-boxes can be directly ascribed to this form of training.

On 12th June the 51st was transferred to the XVIIIth Corps, and on the 15th General Harper was informed by the Corps commander, General Sir F. I. Maxse, that the Division would shortly occupy a portion of the Ypres salient, from which it would take part in a great attack.

The situation in the salient as summarised in the commander-in-chief's despatch was as follows : " The positions held by us in the Ypres salient since May 1915 were far from satisfactory. They were completely overlooked by the enemy ; their defence involved a considerable strain on the troops occupying them, and they were certain to be costly to maintain against a serious attack, in which the enemy would enjoy all the advantages in observation and in the placing of his artillery. Our positions would be much improved by the capture of the Messines-Wytschaete Ridge and of the high ground which extends north-eastwards for some seven miles, and then turns north through Broodseinde and Passchendaele."

In operations beginning on 7th June the Messines-Wytschaete Ridge had been captured, so that at this date, 15th June, the capture of the Passchendaele Ridge remained as the ultimate objective to be attained.

The front allotted to the Division lay due north of Ypres. It was not a pleasant sector, as, in spite of the capture of Messines, the salient still remained sufficiently pronounced for shells to arrive in the front-line trenches from the right rear.

The trenches, such as they were, consisted of breastworks. The front line in some places did not afford cover from view, while in others the thistles and wild mustard on the parapet had been allowed to grow so high that men on the fire-steps could not see over them.

The support line consisted of a few earthworks, resembling grouse butts, and fortified farms, while the reserve line was composed almost entirely of the latter.

There were about half a dozen shell-proof dug-outs in the Divisional sector, one at Turco Farm and one at the Willows, both having to be abandoned owing to the shell-fire they attracted. The C.R.E. reported on these dug-outs: " They are shelled extremely heavily always on the slightest provocation and often with none." Two other dug-outs, one at Lancashire Farm and one at Foch Farm, were good, and were retained as battalion headquarters.

About 2000 yards behind the front line ran the Canal de l'Yser. In the banks of this canal lived a large population—reserve companies, battalion headquarters, pioneers, sappers, R.A.M.C., and brigade headquarters. There was hardly a square yard of the canal bank unoccupied. This vast population lived in every type of non-shell-proof residence, from splinter-proof elephant shelters to the worse kind of " Bairnsfather " shack, which did not even keep out the rain.

As regards the enemy's defences, nothing could be seen beyond his front line. This was sited on the crest of a small rise known as the High Command Redoubt, which, though its height was really insignificant, owing to the flatness of the surrounding country, overlooked the whole of the British trench system as far as the canal bank. The only other feature in the enemy's lines which could be observed were the tops of the trees of Kitchener's Wood.

In the preparations for the attack three separate factors required consideration—a tangled mass of derelict trenches and earthworks had to be transformed into a jumping-off place for a great battle ; the troops had to be trained to attack a position that they could not see ; the artillery had to cut countless belts of wire that could not be observed from the ground.

As regards the first problem, the Division was fortunate in having acquired as its C.R.E. Lieut.-Colonel J. Gibson Fleming, D.S.O., R.E. Lieut.-Colonel C. F. Rundle, D.S.O., who had been transferred as C.R.E. to an Army Corps, had been succeeded at the end of 1916 by Lieut.-Colonel H. W. Weekes, D.S.O., who in his turn had gone sick.

Colonel Fleming then joined the Division just before the battle of Arras, but almost on the day of his arrival was wounded by a premature from one of our own guns. He, however, returned to duty in time to organise the work on the consolidation of the chemical works, and to arrange the pontoon ferries on the river Scarpe.

Colonel Fleming was not only possessed of untiring physical energy himself, but he had in a great degree the faculty of instilling energy into others. He was, in fact, adept at what can best be described as "getting a move on." To him was entrusted the responsibility of preparing the Divisional sector for the coming operation, and for this purpose he moved, on 15th June, with the three field companies, R.E., and the 8th Royal Scots to a camp just north-east of Poperinghe.

The Royal Engineers and pioneers, and similarly the Divisional artillery, were seldom allowed the same periods of rest out of the line as the infantry. It is true that they did not suffer the same number of casualties as the infantry, as they were not required actually to accompany the advancing waves in the attack; but they carried on for long periods in the line during active operations with little or no opportunity of settling down to a period of comfortable quarters and of facilities for training.

Owing to the wet nature of the ground, it was decided that the digging of assembly trenches could not be undertaken. Work was therefore concentrated on building up the front line to give cover from view, and, as far as labour would permit, on the construction of a parados to it.

Battalion battle headquarters were constructed immediately behind the front line, elephant shelters sunk flush into the ground with a strong burster course of broken stone on the top of them being used. The communication trenches were improved to give covered access to the front line, and, where necessary, were diverted to avoid particularly shelled areas such as Turco Farm. As the daily bombardments of our lines became more intense, the trenches were continually being blown in, and the work of repairing them became increasingly heavy.

In addition to this work, accommodation had to be

provided for the maximum number of men in the canal bank. Unfortunately, the canal area allotted to this Division contained the high-level broad-gauge railway causeway and the low-level causeway adjacent to Bridge 4, both of which excited great interest and attracted very heavy shelling from the Boches, who made every endeavour to destroy them by bombardment. Bridge 4 was broken so frequently that in July it was decided that it could not be kept open for wheeled traffic, and that the low-level causeway alone would have to be used. Both banks of the canal in the vicinity of these causeways were involved in these bombardments, with the result that much of the work expended on the erection of shelters was destroyed.

During the whole of this period, two field companies, R.E., and the 8th Royal Scots lived in the canal bank, subjected to heavy and continuous shelling, including a lavish use of gas. Throughout the month of July there was barely a single evening in which they were not heavily bombarded.

As regards the preparation of the troops for the attack, it can safely be said that no troops have been given a better opportunity of training for a particular operation than was the Highland Division in this instance.

General Maxse, the Corps commander, took the greatest interest in the training, visiting each brigade and lecturing to all the officers. Large training areas were hired, and so that officers and men might form some impression of the German position, which they could not see, a large model was made, about the size of four tennis courts, in which hills, valleys, streams, houses, roads, woods, trenches, &c., were all accurately represented by models. Platforms were then erected at intervals round it, from which officers could point out to their men the appearance of the area which they would traverse during the operations.

In some battalions each platoon made similar models in the orchards round their billets, showing all the features in the area allotted to their companies for the attack.

An exact replica of the German trenches was also marked out with tracing-tapes on the training ground full size, in which every known trench and farm was represented. The troops were then practised on this course until they could find their way to their objectives according to plan, without any officers taking part in the exercise. The men were also carefully trained in the manner in which each post was to dig itself in during consolidation, and how to pile the earth as it was excavated, so that it at no time obscured their field of fire to their front. The attack was not delivered until 31st July, so that the Division was given six weeks in which to make its preparations. During this period the plans for the operation, as well as the training of the troops, were perfected down to the minutest details.

In consequence, when the day arrived there was a feeling of confidence in all ranks that, providing the artillery could effectively cut the numerous wire entanglements and that the weather was reasonably good, nothing could prevent them from reaching their objectives. Indeed, with six weeks to prepare for the capture of a limited objective, had it been otherwise the Division would have been greatly at fault.

On 22nd June the 152nd and 153rd Brigades moved to the St Momelin and Lederzeele training areas respectively, and Divisional headquarters to Lederzeele. On the night 22-23rd June the 153rd Brigade took over the Divisional front from the 29th Division, remaining under the command of the G.O.C. of that Division.

The sector at first was reasonably quiet; but as the preparations for the attack began to come to the enemy's notice, his activity increased daily, and finally became intense.

There were two areas in particular to which the enemy artillery paid constant attention: the first was the belt of country running from behind Turco Farm to behind Lancashire Farm, known as the Willows; the second was the canal bank. The bombardment of these two areas was both frequent and violent, and it was often impossible for parties of men to pass through them without running the risk of suffering serious casualties. As the German was at this time fairly active in the air, he could direct his artillery to good purpose. As a result, the crowded canal banks received a large daily ration of shell of all calibres up to 11-inch. The casualties were heavy, and there were several unfortunate cases of heavy shells bursting within crowded shelters and destroying all their inmates.

In fact, the canal bank at times became almost a shambles, and as an unhealthy residence was only surpassed by the Happy Valley in the days of High Wood.

During one of these daily bombardments of this area, a shell burst in the doorway of the headquarters dug-out of the 5th Gordon Highlanders near Turco Farm. Fragments from the back-blast of the shell came in through the doorway, killing 2nd Lieutenant A. S. Milne of the 5th Gordon Highlanders, and wounding four trench-mortar officers who were holding a conference there, including Captain Gillespie, the Divisional trench-mortar officer.

In this period the enemy also considerably developed his activity with high-velocity guns and with aerial bombing, the hutted camps in rear of the trench area, in which the reserve battalions were accommodated, Poperinghe, and the various dumps, all receiving an increasing ration of bombs and high-velocity shells. The value of this form of activity was at once evident, as by a careful employment of high-velocity guns and aircraft, it can be ensured that troops resting behind the line are denied a reasonable night's sleep, and their efficiency can in this manner be considerably impaired.

On 8th July Divisional headquarters moved to a camp in rear of the trench area, and the G.O.C. 51st Division took over command of the line. While the 152nd and 153rd Brigades were carrying out their tour of duty in the line, little change in the situation took place, beyond the introduction of mustard-gas by the enemy. This was the most diabolical form of gas produced during the war. Death from its fumes was a prolonged agony ending in suffocation. Post-mortem examinations of its victims revealed the fact that all their organs from the throat to the abdomen were ulcerated throughout. The health of men who survived its effects was often permanently impaired, while externally, particularly in those portions of the body where perspiration is most profuse, the gas raised large blisters, which gradually chafed into open sores. Fortunately, the British mask was found to be absolutely proof against the effects of this gas. It was, however, found to be most persistent in its effects; the liquid contained in the shells became absorbed in the earth and continued vaporising for many hours. As a result, men who were working

THE THIRD BATTLE OF YPRES

or living in an area that had been gas-shelled were often infected by the fumes many hours after the shelling had subsided. In some Divisions in the Ypres sector casualties from mustard-gas reached alarming proportions.

After the 154th Brigade had taken over the line, the character of the enemy's activity changed for the worse. He continued his constant bombardments of the canal bank, and at the same time persistently shelled the forward area, no doubt in the hope that he might knock out any attack that was impending by overwhelming the troops with shell-fire in their assembly trenches.

Some of those bombardments were of great violence, on one occasion 200 trench-mortar bombs being fired into the trenches on one battalion front.

On 28th July a Chinese attack was carried out at 5 A.M. by the Divisional artillery. A Chinese attack consists in passing a moving 18-pounder barrage across the enemy's trenches exactly as if an attack had begun, except that no infantry take part. The troops in the front line make a considerable noise and hoist dummies on to the fire-step. The German sentries then give the alarm, and as soon as the barrage has passed the garrisons leave their shelters and man their fire-steps. The barrage is then suddenly brought back on to the trenches, and is upon the Germans before they have time to regain their shelters. This is excellent medicine, and after he has been treated to a Chinese attack two or three times, the enemy rather hesitates to man his fire-steps immediately the barrage has passed. Thus, when the day of attack arrives, our infantry, if they can keep close on the heels of the barrage, have an excellent opportunity of " chopping him in cover." The exposure of the dummies, which have the appearance of troops mounting the parapet, also compels him to disclose the position of his machine-guns, which he normally keeps secret until an infantry attack has begun.

By July 15 each infantry brigade had carried out a tour of duty in the line, so that officers and men had all been given an opportunity of studying the area from which the attack was to be launched. On that date the infantry was therefore all relieved and moved back for training, though the command of the sector still remained in General Harper's hands.

As regards the area to be attacked, the width of frontage allotted to the Division was slightly over 1400 yards. The enemy's defences consisted of a front system, including front, support, and reserve line trenches, some 300-500 yards in depth, supported by fortified farms and concrete blockhouses.

About 800 yards in rear of the front system lay a deeply wired line of trenches, supported in front and rear by more fortified farms and blockhouses. This line was known to the Germans as the Stutzpunkt line. To the rear, again, lay further numerous blockhouses and fortified farms. In all cases the blockhouses, as opposed to the farms, which were marked on the map, were not known to exist until they were actually encountered during the operations.

At a distance varying from 1500 to 2000 yards in rear of the Stutzpunkt line lay the Steenbeek, a river which in normal conditions, such as on the morning of the battle, was fordable, but which was liable after rain to rise suddenly and become a serious obstacle, as it did on the afternoon of the battle.

One thousand five hundred yards beyond the Steenbeek lay a strongly-wired line known as the Langemarck-Gheluvelt line.

From the High Command Redoubt in the German front system the ground falls gradually down to the Steenbeek with no pronounced irregularities. Immediately in rear of the Stutzpunkt line and just east of the Divisional right boundary, lay a large copse, Kitchener's Wood, while the whole area was dotted throughout with numerous spinneys and small orchards.

The main objective of the Division, known as the Green line, was the river Steenbeek, but two companies were detailed to cross the river after its capture and establish bridgeheads on the northern bank, the actual distance to be traversed by the troops detailed for the capture of these bridgeheads being 2600 yards on the right, and 3200 yards on the left.

The attack was divided into four stages, three definite intermediate objectives being selected. These were :—

First objective—the Blue line. This included the enemy's front system.

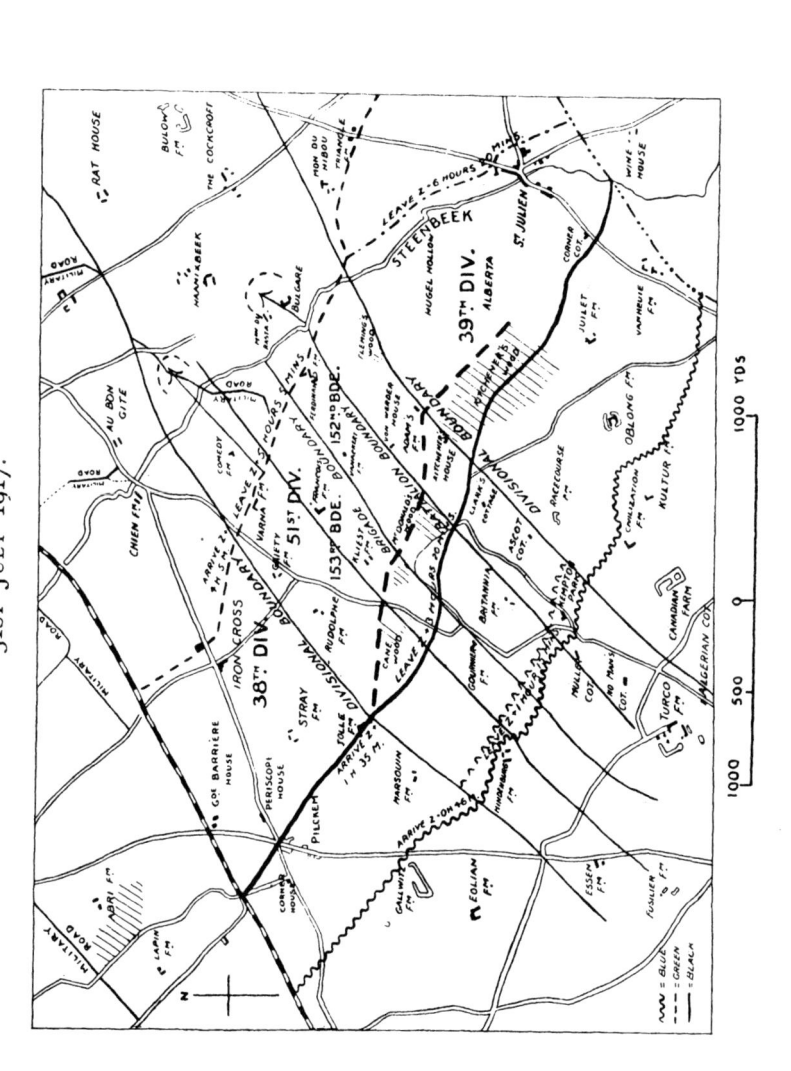

MAP VI.—THIRD BATTLE OF YPRES: ADVANCE TO THE STEENBEEK, 31ST JULY 1917.

Second objective—the Black line. The Stutzpunkt line, with its supporting farms and blockhouses.

Third objective—the Green line. The line of the river Steenbeek.

Fourth objective—one company post at Mon du Rasta, 200 yards beyond the Steenbeek, on the right front; and one company post on the military road, a similar distance beyond the river, on the left front.

In actually defining the objective lines on the map, the question of the various farm buildings to be encountered had to be taken into consideration. It was not known whether the enemy had incorporated them into his system of defence. However, to leave nothing to chance, it was assumed that this had been the case, and, further, that they had been fortified with concrete.

It was therefore decided to arrange the attack so that all farm buildings not more than 200 yards in advance of the main objectives should be assaulted under the barrage without any pause after the capture of each objective. It was thus ensured that no bodies of the enemy would be left undealt with who might interfere with the troops forming up for the assault of the next subsequent objective, and disorganise the attack by their fire before the troops were properly under way. Thus in front of each main objective a dotted line was drawn on the map including all such farms, &c. These lines were known as the Blue outpost line and the Black outpost line.

The assumption that the farms had been fortified with concrete was confirmed on 29th July by Lieutenant F. C. Jack, R.F.A., who, with an orderly, carried out a daring reconnaissance in broad daylight. This officer penetrated into the German lines in two places for about 200 yards depth, and reported that Hindenburg Farm and some other farms were apparently still undestroyed. As they had been hit repeatedly by heavy howitzer shells and much damaged externally, it was evident that concrete had been used in large quantities.

The Division attacked on a two-brigade front, the 152nd Brigade being on the right and the 153rd on the left. Each brigade attacked on a two-battalion front, the leading battalions taking as far as the Blue line inclusive, the remaining two battalions taking up to the Green line.

In this attack Lieut.-Colonel H. G. Hyslop, D.S.O., commanding 7th Argyll and Sutherland Highlanders, commanded the 153rd Infantry Brigade. On 17th May 1917, Brigadier-General D. Campbell, C.B., after having commanded the 153rd Brigade in the field for over two years, had returned home for a well-earned period of rest. General Campbell will always be remembered by those who served with him for his unfailing courtesy to all, and for the evenness of his temperament, no matter how adverse the circumstances. With his departure the Division lost the last of its earliest Brigadiers who had guided it through its infancy and adolescence.

General Campbell was succeeded by Brigadier-General Alistair Gordon, C.M.G., D.S.O., Gordon Highlanders. General Gordon had been seriously wounded in the early days of the war, and had, after his recovery, been employed as a Brigadier-General on the Staff at the War Office. In the short period that he served with the Division, it became evident that had he survived a distinguished career would have awaited him.

On the day before the battle General Gordon and his brigade-major, Hugh Lean of the Highland Light Infantry, while walking round the trenches, were struck by the same shell, Lean being killed and General Gordon mortally wounded.

Lean had always been unlucky. Very early in the war he had been severely wounded, for a time losing his sight. At Arras he received a severe scalp wound from the same shell that killed the brigade intelligence officer with whom he was walking. He, however, gallantly remained at duty. In his next tour in the line he was struck a severe blow on the elbow by the nose-cap of a bursting shell, but again remained at duty.

A few days before going into the line on the last occasion, in conversation he expressed a definite opinion that he would be killed in the coming operations, as indeed he was.

Colonel Hyslop, who at the last moment assumed command of the 153rd Brigade, had been the first regimental officer to land in France with the Expeditionary Force, and had the unique record of having served with a battalion continuously from the date of landing.

Opposed to the Highland Division, and holding a slightly

more extended front, was the 23rd (Reserve) Saxon Division, in process of being relieved by the 3rd Guards Division. The Guards had already taken over the rear lines up to the Black line, and were actually carrying out the relief of the front systems when the attack was launched. The enemy held the trenches with four battalions from the front line to the river Steenbeek inclusive, and with five battalions in reserve north of the Steenbeek.

For this attack the Divisional artillery was reinforced by the two brigades of the 11th Divisional artillery and by two army brigades, the 77th and the 282nd. These six brigades were divided into two groups of three brigades each, one group under the command of Lieut.-Colonel L. M. Dyson, D.S.O., covering the 152nd Brigade; the other, under the command of Lieut.-Colonel M. M. Duncan, C.M.G., covering the 153rd. A brigade of artillery covered each of the four battalion frontages, while the remaining brigade in each group covered the whole brigade front. This plan gave one 18-pounder gun to every twelve and a half yards of the front.

One hundred and twelve machine-guns were available for this attack, as a fourth machine-gun company, the 232nd, had now joined the Division, and forty-eight guns from the 11th Division were also placed at the disposal of the 51st. Of these, sixty-four fired three successive barrages, covering the ground in front of the Blue, Black, and Green lines. Sixteen were placed under the orders of the Brigadiers for purposes of consolidation, and thirty-two were kept in reserve.

As the attack was launched 206 drums of burning oil were projected from mortars on the enemy's support and reserve lines, while to discourage the enemy further 150 shells filled with thermite were thrown at Fort Caledonia in the German reserve line three minutes after zero. There seemed to be rather a mediæval touch about the employment of drums of burning oil; but according to the statements of prisoners who experienced it, it appeared to have been as effective as ever.

One squadron of the 1st King Edward's Horse and eight fighting tanks, with one supply tank, were also placed at the disposal of the Divisional commander.

The artillery had begun the cutting of the enemy wire

on the 16th July, and for a fortnight were firing with great intensity, their average daily expenditure being 3500 rounds by the 18-pounders, 1000 rounds by the 4·5 howitzers, and 400 rounds by the 2-inch trench-mortars.

Naturally this great activity on the part of the gunners drew considerable retaliation from the enemy; nevertheless, they carried out their task with a precision that was little short of amazing when the fact is taken into account that they had to work entirely by aerial observation.

The concentration of the troops in the assembly trenches was a matter which required elaborate arrangements. On the night of the 28-29th the two brigades took over their battle fronts each with four companies, the remainder of the troops moving up to the trenches on the night before the battle. "To ensure secrecy, it was impossible, owing to the enemy's activity in the air, to move from the camps in which the brigades were assembled before 8.30 P.M. There was thus barely time for the attacking force to arrive in its position of deployment before zero hour. It was therefore necessary to eliminate by careful arrangement all likely causes of delay. To avoid loss of direction, overland routes to the entrances of the communication trenches were marked out by stakes and tapes. Men who had been made familiar with these routes were employed as guides. Police were also posted at all junctions of tracks and of trenches, to ensure that in the event of gas being encountered the men would adjust their respirators as quickly as possible and continue their march. The troops were also instructed that in no circumstances was the march to the position of deployment to be delayed by enemy action. Previous to the attack this march had been rehearsed in the dark by bodies of troops both with and without respirators, so that it could be ensured, in selecting the zero hour, sufficient time was allowed for the operation. A hot meal was issued at the place of assembly, and soup and tea were issued from hot-food containers at the positions of deployment."[1]

These arrangements proved adequate. The hostile artillery was exceptionally quiet, and the assembly was completed without incident.

---

[1] This passage is quoted from Lieut.-General Sir G. M. Harper's 'Notes on Infantry Tactics and Training.' Appendix, p. 126.

At 3.50 A.M., 31st July, the third battle of Ypres opened. At that hour the sky was covered with clouds, and in consequence there was little natural light. However, the burning oil thrown on the enemy lines by the trench-mortars at zero hour illuminated the whole front. The troops had little difficulty in forming up under the barrage, except that the numerous water-filled shell-holes made the maintenance of direction and of proper extensions no easy matter. The going was also very heavy.

The enemy's artillery did not open in reply to our barrage for some ten minutes, and fell on and in rear of the old British front line. The leading battalions were, from right to left, the 5th Seaforth Highlanders, the 8th Argyll and Sutherland Highlanders, the 7th Gordon Highlanders, the 7th Black Watch. These four battalions advanced to the Blue line without a check. The trenches were found to have been almost obliterated by the artillery. Some of the farms had been so demolished by shell-fire that they could not be located until the sun was above the horizon. The gunners had, indeed, carried out their tasks.

Points of resistance being scattered rather promiscuously about the area, in the half-light it did not always happen that the German garrisons were dealt with immediately as the barrage lifted. The Jocks, however, in this and in their next battle, were at the very top of their form, and showed extraordinary initiative. Whenever a point of resistance disclosed itself, it was attacked immediately by the troops in its vicinity with great dash—not, however, by wild frontal expensive charges, but by the skilful use of ground and their weapons, in accordance with their training. In fact, as infantry fighters they completely outclassed the Germans, and by using their Lewis guns and rifle grenades with considerable effect they promptly swamped every party of the enemy which opposed them.

In the two attacks carried out by the Division in the third battle of Ypres, the Germans, in spite of the strength of their defences and of the splendid resistance they offered, utterly failed to prevent the Jocks from reaching their final objective. It was no doubt on this account that they published the fact that at this time they considered the 51st the most formidable Division on the Western Front.

In the advance to the Blue line the 7th Gordon Highlanders had probably the most serious minor encounter in the capture of Hindenburg Farm. Under cover of rifle grenades and Lewis guns the farm was captured, ten Germans being killed and wounded, and an officer and twenty-two men being captured. The 7th Black Watch were opposed by the remnants of a more elaborate trench system than other units, but they swept through them with "unco precision," and reached their objective with the other battalions.

The Blue line was thus captured according to plan, and consolidation was well advanced before the troops detailed for the capture of the Black line passed through it on their way to form up under the barrage.

By 5.15 A.M. orders were given for two batteries to move forward to more advanced positions.

So far some 400 casualties had been sustained, including 3 officers killed and 8 wounded. Many of the enemy were killed in the assault, or found lying dead in their trenches, and some 100 prisoners had been taken.

In the advance to the Black line after the capture of the Blue line, the character of the fighting changed. Up to this point the attack had been directed against a trench system badly damaged by shell-fire and only thinly held.

From the Blue line onwards the enemy was in greater strength, and his system of defences was mainly composed of isolated fortified farms and of reinforced concrete blockhouses with double walls, cellars, and wide machine-gun loopholes. The Black line had been so seriously damaged by the artillery that it did not in itself present a serious obstacle; on the other hand, the concreted farms and blockhouses were almost intact. These were particularly troublesome between the Black line and the Black support line.

In this phase of the advance the condition of the ground was appalling, the movements of the infantry being seriously handicapped by the mud, which made it impossible for them to move out of a walk.

The order of battle of the troops detailed for the capture of the Black and Green lines from right to left was as follows: 6th Gordon Highlanders, 6th Seaforth Highlanders, 5th Gordon Highlanders, 6th Black Watch.

THE THIRD BATTLE OF YPRES

On the right the 6th Gordon Highlanders reached the Black line with little difficulty. A machine-gun in rear of Ascot Cottage checked the advance for a short time; the infantry, however, hailed a passing tank, which joined in the action, the cottage being carried and twelve Germans being killed or captured.

Similarly the 6th Seaforth Highlanders captured the Black line behind the barrage except in the neighbourhood of Macdonald's Farm and Macdonald's Wood. Here a considerable engagement took place. Two platoons, whose real objective was the northern edge of Macdonald's Wood, first tackled the farm; while a platoon of the 6th Gordon Highlanders, which had been ordered to the Black line to gain touch with the 6th Seaforth Highlanders, realising the situation, joined in the fight and engaged the enemy in Macdonald's Wood with enfilade rifle and machine-gun fire. Tank G 50 also arrived, and promptly fired six shells into Macdonald's Farm. These shells, arriving in company with a storm of bullets and rifle grenades, proved too much for the Germans, who surrendered. Seventy prisoners were taken, many dead lay round the farm, and a 4·2 howitzer and two machine-guns were captured.

On other parts of the front of the 6th Seaforth Highlanders between the Black and the Black outpost lines some fighting took place, and much gallantry was displayed. In one instance two privates captured four Germans and a machine-gun which had been firing on their platoon, one of the privates alone killing six Germans in the process. This battalion also cleverly captured Canister Trench, a trench running at right angles to the line of advance. A half-platoon entered it at each end, and then fought along it until they met in the middle, having wiped out its entire garrison.

The 6th Black Watch on the left of the 6th Seaforth Highlanders had severe fighting in clearing the Black and Black outpost lines. Of the battalions engaged on the Divisional front, the 6th Black Watch sustained most casualties, 9 officers and 292 other ranks. This battalion had suffered considerably in the half-hour before zero while lying assembled immediately in rear of the old British front line, and again while waiting for the barrage to move forward from in front of the Black outpost line. In this position the men were swept by a machine-gun firing from Gournier Farm. Accordingly, when the barrage lifted, No. 1 platoon made at once for this farm. By working round its flanks from shell-hole to shell-hole they rounded it up, taking two machine-guns and twenty prisoners, and later a field-gun. By 6.40 A.M. the Black outpost line was captured on the whole battalion front.

The 5th Gordon Highlanders met no defended farms during their advance to the Black line, but machine-guns had been posted in front of the line in strong concrete emplacements. These were vigorously assailed, and by the skill and gallantry of the men were speedily silenced. In one of these encounters 2nd Lieutenant Maitland, commanding " C " Company, performed a conspicuous act of bravery. Seeing a machine-gun firing from a shell-hole, he advanced alone, moving from shell-hole to shell-hole until he had worked round to the flank of the gun. He then rushed into the emplacement, shot two of the team, and clubbed a third with the butt-end of his rifle, capturing the gun. This officer was, unfortunately, shortly afterwards wounded.

Severe fighting occurred on the right flank of the 5th Gordon Highlanders, where a pocket of Germans resisted stubbornly. Lieutenant J. Rutherford, adjutant of the 6th Black Watch, seeing that the advance was checked at this point, organised the troops at hand, both Black Watch and Gordon Highlanders, and, supported by a Stokes mortar, advanced from shell-hole to shell-hole against the flank of the Germans. The troops held up meanwhile opened a heavy fire on the enemy, who, seeing themselves engaged both frontally and from a flank, gave up the contest and surrendered. The trench they had occupied was found to be choked with enemy dead, most of whom had been killed by bullets. About 100 prisoners were taken in this local action.

By 7.45 A.M. all arms, in addition to the infantry, were moving forward. The first batteries were now in action just in rear of the old British front line. The Stokes guns were up ready to support the fighting troops, as they had, indeed, already done.

The machine-guns, which had been ordered to move up to the Blue line to fire in the later stages of the barrage, had also begun their advance, though many were delayed owing to the men finding great difficulty in carrying their loads through the mud.

The 8th Royal Scots had also begun work on a road and a trench across the old No Man's Land.

The fighting round the Black outpost line was still in progress when the barrage moved forward to the Green line. In consequence, troops whose real objective was the Green line became involved in the fighting both at Cane Wood and Macdonald's Wood on their way to form up under the barrage.

In spite of this the whole line managed to defeat the Germans who were still holding out, overtake the barrage, and advance behind it.

On the right the 6th Gordon Highlanders reached the Green line at 7.50 A.M. with little opposition, and began to consolidate about 250 yards south-west of the Steenbeek. German low-flying aeroplanes, however, shortly arrived, and took stock of their positions. The company commander, guessing what their business was, as soon as they had gone, moved his front line 100 yards forward and his support line 100 yards back. He thus had the satisfaction of seeing the position he had originally occupied thoroughly well shelled, while his own lines entirely escaped the bombardment.

This battalion had captured in its advance to the Green line 4 officers, 130 other ranks, 3 machine-guns, 2 trench-mortars, and 2 anti-tank guns, its losses being 6 officers and 130 other ranks. Curiously enough, the company which reached the Steenbeek only lost 2 men killed and 19 wounded during the whole period that it was engaged in these operations.

In this advance Private G. I. M'Intosh of the 6th Gordon Highlanders performed an act of conspicuous gallantry, for which he was awarded the Victoria Cross. Machine-guns across the Steenbeek were firing on his company. Private M'Intosh, entirely on his own initiative, crossed the stream alone under fire, armed with a bomb and a revolver. Working round to the rear of the emplacement he hurled his bomb into it, killing two Germans and wounding a third. He found two light machine-guns, which he brought back with him.

On the left of the 6th Gordon Highlanders, the 6th Seaforth Highlanders had detailed one company to cross the river Steenbeek and establish a post at Mon du Rasta, and three platoons to dig in on the Green line. These troops passed through the Black outpost line while fighting was still in progress, and joined in the reduction of Macdonald's Wood.

The advance thus continued without incident until the platoons were approaching the Green line. At this point they came under a heavy rifle and machine-gun fire from the opposite side of the river. Lewis guns therefore swept the farther bank, a tank was called up to give covering fire, and the Green line platoons were thus enabled to dig themselves in as arranged. The company for Mon du Rasta, finding all bridges and the river bank swept by hostile machine-gun fire, dug in 100 yards from the stream and awaited an opportunity to cross.

Meanwhile the 6th Black Watch had, after some stiff fighting, overcome the numerous blockhouses and fortified farms that they encountered, and had captured a number of prisoners. The behaviour of this battalion was magnificent, as every advance it made was carried out in the face of obstinate resistance. The platoons for the Green line were first engaged in the Black outpost line, particularly about Cane Wood. They next captured Rudolf Farm with 20 prisoners, and later, in conjunction with platoons of the 5th Gordon Highlanders, a blockhouse near François Farm with 3 machine-guns, 4 officers, and 40 other ranks. The Green line platoons, though greatly reduced in numbers, finally reached their objective and dug in.

At 10.30 A.M. Lieut.-Colonel T. M. Booth, D.S.O., commanding the 6th Black Watch, made a reconnaissance of the Green line. Appreciating that it was then possible to rush men across the Steenbeek, he collected thirty to forty men of " D " Company, and led them with few casualties across the river by a bridge just north of the Military Road. He then disposed them in four posts north of the road, and a message was sent back to the cavalry at Gournier Farm that the posts were successfully established across the stream.

As this was to be the signal for the squadron of the

THE THIRD BATTLE OF YPRES

King Edward Horse to advance and patrol north of the Steenbeek, the men mounted, moved forward, and deployed in front of the Palace Farm. On reaching a line 150 yards from the stream, they suddenly came under heavy machine-gun fire, and immediately suffered such losses in men and horses that any attempt at a further advance was out of the question. They therefore dug in under orders of Colonel M'Donald of the 6th Seaforth Highlanders, in a position which covered Mon du Rasta.

It was at this moment that Sergeant Edwards, 6th Seaforth Highlanders, performed one of several acts of conspicuous gallantry for which he was awarded the Victoria Cross. Major Swan, commanding the squadron of King Edward Horse, fell wounded. Sergeant Edwards went out under heavy fire, dressed the officer's wounds in a shell-hole, and helped him back into a trench. He had already led his platoon against a machine-gun in Macdonald's Wood and wiped out the team. He had also, though wounded in the arm, alone stalked and killed a sniper. The following day Edwards was wounded in the leg, but refused to leave his platoon.

The 5th Gordon Highlanders were also by this time established on the Green line. They had overcome two strongly-defended posts—the blockhouse near François Farm, in conjunction with the 6th Black Watch, as already described ; and Varna Farm, in conjunction with troops of the 38th Division.

In each case the men " dribbled " towards their objective—that is, they worked their way individually from shell-hole to shell-hole, and by this means were able to reach the flanks of the point of resistance opposing them. So skilfully did they carry out this manœuvre that the German machine-gunners could not check their advance, and in both cases the garrisons surrendered before the Gordon Highlanders had closed with them, a number of dead being found in the neighbourhood of the captured posts. This battalion took 7 officers and 160 other ranks (excluding wounded) prisoners, and 10 machine-guns ; while they lost 1 officer killed, 7 wounded, and 58 other ranks killed, 171 wounded, and 7 missing.

Two tanks had by this time arrived on the Green line,

and patrolled it for about two hours, engaging any targets that offered, and thus protecting the infantry from the enemy's activity.

Between 3 and 4 P.M. in the afternoon the enemy put down a heavy barrage on the Black outpost line, and the infantry began advancing on the left flank towards the Steenbeek. This attempted counter-attack, however, failed, the fire of rifles, Lewis and machine guns sending the enemy running back, and causing him many casualties. Taking advantage of the disorganisation caused by the failure of this enterprise in the enemy's dispositions north of the Steenbeek, the company of the 6th Seaforth Highlanders, reinforced by two platoons of the 8th Argyll and Sutherland Highlanders, dashed across the stream, seized the bridgeheads opposite Ferdinand Farm, and rushed Mon du Rasta. Posts were then established at Mon du Rasta and Mon Bulgare. These were next reinforced by a Stokes mortar which was pushed across the stream, and which was soon in action, firing thirty rounds on parties of the enemy on the road running north - east from Mon du Rasta.

The 6th Seaforth Highlanders had now also occupied their farthest objective. This battalion had captured during the day 2 officers, 276 other ranks, a 4·2 howitzer, and 9 machine-guns, and had sustained the following casualties : 3 officers killed and 7 wounded, 38 other ranks killed and 174 wounded, and 21 men missing.

The operation had thus been a complete success ; each platoon was on the objective to which it had been detailed, machine-guns and Stokes guns were in position, and the work at consolidation was well advanced.

Later it was found necessary to withdraw the posts on the north bank of the Steenbeek. The enemy had counter-attacked the 6th Black Watch at 3.45 P.M., 4 P.M., and 4.30 P.M., but in every case the battalion had held their ground and broken up each attack. At a low estimate eighty Germans were killed and wounded by rifle and Lewis gun fire during these actions. At 6.5 P.M., after a heavy bombardment, including a lavish use of gas shells, a further and more serious attack was delivered. Owing to the casualties they had sustained in the previous attacks and to the withdrawal of troops on their left, the 6th Black

Watch were forced to return to the south bank of the Steenbeek, where they again dug in.

Meanwhile the posts of the 6th Seaforth Highlanders and the 8th Argyll and Sutherland Highlanders at Mon du Rasta and Mon Bulgare were in danger of being isolated. Not only were their flanks in the air, but also, owing to heavy rain which had set in during the early afternoon, the Steenbeek was being transformed from a fordable stream into a rushing torrent.

It was therefore decided to withdraw the outlying posts and hold only the bridges. Thus at the end of the day the Steenbeek divided the opposing forces.

In each phase of the operations the infantry advance was closely followed by the other arms of the service in exact accordance with the prearranged plans, with the result that before nightfall the whole of the captured area had been powerfully organised.

By 12 noon four batteries of artillery were in action in and about the old No Man's Land. Eighteen machine-guns were in position in the Black line in time to answer an S.O.S. signal in the afternoon, while sixteen other machine-guns were established in their prearranged positions during the day, with a good supply of ammunition. The 152nd Machine-Gun Company's barrage guns alone were able to fire 20,000 rounds in answer to a single S.O.S. call.

The engineers had also performed a number of tasks. By the afternoon they had constructed posts at 23 Metre Hill, Cane Avenue, and von Werder House. They had repaired the Pilkem Road up to the 5 Chemins Estaminet, and Boundary Road as far as Kempton Park, so as to be suitable for wheeled transport. They had also made a track across No Man's Land which joined up with an old road at Below Farm. They had, in addition, constructed a water-supply point at Lancashire Farm with a track connecting it to the nearest road.

Rations for the following day were dumped at the Black line by 7 P.M., a fact which provides an illustration of the remarkable work done by the Divisional pack-train under the command of Captain Smith of the 51st D.A.C. This train consisted of 328 mules. The first pack-loads of ammunition were on their way to dumps at Hurst Park and Gournier Farm three hours after zero. Throughout the day ammunition, sandbags, Lewis gun drums, Very light cartridges, water, and rations were carried forward in a continual stream.

Only one mule was hit during these operations, an instance of the benefit which results from carrying out a task of this nature quickly and in daylight during the comparatively undisturbed hours which always occur behind the fighting line during an actual attack. At this period the enemy's artillery is too preoccupied in trying to check the attacking infantry to pay much attention to the activities that may be going on in rear of the attack.

Throughout the battle little trouble was experienced as regards communication. A cable-tank had carried signal gear to a prearranged dump between Sandown and Hurst Park. Wires were then quickly laid to the battalion headquarters which were established in various fortified farms.

A message-carrying dog sent from the Green line during the engagement reached its destination two days later, minus its collar and message.

As was usually the case when the Division carried out a trench-to-trench attack, rain fell heavily during the night. In many cases men were flooded out of their trenches and had to lie in the open. Throughout the whole captured area movement became a matter of the greatest difficulty. Luckily the enemy suffered equally, and remained quiet.

The troops on the Green line, however, remained in good heart, and reported the situation as " water two feet deep, but spirits very high."

The eight tanks which supported the attack in some cases did valuable work; their doings, briefly summarised, were as follows :—

G 49 stuck in the Blue line; G 41 stuck 200 yards beyond the Blue line; G 51 reached Kitchener's Wood; G 44, 45, and 52 reached the Green line after having dealt with several machine-guns. G 50 reached Varna Farm after several engagements with machine-guns. G 42 reached the Black line and worked along it.

The 152nd and 153rd Brigades had each gone into action with the approximate strength of 80 officers and 2700 other ranks. Their casualties totalled 52 officers (32·5 per cent) and 1516 other ranks (28·07 per cent).

THE THIRD BATTLE OF YPRES

As opposed to this, 15 officers and 624 other ranks, 2 field-guns, 4 trench-mortars, and 29 machine-guns were captured, many enemy killed and many machine-guns and trench-mortars destroyed.

This attack can be summed up as the neatest and cleanest performance which the Division had carried out. It was delivered against the Germans while their fighting efficiency was still unimpaired, and while their numbers were still unappreciably diminished. Moreover, it was delivered against a position hidden from view, which had been deliberately fortified during the preceding years with every artifice the ingenuity of the Boche could devise, and contained the concrete barrage-proof farms and the entirely unexpected concrete blockhouses.

The success, indeed, was so complete that, even after the battle was over, nothing which would have been an improvement in the plans of attack suggested itself.

During the afternoon and evening of 1st August the 154th Brigade, which had as yet not been employed in the operations at all, relieved the 152nd and 153rd Brigades, and remained in the line until 8th August, when the whole Division was relieved.

CHAPTER XII.

POELCAPPELLE.

FROM the 8th August until 29th the Division remained at rest in the St Janster Biezen area, with the exception of the 154th Infantry Brigade, which moved back to the Eperleques area. Training was carried out as usual, particular attention again being given to the practising of platoons in attacking under cover of their own fire.

On 17th August Brigadier-General A. T. Beckwith, C.M.G., D.S.O., Hampshire Regiment, took over command of the 153rd Brigade, having already had a distinguished career as a battalion commander in the 29th Division. He had left one Division with a distinct identity of its own to join another with an equally distinct identity. His great capacity for detail being admirably adapted to the system on which the 51st worked both in attack and defence, enabled him quickly to become one of its main supports.

On 20th August the G.O.C. 51st Division assumed command of the left sector of the XVIIIth Corps front, the 152nd Brigade having taken over the line. The trench area was situated some half a mile away from the remains of the village of Langemarck and just east of the Langemarck-Gheluvelt road, the Divisional frontage being about 1500 yards in breadth.

The Division continued holding this line until 20th September, when an attack was launched. This period was remarkable on account of three things. First, the mud, which reproduced conditions similar to, if not worse than, those at Courcelette. The ground throughout the whole front was so sodden with rain and churned up by shell-fire as to be impassable to troops in any numbers.

The second feature was a consistently lavish use of the recently-introduced mustard gas, which caused numerous cases of slightly-gassed men, and a lesser number of men seriously gassed. The latter suffered indescribable agonies, and either ultimately died, or made an insufficient recovery ever to return to the ranks as whole men. The mustard gas shell proved itself to be a weapon that was liable to cause serious losses unless all measures for anti-gas defence were maintained at a high level of efficiency. It was, however, a persistent gas, and might cause casualties hours and even days after it had been used, so that the enemy could never employ it on an area which he intended to attack in the immediate future.

The third feature of this period was great activity in aerial bombing, which the Germans suddenly developed, and which they maintained in an increasing degree to within a few weeks of the armistice. Both bombing and long-range guns, which the enemy freely used in this front, were difficult to deal with, as shelter for the men could not be provided by means of dug-outs in the clay soil of Flanders. In consequence, both men and horses suffered a number of casualties from bombing, particularly in the camps and rest billets behind the line. On one occasion alone three bombs dropped in Siege Camp caused thirty-two casualties.

On 6th September the 5th Seaforth Highlanders attempted a raid on the enemy's posts in front of Pheasant Trench (see Map VII.), 3 officers and 100 other ranks being employed. The raiding party failed to reach the enemy's lines owing to the intensity of his rifle and machine-gun fire; but they obtained some valuable information, and caused the enemy serious losses by the energetic use of their rifles. They observed that Pheasant Trench was protected by an uncut belt of wire about fifteen yards in depth. They also found that in some parts Pheasant Trench was manned by dummies, and in others by men holding it in two ranks, the front rank using their rifles while the rear rank threw bombs. They took advantage of this close grouping on the part of the enemy by shooting twelve of them. During the advance a party of about twenty of the enemy left two advanced saps and made for the rear, but only four of them reached cover.

The raiders could not regain our lines during daylight, and remained in shell-holes until dusk, when they returned, having lost 1 officer and 19 men killed, 2 officers and 18 men wounded, and 9 men missing.

On 19th September the artillery and trench-mortars began a bombardment preparatory to the attack.

The object of the operations was to secure a satisfactory " jumping off " place for an attack against Poelcappelle, and to secure positions in the valley of the Steenbeek from which the artillery could cover this attack.

The area which the Highland Division was detailed to capture was some 1500 yards in depth, about 1500 yards in breadth in the first instance, but widening to some 1900 yards on the final objective. In this area the ground gradually rises from the river Steenbeek except in the centre, where a depression marks the course of the Lekkerboterbeek, a small stream running east and west about six feet broad, two feet deep, with banks five feet in height. On the left a slight ridge above Pheasant Farm forms the highest ground from which close observation of Poelcappelle is obtained, and which covers the Steenbeek Valley. On the right a depression is formed running north and south by the Stroombeek, a tiny stream beyond which lies a slight ridge about Quebec Farm. From here also observation of the surroundings of Poelcappelle is obtained. About the position of assembly the ground is broken by swamps and pools, but becomes drier and firmer as the higher ground is reached.

The 154th Infantry Brigade was allotted the task of carrying out the attack. In this stage of the war the detailing of troops for the attack required more than ever careful consideration. Dug-outs could not be constructed in Flanders; the Germans had therefore to rely for protection against shell-fire on concrete pill-boxes and shelters and reinforced farms. Any troops to whom this form of protection was not available would have little chance of surviving bombardments of the intensity which had by this time become the fashion. The German therefore tended to restrict the numbers of troops he employed on the stationary defence in accordance with the number of shelters available. It was therefore to be anticipated that the garrison would be a light one, but that it would in the main survive the artillery bombardment. It was thus evident that should large numbers of men be employed in the attack, if they were successful they could not hope for a big bag of killed and captured Germans, whereas if they failed heavy casualties would result in an endeavour to overcome comparatively few of the enemy.

In these circumstances the Divisional commander decided to employ only the 154th Brigade on the initial attack. Had the operation been a failure, critics would no doubt have said that the attack had been too light. As it turned out, the troops detailed for the assault reached their final objective, overcame all resistance, and with the assistance of two battalions of the 152nd Brigade which were sent forward to support them, defeated six counter-attacks delivered by four different German Divisions. In killed and missing in this operation the Division only lost 17 officers and 184 other ranks.

The conditions under which the action was fought were in some respects new. There was a well-defined trench line, running right across the Divisional front about 150 yards from the British front line, known as Pheasant Trench and New Trench; and, again, some 1200 yards in rear, Kangaroo and Beer Trenches also traversed the Divisional front. The defence, however, primarily consisted of concrete pill-boxes and fortified farms distributed throughout the area to be attacked, supported by troops concealed in shell-holes.[1]

To meet these conditions every known "pill-box," farm, or fortified post had a specific body of troops detailed for its capture. The sole business of these troops was to follow the barrage until they reached their own particular objective, to overcome the enemy in the objective as quickly as possible, and then take their appointed place in the scheme of consolidation.

In addition, the very fullest use was made of the enormous artillery and vast supply of ammunition at the disposal of the Divisional commander. The part played

[1] To protect the troops in the shell-holes from the shrapnel barrage the Germans had about this time equipped them with body armour, proof against shrapnel bullets and against rifle bullets from a range of 400 yards and over. This armour, which could be worn either on the back or the front, according to whether a man was standing or lying down, proved too heavy and was soon discarded.

by the gunners in this attack was indeed considerable, the Divisional artillery, as usual, carrying out its allotted programme faultlessly.

Briefly the artillery plan was as follows : The barrage was organised in depth in four zones.

First came the main creeping barrage. This was fired by the 18-pounder batteries of the 255th, 256th, 58th and 59th Brigades, R.F.A., and advanced at the rate of 50 yards every two minutes for the first 200 yards, every three minutes up to the first objective, and finally 50 yards every four minutes up to the Blue line. In other words, the maximum average rate at which the infantry following the barrage could advance was 1500 yards per hour, the minimum 720 yards per hour—a cold-blooded operation which allows plenty of time for reflection.

The 18-pounders of two further brigades of artillery fired a creeping barrage 100 yards beyond the main barrage.

When the first objective had been captured, a pause in the advance of an hour was arranged, to allow time for cleaning up any pockets of the enemy still holding out, and for the troops for the final objective to move forward and deploy behind the barrage before it moved on. During this pause the No. 3 guns of each battery fired smoke shells, so that a screen of smoke was provided which concealed the infantry from the enemy's view.[1]

Two hundred yards beyond the creeping barrage came the combing barrage. This was composed of all the 18-pounder batteries of the 65th Brigade Army field artillery, while a further 300 yards beyond all the howitzer batteries of the artillery at the disposal of the Division were employed. The combing barrage dwelt on all " pill-boxes," strong posts, &c., and also worked up and down the communication trenches.

Beyond the combing barrage was a neutralising barrage of 6-inch howitzers and 60-pounder guns, which also dwelt on pill-boxes, &c.

Finally, there was a standing barrage of heavy howitzers and 60-pounder guns, which dwelt on avenues of approach or likely places for assembly of the enemy's reserves.

As the infantry advanced the whole of these different

[1] On the arrival of the first smoke shells the enemy, thinking they were some new form of frightfulness, put on gas masks.

barrages advanced also, so that by the time the infantry reached the Germans the latter had had during the morning a good sample of most of the types of shells employed by the British artillery.

Altogether this one brigade of infantry was supported by (*a*) twenty-two 18-pounder batteries, which fired 67,000 rounds on the day of the attack and the same number on the following day ; (*b*) six 4·5 howitzer batteries, which fired 14,000 rounds on the day of the attack and the same number on the following day ; (*c*) twelve batteries of 6-inch howitzers, which fired 5551 rounds during the first four and a half hours of the attack ; (*d*) the following batteries of heavy guns, which fired in the first four and a half hours the ammunition as stated :—

One battery 6-inch Mark VII. guns	114 rounds.
One battery 8-inch howitzers . .	114 ,,
One battery 9·2 guns . . .	49 ,,
Three batteries 9·2 howitzers . .	685 ,,
One 15-inch howitzer . . .	20 ,,

In addition, the 2-inch trench-mortar batteries and Stokes mortar batteries all joined in the bombardment, the latter firing 2700 rounds in the initial stages of the attack.

Before the attack barrage was opened the enemy's position was subjected to twenty-four hours intense bombardment.

The infantry were also preceded by a barrage fired by thirty-two machine-guns, which engaged all strong posts, pill-boxes, &c. Twenty machine-guns went forward and assisted in the consolidation of the captured positions.

Each of the three brigades had, previous to the attack, carried out a tour of duty in the line, while the 154th Brigade had also spent five days in practising the attack over a taped-out course representing the German trench system in full size. There had not been the same amount of time available for training as had been the case before the attack on 31st July ; platoons had, however, been constantly practised in attacking small objectives under cover of their own weapons—the rifle, the Lewis gun, rifle grenades, and the bomb. In this respect they had reached a high standard of efficiency.

Two objectives were selected, the first being the dotted

Blue line, the line of the Stroombeek continued in a northwest direction to Delta Huts. The final objective, the Blue line, was a line through Quebec Farm, Bavaroise House, Church Trench, Delta House. The 58th Division on the right and the 20th Division on the left were allotted similar objectives.

Brigadier-General J. G. H. Hamilton, D.S.O., commanding 154th Infantry Brigade, decided to attack on a two-battalion front. The plan of attack was that the two leading battalions, the 9th Royal Scots and the 4th Seaforth Highlanders, each on a two-company front, should take as far as the dotted Blue line; the 7th Argyll and Sutherland Highlanders and the 4th Gordon Highlanders were then to pass through the leading battalions, each on a three-company front, to the capture of the final objective.

Special parties were also detailed to go forward in rear of the attacking waves in the attack on the dotted Blue line, so as to be ready immediately to counter any attempt on the part of the enemy to counter-attack.

The 8th Argyll and Sutherland Highlanders, assembled about the river Steenbeek, and the 5th Seaforth Highlanders, assembled on the banks of the Canal de l'Yser, were held in readiness to move forward to assist the 154th Brigade should they be required.

Twelve tanks were allotted to the Division, but only one was able to come into action effectively against the enemy.

Facing the 154th Brigade was the 36th German Division, whose frontage almost corresponded with that of the Highland Division. The assembly was carried out successfully with casualties to 2 officers and 25 other ranks, after an arduous march. The ground through which the routes to the forward area lay had been badly ploughed up by shell-fire. The difficulties of traversing it were much aggravated by a heavy fall of rain, lasting for two hours, which occurred during the night. Each shell-hole became a miniature pond, while the natural marshes and pools increased in size, and the mud became softer and more slippery than ever. However, these were the normal conditions of the Ypres salient in those days, and the men were learning to expect nothing else.

MAP VII.—POELCAPPELLE, 20TH SEPTEMBER 1917.

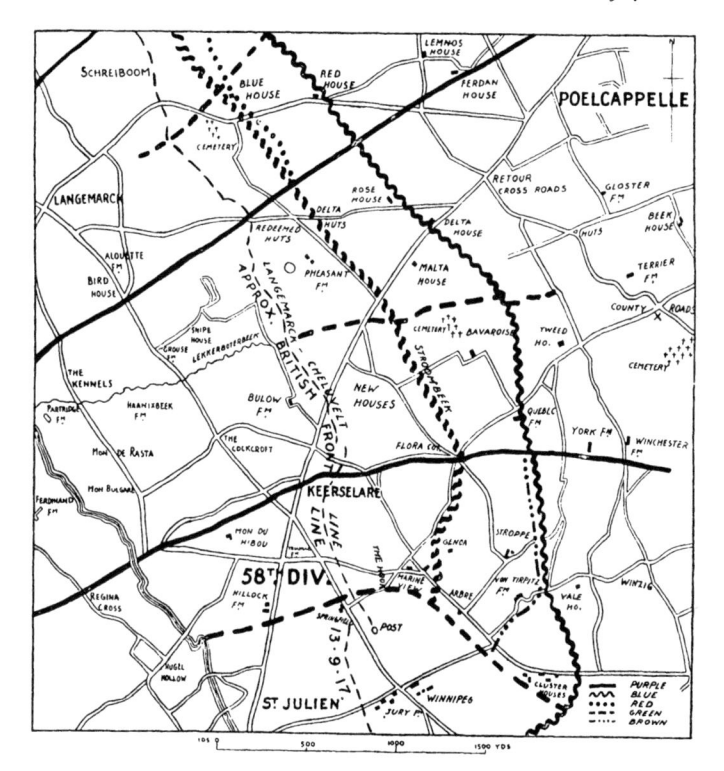

The attack was launched in the grey of the morning at 5.40 A.M.

In the first phase strong resistance was encountered in and in front of Pheasant Trench. On the right " A " and " B " companies of the 9th Royal Scots were engaged with rifle and machine-gun fire from the start. " A " company assisted by " C " Company, whose real objective was the dotted Blue line, advanced with the greatest skill and gallantry, moving from shell-hole to shell-hole in twos and threes, pouring into the German trenches rifle grenades and rifle fire. By this means they gained their objective, and enabled the advance to the dotted Blue line to be continued.

On the left, where " B " Company 9th Royal Scots, followed by " D " Company (dotted Blue line), was engaged, Pheasant Trench was occupied in the centre of the company front almost at once. The left two platoons of the company front reached the trench, but were heavily engaged by machine-gun fire, and returned to our lines. Thereupon the company commander, the battalion intelligence officer, and the artillery liaison officer rapidly reorganised the men, and led them forward again, accompanied by some of the 7th Argyll and Sutherland Highlanders, who were destined for the capture of the Blue line. Assisted by the platoon which had already gained a footing in Pheasant Trench, and which fought its way along the trench to its left flank, this party captured its objective. The gallantry and initiative of these officers and men bore important results, as had Pheasant Trench not been captured, the whole attack of the left battalion would have been held up, and the final objective could not have been reached. It was a typical example of that combination of tactical skill and gallantry which contributed so much towards the success of the Division.

The 4th Seaforth Highlanders on the left also encountered serious resistance, and hand-to-hand fighting developed in which they completely outmatched the Boches. It was in Pheasant Trench between Point 85 and the Lekkerboterbeek that they experienced the fiercest fighting. Here the trench was very strongly held, with newly-constructed posts in front, some being as much as forty yards in advance of it. Machine-guns were fired from the tops of blockhouses, while bombs and rifle-fire came from the trench itself. The company detailed for the capture of the trench advanced by twos and threes from shell-hole to shell-hole, rifle grenades, Lewis guns and rifles being freely used. Meanwhile the company detailed for the capture of the dotted Blue line, seeing what was afoot, moved round and attacked Pheasant Trench from a flank. The advance culminated in hand-to-hand fighting, in which the 4th Seaforth Highlanders signally triumphed.

Their left company was engaged by three machine-guns firing from Pheasant Trench and from a pill-box west of it. These were all knocked out, but not before thirty Germans had been killed who fought most gallantly round the pill-box.

After the capture of Pheasant Trench the advance on the dotted Blue line was continued. " C " Company of the 9th Royal Scots had some hard fighting round Flora Cot, in which they killed fifteen Germans. Later they came under enfilade fire from machine-guns on Hubner Farm (300 yards south of the Divisional right boundary). The company commander immediately detached two Lewis guns and two rifle sections to deal with Hubner Farm. This detachment fought for twenty minutes, during which they inflicted such losses on the occupants of the farm that the 2/8 London Regiment was able to capture it frontally.

On their left " D " Company of the 9th Royal Scots reached the Blue line successfully, but was much reduced in strength, having suffered serious casualties in the fighting round Pheasant Trench.

The 4th Seaforth Highlanders had little difficulty in capturing the Blue dotted line, and in consolidating according to prearranged plan. Pheasant Trench on both battalion fronts was in some parts literally choked with dead. In one stretch of about 200 yards in the left sector alone 150 German bodies were counted. Many dead were also found amongst the garrisons of the enemy's shell-hole posts, the artillery barrage having been most effective in this respect.

When one remembers the amount of shells which had been deluged on the Germans in the Pheasant Trench position, one cannot but admire the resolute manner in which they resisted our attack. It was indeed the strength of their resistance which made the capture of this line by the 4th Seaforths and 9th Royal Scots such a magnificent performance. One can gauge the severity of the fighting by the fact that so much rifle ammunition had been used by the infantry in this attack that 12,000 rounds had to be sent up to the parties consolidating the Blue line.

The enemy's barrage did not open until five minutes after the attack was launched, and was then particularly heavy on the area between our original front line and the Langemarck road.

Both the battalions detailed for the capture of the Blue line, the 4th Gordon Highlanders and the 7th Argyll and Sutherland Highlanders, had suffered serious casualties from having become involved in the fighting for Pheasant Trench before they formed up under the barrage. "D" Company of the 7th Argyll and Sutherland Highlanders had also suffered heavily from shell-fire when advancing from the old British front line.

The 7th Argyll and Sutherland Highlanders reached the Blue line after having overcome, chiefly by means of rifle grenades, Flora Cot, Quebec Farm, and Bavaroise House, capturing four machine-guns, of which one was turned on the enemy with good results, and about thirty prisoners.

The 4th Gordon Highlanders, who had already lost five officers before forming up under the barrage, had their first fight after the barrage moved forward at Pheasant Farm Cemetery. Here a lance-corporal was responsible for capturing two machine-guns and twenty-eight prisoners. Malta House, Rose House, and Delta House were all captured after stiff fighting, several machine-guns being destroyed.

By the time the 4th Gordon Highlanders had reached the Blue line, they had only three officers and six platoons of about ten men each in the front line; the remainder of the reserve company with two officers was therefore sent up as a reinforcement.

The situation on the left was a delicate one, as the neighbouring Division attacking on that flank had been unable to make progress, so that the two battalions on the left had between them to form a defensive flank some 1000 yards in depth. The Blue line was thus consolidated,

P

as had been intended, as far as Rose House, and the line then bent round towards White House.

The 9th Royal Scots reported that they could not supply the two platoons which they had been ordered to send to support the 7th Argyll and Sutherland Highlanders as counter-attack troops. Two platoons of the 8th Argyll and Sutherland Highlanders therefore moved forward in their place. Of these only thirty men reached their destination owing to heavy casualties suffered in passing through the hostile barrage.

Consolidation had not long been in progress before that series of enemy counter-attacks began which culminated in the late afternoon in a most determined assault backed by heavy masses.

Our advance had not seriously threatened the enemy's gun line; he was therefore able to employ his artillery fully throughout the operations. The valley of the Steenbeek was heavily and continuously shelled, and after the capture of the Blue line, the area subjected to heavy bombardment extended up to the Pheasant Trench Ridge and across the Stroombeek. In consequence many casualties were sustained by reserve troops, machine-gun teams, &c., moving forward, while heavy losses sustained by the runners made communication difficult.

In these days a runner, if he was to survive, had to be a runner in the true sense of the word. Starting from his platoon or company headquarters, during a battle, he stood a good chance of being shot, particularly by that unpleasantly accurate weapon the telescopic-sighted machine-gun. As soon as he was clear of the bullet zone he then had to dodge the shells, the shell with the instantaneous fuze, since it had a missile effect of several hundred yards, being a particularly difficult one to avoid.

Having delivered his message, he then had to return whence he came, and compete with the same risks on his return journey. The company and platoon runners were usually officers' servants, and belonged to that class which an agitated Press described as able-bodied men doing menial work.

It was not long before the enemy tested the strength of the defensive flank, and at 11.45 A.M. he made a demonstration against the left of the 4th Gordon Highlanders.

The defensive flank made short work of this attack. At 12.30 P.M. he repeated the experiment, but in greater numbers. The defensive flank again wiped out the attack. Meanwhile, so as to strengthen the line, "A" Company of the 8th Argyll and Sutherland Highlanders were sent forward as reinforcements, and were disposed two platoons on a line from the Poelcappelle road through Pheasant Farm Cemetery to north of Delta Huts, two platoons just west of the Poelcappelle road in Stroom Trench.

By this time Tank D 44 had reached a point on the Poelcappelle road near Malta House, where it broke down. It was therefore taken into use as a company headquarters. One Lewis gun from it was sent forward to Delta House, two were sent to Beer Trench, and one was retained in the tank, while 200 rounds of ammunition were distributed from it to each man in Beer Trench. A corporal was also detailed to work the tank's 6-pounder gun.

Throughout the morning machine-guns had been taking up their prearranged positions. On the right two were in action at Bavaroise House, two a hundred yards in front of Flora Cot, two between the Steenbeek and New House. On the left four were in the vicinity of Pheasant Farm Cemetery, two at Malta House, and one at Rose House.

During the afternoon, then, the Blue line was held along its length up to Rose House, where the line bent back forming a defensive flank, until touch was obtained with the Division on the left. The troops which had carried out the assault had been reinforced by two platoons of the 8th Argyll and Sutherland Highlanders, and the bulk of the machine-guns had reached the positions allotted to them for consolidation.

Meanwhile from the direction of Poelcappelle parties of the enemy moving from shell-hole to shell-hole in ones and twos were dribbling up through the afternoon towards the captured position, and concentrating for a counter-attack in dead ground. Further in rear, out of range of rifles and machine-guns, larger bodies of the enemy could be seen massing.

At 5 P.M. the counter-attack, accompanied by a barrage of unusual intensity, was fairly launched, the Houthulst, Poelcappelle, and Passchendaele groups of artillery all actively co-operating in support of the German infantry.

On the right the 451st Infantry Brigade of the 234th German Division advanced between York House and Tweed House, but it never reached the Blue line. In fact, the attack carried out by the regiment was completely broken by our artillery, rifle, and machine-gun fire, the artillery in particular causing heavy losses.

In the centre the 452nd Infantry Regiment of the 234th Division continued to attack, the 5th Grenadiers of the 36th Division and the 208th Division attacking on the battalion left flank. The attack was firmly held all along the line until the rifle and Lewis-gun ammunition, of which there had been an extraordinary expenditure, was exhausted. Rose House continued to hold out, but was isolated. After the front line had given, the three platoons of the 8th Argyll and Sutherland Highlanders north of the Lekkerboterbeek held firm and broke up attack after attack, punishing the enemy severely. On their right, after every officer of the 4th Gordon Highlanders who had taken part in the initial attack had become a casualty, the small party in Beer Trench gave. Malta House was next overwhelmed, and the platoon garrisoning Stroom Trench was forced back.

About 6 P.M. a general withdrawal of the troops inside the V formed by the Poelcappelle road and the Lekkerboterbeek took place.

During this withdrawal the local commanders, realising the necessity of reducing the area of the enemy penetration to a minimum, formed defensive flanks. On the right "C" Company 7th Argyll and Sutherland Highlanders, two platoons of the 8th Argyll and Sutherland Highlanders, and "D" Company of the 9th Royal Scots; and on the left the 8th Argyll and Sutherland Highlanders and the 4th Seaforth Highlanders, were all so disposed as to pin the enemy into the V; in this position he was caught under enfilade fire from both flanks, and suffered heavily.

Meanwhile the troops who had withdrawn from the V were rallied, and having collected ammunition from the dead and wounded, were led forward from Pheasant Trench. At the same time the company of the 8th Argyll and Sutherland Highlanders which earlier had been sent forward to assist in countering any enemy counter-attack, also launched an attack from the same trench. This attack was successful in clearing the enemy out of the angle of the V, and it left him with his farthest point of penetration about Point 82 on the Poelcappelle road.

The front line was then reorganised so as to run from a point 500 yards north of Delta Huts through Pheasant Farm Cemetery on the south side of Point 82 to the Lekkerboterbeek, thence along the stream until it joined the original Blue line.

As soon as it was dusk the remaining company of the 8th Argyll and Sutherland Highlanders was brought up to reinforce the left, and consolidation was continued throughout the night.

During the same night the Germans found that the 452nd Regiment which had penetrated the V had been so severely handled that it was necessary for them to be relieved. Accordingly the 371st Infantry Regiment from a fresh Division took over from them.

The position remained substantially unaltered until the night of the 21-22nd, when the 152nd Infantry Brigade relieved the 154th.

During the afternoon of 23rd September an intense barrage broke out all along the brigade front, culminating just after 7 P.M. in a heavy German attack. This attack came from south of Poelcappelle towards the centre of the position.

The enemy first advanced in great columns, and while extending to the south and east of Malta House, were caught in an artillery barrage and in the fire of Lewis guns and Vickers guns and rifles.

As a result the attack melted away, and the morning disclosed the enemy's dead strewn in heaps about Malta House. The right battalion, the 6th Seaforth Highlanders, had most opportunities of inflicting losses on the enemy, and fully availed itself of them. One company alone had five Lewis guns firing on the enemy at the same moment, of which one fired twenty-eight drums.

Later the left battalion, the 5th Seaforth Highlanders, carried out some satisfactory shooting. On one occasion in the early morning they arose to find a platoon of forty strong, in marching order, advancing within close range of them. They immediately wiped it out. On another occasion they inflicted by enfilade fire such heavy losses on a storm trupp attempting to raid the 12th Battalion King's Royal Rifles on their left that the survivors of the storm trupp, twenty-three in number, ran towards the King's Royal Rifles with their hands up and surrendered.

The total casualties to the Division during the operations were 45 officers and 1110 other ranks, the 154th Brigade, which carried out the attack, losing 32 officers and 891 other ranks, and the 4th Gordon Highlanders 12 officers.

On 26th September the 152nd Infantry Brigade was relieved by the 32nd Infantry Brigade, 11th Division, and on the 27th the G.O.C., 11th Division, took over the command of the line.

This battle affords an admirable illustration of the economic use of troops. It must be remembered that only five battalions were employed in the attack and subsequent counter-attacks; that these five battalions—though through want of ammunition they did not hold their entire gains—had established themselves for a while in their final objective, and had accounted for every German garrisoning the area allotted to them for attack. Moreover, these battalions were fighting not only facing their front, but also facing their left flank, as the Division on their left had not made equal progress in the attack. That it was possible for so few men to do what they did was due to two things: first, to the combination of gallantry and skill on the part of the men and the leadership and initiative on the part of the officers and N.C.O.'s. The men had been trained in the use of ground, movement supported by fire, and in platoon tactics in general, and they put what they had learned into practice from the outset of the attack. The enemy fought bravely, perhaps as bravely as our men, but he was outmatched in tactical skill, and was in consequence defeated.

Secondly, the handling of the troops by the senior commanders was such as to forestall every move on the part of the enemy. It was anticipated that the enemy would do his utmost to prevent us from making ground towards Poelcappelle, and rightly so, for on the evening of the attack nine out of ten battalions massed against the XVIIIth Corps were directed against the 51st. The Divisional commander, having rightly appreciated the situation, solved absolutely the problems connected with the two important factors of time and space,—the problem of having the right number of troops at the right place at the right time. The reserve did not require to be moved after the enemy had disclosed his intentions; but his intentions were anticipated, so that in each case reserve troops (counter-counter-attack troops) were ready to deal with hostile enterprises. Thus the weak points in the line were strengthened before they were threatened and not after the line had been pierced, and the main counter-attack was delivered by the 8th Argyll and Sutherland Highlanders while the enemy's troops were still on the move and before they had had time to reorganise or consolidate their gains. In fact, the Germans were on this occasion completely outmatched in generalship, leadership, tactical skill, and skill at arms.

On the conclusion of these operations, the following messages were received :—

1. From Lieut.-General Sir I. Maxse, K.C.B., D.S.O., commanding XVIIIth Corps.

" Before the 51st (Highland) Division quits the XVIIIth Corps, I desire to express to its commander and to all ranks in the Division how highly I have appreciated their services throughout three months of strenuous fighting.

" What has struck me most is the thoroughness of the organisation within the Division, and the fact that all usual war problems have been thought out beforehand, discussed in detail, and are embodied in simple doctrines well known to all ranks. The result is the Division fights with gallantry, and can be depended upon to carry out any reasonable task allotted to it in any battle. For this reason I venture to place it among the three best fighting Divisions I have met in France during the past three years.

" Its record in this Corps comprises :—

" (1) *On 31st July* 1917, a shattering assault on High Command Redoubt, the capture in their entirety of three separate systems of German defence lines, an advance of two miles in depth into hostile territory, and the consolidation and retention of the line of the river Steenbeek and all the objectives allotted to the Division.

" (2) *On the 20th September* 1917, an assault on a sector

of the Langemarck-Gheluvelt line which had resisted capture for more than a month, an incursion into hostile territory, and the consolidation of important hills south-west of Poelcappelle and at Bavaroise House. The same afternoon these two hills were repeatedly attacked by five Prussian battalions, all of whom were defeated with sanguinary losses.

" In conclusion, I wish good luck to all ranks, and hope to serve with them again in this war."

    2. From General Sir H. de la P. Gough, K.C.B., K.C.V.O., commanding Fifth Army.

" In bidding farewell to the Highland Division, the Army Commander wishes to express his great admiration for and appreciation of their splendid record during the fighting of the past two months.

" Their fine advance, their gallant defence of ground, even against repeated enemy attacks, and the severe punishment they inflicted on the enemy during the last battle, will ever remain one of their proudest records, and has helped materially towards the enemy's final defeat. He heartily wishes them all success in the future. Scotland for ever."

CHAPTER XIII.

THE BATTLE OF CAMBRAI.

AFTER relief in the Ypres salient the Division, less its artillery, moved to the VIth Corps area, with headquarters at Achiet le Petit. By 5th October, ten days after coming out of their last battle, the 154th and 153rd Brigades were back in the trenches in the Heninel-Wancourt sector, with Divisional headquarters at Boisleux au Mont.

On this occasion the Division was for the first time introduced to the area which the Germans had wilfully devastated prior to their withdrawal from it to the Hindenburg line just before the battle of Arras.

One cannot do better than allow a German newspaper, the 'Local Anzeiger' of 18th March 1917, to describe this area. It says : " In the course of these last months great stretches of French territory have been turned by us into a dead country. It varies in width from ten, twelve, to thirteen kilometres, and extends along the whole of our new positions. No village or farm was left standing, no road was left passable, no railway track or embankment was left in being. Where once were woods, there are gaunt rows of stumps ; the wells have been blown up. In front of our new positions runs like a gigantic ribbon our Empire of Death."

One could not fail to appreciate the diabolical efficiency with which the work had been carried out. Where time had been too short to enable fruit-trees to be felled, their bark had been ringed. Wells before destruction had been turned into cess-pits. The effect on every unit on first entering the devastated area was the same. It produced a determination in all ranks to kill every German that it was possible to put out of the world with any degree of decency. By this wanton act of vandalism the Hun had turned himself, in the eyes of the British soldier, into a vermin fit only for extermination.

"Our new positions" mentioned above were the Hindenburg Line. The Hindenburg Line was not a line in the true sense of the word, since, in addition to having length, it also had considerable breadth. It was, in fact, a highly-elaborated system of trenches running roughly from St Quentin to just south of Arras. The trenches were skilfully sited, so as to have every advantage of observation; they were of immense breadth and depth; they contained numerous concrete machine-gun emplacements and dugouts; they were connected with one another by underground tunnels; they were protected by tremendous belts of wire many yards in depth. Yet, in spite of the skill with which it had been constructed, several portions of the Hindenburg Line were twice captured by the British army.

From this point onwards the Highland Division was so continuously involved in important operations that space cannot be given to detailed accounts of uneventful periods in quiet parts of the line. It must, however, be understood that uneventful is a relative term, and that even the quiet periods were often eventful enough for those in immediate contact with the enemy.

As regards the sojourn in the Boisleux au Mont area, suffice it to say that all three brigades carried out tours of duty in the line there, and that the Division was relieved on 2nd November. On completion of this relief the Division moved to Hermaville, the infantry brigades being billeted at Warlus, Hauteville, and Izel les Hameaux.

Prior to taking over the line in this sector a change in command had taken place in the 154th Brigade. Brigadier-General J. G. H. Hamilton, D.S.O., who had commanded the brigade since General Stewart's death in September 1916, gave up his command, and returned home for a period of rest. General Hamilton had come to the brigade from the command of a battalion, and had been with it through many trying ordeals, including Beaumont Hamel, Courcelette, Arras, and Ypres. By many of his officers, both senior and junior, he was regarded not only as their brigade commander, but also as an intimate friend, and his departure was in consequence keenly felt.

THE BATTLE OF CAMBRAI

He was succeeded by Brigadier-General K. G. Buchanan, D.S.O., Seaforth Highlanders. General Buchanan possessed not only consummate judgment in all matters of tactics, but also a charming personality, with the result that his brigade throughout the period of his command could be relied on to render a splendid account of itself. His coolness in action and his tactical instincts enabled him so to dispose his troops in the varying phases of a battle that they were always ready to meet any sudden emergency. Moreover, his personality was such that officers and men would at all times make any sacrifice to carry out what he asked of them. The magnificent resistance offered by the 154th Brigade on the right flank of the Division both in March and again in April of 1918 afford in themselves ample proof of General Buchanan's powers as an infantry commander.

The Division had not been long in rest in its new area before it transpired that it was again required to take part in active operations. The news that this was the case came rather as a shock, as the Division had already fought battles in the year 1917 on 9-12th April, 23-24th April, 16th May, 31st July-1st August, 20-23rd September, and had lost in casualties since 9th April 457 officers and 9966 other ranks—a total of 10,523.

Moreover, the forthcoming operations were to be of an experimental nature, since the plan of attack was to attempt to break through the Hindenburg Line by employing a large number of tanks in an offensive which was to be a complete surprise.

To quote Sir Douglas Haig's despatch : " The object of these operations was to gain a local success at a point where the enemy did not expect it. Our repeated attacks in Flanders, and of our Allies elsewhere, had brought about large concentrations of the enemy's forces on the threatened points, with a consequent reduction in the garrisons of certain other sectors of the line. Of these weakened sectors the Cambrai front had been selected as the most suitable for the surprise operations in contemplation."

In order to maintain this element of surprise up to the last moment, various measures had to be taken. In the first place, the Division was left in its present quarters in the neighbourhood of Hermaville, so as not to draw the attention of the enemy to the area to be attacked. For the same reason the usual full-sized replica of the enemy's trenches was taped out west of the town of Arras, and all training took place in that area.

Further, the Division was not allowed to take over the trenches from which it was to deliver the attack. It had therefore little opportunity for preliminary reconnaissances of the battle area, with the exception that parties of officers and N.C.O.'s daily visited the trenches to spy out the land. These parties were all clothed in trousers to prevent the enemy's observers from suspecting the presence of the Highland Division in the neighbourhood of the position to be attacked.

The Division was given every opportunity of practising the attack with tanks, the platoons carrying out their training with the actual tanks and crews which were to accompany them in the operations. It will be seen that, as usual, liaison was synonymous with success, and that on the day of the attack the co-operation between the tanks and the infantry was admirable.

An additional difficulty lay in the fact that somehow or another the Division had to be concentrated in the battle area some thirty-six to forty-eight hours before the battle, so as to allow the troops adequate rest before proceeding to the assembly trenches.

On this account the C.R.E. and the three field companies, R.E., with the 8th Royal Scots, moved to the IVth Corps area early in November to prepare hidden shelters in which the troops might be accommodated during this period. The sappers and pioneers worked with such effect that between the 2nd and 19th November camouflaged accommodation had been provided for 5500 men in the ruined village of Metz and for 4000 men in Havrincourt Wood. The necessary dumps of material were also formed by the C.R.E., tracks for moving guns forward prepared, and, as cavalry were also detailed to take part in the operations, six water points with a capacity for watering 7000 horses per hour were constructed. Forward routes for infantry were also laid out and advanced dressing stations completed; no mean record for a little over a fortnight's work.

All undertakings of this nature were made more difficult than usual by the fact that no increase in the normal

THE BATTLE OF CAMBRAI

amount of lorry traffic on the roads during the hours of daylight was allowed. Further, no new work was carried out in the forward area, in case it might be noticed by enemy airmen. As it turned out, the weather was fortunately cloudy and misty, so that observation from the air became practically impossible throughout the period of preparation.

The area through which the Division was destined to advance was traversed by three separate trench systems, each forming integral parts of the Hindenburg system. Of these, the first, known as the Hindenburg front system, was composed of a maze of wide, heavily-wired trenches, supplemented by numerous saps, the whole presenting such a tangle of excavations that it was impossible to foretell accurately where the principle points of resistance were most likely to be found.

The main framework of this front system was, however, composed of a lightly-held outpost line, a front line, and a support line.

In rear of the front system, and just south of the village of Flesquières, lay the Hindenburg support system, composed of two lines of heavily-wired deep trenches, connected with each other and with the front system by numerous communication trenches.

Four thousand yards in rear of the support system lay a third double line of trenches, south-west of the village of Cantaing. The area allotted to the Division was not uniform in shape, being in the Hindenburg front system 1500 yards in breadth, 2700 yards at the second system, 3500 yards at the third, and ending just north of the village of Fontaine Notre Dame at a breadth of 2200 yards.

Our assembly trenches rested on the summit of a spur, from which the country gradually sloped down to the Grand Ravine, a feature which traversed the Divisional front just north of the Hindenburg front system.

From here it switchbacked up to the village of Flesquières, thence it declined in a series of gentle undulations to Cantaing and Fontaine Notre Dame.

Just west of Fontaine stood Bourlon Wood, a hanging wood on the summit and slopes of a spur, from which the whole countryside could be surveyed, and from which it was always difficult to hide.

The position to be attacked was, in the first instance, divided into three main objectives : the Blue line, which included the Hindenburg front system and Chapel Trench ; the Brown line, which included Flesquières and the Hindenburg support system ; and the Red dotted line, which was the sunken road running from Marcoing to Graincourt.

For the first phase, the plan was for the Division to attack on a two-brigade front, the 152nd Brigade on the right, the 153rd on the left. Each brigade was to work on a two-battalion front, the leading two battalions to take as far as the Blue line in the case of the 153rd Brigade, and the Grand Ravine in the case of the 152nd Brigade.

The order of battle of the leading battalions from right to left was as follows : 5th Seaforth Highlanders, 8th Argyll and Sutherland Highlanders, 6th Black Watch, 5th Gordon Highlanders. The remaining battalions of the two brigades were detailed for the capture of the Brown and Red dotted lines, the order of battle from right to left being 6th Gordon Highlanders, 6th Seaforth Highlanders, 7th Black Watch, 7th Gordon Highlanders.

Each battalion taking part in the attack of the Blue line detailed two companies for the capture of the enemy front system up to Mole Trench, a third company to cross the Grand Ravine, while the fourth company was kept in reserve. The battalions detailed for the capture of the Brown and dotted Red lines allotted objectives to each of their four companies.

For the first day's fighting, seventy-two of the 1st Brigade Tank Corps were allotted to the Divisional front, of which seventy actually took part in the operation. One-half of the tanks, "E" Battalion, were allotted to 152nd Brigade, the other half, "D" Battalion, to the 153rd.

They were divided into three waves. The first, formed of twelve "Rovers" or wire-crushers, moved forward at zero, 150 yards in advance of the second, to crush the wire protecting the enemy front and support trenches, and then to engage machine-guns and any special posts outside the main trenches. The second wave, formed of thirty-six "Fighting" tanks, dealt with the trenches up to and including the Blue line. The third, composed of all the remaining fighting tanks, was detailed to form up an hour and a half after zero just south of the Grand Ravine,

THE BATTLE OF CAMBRAI

and to proceed with the survivors of the first two to attack the Flesquières Ridge.

The distribution was on the basis of one section of three tanks to a platoon frontage (*i.e.*, about 150 yards). The general principle on which sections were to work was for the two outside tanks to cross a trench, turn alongside it and help to clear it, while the centre tanks carried on to the next trench, there to be joined by the two others as soon as the infantry had reached the first trench.

However, in tackling a system which contained many crater posts and sapheads, and which was thickly interlaced with short communication trenches and backed by many subsidiary trenches and detached posts, some modifications of the general principles were necessary.

Special tasks were therefore given to many of the second wave sections of tanks, in which each tank was given some saphead, crater post, or communication trench to deal with in addition to assailing the main trenches.

Similarly, detailed instructions were given as to routes and individual objectives in the village fighting that was anticipated.

Each tank carried on its back a huge fascine or faggot, resting on a giant pair of arms. A contrivance existed by which these arms raised the fascines off the back of the tank, and dropped them into any unusually wide trenches encountered, so as to form a stepping-stone, which enabled the tanks to keep their noses from dropping into the bottom of the trench.

In spite of this precaution the Hindenburg Line was in some parts so broad and deep that a number of tanks were ditched in spite of the fascines.

The first wave of the infantry followed the tanks at a distance of 150-200 yards, their orders being to assault immediately the tanks reached and opened fire on a trench. On reaching their objectives, the infantry marked with red strips of cloth the gaps in the wire, and filled in portions of the trenches to make crossing-places for subsequent tanks, cavalry, and artillery.

Each tank carried for the use of the infantry Lewis gun drums, rifle ammunition, bombs, and rifle grenades.

The field artillery supporting the attacks was divided into two groups, each composed of two field artillery brigades and one R.H.A. brigade. Each brigade was supported by one of these groups, that containing 256th Brigade, R.F.A., being on the right and that containing 255th Brigade, R.F.A., on the left.

One brigade of artillery covered each battalion front, while the 3rd Brigade of artillery covered its whole infantry brigade front. The fifteen 18-pounder batteries firing in the creeping barrage fired 33 per cent of smoke shells, so as to screen the movement of the tanks.

Two 4·5 howitzer batteries also kept a standing smoke barrage in front of Flesquières Ridge.

No registration was carried out, so that the presence of fresh batteries in the area might not be disclosed. The whole of the firing was therefore carried out from the map and by calibration.

The concentration of artillery, tanks, and infantry immediately behind the line from which the attack was to be launched was successfully effected between 17th and 19th November with great rapidity and complete secrecy, mainly under cover of darkness.

The artillery was moved up on 17th November; the tanks were assembled on the night of 18th November in Havrincourt Wood, and travelled to their assembly positions in the early hours of the 20th. The infantry came into Metz on the evening of the 18th, and began taking over the line on the 19th.

It must be borne in mind that a similar concentration of tanks, guns, and troops was taking place simultaneously on the fronts of Divisions on either flank. The fact that all the necessary moves took place, and that the troops were eventually formed up in the assembly trenches without any suspicions being aroused in the mind of the enemy, shows how admirably the arrangements for ensuring secrecy were carried out.

A taped line was laid out in front of the assembly trenches to ensure that the main wave of tanks formed up on its proper alignment. By zero hour the bulk of them were on this line, while the remainder which had been delayed from one cause and another were crossing the British front line.

The twelve " Rovers " were formed up beyond this line, the third wave being deployed behind the support line.

THE BATTLE OF CAMBRAI

The platoons to form the first two waves in the attack took over the line on the morning of the 19th, and thus had an opportunity of viewing the ground to their front. At midnight the remainder of the four leading battalions arrived in their assembly trenches.

Before zero hour the four battalions for the later stages of the initial attack were assembled in rear of the trench area, with their leading platoons on the Charing Cross-Trescault road.

As soon as darkness set in the platoons which had arrived first set to work to make causeways across their trenches for the passage of the tanks. They also freed the troops that were to assemble during the night from any chances of confusion and unnecessary fatigue by placing in position red lamps, flags, signboards, and markers to show routes and positions of platoons.

Before zero hour all ranks were issued with a hot meal.

Naturally considerable anxiety was felt, as it was feared that the noise of the engines of the assembling tanks might be heard by the enemy and cause him to open a heavy bombardment of our trenches. However, though a light southerly breeze carried the noise made by the seventy tanks on the move towards the enemy, there was between 2 A.M. and 6 A.M. only slight hostile artillery activity, and that only on the left front.

During the whole period of assembly there were a few casualties in the forward battalions of the 153rd Brigade, and none on the 152nd Brigade front.

At 6.30 A.M., 20th November, the advance began on a fine but cloudy morning, the visibility being such that a man could be seen at a distance of about 200 yards. As the artillery barrage opened, the twelve wire-crushing tanks moved off, accompanied by small parties of infantry detailed for the capture of the outpost line.

Four minutes later a light artillery barrage came down on and just in front of our assembly trenches, causing slight casualties. Considerable hostile machine-gun fire was also opened, but it was wild and harmless. Between 9.15 and 9.40 A.M. all the leading battalions had reached their objectives.

The 5th Seaforth Highlanders on the right carried out their advance practically without a check, making a bag of 9 machine-guns and 230 prisoners, including 14 officers. The total number of casualties sustained by the battalion in this operation was twenty-five.

On arrival at the railway, " A " Company, 5th Seaforth Highlanders, found that the situation at Ribécourt was obscure, hostile machine-guns still being active there. Lance-Corporal R. MacBeath was therefore sent out with a patrol to report on the situation. Having proceeded 150 yards from his company MacBeath discovered the first machine-gun, and killed the gunner with his revolver. A tank then arrived and drove the teams of some of the other machine-guns down a deep dug-out. MacBeath bounded down the dug-out steps after them, killed a German who resisted him on the staircase, and drove the remainder—3 officers and 30 other ranks—out of the dug-out by another exit. Sending these men to the rear as prisoners, he again entered the dug-out and thoroughly searched it, accounting for two more Germans. In all, five machine-guns were found mounted round the dug-out, which proved to be a battalion headquarters.

The capture of these guns not only freed the right flank of the 5th Seaforth Highlanders, but also considerably helped the advance of the 9th Norfolks on the right.

For his courage and initiative on this occasion MacBeath was awarded the Victoria Cross.

The 8th Argyll and Sutherland Highlanders had rather more fighting than the 5th Seaforth Highlanders, as active machine-guns and bombing-posts were encountered in the first and second German lines and between them.

In the case of the former the Argylls overcame the resistance by advancing in short rushes, while the advent of the tanks encouraged the enemy to surrender in other parts of the front. During these operations a private soldier led his platoon to its objective in Mole Trench, his platoon commander and two sergeants having become casualties as the advance began.

On the left of the 8th Argyll and Sutherland Highlanders the 6th Black Watch met no resistance until they had passed the Hindenburg front line. In the later stages of their advance many machine-guns had to be tackled.

The front line proved a serious obstacle to the tanks, in spite of their fascines, four of them becoming ditched in it on this battalion front. In consequence, portions of the second wave came under close-range machine-gun fire. Of these guns one was disposed of by a sergeant, who, crawling forward, threw a hand-grenade amongst its team. The remainder were destroyed with the assistance of tanks.

In the advance to Mole Trench further resistance was encountered by the 6th Black Watch. First two machine-gun posts on the right held up the advance; but in one case a sergeant, in the other a corporal, worked forward alone and knocked out the teams with hand-grenades.

On the left the advance was held up by uncut wire; but the infantry summoned by signals three third-wave tanks from the next battalion front, which crushed the wire and enabled the advance to be continued.

On arrival in Mole Trench the 6th Black Watch were raked with enfilade machine-gun fire from Sammy's Trench. A platoon was therefore immediately detached, which, advancing by section rushes under cover of the fire of its Lewis guns, wiped out the entire garrison of Sammy's Trench. The Germans here offered a magnificent resistance, and fought until the last man was killed.

Still further fighting occurred, heavy machine-gun and rifle fire being opened on the advancing 6th Black Watch from the Grand Ravine. Individual skill and initiative were again displayed. The first machine-gun was put out of action by a private soldier, who, working towards it alone, killed five and wounded two of the team with rifle grenades. A tank at that moment arrived, and the Grand Ravine was cleared, 6 officers and 100 other ranks being taken prisoner.

Meanwhile Lieut.-Colonel N. D. Campbell, commanding this battalion, in making a reconnaissance of the captured ground, came across a dug-out which had not previously been noticed, and with the help of his orderly captured twelve prisoners in it.

On the extreme left the 5th Gordon Highlanders made a surprisingly big bag in the outpost line, capturing 21 prisoners in one saphead, and capturing or killing 22 in another. The Hindenburg front line was entered without difficulty with the tanks, the bulk of the garrison having run back to Triangle Support. Up to this point 2 machine-guns and 200 prisoners had been captured.

It was some time before the garrison of Triangle Support could be overcome, as only one second-wave tank on the battalion front managed to cross the Hindenburg front line.

Subsequently the resistance collapsed on the arrival of some third-wave tanks, but not before odd platoons had gallantly fought their way into the trench.

Wood Trench and Mole Trench were occupied without particular effort; but beyond Mole Trench lay a sunken road, into which large numbers of the enemy had fled at the first sight of the tanks. This road was cleared with the assistance of a tank, which did magnificent execution with its 6-pounder gun, shell after shell bursting in the midst of parties of panic-stricken Germans.

By this time the 7th Black Watch, who were detailed to pass through the 5th Gordon Highlanders for the second phase of the attack, came up, and with some of the latter crossed the Grand Ravine and moved towards Chapel Trench. Here again the Germans fought stubbornly, some 40 of them being killed before the trench was occupied. The 5th Gordon Highlanders thus arrived on their objectives, having captured a total of 10 machine-guns, 2 trench-mortars, and 400 prisoners, including a battalion commander complete with his staff.

So far the attack had proceeded smoothly enough, but in the next phase the conditions under which the advance was to be carried out changed considerably. Up to the present the main difficulty of the tanks had been the width and depth of the trenches which they had to traverse, effective action against them on the part of the enemy having been negligible.

In the next stage the advance was to be carried out through the enemy's gun line, with the result that the tanks had not only to contend with the crossing of the trenches, but were also exposed to the close-range fire of field-guns. As the infantry depended absolutely and entirely on the tanks for the crushing of the large belts of wire opposed to them, any losses sustained by the tanks, as will be seen, seriously prejudiced the infantry's chances of success.

The enemy's support system, which was to be overcome in the next bound, consisted of a strong fire-trench known as the Hindenburg Support, protected by two to four belts

THE BATTLE OF CAMBRAI

of heavy wire, and supported by a trench some 100 yards in rear known as Flesquières Trench—a trench in many places shallow, and protected by little wire. Of these the former lay on the crest of the Flesquières Ridge, and the latter just behind it. Both skirted a chateau at the south-west corner of the village, which, with its walls and wooded grounds, offered great possibilities for concealed defences.

On the right, the 6th Gordon Highlanders advanced on a two-company front, the leading two companies being detailed for the capture of the Hindenburg support system. These companies were preceded by six tanks. On arriving at the enemy wire the tanks came within view of a field battery some 500 yards distant, which immediately opened on them, and by a succession of direct hits knocked out all six in the space of a few minutes, an admirable exhibition of shooting on the part of the German gunners.

Owing to the formation of the enemy's entanglements, which projected in irregular V shapes for over 180 yards from the trench, the infantry did not appreciate, until they were held up by the wire, that the tanks had failed to penetrate it. In this position they were suddenly swept by close-range machine-gun fire, and in a few moments had lost some sixty men killed and wounded.

As a farther advance in face of the uncut wire was out of the question, the companies were immediately withdrawn to Station Avenue and the sunken Ribécourt-Flesquières road. An advance up Station Avenue was then organised with the intention of breaking into the Hindenburg support line on the right and of working inwards along it. Though it turned out that Station Avenue did not join up with the Hindenburg support line, one platoon was successful in dashing across the open, entering the support line, and capturing two machine-guns. This platoon, in attempting to work along the trench towards its left flank, found portions of it so shallow that they could not continue their advance in face of the intense machine-gun fire coming from Flesquières.

Meanwhile the remaining two companies of the 6th Gordon Highlanders had been collected in the Ribécourt-Flesquières sunken road.

The 6th Seaforth Highlanders fared better. Seven tanks on the left and centre of the battalion front passed through the wire, and enabled the left company to enter the trench with only three casualties.

On the right of the battalion front the tanks appear to have lost their direction, as no gaps were cut in the wire. "C" Company, however, discovered a gap on their left flank, and having passed through it, pushed on towards the trench. Here they had some severe fighting before they finally established themselves in it, inflicting heavy losses on the enemy and capturing many prisoners.

This company then tried to force their way along the Hindenburg support line towards their right to join up with the 6th Gordon Highlanders. By leaving the trench and running along the parapet, shooting and bombing the Germans, they cleared some fifty yards of the trench. The rifle and machine-gun fire from Flesquières, however, became so heavy that they were forced to take to the trench again and establish a bombing-block on their flanks between them and the enemy.

While this fighting was in progress the surviving tanks were pushing on towards Flesquières Trench; but they, too, came under artillery fire, and were knocked out by direct hits.

The personnel of the tanks suffered heavy losses, as in some cases the tanks burst into flames on being struck by a shell, and their crews were burnt to death before help could be brought to them. There is no need to describe the sufferings of the unfortunate men who died in this manner, imprisoned in the flaming tanks.

The tanks which still survived shortly became non-effective for the time being owing to shortage of petrol. The crews which survived, however, still continued to assist the infantry after their tanks were out of action. For example, 2nd Lieutenant Blow, after his tank, the Edward II., was struck by a shell, took his Lewis guns from it, placed one in action at the head of a communication trench, and himself fired a Lewis gun from the roof of his tank until the gun became too hot to hold. He then attached himself to the Seaforths for the remainder of the action.

The second wave of the 6th Seaforth Highlanders, in spite of a heavy fire directed against them from Flesquières Trench, made repeated attempts to enter it, in which all officers except one per company became casualties.

THE BATTLE OF CAMBRAI

One officer in particular, 2nd Lieutenant Donald Grant, displayed great courage and initiative in his efforts to gain his objective. Leading his platoon along a communication trench, east of Flesquières Wood, he drove the enemy before him, bayoneting many himself. When all his men but one were casualties, he climbed out of his communication trench and attempted to rush Flesquières Trench from above ground. He and his companion were, however, immediately shot dead.

The 7th Gordon Highlanders, just as they had done at Beaumont Hamel and again at the chemical works, carried their advance to the farthest point reached in the attack. They made short work of the Hindenburg Support, where they picked up 100 prisoners. On approaching Flesquières Trench their tanks became subjected to close-range field-gun fire, and drew most of the fire of the riflemen and machine-gunners. The infantry were thus able to enter the trench and establish themselves in it after some heavy fighting.

On the right at first only one section gained a lodgment in this trench, but a platoon advancing over the area which the section had just traversed followed it into the trench, and then fought its way along it with bombs and rifles until it reached the battalion right boundary.

The next waves thus passed on to assault the village, unsupported by tanks, and in the face of a terrific fire. At one period they were able to sweep the main street of the village with Lewis-gun fire; but subjected to machine-gun fire from all sides, they could not maintain their position, and were forced back into Flesquières Trench.

The Germans then delivered a counter-attack against the right of the 7th Gordon Highlanders, and forced them out of Flesquières Trench, which in this sector was in many places only a few inches deep.

The 7th Gordon Highlanders were thus left, holding the Hindenburg support line throughout the battalion front, and with three platoons in Flesquières Trench.

The 7th Black Watch on the left flank of the Division encountered a series of misfortunes. In the first place, two of their tanks were ditched in crossing the front line. Secondly, before encountering Hindenburg support line, they met tremendous resistance from Cemetery Alley.

Here both their second and third waves became involved in heavy fighting, and after a severe engagement, in which the attackers were subjected to a considerable volume of machine-gun fire from Cemetery Ridge, the trench was captured with 200 prisoners.

Hindenburg support line was thus successfully captured in conjunction with tanks; but on crossing this trench, all the remaining tanks were knocked out. As uncut wire lay in front of them, and a great volume of fire was being directed against them from the village, the waves could not continue their advance. Attempts were made to get forward by small parties, but with no success, and the battalion was ordered to consolidate its gains as it stood.

At this stage the prospects of a farther advance were not good. The German gunner, always an unpleasantly efficient person, seemed to have got the measure of the tanks, and without them it appeared impossible in the near future to give the advance further impetus.

Meanwhile, Lieut.-Colonel S. MacDonald, D.S.O., commanding the 6th Seaforth Highlanders, had arrived at the Hindenburg support line, and had reorganised his two companies there for further efforts. He found that the village, wood, and chateau were a series of strong nests of machine-guns. However, employing tanks in the vicinity, which had run out of petrol, to open on the village with their 6-pounders and Lewis guns, he led his battalion forward in person, and gained a foothold in Flesquières Trench, which extended from the Ribécourt-Flesquières road for 300 yards to the left.

From this position Colonel MacDonald, showing splendid qualities of leadership, organised two determined attempts to reach the village under cover of rifle and Lewis-gun fire. Though one or two machine-guns were put out of action, the intense fire which this enterprise attracted from the high walls of the chateau grounds and the houses in the village, checked the advance on both occasions. During one of these attempts a private soldier, single-handed, killed the team of a machine-gun and carried the gun back to the British lines.

About 5 P.M. seven more tanks arrived, of which six entered the village. They were not, however, sufficiently closely supported by the infantry, and the attack failed.

THE BATTLE OF CAMBRAI

The enemy, with great cunning, offered no resistance to the tanks in the streets, either lying motionless in his emplacements or retiring into dug-outs and cellars while the tanks were passing. The tanks, after cruising about the village until the light began to fail, returned after an uneventful voyage.

Meanwhile, in support of the tanks two platoons of the 6th Seaforth Highlanders were ordered to advance through the wood, and two to enter the village from the north. The first party was held up in the wood by machine-guns, and the second entered the village only to meet the tanks withdrawing. They therefore attempted to establish a chain of posts round the village; but, fired at from front and flanks, were compelled to withdraw.

Arrangements were now made to prevent the enemy from evacuating his guns during the night by placing a machine-gun barrage on the northern slopes of the Flesquières Ridge. With this object the 152nd Machine Gun Company alone fired over 19,000 rounds before daylight. By dawn, however, the enemy had withdrawn from Flesquières Trench and the villages.

A patrol of the 7th Gordon Highlanders had left their trenches as early as 3.45 P.M., circled the north-west side of the village to the north-west corner, and reported that that flank was only held by a few machine-guns and snipers. At 4 P.M. a patrol of the 7th Black Watch found Flesquières Trench unoccupied, and the battalion moved into it.

At 2.45 A.M. three patrols of the 7th Gordon Highlanders returned and reported that they had advanced as far as the Brown line, and that the whole area was clear of the enemy. About the same time a patrol of the 7th Black Watch returned with similar information. These two battalions therefore advanced and occupied the Brown line, troops of the 7th Gordon Highlanders passing right through the village and encountering only slight machine-gun and rifle fire.

At 6.15 A.M. on the following morning troops of the 6th Gordon Highlanders and 6th Seaforth Highlanders also established themselves on the Brown line without opposition.

Thus within twenty-four hours of the attack having been launched the Brown line was occupied in its entirety, largely owing to the vigilance with which the 153rd Brigade had kept in touch with the enemy's movements by patrolling.

During the final advance to the Brown line considerable booty was taken, the following guns being captured by the 6th Gordon Highlanders: two 5·9 howitzers and two 4·2 guns; by the 6th Seaforth Highlanders, five field-guns; by the 7th Gordon Highlanders, two 8-inch howitzers, five 5·9 howitzers, and a field-gun.

By nightfall on the day of the attack the artillery had considerably advanced their positions, one brigade being at the Grand Ravine, and two in No Man's Land.

The advance to the Red dotted line was now accomplished without difficulty. On the right the 5th Seaforth Highlanders passed through the 6th Gordon Highlanders, reached the Red dotted line, and made a reconnaissance in force towards Cantaing with a total of fourteen casualties. On their left the 8th Argyll and Sutherland Highlanders also reached the Red dotted line, having killed five Germans and captured thirty-three in an attack by section rushes against a sunken road. They also reconnoitred towards Cantaing, but found it strongly held.

Similarly, the 6th Black Watch and the 5th Gordon Highlanders occupied the Red dotted line with a total of two and three casualties respectively. The former captured three field-guns and four 4·2 howitzers, and the latter three field-guns.

During these operations the 154th Brigade, which had assembled at Metz at 5 A.M. on the day of the attack, had at 10 A.M. moved two battalions to the old British front line and two just clear of Metz, in readiness to move forward should Flesquières fall.

On the evening of the 20th it was decided that should the Red dotted line be captured during the night, the 154th Brigade should pass through the 152nd and 153rd Brigades, capture the Cantaing Line and Cantaing, and advance on the village of Fontaine Notre Dame.

Of these objectives Cantaing and the Cantaing Line proved themselves to be formidable obstacles. The latter, though the trenches were for the most part only traced out, contained numerous completed dug-outs and machine-gun emplacements, and was for the greater portion of its length

THE BATTLE OF CAMBRAI

protected by a double belt of wire some fifteen yards in depth. The defences of the village of Cantaing were also considerably strengthened by a well-traversed trench encircling its south-western corner.

The 154th Brigade began its advance with the 4th Gordon Highlanders covering the front of the 152nd Infantry Brigade, and the 7th Argyll and Sutherland Highlanders covering the 153rd. In rear were the 9th Royal Scots on the right, and the 4th Seaforth Highlanders on the left.

The 4th Gordon Highlanders passed through the Red dotted line at 10.30 A.M., and continued their advance at first uneventfully. As, however, they began to approach Cantaing Trench, machine-guns from the trenches and from buildings in the village, as well as light trench-mortars, opened on them in sufficient volume to hold up the advance until shortly after noon. At that hour ten tanks arrived from Premy Chapel, and made towards the village, followed by " B " Company of the 4th Gordon Highlanders. Cantaing was entered, and after a little street fighting 300 prisoners were taken from it.

Meanwhile about the south-western end of the village, in the trenches in that vicinity and in the sunken road running to Cantaing Mill, bodies of the enemy continued to offer a magnificent resistance. " D " Company of the 4th Gordon Highlanders managed to force their way through the wire into a position on the Cantaing-Flesquières road, but could make no farther progress. Two Stokes guns were then brought into action, but even these failed to dislodge the enemy. Indeed, it was not until 3 P.M., when one of the tanks *en route* for Fontaine arrived, that the pocket was finally cleared. This gallant stand made by the enemy had disorganised this attack, which came to a standstill with " B " and " D " Companies of the 4th Gordon Highlanders consolidating the line north and northeast of the village, and with " A " and " C " Companies connecting them on the right flank with the 29th Division, who were by this time in Nine Wood. Subsequently three squadrons of the Queen's Bays and the 9th Cavalry Brigade M.G. Squadron arrived, and took up defensive positions round the perimeter of the village in conjunction with the 4th Gordon Highlanders.

While this operation was in progress, the 7th Argyll and

Sutherland Highlanders, on the left of the 4th Gordon Highlanders, could not join in the advance until 11.20 A.M., as they were held up by heavy fire from the village of Anneux. However, at that hour the village was captured by the 62nd Division, and they were able to move forward again.

By noon the advance had again been completely held up about 300 yards from the Cantaing Line by heavy enfilade fire from Cantaing on the right and Bourlon Wood on the left. As no tanks had as yet arrived, the battalion therefore began to dig in.

During this time and until the end of the day low-flying enemy aeroplanes, sometimes only 150 feet from the ground, patrolled our lines, observed the position of our troops, disclosed them by dropping lights, and fired with machine-guns on the men.

Meanwhile, the 4th Gordon Highlanders having been led away rather to the right to deal with Cantaing, touch had been lost between the two battalions. A company of the 4th Seaforth Highlanders was therefore ordered forward to fill the gap between the Gordons and the Argylls.

At 3.30 P.M. the situation was cleared up by the arrival of seven tanks, which moved forward, followed by the 7th Argyll and Sutherland Highlanders and the company of the 4th Seaforth Highlanders. At the sight of the tanks the Germans in the Cantaing Line surrendered, 130 men being taken prisoners.

The advance on Fontaine Notre Dame was thus begun, and was carried out without any opposition being met beyond a few shots fired by riflemen in Bourlon Wood. The village was in our hands by 5 P.M.

The 7th Argyll and Sutherland Highlanders were then disposed so as to defend Fontaine, the point of junction being north of the village, with the 7th Argyll and Sutherland Highlanders on the left and the 4th Seaforth Highlanders on the right. One company of the latter was also detached to connect up the 62nd Division north of Anneux with the reserve platoons of the 7th Argyll and Sutherland Highlanders garrisoning the Cantaing Line.

During the night the enemy infantry remained inactive. Fontaine was found to be a large village little damaged

MAP VIII.—THE BATTLE OF CAMBRAI: POSITION AT 7 P.M., 21ST NOVEMBER 1917.

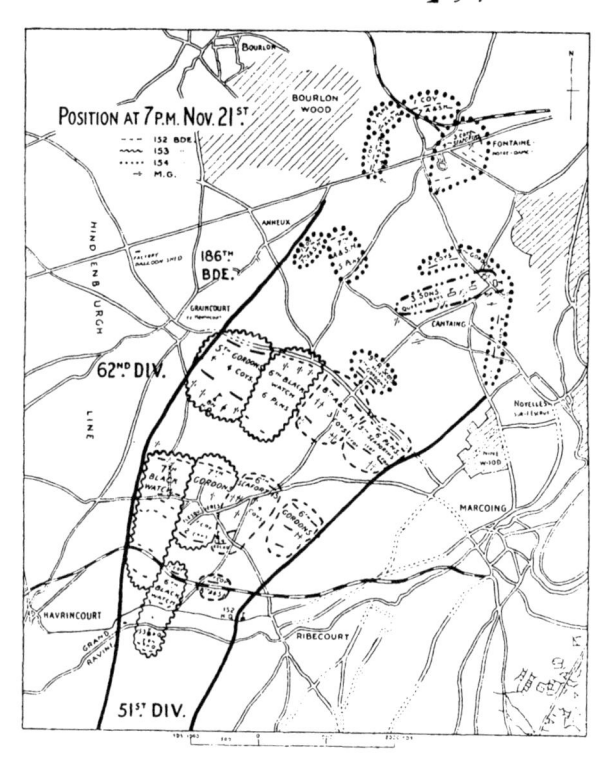

THE BATTLE OF CAMBRAI

by shell-fire, but as darkness had fallen shortly after its capture, it was impossible to make a systematic search of all the cellars and dug-outs contained in it, in which parties of Germans might be hiding.

But though the enemy remained quiet, the position in Fontaine was a desperate one. The enemy still held Bourlon and La Folie Woods. The village was, in fact, like a nut gripped by the crackers.

At 6.30 P.M. steps were taken to ensure that the flanks of the defenders of Fontaine were securely connected with the neighbouring troops, the 9th Royal Scots, who had relieved the 4th Gordon Highlanders in Cantaing, being ordered to swing forward their left flank until they were definitely in touch with the right of the 4th Seaforth Highlanders. At the same time the 7th Argyll and Sutherland Highlanders were instructed to make certain that no gap existed between the troops on the west side of Fontaine and the Cantaing Line. It was imperative that no such gaps should exist, as should the enemy succeed in penetrating between Fontaine and the Cantaing Line during the dark, there was every chance of the entire garrison of Fontaine being cut off.

At 8 P.M., as there was no activity on this part of the front, the brigadier ordered the 4th Seaforth Highlanders to take over the defences of Fontaine, thus relieving three companies of the 7th Argyll and Sutherland Highlanders, who were to be used in their turn to defend the flanks in rear of the village. The object of these orders was to place the defence of the village under a single command.

Fontaine Notre Dame was subsequently lost in a counter-attack. It has often been urged that this would not have been the case had a stronger garrison been detailed for its defence. This is not true. Fontaine could only have been secured by a successful attack on Bourlon Wood. Sufficient troops could have at any time been moved into Fontaine to give such an attack adequate support on its right flank. No number of troops could be expected successfully to hold Fontaine against counter-attack so long as the enemy held Bourlon Wood.

The village was indeed merely the point of junction of two defensive flanks. Only two policies appeared possible :

either an attack must be delivered against Bourlon Wood by the Division on the left, or Fontaine must be evacuated. To put more men into the village would have been to expose more men to certain defeat in the event of counter-attack. It would have been the equivalent of putting a large nut within the grip of the crackers instead of a small one.

The perimeter of the village was some 3500 yards, the strength of the 4th Seaforth Highlanders roughly 400, or approximately one man to eight and three-quarter yards of front. In addition, six Vickers guns had also taken up defensive positions in the village.

Immediately after the completion of the relief by the 4th Seaforth Highlanders, it was reported that the enemy were massing for attack in Bourlon Wood, and shortly afterwards that they were dribbling forwards on to the Cambrai road, in just the same manner as they had done for the counter-attack near Poelcappelle on 20th September 1917.

At 5.30 A.M. on 23rd November, Lieut.-Colonel Unthank, D.S.O., commanding the 4th Seaforth Highlanders, who had established his headquarters in the centre of the village, sent an officer and the battalion scouts to establish four posts of observation on the Cambrai road north of the village. These were in position by 7 A.M.

As soon as dawn broke a fleet of twelve enemy aircraft circled over Fontaine at a low altitude. The battalion headquarters staff were lined up in the main street, and forced the planes to fly at a higher altitude by their rifle-fire. They, however, continued to observe and to engage our troops with machine-gun fire all morning.

At 10.30 A.M. the first S.O.S. signal was fired by the infantry, and a fierce battle was soon raging. The enemy's plan was to attack the village from both flanks simultaneously, from the Cambrai-Bapaume road on the right, and from Bourlon Wood on the left. At the same time, he delivered a holding attack from the north.

The Germans advanced most gallantly in five waves, separated from one another by a distance of about ten yards. Numbers of officers were conspicuous directing the advance. These waves advanced determinedly, regardless of casualties, on the left to within bombing distance of the front line.

Meanwhile parties of the enemy, who had no doubt remained hidden in the village all night, opened fire on the backs of the defenders from the church and adjoining houses.

On the right the enemy was first checked by troops holding the last house in Fontaine on the Cambrai road. The enemy, not being able to dislodge them, turned northwards and entered the railway cutting, driving the small posts from it into the outskirts of the village. To check his farther advance in this direction two platoons were brought from the reserve south of the village to the station, and Colonel Unthank led his headquarters personnel along the Cambrai road. On the way the colonel met the two platoons falling back from the station; these he ordered back again, and advanced with his party also in that direction. He found the enemy two hundred yards from the station buildings in great force. For a short time he kept them in check with the troops at his command, but after a few minutes was driven by weight of numbers into the street running parallel to the Cambrai road and north of it.

The pressure now increased as Captain Peverell, the adjutant who was in charge of the party defending the Cambrai road on the extreme right, was wounded and his party driven in. At the same time the company defending the north-west and western edges of Fontaine were forced back by weight of numbers, first on to the Cambrai road, and then into a sunken road running into the village at its south-western corner. During this withdrawal the company was heavily engaged and suffered severe losses, the company commander being wounded.

South of the Cambrai road on the right two platoons holding the sunken road running from Fontaine to La Folie Wood offered a most heroic resistance. They held the ground until they had fired every round of ammunition that they carried or could collect from the dead and wounded. Then covered by a gallant band of four men, they fell back into the sunken Cantaing-Fontaine road.

While these actions were in progress, Colonel Unthank with his small party had withdrawn to the centre of the village. The enemy was now pressing them on three sides, and they had no alternative but to extricate themselves from a most dangerous situation. They accordingly withdrew southwards. At the edge of the village they found the enemy advancing in waves on both flanks. Though they were now reduced in number to seven, they halted, faced the enemy, and opened rapid fire on him for a minute, and then dashed across the open under a heavy cross-fire to the Cantaing-Fontaine road.

Colonel Unthank and his men had fought magnificently against overwhelming odds ; he did not withdraw from the village with the remnants of his headquarters until 2.30 P.M., a few moments before the German cordon round the village was completed, and even then paused to take a final toll from the Boches. As he withdrew a British machine-gun was seen on the Cambrai road still in action with Germans all round it.

The survivors of the defenders of Fontaine were now all gathered together in the two sunken roads running southwards from the village. The enemy were continuing to advance on the right, and the defenders of the road with their ammunition almost spent made a gallant attempt to relieve the pressure by a counter-charge. The men were, however, so terribly exhausted that the charge lost its impetus just as the enemy were beginning to retire. The troops then returned to the road.

A line was now organised, so that a continuous line of resistance was formed connecting the Cantaing Line on the left with the sunken roads. The troops in the eastern sunken road also gained touch with the 9th Royal Scots. The enemy thus found it impossible to debouch from the village or to work round the left flank. Several times he attempted to throw back the 154th Brigade and continue his advance, but each attempt was shattered by the rifle and Lewis-gun fire of the defenders. He could do no more than occupy the trench at the south-western corner of the village. The organisation of this line, which brought the enemy's initial success to a standstill, was a fine piece of tactical work, and reflects great credit on the local commanders and the troops.

Meanwhile the 9th Royal Scots had had some splendid shooting during the afternoon. Five times the enemy attempted to deliver an attack across the country intervening between Fontaine and La Folie Wood, but on each occasion the Royal Scots delivered such a fire that his

THE BATTLE OF CAMBRAI

troops withered away, and contented themselves with digging in behind a ridge. Quiet prevailed along the whole front in the evening, the enemy not feeling disposed to test our line again. Patrols reconnoitred the country immediately in front of our line, but met none of the enemy.

During the night the 7th Black Watch relieved the 4th Seaforth Highlanders and the 7th Argyll and Sutherland Highlanders, and the Queen's Bays were withdrawn from Cantaing. The front held by the Division was also contracted on the right, so as just to include Cantaing.

On the evening of the 22nd orders were issued for a combined attack to be delivered on Bourlon Wood and Fontaine on the following day, the wood being allotted to the 119th Brigade, 40th Division, and the village to the 152nd Brigade.

This attack, delivered as it was from the point of a salient, included all the natural disadvantages that attend such operations, as a defensive flank had to be formed progressively as the attack advanced.

The 6th Gordon Highlanders on the right and the 6th Seaforth Highlanders on the left were detailed by the 152nd Brigade to carry out the operations, the 8th Argyll and Sutherland Highlanders being employed to form the defensive right flank as the attack progressed. That is to say, the two former battalions were to capture Fontaine, while the last, facing north-east, was to connect up the defences of Fontaine with the defences of Cantaing.

Twelve tanks were allotted to the 152nd Brigade for the operation, a number which was more than doubled by reinforcements which arrived during the day.

An artillery barrage was also arranged which opened for twenty minutes south of the village, and then moved across the area to be attacked at the rate of 200 yards every ten minutes.

The tanks moved off at 10 A.M., the plan being for those destined for the village to enter it from the flanks. On the right the 6th Gordon Highlanders advanced on a two-company front, their objective being the high ground north of Fontaine village; the 8th Argyll and Sutherland Highlanders followed in rear, ready to form the defensive flank.

As is liable to happen when an attack is delivered from

the point of a salient, the advancing infantry were badly enfiladed by machine-guns from the direction of La Folie Wood on their right flank. In addition, every house on the south side of the village seemed to hold one or more machine-guns, which the tanks, having entered the village from the flanks, had left undamaged.

Repeated attempts were made to cross a zone swept from end to end by bullets fired from the front and flank; but though part of " C " Company, 8th Gordon Highlanders, managed to reach the outskirts of the village, they could not maintain themselves there, the battalion being compelled to dig in on a line about 500 yards south of the village.

On the left the 6th Seaforth Highlanders advanced with the task of capturing the ground lying between the wood and the village, and of joining up with the 6th Gordon Highlanders north of the village.

This battalion, too, suffered heavily from enfilade fire from houses in the village which had escaped the tanks.

However, chiefly owing to the gallantry of individual officers and men, the enemy resistance was overcome. One officer, for instance, advancing ahead of his platoon against a machine-gun in a ditch alongside the Bapaume-Cambrai road, shot two of the team, and then carried back the gun under fire. A sergeant put a gun out of action by heading an attack along a trench occupied by a party of about thirty Germans, of which he bayoneted three himself, thus cowing the others into surrendering. A dash through the German barrage by an officer and one N.C.O. captured fifty Germans garrisoning a trench.

By means of these and similar exploits " C " Company, pushing in by section rushes, and closely supported by " D " Company, reached the north-east corner of Bourlon Wood. " D " Company from this point tried to gain the high ground north of the village, but the fire from Fontaine was so intense that their efforts had to be abandoned.

Meanwhile " A " and " B " Companies with the tanks were endeavouring to enter the west side of the village. They successfully cleared the outskirts, but every endeavour made to enter the main streets failed. Machine-gunners or riflemen seemed to be manning the windows of every house.

THE BATTLE OF CAMBRAI

During this action the enemy made several attempts to defeat the whole attack by cutting in across the Bapaume-Cambrai road (south-west of the village), a form of counter-attack to which an attack from a salient is particularly liable. All his attempts in this direction collapsed under the fire of rifles and Lewis guns.

By the early afternoon the situation had become stationary, the surviving tanks all having returned from the village.

A fresh attack was therefore planned, as it would have been impossible for the 6th Seaforth Highlanders to maintain themselves in their advanced position unless some effort was made to relieve the pressure on their flanks. Two companies of the 5th Seaforth Highlanders were therefore ordered to advance through Anneux to the south-east corner of Bourlon Wood, now in the hands of the 40th Division, and forming up there, to attempt to clear Fontaine by bombing in conjunction with a fresh company of twelve tanks. At the same time, it was arranged that 100 rifles of the 6th Gordon Highlanders and two companies of the 8th Argyll and Sutherland Highlanders should form up on the right flank and co-operate in the attack.

Immediately before the hour fixed for the operation to begin, the enemy successfully counter-attacked the 40th Division in Bourlon Wood, and uncovered the left flank of the 6th Seaforth Highlanders. They had, in consequence, to fall back, with the result that the situation west of Fontaine became uncertain.

However, while this withdrawal was taking place, the tanks had begun their advance through a heavy artillery barrage, which accompanied the German counter-attack on Bourlon Wood. Several of them were put out of action by direct hits, in consequence of which some confusion and disorganisation arose, which resulted in none of the tanks entering the village on the front of the two companies of the 5th Seaforth Highlanders.

In view of the intensity of the machine-gun fire which was being poured out of Fontaine, it seemed clear that an attack unsupported by tanks had no possible chance of success. The enterprise was therefore abandoned, and the men withdrew and dug in so as to form a connecting link between the 6th Seaforth Highlanders and the troops south of the village.

This gallant attack on Fontaine illustrates the extreme difficulty of taking an undemolished village with or without tanks, if strongly held and organised for defence, unless there is sufficient time available to subject it to a severe and thorough bombardment.

No further changes in the situation occurred, except that after dusk the line was so adjusted as to be continuous from the left of the 6th Seaforth Highlanders in the south-east corner of Bourlon Wood to the right of the 9th Royal Scots south-east of Cantaing.

During the night of the 23-24th the Division was relieved by the Guards Division, and a continuous line was handed over five miles in advance of the trenches occupied by the Division at zero hour on the 20th.

The part played by the Highland Division in the battle of Cambrai was a great one. It had reached its final objective, though Fontaine was ultimately lost; it had captured 2609 unwounded prisoners, including 66 officers, with a loss of 27 officers and 312 men killed and missing, and of 41 officers and 1190 men wounded.

In the action the tanks certainly played a gallant and conspicuous part, and since they were alone responsible for crushing the wire throughout the varying phases of the attack, contributed largely to the success of the infantry. It must, however, be borne in mind that the tanks suffered serious losses. In "D" Battalion ten tanks were knocked out by direct hits, and in "E" eighteen. Many others, through mechanical trouble, were unable to reach their objective. Indeed, of the seventy that took part in the first day's action, only twenty-six rallied at the conclusion.

It will thus be seen that in many cases the infantry gallantly continued their advance without the support of their tanks, so that the success was equally due to their splendid qualities, which enabled them to reach their objectives by substituting for the help they anticipated from the tanks their own initiative and resource. Those tanks that remained in action did magnificent work, as is testified by the following figures. In one day "Z" Battalion fired 2000 6-pounder shells, and 95,000 rounds of small-arms ammunition, excluding any rounds fired by the tanks that were knocked out. In many cases tanks not only fired every round of their own ammunition, but also all the ammunition that they were carrying for the infantry.

One has now reached a point at which one may pause and consider the last three attacks carried out by the Division. They were delivered at the height of the German's defensive power; two of them against trench systems perfected by every modern artifice, deliberately constructed with ample leisure in which to complete them; one against the barrage-proof pill-box; all of them before the German had exhausted the flower of his army in his violent attacks of the first six months of 1918.

In every case the Highland Division reached the final objective allotted to it; true, in two cases, with an exposed flank, counter-attacks ultimately reduced its gains, but only inconsiderably. In the aggregate of its three attacks, it advanced 14,000 yards, accounting for practically every German in the area traversed, capturing as unwounded prisoners 87 officers and 3403 unwounded men, irrespective of the wounded collected by the R.A.M.C.; defeated at least a dozen counter-attacks; and lost in the three actions in killed, wounded, and missing a sum total of only 162 officers and 4128 other ranks. That is to say, its losses in these attacks exceeded the number of unwounded prisoners captured by only 75 officers and 725 other ranks, the German killed, wounded, and wounded prisoners not being taken into account in this balance.

Many Divisions reached their final objectives, but few can have done so three times in four months with the balance of dead loss in man-power, as opposed to the Germans, so immeasurably in their favour. The three battles were, indeed, immense successes, and proved indisputably that in 1917 in the Highland Division the Germans had an opponent for whom they were no match.

How, then, was this success achieved? One can say with truth that the leap-frog system of attack gave the infantry the best possible chances of success; one can say with equal truth that in Generals Harper, Oldfield, Pelham-Burn, Buchanan, and Beckwith, and its unit commanders, the men had magnificent leaders; one can say that the men themselves were as gallant and courageous as soldiers can be ; but there was something further.

It was that the Division was trained throughout to act intelligently. It had learned to fight scientifically by the combination of skill and gallantry, and not by animal courage alone, untempered by intelligence.

The success of the Division and the cheapness in life of its successes was due, as General Maxse had put it, " to the fact that all usual war problems had been thought out beforehand, discussed in detail, and embodied in simple doctrines well known to all ranks."

One cannot leave this battle without a word of praise for the courage and steadiness of the German soldier in the face of one of the heaviest attacks of the war. Without warning the Germans were assaulted in the early dawn by tanks, against which the infantryman is practically defenceless, in numbers which had not previously been contemplated. At the same time, they were bombarded and barraged by a vast artillery, subsequently they were attacked again and again by tanks. Yet though, it is true, certain of them broke and fled or surrendered, in the main they stood their ground, and set a magnificent example of stubborn and skilful defence, in which their gunners supported the infantry with the greatest devotion.

The battle of Cambrai was the first occasion on which troops of the Highland Division had penetrated the enemy's positions to such a depth as to liberate French civilians. All who took part in the battle will never forget the gratitude of these French people, who, having lived for three years behind the German lines, were ultimately released as the result of a great battle fought in their presence round their homes.

CHAPTER XIV.

THE GERMAN OFFENSIVE.

THE year 1917 closed in an atmosphere of depression. Most Divisions on the Western Front had been engaged continuously in offensive operations. Some had been hurried off to Italy; all were exhausted, and either numerically weak or had been reinforced by rather indifferent material. The drain on officers had been severe during the last twelve months, and deficiencies in this respect were hard adequately to replace. The signing of the Brest-Litovsk Treaty and the complete defection of the Russians had, at the same time, enabled Germany not only to make up the wastage in her ranks, but even to increase the number of Divisions on the Western Front.

There was a universal feeling that, in spite of the sacrifices of Arras and Passchendaele, and the bitter fighting at Messines, Ypres, and Cambrai, the initiative could but pass into the hands of the Germans, and that they were soon to become the aggressors.

There had also been the painful incident of the ringing of the joy-bells in London, which had heralded the Germans' successful counter-attack against the shoulders of the Cambrai salient.

This counter-attack had fallen on, among other Divisions, the 56th Division. It had necessitated urgent orders being sent on 30th November to the 51st Division, which was resting in the neighbourhood of Baisieux, to move at once to the Lechelle area. These orders arrived most inopportunely, as, in the first place, it was St Andrew's Day, and the numerous dinners which were to be eaten in memory of the patron saint were actually being cooked, and had to be left untouched. Further, General Harper's horse had come down with him in a hidden wire-entanglement, the General being severely shaken, and had sustained a badly-damaged wrist.

On 1st December two battalions of the 153rd Brigade relieved two battalions of the 56th Division in the old British front, and on 2nd December the 154th and 153rd Brigades relieved the 56th Division in the front trenches. On 3rd December the G.O.C. 51st Division took over command of the line.

The situation was a precarious one. Our troops occupied the Hindenburg front line as far as Tadpole Copse inclusive, a trench had thence been hastily dug across No Man's Land to protect the left flank. This flank was thus highly vulnerable and liable to be heavily counter-attacked. Indeed, the Germans maintained constant pressure against our troops in that part of the field by means of bombing parties, and in this respect could only be kept in check by a systematic use of rifle grenades.

To relieve this situation on 5th December our troops were withdrawn to the old British front line. After various adjustments of the frontage held, the Divisional sector was finally fixed, and ran from Betty Avenue east of Demicourt on the right to the Strand on the left, the village of Boursies on the Bapaume-Cambrai road being a little south of the centre of the sector. The total frontage held by the Division was roughly 6000 yards.

The trenches—for the defences could not be called a trench system—consisted of a front line and portions of a support line sited for the most part so that it could not perform the functions for which it was designed. About 2000 yards in rear lay some reserve line posts. The trenches were, in fact, merely those in which men had dug themselves in in front of the Hindenburg Line when following the retreating Germans in their withdrawal in the spring of 1917. With no prospect of the enemy attacking in this sector, they had provided reasonable summer accommodation for their garrisons; at this moment, however, it was not only winter, but it was also morally certain that the Germans were preparing for a spring offensive.

The trenches were therefore wholly unsuitable both in construction and siting for the purpose for which they were now required. Indeed, they were little more than a few " Bairnsfather " villas, connected by short lengths of narrow crumbling ditches, which, partly owing to the rank growth of thistles and other weeds, and partly to their siting, had practically no field of fire.

It can therefore be said that the Division was given an area 6000 yards in breadth in which to construct a defensive system *de novo*.

The front line crossed three spurs and two valleys all running in a north-easterly direction from the main feature of the position, the ridge running from Hermies to Lebucquière.

The country was similar in nature to the upland country of the Cambrai battle, and was similarly completely dominated by Bourlon Wood. One was even in view of Bourlon Wood at the Divisional race meetings.

The enemy occupied the Hindenburg Line some 2500 yards from the British front line with outposts in an uncompleted line some 300 to 700 yards in advance of it.

It was a comfortable sector, the unpleasantness attendant on being in close contact with the enemy, such as mining, trench-mortars, rifle grenades, sniping, and indirect machine-gun fire, being absent. As a rule, the German gunners, in spite of their magnificent observation of our lines, remained inactive.

In view of the fact that so much new work was necessary in the sector, General Harper published a memorandum containing certain principles of defence and of trench construction, a document which at their own request was circulated to a number of Divisions, and adopted by them.

The chief innovation in this document was the construction of trenches of a far larger size than had been the case in the past. The depth for all trenches was laid down as six feet, their width at the top as eight feet, later increased to nine feet six inches. Each fire-bay was to be fifteen yards in length, with a twenty-three feet traverse separating it from the next one. The minimum breadth of the berm was laid down as three feet.

The document ended with the following sentences :—

" Nothing indicates the standard of discipline and the *morale* of a Division more clearly than work done on a defensive front. It may be assumed with certainty that a Division that digs well will attack well, and that bad trenches are the work of a Division that cannot be relied on in the attack.

"Officers and men must realise that good work stimulates interest, and consequently tends to keep up *morale*, and that a good trench system economises men and minimises losses. There is, perhaps, nothing more demoralising to infantry than taking over badly-constructed and badly-kept trenches, except actually constructing and keeping them in such a condition."

To ensure continuity of effort within the Division, General Harper in his memorandum laid down fixed principles on the system on which a sector was to be defended, on the system on which trenches were to be sited, and on the actual method of construction of trenches, dug-outs, entanglements, &c., and standardised their dimensions.

Thus within the Division, if men were ordered to make a trench, dug-out, or entanglement, or to finish some work begun by another unit, they and their officers knew exactly how to carry on.

The employment of all available labour was also reduced to a system. The Division was made responsible for all work in front of and including the line which ran through Hermies and Doignies, work in rear of this line being carried out under arrangements made by the Corps.

In the Divisional area it was arranged that each of the three field companies was allotted a sector of its own, and worked continuously in that sector, finding its own reliefs.

Each brigade was made responsible for its own front and support lines, and for the communication trenches connecting them and for wiring them.

The pioneer battalion placed at the disposal of the C.R.E. was made responsible for the construction of communication trenches, of which none existed.

The sappers in each sector organised the infantry parties and supervised the work as regards its quality, and were generally employed as technical advisers. It was definitely laid down that the work of trench construction and wiring was the duty of the infantry and not of the R.E., and also that the infantry officer and not the R.E. officers

THE GERMAN OFFENSIVE

was responsible for the amount of work performed by the infantry and for its quality.

Each infantry battalion had also to provide a mining platoon, which, with the assistance of a few sappers, was employed on the construction of deep dug-outs. Troops in reserve were employed in digging the Corps line, which ran west of Hermies and east of Beaumetz and Morchies. On this line the reserve battalions were trained in digging and drilled as working parties, and considerably benefited from the instruction given there.

In order to simplify the work, reliefs were, as far as possible, arranged so that battalions always occupied the same sector.

The artillery, who had many professional miners in their ranks, made their own dug-outs, with some slight assistance from the R.E.

No new work was allowed to be undertaken without the approval of Divisional headquarters ; a definite programme could therefore be laid down and adhered to, and, as a result, the minimum of labour was wasted.

This system proved highly satisfactory. The Jocks showed a keen interest in the work of trench construction, worked admirably, and took the greatest pride in the result of their labours.

An orderly, who was taken on a reconnaissance into the trenches held by a neighbouring Division, summed up the opinion of the Jocks excellently by looking at the narrow trenches with their small sandbagged traverses, and saying, "It's easy seen these trenches belong to some other bodies."

So successful in fact was the system, that between 3rd December and 21st March, during which period (with the exception of a three weeks' rest at Achiet le Petit) the Division held this sector, the following work was carried out :—

The front line had been reorganised and the occupied sections made habitable.

The support line had been dug throughout its 6000 yards' length, and contained deep dug-outs for its entire garrison.

Three main communication trenches had been dug from the Corps line to the front line.

The reserve line had been partially completed, and had many dug-outs constructed in it.

The Hermies-Doignies-Louverval line had been dug through to make a continuous line.

The Hermies-Beaumetz-Morchies line had been dug through to make a continuous line.

Many machine-gun emplacements leading from deep dug-outs had also been made, as well as brigade, battalion, and company battle-headquarters.

In this area a total of over sixty new dug-outs had been completed.

Every trench had been so heavily protected with barbed wire that even the army R.E. park ran dry, and the supply of barbed wire almost ceased.

This magnificent record of eight weeks' work, coming at the end of eight months' almost continuous fighting, when the dimensions of the trenches constructed is remembered, clearly proves the value of the system which had been brought into force.

General Sir Julian Byng, commanding the Third Army, on visiting the trenches, was so satisfied with the work done that he addressed the following letter to the Divisional commander :—

"The Third Army commander wishes to express to all ranks of the 51st (Highland) Division his keen appreciation of the extremely good work done by the Division in the strengthening of the defences of the line.

"He is fully aware of the fact that the Division has been continuously engaged throughout 1917, and considers that the way in which all ranks, in spite of their recent efforts, tackled the heavy work in front of them is all the more commendable.

"The Army Commander wishes all ranks to know that their good work in defence, as much as in attack, is fully realised."

Probably in this sector "Q," as the quartermaster-general's branch of the staff is known, was at the zenith of its efficiency.

There was hardly a single room, much less a house, in the whole Divisional area that had not been destroyed, except one in Bapaume that was marked "dangerous." The buildings of the various Divisional institutions had therefore all to be improvised. These included hot bathhouses for officers and men, at which the latter were issued with clean underclothes ; Divisional canteens, both retail and wholesale, at which battalion canteens could purchase their stock ; wet canteens, a fresh fish, vegetable, and egg store, a picture palace, a Divisional theatre, a Divisional soda-water factory, a rest camp for officers and men, and hot soup kitchens. In fact, there was practically nothing which civilisation supplies which "Q" did not produce in the Fremicourt-Lebucquière-Beugny wilderness.

Lieut.-Colonel J. L. Weston, D.S.O., who had been A.A. and Q.M.G. since the April of 1917, had a gift for liaison with the various units, and he thus kept himself fully informed of their wants, and by collecting round him some valuable subordinates, in addition to his two staff officers, was almost invariably able to supply them. The R.E. also co-operated with "Q" admirably, and were of the greatest assistance in helping to change ruined houses into Divisional institutions.

It was while the Division was resting in the Achiet le Petit area that Captain Stanley first produced his original comic opera, 'Turnip Tops,' which was played over a hundred times by the "Balmorals." Captain Stanley wrote the words, the music, and the songs, and himself played the leading part, most ably supported by "Gertie" as the heroine.

So successful was 'Turnip Tops' that a special theatre was built for it at Lebucquière, which was unfortunately captured by the Boche on the day that it should have been opened.

By the first days of 1918 night bombing had become so frequent that it became dangerous to allow audiences to collect in buildings after dark ; theatres and cinemas had therefore for a time to be discontinued.

Casualties from bombing to men and horses, particularly to the latter, occurred on several occasions. Towards the end of December 1917 Fremicourt, where Divisional headquarters lived, was bombed one evening by relays of Gothas for over an hour. Many men were killed and wounded. No. 2 mess was struck by a direct hit, Colonel

Fleming, the A.D.M.S., was killed, and the A.P.M. wounded. One of the Gothas was happily brought down, its crew of three being captured.

Colonel Fleming had been A.D.M.S. of the Highland Division for over two years, and had been with it through all its chief engagements. He was succeeded by Colonel David Rorie, D.S.O., who was at the time commanding a field ambulance. Colonel Rorie was one of the best known and most popular officers in the Division. He was not only highly efficient, as he had proved when acting as A.D.M.S. to the Division at Beaumont Hamel, but he also possessed an inexhaustible fund of humour. In fact, to spend an hour talking to Colonel Rorie in the mess was to obtain as good a tonic as any he possessed in his medicine-chest.

In March signs that an attack was impending began to appear. In the first place, information was received from the intelligence staff at general headquarters that an attack on a large scale was being prepared. Locally on the Divisional front there were also unmistakable signs. It was noticed that the enemy was taking elaborate precautions to avoid any of the trench garrison being captured. Raiding parties either found his outpost line empty or the garrisons withdrew as soon as the raiders approached. His object doubtless was to prevent us from capturing a prisoner and extracting from him information regarding his preparations. His activity in the air became increasingly marked, and he made every effort to keep our reconnaissance machines from crossing his lines, both by anti-aircraft fire and by aerial attack.

A number of new trench bridges, work on new roads, &c., appeared daily in air photos of his position.

He laid a line of telegraph wires on poles right up to his front line. Lines of white posts, presumably marking the position of routes, also appeared, and increased daily.

Finally the air photos became spotted with curious small rectangular mounds, which from their appearance on the photos came to be known as "lice." The idea of trying the effect of a direct hit on one of these "lice" with a 4·5 howitzer occurred to General Oldfield, and a shoot was in consequence arranged. The result was conclusive; every time a "louse" was hit it exploded. They were, in fact, dumps of ammunition scattered broadcast about the valley of the river Agache. The 256th Brigade, R.F.A., caused over a hundred of these explosions within an hour and a half.

It was then decided to test the gun emplacements, and see whether ammunition had been stored in them. The result showed that every gun position, whether it was occupied by a gun or not, contained ammunition.

These signs were unmistakable.

Prisoners captured on various parts of the front also reported that the Germans were building tanks in large numbers. Two measures of anti-tank defence were therefore taken. Fields of anti-tank mines were laid, covering all the main avenues of approach, such as valleys and roads. The mines used were the old 60-pounder trench-mortar bomb, fitted with a special fuze, which were sunk just level with the surface of the earth. In laying one of these mines, a most unfortunate accident occurred. A bomb from some unknown cause exploded, killing and wounding one officer and eighteen men of the 152nd Trench-Mortar Battery.

Seven 18-pounders and three 15-pounders were also employed as anti-tank guns, being placed in positions about the support and reserve line from which they could cover the main avenues of approach over open sights.

By the middle of March the trench system consisted of the following: The front system, composed of the front, support, and reserve lines, the two former being continuous trenches held by section and double-section posts, the third a series of defended localities and portions of trenches, all heavily wired. The intermediate line, running from the north of Hermies, north of Doignies, north of Louverval, through Louverval Wood to the Divisional boundary.

The Corps line—*i.e.*, the Hermies-Beaumetz-Morchies line.

Behind this trench system the Army (Green) line traversed the Divisional sector. It consisted of an old German trench, heavily wired, running from Ypres to Beugny, and thence northwards.

By this time the brigades had all been reduced from four to three battalions, the 9th Royal Scots, the 5th Gordon Highlanders, and the 8th Argyll and Sutherland

Highlanders having been transferred to the 62nd Brigade. The departure of these units was a great blow both to the Division and to the battalions, but it was due to a definite change in organisation throughout the Expeditionary Force in France, to which no exceptions could be made. With only nine infantry battalions available, all three brigades were in the line—154th Brigade on the right, 152nd in the centre, and the 153rd on the left. Each brigade had two battalions holding the trenches in depth from the front line to the Corps line inclusive.

The order of battle ran from right to left, 4th Gordon Highlanders, 7th Argyll and Sutherland Highlanders, 6th Gordon Highlanders, 5th Seaforth Highlanders, 7th Black Watch, 6th Black Watch, the battalions in brigade reserve being the 4th and 6th Seaforth Highlanders in Lebucquière, and the 7th Gordon Highlanders at Beugny, all ready to man the Beaumetz-Morchies line (Corps line) if required.

Each brigade was covered by a brigade of field artillery as follows :—

154th Brigade by the 293rd Army Brigade, R.F.A., Lieut.-Colonel A. Main, D.S.O., commanding.

152nd Brigade by the 255th Brigade, R.F.A., Lieut.-Colonel F. Fleming, D.S.O., commanding.

153rd Brigade by the 256th Brigade, R.F.A., Lieut.-Colonel L. M. Dyson, D.S.O., commanding.

These brigades were disposed with nine forward 18-pounders and four forward 4·5 howitzers, and with the remainder of the guns in main battery positions 3500 yards behind the front line. The forward guns only were active, the remainder remaining silent so as not to disclose their positions.

Four 6-inch Newton trench-mortars covered the front line in each brigade front, while four were in positions from which they could cover the intermediate line.

The guns of all four machine-gun companies were in position with the exception of six held in reserve. They were distributed for the most part in pairs as follows : Fourteen in the support line, fourteen in the reserve line, sixteen in the intermediate line, eight in the Corps line, and six in supporting points between the intermediate line and Corps line. The positions of these guns were all selected entirely with a view to obtaining good fields of fire over the sights, their uses for purposes of firing a barrage being treated as a secondary consideration.

On 11th March 1918 Major-General Sir G. M. Harper, K.C.B., D.S.O., was promoted to the command of the IVth Corps. Though his promotion came as no surprise, and was indeed confidently expected, the departure of the General came nevertheless as a severe blow.

There were strong feelings towards the General which animated the Division other than those of confidence in his command, and deep respect for his qualities as a soldier. General Harper's personality was one which won for him the genuine affection of all ranks with whom he came in contact. In constant touch with his troops, both in and out of the line, he was known personally to many of them. He never confined his conversation with them to matters of military interest alone, and in consequence they appreciated that he regarded them in the light of normal sympathies, and not merely as units in a fighting machine.

It can safely be said that the Jocks regarded " Uncle " or " Daddie," as the General was known to them, not merely as a commander in whom lay the origin of their success, but as a friend who had their constant welfare in mind.

Being in the IVth Corps the Highland Division now found General Harper as its Corps commander, and fought its last fight under him in those very trenches which had been constructed under his presiding genius.

General Harper was succeeded as commander of the 51st Division by Major-General G. T. C. Carter-Campbell, C.B., D.S.O., Scottish Rifles, who remained in command until after the armistice. General Carter-Campbell had been seriously wounded at Neuve Chapelle, in which action his battalion sustained more severe casualties to officers than had ever before occurred in a single engagement. For his conspicuous gallantry and leadership in this action he had received an immediate award of the D.S.O.

General Carter-Campbell could not have been more unfortunate in the period in which he took over command of the Division than he was. Within a few days of his arrival tremendous losses were sustained in the German offensive in March, only to be followed by a further engagement in April with an almost equal number of casualties.

The losses, in fact, were such, particularly in senior officers, that the old Division had virtually disappeared.

In spite of these misfortunes under General Carter-Campbell's command, the efficiency of the Division continued. It became as often and as heavily engaged as ever, yet in spite of its losses fully maintained its reputation to the end.

During the afternoon of 20th March a scout of the Black Watch, lying out in No Man's Land, observed between 6000 and 7000 men, not wearing their packs, enter the enemy's trenches. It was therefore evident that the enemy was assembling for the attack; and all active guns, with some additional batteries of the corps heavy artillery, opened on his assembly positions and on the Agache valley.

The night remained as quiet as usual, the whole sector having been little disturbed by artillery for many weeks, with the exception of a heavy bombardment of battery positions near Beaumetz during the last day or two.

At 5 A.M., 21st March, a violent barrage broke out, which, as some one put it, extended from the front line to Paris. At the same time as the first salvo was fired, the observation balloon in front of Divisional headquarters was brought down in flames by an enemy aeroplane.

On the front and support lines the barrage was most severe on the 6th Division on the left, and on the 153rd Brigade. Here it was overwhelming, countless heavy trench-mortars adding their support to the artillery.

All battery positions, whether they had been active or silent, were engaged, and, in addition, heavily gassed.

All villages were involved, particularly Beaumetz, Doignies, and Louverval, and the intermediate and Corps lines were also bombarded.

All battalion and brigade headquarters had been marked down and were continuously shelled, while high-velocity guns fired quantities of rounds into Beugny, Lebucquière, Velu, Fremicourt, and along the Bapaume-Cambrai road. The first shell falling in Fremicourt burst in Divisional headquarters, killing a signaller.

In rear of the Divisional area places such as Bapaume, Albert, and even Doullens, Frevent, and St Pol were all

T/Major-General G. T. C. CARTER-CAMPBELL, C.B., D.S.O.

21st March 1918.

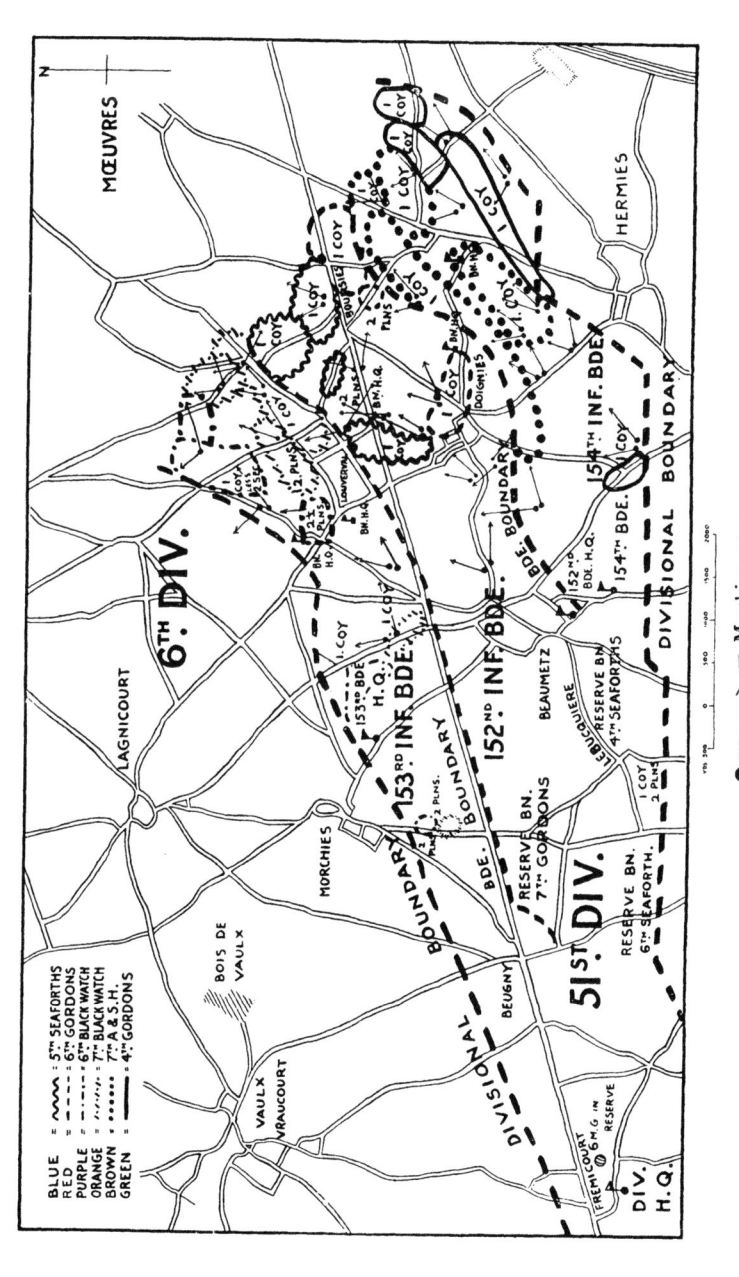

shelled by long-range guns, while Paris was engaged by "Big Bertha."

In a quarter of an hour practically all signal communications in the Divisional area had been destroyed; moreover, observation was made impossible by a thick ground mist, which did not rise until midday.

The bombardment continued for over four hours; by 7 A.M. it had quietened on most of the Divisional front, but it remained intense on the front of the 6th Division and on the left of the 153rd Brigade.

No information could be obtained as to the movements of the German infantry until 9.53 A.M., when information was received from an observation post which still was in telephone communication with the C.R.A. 2nd Lieutenant W. H. Crowder and 2nd Lieutenant J. Stuart of the 256th Brigade, R.F.A., manning this observation post, reported first that men could be seen moving between the front and support lines. Two minutes later they confirmed that these men were Germans, and at 10 A.M. they reported that the enemy were round the observation post, and were throwing bombs into it. After that, though the line still showed a circuit, no message was received. These officers had stayed at the telephone to the last, even while being bombed. Fortunately, Lieutenant Crowder was later reported wounded and a prisoner of war, and for his gallant conduct on this occasion was awarded the D.S.O. a year after the armistice.

The exact happenings when the German infantry were first encountered are not known, as none of the 6th Black Watch in the front and support line survived. These unfortunate men were subjected to a continuous bombardment of over four hours, which was concentrated on the trenches they occupied. If any of them survived the ordeal, they must have been overwhelmed when the masses of German infantry emerged through the fog.

The enemy's plan of attack is, however, clear. By a tremendous weight of artillery and trench-mortars he blasted his way through the defences of the left of the Highland Division and the right of the 6th Division. Then his troops, having poured through this gap, turned to their flanks, and, assisted by the fog, attacked each successive line of trenches in enfilade.

The parties working against the flanks thus created were highly organised, and included flame-projector detachments, light and heavy machine-guns, light trench-mortars, countless bombers, and, in close support, field artillery.

In the front and support lines the attack progressed for some distance. After putting up a stout resistance, a post of the 7th Black Watch was overwhelmed, only one survivor returning. Other posts were taken in succession until the remnants of the 7th Black Watch were rolled up amongst the 5th Seaforth Highlanders. They, in their turn, burnt by the flames of the projectors, bombed and raked by enfilade machine-gun fire, were driven in on the 6th Gordon Highlanders. The 5th Seaforth, however, fought stubbornly, two Lewis guns in the front line firing twenty and fifteen drums respectively into the German masses.

Not until the 6th Gordon Highlanders were reached was the progress of the enemy checked. In this battalion sector the remnants of the front and support line companies of the 7th Black Watch and 5th Seaforth Highlanders and the 6th Gordon Highlanders formed a block in Sturgeon Avenue, and occupied that trench south of Sturgeon Support. Here they maintained themselves for the remainder of the day. The front and support lines had, however, been lost throughout the 152nd Brigade front, with the result that the 7th Argyll and Sutherland Highlanders, who had not been attacked frontally, were assailed in the front and support line by parties bombing along the trenches. Though the Argylls were driven in at first, they established blocks at Aldgate, and checked the enemy's farther progress. In this portion of the field, then, we were for the remainder of the day left in possession of the front and support lines as far as Aldgate, thence the Demicourt-Boursies road was held, and Sturgeon Avenue south of the support line.

In other parts of the front, however, great changes had taken place. Almost simultaneously with the capture of the front line, the whole left flank as far as the intermediate line was assailed by vast numbers of the enemy.

In rear of the support line some of the 7th Black Watch, two sections of the 400th Field Company, R.E., and some machine-guns were in turn overwhelmed in the mist. One machine-gun in the encounter alone fired over 10,000 rounds before its section was put out of action, only two survivors returning.

Favoured by the mist and smoke, the enemy then assaulted the posts in the intermediate line north and west of Louverval Wood, and captured them. The highest ground in this neighbourhood thus won, he quickly brought up machine-guns, and with them swept Louverval Wood and Chateau. Two machine-guns, however, in the neighbourhood of Sole Post held up the enemy here for a considerable time, one gun ultimately having to be mounted on the parados and engage the enemy to its left rear. These guns skilfully extricated themselves when almost surrounded, and withdrew to the Beaumetz-Morchies line.

At this time the enemy began to advance down the Cambrai road from Boursies; here the 6th Gordon Highlanders resisted magnificently; one platoon just west of Boursies was last heard of fighting completely surrounded, while two other platoons made a gallant attempt to relieve the pressure by counter-attack. They were, however, overwhelmed by the volume of hostile fire.

The defence of Louverval finally collapsed, with the enemy on three sides of it.

Meanwhile, the headquarters of the two Black Watch battalions, situated in the intermediate line near the Divisional left boundary with the posts on their right and left, were offering a most effective resistance. Assailed with machine-gun fire by low-flying aeroplanes, and repeatedly attacked by numbers of the enemy, they held their ground for some two hours, with both flanks turned.

Subsequently, in imminent danger of being surrounded, they fell back to the road immediately in rear of the intermediate line, and finally to the Beaumetz-Morchies line. When the remnants of the 7th Black Watch were assembled in this line, it was found that out of three companies there were only twenty-eight survivors.

Thus Boursies, Louverval, and the whole of the intermediate line north of the Cambrai road were lost.

During these operations the artillery had fought magnificently. Most of the forward and anti-tank guns were destroyed by shell-fire during the preliminary bombardment; the survivors, however, did splendid work before they were withdrawn.

One gun in charge of 2nd Lieutenants M'Readie and M'Neill of "A" Battery, 255th Brigade, R.F.A., fired over one hundred rounds into the enemy over open sights. M'Readie was then killed by a sniper, so M'Neill, with the enemy already pressing him, destroyed his gun, and withdrew with the survivors of the detachment to Doignies.

2nd Lieutenant A. B. M'Queen of "A" Battery, 256th Brigade, R.F.A., engaged large parties of the enemy at ranges from 400-800 yards, inflicting many casualties. The enemy then opened heavy enfilade machine-gun fire on his emplacement at a range of 400 yards. M'Queen therefore destroyed his gun by putting one shell in the breech and one in the muzzle, and firing it by attaching a dragrope to the firing-lever. He then withdrew with his detachment and a Lewis gun into a sunken road, and engaged the enemy with Lewis-gun fire until he had only two drums left. He then retired to Beaumetz, carrying a wounded sergeant of the Black Watch.

The enemy's artillery was also active, shelling the parts of the intermediate line still held, the corps line and the back areas very heavily. His field-guns closely supported his infantry, and well before noon his batteries were in action in the old No Man's Land.

The enemy's next objective was the village of Doignies. The 5th Seaforth Highlanders with their battalion headquarters, which had moved from Louverval with two sections of the 404th Field Company, R.E., were protecting Doignies by retaining their hold of the intermediate line. The enemy therefore moved machine-guns so as to rake this trench from higher ground with enfilade fire. In consequence the 5th Seaforth Highlanders suffered serious casualties, many men, including Captain M'Kenzie, the adjutant, being shot through the head. They therefore withdrew westwards, and attempts were made to form a defensive flank covering Doignies on the north. The enemy's fire was, however, too accurate to carry out this movement, the men being shot down as soon as they left the trench. The attempt had therefore to be abandoned.

While these events were in progress, the enemy advanced against Doignies from the north in close order. They were engaged by two machine-guns and a Lewis gun, which, though under fire from the front and flanks, inflicted heavy losses on them. These guns remained firing under the superintendence of Lieutenant Muntzer until they were put out of action. Two other guns were then taken from their emplacements, and from positions in the open continued to deal with large bodies of the enemy advancing from Louverval.

About 2 P.M. the enemy was found to have entered Doignies from the left, and a general withdrawal of the troops in Doignies and its vicinity to the Beaumetz-Morchies line began.

Sturgeon Avenue and the intermediate line south-east of Doignies, and the area south of the village between the intermediate line and the Beaumetz line, still remained in our hands.

The enemy's next objective was the Beaumetz-Morchies line. On the right, owing to the magnificent handling of the machine-guns, particularly those under the command of Lieutenant Potter, all his attempts to debouch from Doignies broke down, and in this area he was definitely pinned to the ground. Indeed these guns, notably those in Bruno Mill and on the sunken road west of Doignies, not only performed this rôle, but they also inflicted heavy casualties on the enemy moving along the Cambrai road.

He, however, made numerous attempts to reach the Corps line on the left. Here the garrison had been considerably weakened, as the remaining company of the 6th Black Watch had attempted a counter-attack about noon to relieve a post which was reported still to be holding out in the intermediate line. This company advanced some 300 yards, but having already suffered 50 per cent casualties, took up a position in some gun-pits north of the Cambrai road. Here they helped considerably to break up various attempts made by the enemy to reach the Beaumetz-Morchies line.

Machine-guns also played a large part in defeating these attacks. Lieutenant Menzies, with his gun between the Beaumetz and intermediate lines, had effectively engaged the enemy trying to advance from the latter, and refused to leave his gun, even though wounded in six places. He subsequently fell back into the Beaumetz line, where he rallied many stragglers, and organised the defence of the line.

In the late afternoon the situation was as follows : On the right, 154th Brigade remained with troops of 152nd Brigade in Sturgeon Avenue, as they were in the morning. Machine-guns encircled Doignies, and prevented the enemy from moving southwards from it between the intermediate and Beaumetz line. The Beaumetz line was held by the 4th Seaforths on the right, the 6th Seaforths in the centre, two and a half companies of the 7th Gordon Highlanders, and some remnants of the other three companies of the 7th Black Watch. The 8th Royal Scots and some sections of field companies remained in reserve, and had not as yet been engaged.

The Division, though seriously depleted in numbers, retained a continuous front.

Meanwhile the Corps commander had moved a brigade of the 19th Division to secure the Hermies-Lebucquière ridge, should the 152nd Brigade front be penetrated. A brigade of the 25th Division had also been moved forward to take up a position astride the Bapaume-Cambrai road in rear of the 153rd Brigade. Here also the companies of the 8th Royal Scots were held in readiness for an immediate counter-attack in case it became necessary.

It will be seen in the ensuing pages how the battle resolved itself into a series of attempts made by the enemy to roll up one or other of the Division's flanks, how every move of the enemy was successfully countered, and how, in spite of the fact that there never was a point in which one or other flank was not being seriously threatened, the Division was able to maintain a solid and continuous front for five days of rearguard fighting.

At 7 P.M. a counter-attack was delivered to regain Doignies by two battalions of the 57th Brigade (19th Division), the 8th Gloucesters and 15th Worcesters, with one company of tanks. The tanks successfully passed through Doignies, but the co-operation of the infantry was not sufficiently close to enable them to regain the village, with the result that the troops were only able to occupy the Beaumetz-Doignies road and the south-eastern outskirts of the village.

Meanwhile the situation at Morchies towards the left flank of the Division was giving cause for some anxiety. A battalion of the 74th Brigade, 25th Division, was therefore moved so as to form a flank just west of Morchies, and two sections of the 404th Field Company, R.E., were ordered to cover Beugny on the north-east and east.

Just prior to the counter-attack on Doignies, some gallant attempts had been made to withdraw guns from the Beaumetz-Doignies valley. Captain Manuel, R.F.A., succeeded in extricating " D " 255 by a daring piece of work, and later " C " 293 also managed to get their guns back. The attempts of " A " 255 and " C " 255, however, both failed owing to heavy machine-gun fire. " B " 255 was already in the hands of the enemy, all the guns having been destroyed.

The losses were in some degree made up by the arrival of the 112th Brigade, R.F.A., two batteries of which were placed under 256th Brigade, R.F.A., and two under 255th Brigade. At midnight 235th Brigade, R.F.A., also arrived, and was placed under the command of the 255th Brigade. At 4 A.M. a third brigade of artillery arrived, the 104th Army Brigade, and was placed under orders of 293rd Brigade, R.F.A.

The machine-gunners at the end of the day had forty guns in action out of an original total of sixty-four. These were reinforced during the night by a machine-gun company of the 25th Division.

The Division therefore presented a solid front, was organised in depth, and was adequately covered by machine-guns and artillery, and, as far as its own line was concerned, could await the morning with confidence.

However, during the early hours of the 22nd, orders were issued that to conform with the movements of the 17th Division on the right flank, the 154th Brigade was to fall back with its right on the defences of Hermies, and its left on the Beaumetz-Morchies line. This move was necessary, as farther south the enemy had driven back the Fifth Army to such an extent that the evacuation of the Flesquières Ridge had become necessary.

The line was thus recast without incident so as to run from Hermies along a partially dug trench connecting Hermies and the Beaumetz line, known as the Hermies Switch, thence as it had been overnight, with the exception that parts of the battalions which had counter-attacked

Doignies, the 8th and 10th Worcesters, were now also in the Beaumetz line.

The night was quiet, the enemy no doubt being busy moving his guns and bringing up ammunition. His infantry, however, made many gallant attempts to cut the wire of the Beaumetz line by hand. At 6 A.M. a bombardment of our positions opened, which continued until 10 A.M., when his infantry launched a strong attack. This was particularly heavy about the Bapaume-Cambrai road and the Hermies Switch; the enemy, however, only succeeded in driving in our outposts, and the line held firm in spite of all his attempts.

The fighting continued throughout the morning and afternoon. Continuous attempts made by the enemy to dribble up were dealt with by machine-guns, rifles, and rifle grenades, while the artillery several times dispersed masses of Germans forming up for attack between Louverval and Doignies.

The Jocks were at the top of their form, were inflicting great losses on the enemy, and were complete masters of the situation. Only once did the Germans penetrate our lines, just south of the Cambrai road. They were immediately ejected by a bombing attack delivered by the 6th Seaforth Highlanders. All ranks had, in fact, the greatest confidence in their ability to defeat the enemy's attempts so long as the line north and south of them held firm and secured their flanks.

Unfortunately this was not to be the case. On our left flank the enemy's attack in the morning had been successful. The Corps line was broken 2000 yards north-west of Morchies, and the Divisional line began to be enfiladed by artillery fire from the north.

To prevent the enemy from exploiting this success and turning the left flank of the Division, two companies of the 3rd Worcesters were ordered to take up a position west of Morchies facing north, and at the same time the 19th Division ordered the 58th Brigade to dig-in on the spurs 1000 yards north of Beugny, also facing north.

During this day 256th Brigade, R.F.A., played a memorable part. During the morning its batteries brought effective observed fire to bear on the enemy east of the Beaumetz-Morchies line, doing considerable damage to his attacking troops. In the afternoon they ran their guns out of the pits, and engaged over open sights masses of the enemy on the left flank of the Division, particularly near Maricourt Wood, where several big concentrations were broken up. Later, when a counter-attack accompanied by tanks took place in this area, " B " 256 covered their advance with smoke, upon which large numbers of the enemy were thrown into confusion, and were subsequently heavily engaged by the concentrated fire of the whole artillery brigade. This battery, commanded by Major R. Will, about the same time completely neutralised an enemy battery that was endeavouring to come into action near Maricourt Wood. For four hours on the afternoon of the 22nd the 256th Brigade, R.F.A., fired continuously over open sights, the howitzers using instantaneous fuzes, and caused very considerable casualties to the enemy.

The amount of ammunition expended by this brigade on the first two days is of interest :—

	Battery.	No. of guns.	No. of rounds.	Rounds per gun.
21st March	A	5	4800	960
	B	4	3600	900
	C	5	4000	800
	D	4	3700	925
22nd March	A	5	5100	1020
	B	4	7000	1750
	C	5	6000	1200
	D	4	2500	625

—a total of 36,700 rounds fired by eighteen guns. Imagination can easily picture the efforts made by the drivers and horses of the ammunition waggons in bringing this amount of ammunition through the barraged roads to the guns.

About 7 P.M. 235th, 255th, 256th, and 234th Brigades, R.F.A., all withdrew to positions farther in rear, Colonel Dyson assuming command of all field artillery covering the Divisional front. This latter arrangement was necessary, as communication between artillery brigades and Divisional headquarters no longer existed.

The machine-gunners had also reaped a fine harvest. Four guns under Lieutenant Menzies had almost more targets than they could engage. Lieutenant Broadbent, just south of the Cambrai road, was able to fire six belts into a large number of Germans who suddenly emerged from a disused trench on to the Cambrai road at a range of under 100 yards.

In the attack on the left of the Division north of Morchies, Lieutenant Birchwood fired many thousand rounds into the attacking waves as they topped a ridge. The machine-gunners were, in fact, thoroughly pleased with their day's work, and justifiably so.

Towards the evening the enemy's success on the left began to make itself felt, strong pressure being brought against the Division from the north. Just before 6 P.M. a heavy attack developed. The 7th Black Watch were engaged from both sides of the Beaumetz line, and were driven back into the Beaumetz-Morchies road, where a company of the 8th Royal Scots were already in position, and had been doing fine work with their rifles. The remnants of the company of the 6th Black Watch in the gun-pits (see p. 279) were cut off from the Beaumetz-Morchies line, and fell back in a southerly direction, lining the Bapaume-Cambrai road. Here they were reinforced by a platoon of the 8th Royal Scots and the remnants of the 7th Gordon Highlanders, and were supported in rear by men of the 6th Gordon Highlanders and 6th Seaforth Highlanders, lining the Beaumetz-Doignies road. These movements had become necessary, as the turning of the Beaumetz-Morchies line and the enemy's progress on the left was compelling us to change front and face north. The enemy advanced as far as the Cambrai road, which he lined on the side opposite to our troops ; and though a certain amount of bombing took place, he made no serious attempt to cross it.

With a view to opposing the enemy's advance more frontally, orders were issued for the evacuation of the Corps line north of Beaumetz, and for the taking up of a new line covering Lebucquière and Velu, the remnants of the 153rd Brigade, the 8th Royal Scots, and the 6th Gordon Highlanders being withdrawn into Divisional reserve at Fremicourt under the command of the B.G.C. 153rd

Brigade. The line then ran from Hermies along the Hermies Switch to the Beaumetz line, thence along the Beaumetz line, from which it bent back between Beaumetz and Lebucquière, to a point west of Chaufours Wood. The 154th Brigade, with the 8th Gloucesters and 10th Warwicks of the 57th Brigade (19th Division) on the right, held this line as far as the southern corner of Beaumetz ; next to them came the 152nd Brigade, with the 10th Warwicks and 401st and 404th Field Companies, thence the line was continued to the Divisional left boundary by the 34th Brigade (23rd Division), with the 11th Cheshires. The 58th Brigade (19th Division) and the 400th Field Company were in position to the north of Beugny, and also extended the left of the Divisional line towards Morchies.

During the evening, owing to the uncertainty of the situation in the north, Divisional headquarters moved to tents at Bancourt, and thence to the late Corps headquarters at Grévillers, while all three brigades moved their headquarters to the old Divisional H.Q. at Fremicourt.

Early in the morning of the 23rd the Division was warned that events in the south were such that their withdrawal to the Army line would become necessary, and that if that were to take place by day, the 154th Brigade were to conform to the movements of the 17th Division on their right.

Subsequent events will show how the magnificent resistance offered by the 154th Brigade in the Corps line materially assisted the withdrawal of the 17th Division.

At 6 A.M. on the morning of the 23rd an intense bombardment of our line again broke out, and between 8 A.M. and 9 A.M. an attack in force was launched by the enemy along the whole front. Stubborn fighting ensued. Before the weight of the attack along the Cambrai road the line fell back, and by 10 A.M. the enemy were working round towards the rear of Lebucquière. At 10.15 A.M. the order was given to the 152nd Brigade to withdraw by Velu Wood through the Army line, which was now garrisoned by the 56th Brigade, 19th Division, and the 7th Brigade, 25th Division. They fell back in perfect order, fighting both to the front and to their flanks. In this operation Major Ernest Johnson, commanding the 6th Seaforth Highlanders, who had shown conspicuous gallantry in organising the defence of the Beaumetz line, was mortally wounded.

Meanwhile the angle in the new line south-east of Beaumetz had also given way; but the 4th Seaforth Highlanders and the 7th Argyll and Sutherland Highlanders, though very heavily attacked, had retained their hold on the Corps line with great determination. The fighting of these two battalions on this occasion certainly constitutes one of the finest performances of the Division.

Shortly before 11 A.M., attacked in front and threatened from the rear, they were compelled to withdraw from the Corps line as far as its junction with the Hermies Switch. They, however, only withdrew a short distance, and disposed themselves facing Beaumetz. In this position they checked the enemy's enveloping movement in spite of his determined efforts to dislodge them. It must be borne in mind that the 154th Brigade remained in this position, fighting to cover the withdrawal of the 17th Division on their right, while the enemy was in Lebucquière, 2000 yards behind them, in their direct line of retreat.

One company of the Argyll and Sutherland Highlanders hung on in a sunken road south of Beaumetz with both its flanks turned until 11.30 A.M. They finally retired fighting to the railway east of Velu, where they formed a line facing west to cover the retirement of their comrades still engaged in the Corps line.

In their heroic resistance the 154th Brigade were magnificently supported, both by the artillery covering them and the machine-gunners. A very gallant action by "A" Battery, 293th Brigade, R.F.A., considerably assisted the withdrawal of the infantry. This battery, commanded by Major Leake, remained in action near Velu Wood until an infantry officer, retiring through the battery, reported to the O.C. that all his men had come back; the battery then limbered up and came out of action with the infantry.

The machine-guns fired an enormous number of rounds, and the difficulty of keeping them supplied with ammunition was considerable. Major Harcourt, commanding the 154th Brigade M.G. Company, however, himself galloped a limber along this line of guns, dropping water and ammunition at the emplacements in the face of close-range fire.

Two guns under 2nd Lieutenant Fenton on the Velu-Beaumetz road did much to hold up the enemy's advance on this portion of the front. On one occasion a party of about a company and a half in strength marched down a forward slope in fours. Lieutenant Fenton waited until they were within decisive range, and then turned two guns on to them simultaneously, wiping them out.

Subsequently the defensive flank facing Beaumetz was driven in, two platoons of the 7th Argyll and Sutherland Highlanders left to cover the withdrawal being surrounded and cut off.

Fighting, however, continued in the Corps line for over an hour, though field-guns in positions between Beaumetz and Doignies fired point-blank at the trench, while machine-guns enfiladed it and infantry attacks were delivered against it.

Finally, when almost surrounded, with Velu in the enemy's hands, the troops withdrew, their retirement being covered by machine-guns. In this phase of the action Major Harcourt again distinguished himself. He placed five guns and some Lewis guns in position between Velu Wood and the railway, and with them held up the German advance for five hours, thus allowing the whole right flank of the Division to effect an orderly retirement. Here he fought with the greatest gallantry until the enemy, by firing the grass and advancing from Velu under cover of the smoke, was almost upon him. His post was then withdrawn southward, Major Harcourt having been severely wounded in the action.

Meanwhile the 152nd and 153rd Brigades had withdrawn through the 19th Division in the Army line, and were organising a line of resistance from Villers au Flos to Bancourt, known as the Red line. The 6th Gordon Highlanders were, however, left as a reserve to the 56th Brigade (19th Division) at Mill Cross east of Fremicourt, and two sections of the 404th Field Company were still forming part of the defences of Beugny.

The line was held as follows : the 152nd Infantry Brigade from about Villers au Flos to Bancourt—the 153rd Brigade defended Bancourt ; while between Bancourt and the Cambrai road the line was continued by the 252nd Tunnelling

Company, R.E., two companies of the 8th Royal Scots, and 100 sappers of the Divisional R.E.

During all this time the battle for the Army line continued, though little information as to how the day was going was received, all that was known being that on the left the enemy, in an attack which was repulsed, had reached the wire of the Army line north-west of Beugny by 10 A.M.

During the afternoon and evening the brigades were gradually assembled and reorganised, the 154th Brigade being collected and formed into a Divisional reserve just east of the Bapaume-Peronne road. A composite unit of the ten surviving machine-guns was also placed in position in the Bancourt line. The artillery were still in action, covering the Green line.

The two sections of the 404th Field Company forming part of the defence of Beugny were also extricated by Captain Duke, M.C., R.E., adjutant to the C.R.E., who had set out on a bicycle to discover them, and were brought into Divisional reserve. In the evening the field-cookers were brought up and the men had a hot meal and were rested. The night was, however, intensely cold, and the absence of their greatcoats—left behind in the trenches—was much felt. In fact, the cold was so extreme, a sharp frost having set in, that anything in the nature of adequate rest for men in shell-holes and open trenches was out of the question.

Touch was obtained at dawn on 24th March on the left with the 57th Brigade, north of the Cambrai road. On the right the results of the calamity which had befallen the Fifth Army were now making themselves felt, and for the remainder of the operations the situation on that flank was obscure when not critical.

It was, however, at this time known that a brigade of the 17th Division was about Rocquigny.

At 9 A.M. information was received that the right flank of the Vth Corps on our immediate south had been turned, and that the Germans were in Bus. The 152nd Brigade therefore threw back its right flank, and took up a line in shell-holes in front of Riencourt. Before noon this flank was strengthened by the arrival of the 6th Gordon Highlanders from Mill Cross, who were placed in the line south-east of Beaulencourt astride the Bapaume-Peronne road. Here they were well hidden in old shell-holes in a position of great natural strength. They also obtained touch on their right with elements of the 17th, 63rd, and 2nd Divisions.

From this point onwards the troops had not only to fight a continuous rearguard action, but had also repeatedly to form a defensive right flank to prevent the Division from being involved in the debacle which had taken place farther south. The point of interest had now changed from the left flank to the right.

Early in the afternoon the Army line east of Fremicourt was penetrated by the enemy, and by three o'clock troops from the 19th Division were retiring through our lines and taking up a position in rear. News was now received that the enemy's progress farther south was becoming more rapid than ever, and that he was advancing from Morval and Les Boeufs and in a general direction towards our right rear. At 4.30 P.M. troops of the Vth Corps fell back through the 152nd Brigade, and there was a general retirement beyond our right flank. From this point onwards touch with British troops on our right was never regained.

Between 5 and 6 P.M. the enemy debouched from Villers-au-Flos under the steady fire of rifles and machine-guns to enfilade our positions. At 6 P.M. the 152nd Brigade, in close touch with the enemy, withdrew through the 154th Brigade, which in turn gradually fell back.

Meanwhile on the left the line had been heavily shelled, and the enemy made several attempts to debouch from Fremicourt. His efforts, however, all broke down under the fire of the machine-gunners, sappers, and 8th Royal Scots.

At 6.30 P.M., in conjunction with the movement on the right, the line here also fell back by successive stages.

Meanwhile the 19th Division had taken up a new position east of Grévillers, through which our troops retired.

The passage through Bapaume during this retirement will leave an ineffaceable memory to many. Shells, steadily arriving from high-velocity guns, some bursting in the air, some on the ground, some containing gas; dense masses of guns, transport, and troops packing the road; the immense Hun dump in flames, with its shells and ammunition exploding with the noise of a big battle in itself; and the emptying of the great Expeditionary Force Canteen. The personnel of the latter had wisely fled, and anything that could be carried away was taken by the troops to save it from falling into the hands of the enemy. The brief interlude in which the Jocks had a free hand to help themselves at the Bapaume canteen was one of the redeeming features of the retirement.

It is rumoured that the Boche expended considerable energy in delivering a set-piece attack on Bapaume after its defenders had evacuated it, but it has been impossible to confirm this report. At 8.30 P.M. orders were issued for the Division to take up a line from Warlencourt-Eaucourt to Loupart Wood, the movement being covered by a force of 1000 men who had arrived as reinforcements with an improvised machine-gun company of sixteen guns. This force was commanded by Lieut.-Colonel S. Macdonald, D.S.O., 6th Seaforth Highlanders, who had just returned from leave.

The Division was in position on the new line at 1 A.M., 25th March, as follows: the 7th Argyll and Sutherland Highlanders facing south-east on the Bapaume-Albert road near the Butte de Warlencourt, thence from right to left came the 4th Gordon Highlanders, 4th Seaforth Highlanders, 6th Gordon Highlanders, 6th Seaforth Highlanders, 6/7 Black Watch, 8th Royal Scots, the 7th Gordon Highlanders and 5th Seaforth Highlanders being in reserve. The left of this line curved round the north-east corner of Loupart Wood.

The artillery had throughout the retirement been conforming to the movements of the infantry. They had, on the morning of the 24th, broken up several concentrations of the enemy between Beugny and Lebucquière near the Cambrai road. They had also repeatedly and successfully dealt with the enemy's attempts to gain a footing in the Army line. About 11 A.M. on the 24th they had, however, owing to the obscurity of the situation on the right of the Division, withdrawn to the neighbourhood of Thilloy. At 7 P.M. they had again been withdrawn, 235th and 256th Brigades, R.F.A., to the north of Irles, 104th, 112th, 255th, and 293rd Brigades to between Irles and Puisieux.

Divisional headquarters had moved to Achiet-le-Petit at 6 P.M., moving again at 4 A.M. with the headquarters of the 19th Division to Puisieux, while all three brigade headquarters were at Irles.

Throughout the night of 24-25th March no touch with British troops could be obtained on either flank, though it was known that the 19th Division was on a line from Le Barque to the east of Grévillers.

At 10 A.M. troops of the 2nd Division could be observed away to our right, with bodies of the enemy penetrating between them and the 154th Brigade near the Butte de Warlencourt. At 10 A.M. the 19th Division was seen withdrawing on our left. At 11 A.M. the enemy was in Le Barque, and were advancing along our front with light field-guns closely supporting the infantry. He was held in front without difficulty, and sustained considerable casualties, machine-guns under Lieutenants Strapp and Broadbent having been repeatedly in action during the day. The right flank was, however, in constant danger of being turned, as the enemy first entered Le Sars and then directed his advance on Pys, so that the 152nd Brigade had to dispose troops facing south and west. Here hand-to-hand fighting occurred, on one occasion the enemy's line being driven back and a prisoner secured in a charge.

However, at 2.15 P.M. the whole line had to fall back to prevent being surrounded, the adjutant and two other officers of the 6th Seaforth Highlanders fighting with a party of men to the end, all being either killed or captured. Lieut.-Colonel Gemmell, commanding the 8th Royal Scots, was also killed, and Colonel Long, commanding the 5th Gordon Highlanders, wounded.

The 154th Brigade therefore took up a position on the high ground east of Pys, and the 152nd and 153rd Brigades east of Irles, and the 8th Royal Scots south of Achiet-le-Petit. Here again the 154th Brigade were in danger of being completely surrounded, and had to fall back to the south of Irles.

In this position the troops engaged parties of the enemy massing for attack successfully ; but the exhaustion of the men had become such that they could no longer offer a protracted resistance. They had been in action continuously since the morning of 21st March ; and at the end of five days, in which the fighting during the day and the intense cold of the nights had denied to them any real rest, their vitality was at its lowest ebb.

The remnant of the Division was thus left still facing the enemy, its three brigade headquarters just in rear of the fighting line still in the same order of battle in which they had begun the engagement, but their fighting efficiency was gone. With no British troops on their right nearer than Albert, there was no other alternative left but to break off the engagement and withdraw. Accordingly orders were issued for the Division to concentrate at Colincamps, where Divisional headquarters had opened at 4.35 P.M.

The withdrawal of all that was left of the Highland Division along the road from Puisieux to Colincamps was a melancholy spectacle: a long line of men and horses, tired and exhausted almost beyond the limits of human endurance, dragging themselves along, many with undressed wounds. The men fell back in groups, not as formed bodies, but not as in a disorderly rout. Every man retained his arms and equipment, and in spirit would have taken up any line ordered and continued the struggle; but in their acute stage of exhaustion further effective resistance was out of the question, and so was not asked of them.

The total casualties sustained by the Division in this action were 219 officers and 4696 other ranks. Of these, the infantry losses amounted to 157 officers and 3744 men. Assuming that the nine battalions of infantry each went into action 600 strong, excluding transport drivers, &c., it will be seen that out of a total of 5400 officers and men only 1500 survived. These figures in themselves show the nature of the fighting. The casualties in officers were also, as is always the case, heavy. Of the 10 commanding officers of the infantry and pioneer battalions, 3 were killed and 3 wounded.

Not only had the men offered a magnificent resistance, but their commanders had handled them admirably. In spite of the fact that after the first few hours of the engagement one or more flanks had at all times to be defended as well as the front, the enemy succeeded in cutting off no considerable body of troops; and yet no withdrawa

MAP X.—THE GERMAN OFFENSIVE: POSITIONS OF 51ST (HIGHLAND) DIVISION, 24/26TH MARCH 1918.

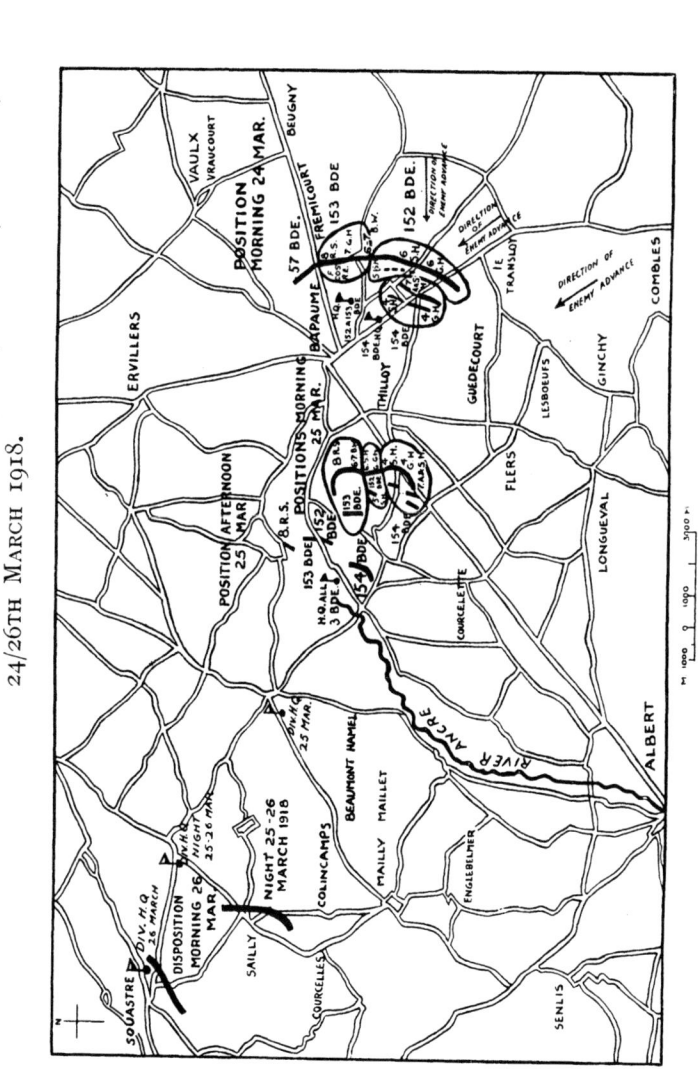

took place until the close of the action, except in close contact with the enemy.

In the first three days alone eight separate German Divisions operated on the Divisional front—the 3rd Guards, the 4th and 5th Bavarians, the 17th, 24th Reserves, the 39th, the 119th, and the 195th. Certainly one other, a Jaeger Division, was engaged on the fourth day, and almost certainly others that were not identified.

The Germans, possibly the 3rd Guards Division, whom the Highland Division had twice before heavily defeated in the Ypres and Cambrai battles, showed their appreciation of the stubborn resistance offered by the Jocks by floating over to our lines a white paper balloon, on which was written, " Good old 51st, still sticking it out." A Jaeger officer captured near Grévillers, on being asked if they had suffered heavy losses, replied, " We have not yet captured sufficient ground to make us a cemetery for our dead." Certainly a tour of the German cemeteries after the country had been recaptured showed a huge increase in new graves.

One of the features of this battle was the work of the " Q " and administrative officers. The movements of battalion transport and the ammunition column were carried out in perfect order through the whole operation. Men were issued with hot food from the field-kitchens whenever a pause in the operations made this possible. Not a single vehicle except those that were unfit for the road fell into the hands of the enemy. The supply of ammunition, though it caused the gravest anxiety, and though the Divisional Ammunition Column was at one time completely empty, never actually failed. As regards the supply of gun ammunition and the making up of deficiencies in guns, the artillery made their own arrangements. Although the demands for ammunition were heavy, it cannot be said, in spite of the enormous quantity expended, that any unit suffered from the want of it. Moreover, every dump of field artillery ammunition was exhausted before our lines retired behind it, the Beugny and Lebucquière dumps being worked even though continually being set on fire by the hostile shell-fire.

By the evening of the 22nd seventeen new field-guns had been issued to replace guns knocked out.

The Divisional and brigade signal sections had considerable difficulty in maintaining any form of communication, but they competed with their difficulties admirably. The linesmen, with great gallantry, laid and maintained numerous lines throughout the operations. In consequence, after the first phase of the battle, it was nearly always possible to talk from Divisional to brigade headquarters. When one considers the volume of shell-fire to which these lines and the men laying and repairing them were subjected, it will be realised that the signallers, though their work is of a kind which often passes unnoticed, must have shown a fine courage and determination. They were assisted considerably in their task by the fact that after the first phase all three brigades occupied the same headquarters.

At Colincamps the troops were collected. It was particularly noticeable to the officers who were sorting the men into their different Divisions and units in the dark, that when a group of men were asked who they were, the Jocks almost invariably replied, not by giving the name of their battalion, but "51st Division," strong evidence that the Divisional esprit, in spite of the last five days, was still unimpaired.

From Colincamps the troops marched to Fonquevillers, where they lay for the night in the most bitter cold, outposts being thrown out at dawn facing south-east, as no information was yet forthcoming as to how far the enemy had followed up the retirement.

At 8 A.M. a further move, protected by rear and flank guards, was made to Souastre.

Here a message was received stating that the enemy were entering Hebuterne in armoured cars. The Division was therefore immediately disposed on a line covering Souastre facing south and south-east, and began to dig in. Happily the report proved false. In the evening the Division marched to Pas, where they bivouacked during the night, moving to the Neuvilette area the following day.

On leaving the Third Army, General Sir Julian Byng, the Army Commander, sent the following message :—

"I cannot allow the 51st Division to leave the Third Army without expressing my appreciation of their splendid conduct during the stage of the great battle which is just completed. By their devotion and courage they have broken up overwhelming attacks and prevented the enemy gaining his object—namely, a decisive victory. I wish them every possible good luck."

The Division had thus not only proved its efficiency in the attack, but it had earned from its Army Commander the highest praise both for the excellence of its work, carried out during a period of stationary warfare, and also its powers of defence.

One important fact had been confirmed from the fighting which is worth recording, as it in some degree accounted for the rolling-up of the front and support lines on the 152nd and 153rd Brigade fronts on the morning on which the attack opened.

A few days before the battle broke out, it had been appreciated that the heaps of earth excavated out of the enormous trenches dug by the Division were so great that it not only prevented the posts from seeing neighbouring posts on their flanks, but the men, even when standing on their fire-steps, could not see to their rear or to their flanks because of the great mounds of soil on the parapet and parados.

Orders were therefore being issued that these mounds were to be levelled down so that a man could stand on the fire-step and have a clear field of fire all round him. The German attack, however, came before this order could be put into effect, with the result that the men in their deep trenches were suddenly assailed from their flanks and rear by an enemy whom they could not see to shoot before he was within bombing range of them. They thus had little opportunity of offering effective resistance to the enfilade attack, and were, no doubt, in consequence rapidly overwhelmed.

The levelling down of the excavated earth during trench construction subsequently became a standing order in the Division.

CHAPTER XV.

THE GERMAN OFFENSIVE (*Contd.*)—THE BATTLE OF THE LYS.

On 1st April the Division moved by train to an area near Bethune, where it remained for a few days resting and refitting. The only event of interest that occurred in this area was the accidental bombing by daylight of the vicinity of Divisional headquarters by a British reconnaissance aeroplane, fortunately without casualties.

On 7th April the Division was transferred to the XIth Corps, and was moved to an area in rear of the Portuguese Divisions, which at the time were holding the line about Neuve Chapelle and Festubert.

Divisional headquarters was established at Robecq, a village which it had occupied on its first arrival in France. The 152nd Brigade were billeted at Ham en Artois, the 153rd Brigade at Busnes—or Business, as the Jocks called it,—the 154th Brigade at Gonnehem, and the Divisional artillery at Amettes.

The units were in the throes of reorganisation under most difficult circumstances. Some three thousand men had joined as reinforcements, but few new officers had arrived; moreover, the authorities at the base had made confusion worse confounded by posting Gordons to Black Watch battalions, and Seaforths to Argylls, and thereby had considerably tried the temper of the men and increased the difficulties of their commanders.

While the Division was resting in this area, there was much speculation as to whether the enemy's effort had not spent itself in the south, and whether he was likely to make a similar attempt in this part of the front, with a view to threatening the Channel ports.

Ultimately the same white directing posts were reported on the enemy's front as had appeared opposite to the Division just prior to the German attack on 21st March, and it was then generally felt that a new offensive in this part of the front could be anticipated with certainty.

At this time arrangements were being made for the relief of the two Portuguese Divisions in the line, with a view to the frontage held by them being taken over by the 50th and another Division. This relief was planned to take place on 10th April.

Meanwhile, certain changes had taken place in the Division. General Pelham Burn, whose health for the last year had been very indifferent, was compelled to give up command of the 152nd Brigade. It is difficult to estimate the loss which not only his brigade but the whole Division sustained at his departure.

Throughout his period of command he had displayed a knowledge of minor tactics and trench craft which had been invaluable both to his own battalions and to the infantry as a whole.

To the satisfaction of all, General Burn was succeeded by the G.S.O. 1, Lieut.-Colonel J. K. Dick-Cunynghame, C.M.G., D.S.O. There was probably no officer into whose hands the traditions of the 152nd Brigade could have been better entrusted. Moreover, this appointment not only secured to Colonel Dick-Cunynghame his promotion, but also secured for the Division a continuance of his services— unfortunately, however, for but a few days.

Colonel Dick-Cunynghame was succeeded as G.S.O. 1 by Colonel A. Symons, C.M.G., 13th Hussars, who had recently been employed at the War Office, and later on the staff of the IVth Corps.

The country in which the Division was billeted and in which it was to become engaged was typical of Flanders— low-lying, studded with hamlets, farms, and orchards, and intersected by dykes, ditches, and fences. In some places it was marshy, and nowhere could trenches be dug to a depth of more than three feet without water being reached.

At 4.5 A.M. on 9th April an intense bombardment broke out on the front of the Portuguese Divisions in the line about Richebourg l'Avoue, Neuve Chapelle, Fauquissart.

At 10 A.M. information was received that the Portuguese had broken.

At 6.30 A.M. the 152nd Brigade, in accordance with instructions issued by the corps, had ordered its battalions to move to positions of reserve—the 5th Seaforth Highlanders to Huit Maisons, the 6th Seaforth Highlanders to Lacouture, the 6th Gordon Highlanders being in reserve at Zelobas and La Croix Marmuse.

At 11.30 A.M. the 152nd Brigade had established its headquarters near La Croix Marmuse, where its battalions were waiting for guides from the units which they were to relieve in Huit Maisons and Lacouture—the Corps Cyclists and King Edward's Horse.

The 152nd Brigade was at this time directly under the orders of the XIth Corps.

As soon as definite information from the front was received, and it became evident that the German attack was making considerable progress, the 154th Brigade was ordered into the 55th Division area east of the Aire-La Bassée Canal, the Divisional artillery to Gonnehem, and the 153rd Brigade to the Le Cornet Malo-Pacaut area. The 51st Division Machine Gun Battalion was also ordered to send one company to join each of the three brigades.

At this time the information concerning the progress of the battle was extremely vague. It was, however, appreciated that the Portuguese had been overwhelmed, and could no longer be considered a fighting force, and that the only troops opposing the Germans in front of the Division were King Edward's Horse and the Corps Cyclists. The 50th Division were known to be on a line east of the river Lawe from Bout de Ville northwards.

At 12.45 P.M. the 5th and 6th Seaforth Highlanders began their advance, guided by troops of King Edward's Horse. It was the intention of the officer commanding 6th Seaforth Highlanders to place two companies in Lacouture. The leading company had, however, only reached the foot-bridge east of the Vert Lannot (subsequently called Boundary Bridge) when it came under hostile rifle and machine-gun fire. In spite of the brisk fire which was engaging them, an attempt was made to continue the advance, but without success. Two companies were therefore placed in position along the western bank of the river

Lawe, from 200 yards south of Boundary Bridge up to the southern bridge at Vieille Chapelle: one was disposed on the western outskirts of that village; one in reserve at Les Lobes. An attempt to blow up Boundary Bridge unfortunately ended only in its partial destruction.

On the front of the 5th Seaforth Highlanders, King Edward's Horse were offering a stubborn resistance against great pressure on a line from a point some 300 yards north of Lacouture to just south of Bout de Ville. The situation was, however, desperate. Both flanks had been turned, the enemy having occupied both Lacouture and Bout de Ville. The cavalry nevertheless held on in their isolated position, and maintained themselves with the greatest gallantry.

At this time Le Marais post was held by troops of the 50th Division. Two companies of the 5th Seaforth Highlanders were therefore ordered to hold the west bank of the river Lawe, while the remaining two companies crossed the river. They reached Huit Maisons, two platoons of the leading company reinforcing the cavalry garrison there, while two platoons lay in support of them. The remaining company was diverted so as to form a flank facing northeast along the road to Fosse. At this period the shelling was intense, being particularly violent on Fosse village and on both banks of the Lawe.

Some desperate fighting ensued, almost immediately after the troops were in position. King Edward's Horse had already been heavily engaged, and had defeated repeated attempts to envelop their left flank. The arrival of the 5th Seaforth Highlanders was most timely, and considerably relieved the pressure, the garrison being able to retain its hold on Huit Maisons for another three hours. In fact, it was not until Le Marais post had fallen, and the enemy appeared to be surrounding Huit Maisons, that the garrison fell back in face of heavy enfilade machine-gun fire and bombing. These troops withdrew to Fosse post, which, with the assistance of the battalion headquarters of the 5th Seaforth Highlanders, they occupied on three sides.

While this action was in progress "A" Company of the 8th Gordon Highlanders, under the command of Captain J. R. Christie, was sent to Vieille Chapelle to reinforce the garrison there of King Edward's Horse under Lieutenant

Stein. This company placed one platoon just west of the bridge across the Lawe, the remainder taking up defensive positions in Vieille Chapelle, in spite of a terrific bombardment to which the village was being subjected.

The remaining three companies of the 6th Gordon Highlanders deployed on a line west of the Lawe due north of La Tombe Willot.

Meanwhile on the left the 153rd Brigade had also been ordered forward. The roads were, however, so congested with Portuguese troops and refugees moving westwards that it was not until as late as 5.45 P.M. that the battalions could move off from Pacaut. At that hour the 7th Gordon Highlanders, with four machine-guns, moved forward to take up a line east of the river Lawe north of the village of Fosse. These battalions, however, during their advance, learnt from troops of the 50th Division whom they met that there was considerable uncertainty as to the situation. Moreover, a change in dispositions became necessary, as the Divisional front was suddenly extended so as to include the whole of Lestrem. As a result, practically none of the 153rd Infantry Brigade were able to cross the river, except for one platoon of the 7th Gordon Highlanders, which formed a bridgehead protecting the bridge just south of the Lestrem Loop.

The 7th Gordon Highlanders and the 6th Black Watch ultimately took up a position on the west bank of the Lawe from just north of Fosse to Lestrem inclusive, the 7th Gordon Highlanders being on the right.

On the right of the Division the 154th Brigade, until the morning of the 10th, was under orders of the 55th Division, the 4th Seaforth Highlanders remaining with the 166th Brigade until 13th April.

The 7th Argyll and Sutherland Highlanders had moved off at 11.40 A.M. on the 9th, and after various vicissitudes and alterations of plans, due to rapidly changing circumstances, were finally disposed with the 7th Argyll and Sutherland Highlanders along the west bank of the Lawe from Pont Tournant inclusive to Boundary Bridge. The 4th Gordon Highlanders remained in reserve about Les Caudrons.

At 7 P.M. the Divisional artillery came into action between the villages of Paradis and La Croix Marmuse.

THE GERMAN OFFENSIVE

Thus at nightfall the Division was in position in the same order of battle as in the operations about Bapaume: 154th Brigade on the right, 152nd Brigade in the centre, and 153rd Brigade on the left. On the flanks touch was maintained on the right with the 55th Division, who were still in their original front line, but had been compelled to form a defensive flank to connect up with the river Lawe; on the left with the 50th Division, who were being heavily engaged about Estaires.

The 51st Division was entirely west of the Lawe, except for the 6th Gordon Highlanders at Vieille Chapelle, the 5th Seaforth Highlanders at Fosse, and the one platoon of the 7th Gordon Highlanders south of the Lestrem Loop.

By dawn on 10th April the whole Division, less the 4th Seaforth Highlanders, had reverted to the command of General Carter-Campbell. No changes had been made in dispositions during the night except that half the reserve company of the Divisional machine-gun battalion had been sent forward to reinforce the 153rd Brigade front, while two companies of the 39th Machine Gun Battalion, due to arrive at Calonne during the day, were placed at the disposal of the Division.

Throughout the day the 152nd Brigade experienced the most sanguinary fighting. The enemy during the night had, in a brilliant enterprise, managed to dribble across Boundary Bridge and push machine-guns and riflemen into the farms just west of it. These he covered by other machine-guns on the eastern bank of the Lawe. From the farms and outbuildings he inflicted numerous casualties to the 6th Seaforth Highlanders by close-range machine-gun fire. When daylight came, he attempted to reinforce them by pushing parties across the bridge, over which only one man could advance at a time. The Seaforths put a stop to this manœuvre by rifle and Lewis-gun fire, and many Germans shot on the bridge were drowned in the river. A counter-attack was launched against the farms by two platoons of the 6th Seaforth Highlanders, supported by covering fire from the 8th Argyll and Sutherland Highlanders, but it broke down under the intense volume of machine-gun fire directed against it.

At 3 P.M. a more deliberately prepared counter-attack was delivered by one company of the 6th Gordon Highlanders sent forward for the purpose. Three of its platoons attacked and successfully occupied the northern of the two farms. The troops were, however, held up in the open in front of the second farm. In this position they were in their turn attacked by some fifty of the enemy. The Gordons held their ground until dusk, when fifteen men out of an original total of ninety-seven rejoined the remaining platoon of their company.

Meanwhile the 6th Gordon Highlanders and King Edward's Horse in Vieille Chapelle, resisting with the utmost vigour, were repeatedly attacked, but gave no ground. A Lewis-gun team on the roof of a cottage remained in action and inflicted many casualties on the enemy, in spite of the building being several times hit by shells.

Throughout the whole day, while the enemy's grip was continuously tightening on them, this company and the cavalry defeated every attempt made by the enemy to drive them in. On the night of the 10th communication between battalion headquarters and Vieille Chapelle was no longer possible. Captain Christie therefore decided to destroy the bridges. An R.E. officer and one sapper were available to carry out the work; but the explosives, for a reason which has never been explained, had been dumped half a mile west of the village.

A party of the 6th Gordon Highlanders, however, made their way under heavy fire to the dump, and successfully carried the charges back to the village. The main bridge was blown up the same night, but the fire directed against the other bridges was so accurate that they had to be left intact.

On the left attempts were also made to blow up the bridges in the Lestrem Loop; but these were only partially successful, and none of the bridges were totally destroyed. At 8 A.M. the enemy, being admirably led by his officers, managed to rush the crossings at the Lock de la Rault and at Pont Riqueul, a subaltern officer being mentioned by name in the German official communiqué for the gallantry and initiative displayed by him in this enterprise. The defenders of the bridges were then driven back, and became absorbed in the line, held as a chord line to the Lestrem Loop, along the Lestrem-Fosse road.

About 10.30 A.M. the enemy also crossed the Lestrem Bridge and entered the village. He was, however, counter-attacked by the 6th D.C.L.I. of the 50th Division and driven back across the river, the bridge remaining in the hands of neither side.

Throughout the afternoon the enemy made repeated attempts to break through the chord line; but the 6th Black Watch, with ten Lewis guns, and the 7th Gordon Highlanders, with eight machine-guns, broke up every attack, and inflicted great losses on the attackers.

During these operations, 2nd Lieutenant R. Scott, 256th Brigade, R.F.A. (since killed in action), observed a party of the enemy digging-in close to the river bank. He at once sent a runner back to his battery to ask for a single gun to be sent forward. He then selected a position for it, and made all arrangements for opening fire on its arrival. The gun came into action at 5.30 P.M., and fired ninety-four highly-effective rounds at close range, causing many casualties, and remaining in action for three hours.

This and many other cases in which a bold use was made of the artillery considerably strengthened the infantry's powers of resistance.

During the night of the 10th orders were received for the Division to extend its front to a point 400 yards north of Lestrem, two companies of the 7th Black Watch being sent forward to take over the additional frontages from the 50th Division. Meanwhile the 61st Division was moving forward in rear of the 50th and 51st, to ensure that no gap should exist between their flanks. Two battalions of the 61st Division, the 2/6 Warwicks and the 1/5 D.C.L.I., were to come under orders of the 51st Division on their arrival.

For some time before nightfall the enemy had been observed collecting, obviously for a renewal of the attack; the artillery had in consequence been harassing all the approaches to the river Lawe from the east. Shortly after dark a heavy attack was launched from the village of Fosse northwards. At Fosse post the enemy managed, after a short struggle, to drive in the north flank, the remainder of the garrison being compelled to fight their way back to the Fosse Bridge. They, however, resisted the enemy's attempt to advance with such vigour that they were able to withdraw in good order, cross the bridge, and successfully destroy it after they had crossed.

In the chord line Lestrem post was also rushed soon after the opening of the attack. The enemy, having thus gained a lodgment in the chord line, developed a strong series of attacks northwards and southwards. In each case he met with some success; to the north the chord line was cleared as far as the northern outskirts of Lestrem, but here he was brought to a standstill by the 7th Black Watch. To the south he reached the village of Fosse, where a defensive flank formed by the 7th Gordon Highlanders held its ground, and stopped his further advance until midnight.

The defenders of this flank, after a gallant resistance in the dark for over three hours, were finally driven back on to a party of about 150 of King Edward's Horse and the 5th Seaforth Highlanders. Here the enemy was again checked, the troops maintaining themselves against several attacks until the pressure became too much for them, and they were driven back on to the Zelobes-Croix Marmuse road.

At this stage the Division still formed a continuous line of resistance. The 154th Brigade, the 6th Seaforth Highlanders, and the company of the 6th Gordon Highlanders at Vieille Chapelle, remained as they had been at check. The remainder of the 6th Gordon Highlanders had been disposed in and about Zelobes, three companies of the 5th Seaforth Highlanders in and about Croix Marmuse, one company of the 8th Royal Scots and the 7th Gordon Highlanders between Croix Marmuse and L'Epinette, the 6th and 7th Black Watch between L'Epinette and the Divisional northern boundary. In rear of this line 500 reinforcements of the 4th Seaforth Highlanders were at Les Croquaux; the 4th Gordon Highlanders at La Tombe Willot; one company of the 8th Royal Scots at Paradis and one at Pacaut; the 39th Machine Gun Battalion with a half company at Paradis, one and a half companies at Pacaut, and two companies at Calonne sur Lys; the 6th Warwicks at Pacaut; and two companies 5th D.C.L.I. at La Pierre au Beurre.

It must, however, be appreciated that though there was a continuous line of resistance opposed to the enemy, the units forming it were in many cases in a state of great disorganisation. They had gone into action considerably deficient of officers, and the continuous fighting in the dark had resulted in not only platoons and companies, but also in men of different battalions, becoming intermingled. Control was therefore becoming increasingly difficult to exercise.

In this position, and before anything in the nature of reorganisation could be completed, a further attack broke out at dawn on the 11th throughout the greater part of the Divisional front.

The enemy pursued his attack along the front with sufficient vigour to find out any weak spots in the defences, with the result that he had soon penetrated to the road between L'Epinette and Croix Marmuse. From this point, as was his usual custom, he made every effort to extend his gains to the north and to the south. After considerable fighting, in which the enemy supported these flank attacks with heavy frontal attacks, our troops were forced back on to the Zelobes-Paradis road. The ground was, however, only given up after desperate fighting, in which the enemy was compelled to pay heavily for his successes. The Jocks were, in fact, in spite of their disorganisation, offering a gallant and stubborn resistance in circumstances in which control was almost entirely dependent on the initiative and leadership of N.C.O.'s.

Owing to the progress made by the enemy, it became evident soon after dawn that the positions in which the field batteries were in action would soon become untenable. Orders were therefore given for both brigades to withdraw to positions previously reconnoitred, 255th Brigade to near the eastern edge of Pacaut Wood, and the 256th Brigade to near Le Cornet Malo. To effect this retirement gun-fire was opened immediately on the advancing enemy, while batteries withdrew singly from both brigades to their new positions, and at once came into action. This covering fire, being mostly over open sights, was highly effective; and though isolated portions of the enemy closed to within 600 yards of some of the batteries and opened fire on them with machine-guns, their main line was checked about 500-600 yards west of the Zelobes-L'Epinette road. Two companies of the 8th Royal Scots established themselves just short of this line, and assisted materially not only in covering the withdrawal of the guns, but also in salving the ammunition of both brigades, very few unexpended rounds being left on the ground.

At about 6.45 A.M. the headquarters of 152nd and 153rd Brigades moved back to the cottages facing one another half-way between Le Cornet Malo and Riez-du-Vinage. At this time Lieut.-Colonel L. M. Dyson, D.S.O., commanding the 256th Brigade, R.F.A., was ordered to take over command of the 153rd Infantry Brigade from Brigadier-General A. T. Beckwith, C.M.G.. D.S.O. The latter had been gassed during the operations in March, and was suffering considerably from the effects. He, however, gallantly continued to carry out his duties until his condition became so serious that he had to be admitted to hospital.

Meanwhile at Vieille Chapelle a company of the 6th Gordon Highlanders and King Edward's Horse were offering a resistance which should become historical. The garrison had denied the enemy passage over the river for two days and two nights, but only by dint of continuous heavy fighting.

They were now completely isolated, the enemy's troops and guns being pushed across the river in large numbers both north and south of them. A German battery of field-guns was in action 600 yards from them to the west. At 7.45 A.M. a pigeon message was received from Captain J. R. Christie, stating that his situation was "almost unbearable." Christie, however, decided with his men that, in view of their orders, surrender was out of the question, and they resolved to make a desperate effort to extricate themselves.

Their best chance seemed to be to make a sortie towards their right, where the enemy did not appear to be in so great strength as he was elsewhere. Machine-guns were posted to cover the withdrawal while the remnants of the garrison emerged on the opposite side of the village. Here they were met by a storm of close-range machine-gun and rifle bullets. Captain Christie was at once hit by a bullet in the right knee, but he managed to rejoin the survivors of his party by crawling to the farmhouse, in which the survivors had been compelled to shelter. Six men in succession advanced to knock out a machine-gun which was pinning them to the farm, each in his turn being shot dead. Captain Christie, unable to walk owing to his wound, next crawled forward himself to attempt to put the gun out of action. He was, however, immediately hit again, his right arm being shattered by a bullet. The enemy then entered Vieille Chapelle and captured the remnants of the garrison, a handful of wounded men.

As Lieut.-Colonel Lionel James, commanding the King Edward's Horse, wrote in his report : " It is impossible to speak temperately of Captain J. R. Christie, 6th Gordon Highlanders, and his officers, and of Lieutenants Stein, Pinckney, and Laurenson of King Edward's Horse."

At 5.15 P.M. on 9th April Lieutenant Pinckney, King Edward's Horse, left Vieille Chapelle with a message to Colonel James, stating that the situation was desperate. This gallant officer made his way back again into Vieille Chapelle, with instructions that the bridgehead was to be held to the end. Thirty-six hours later, at 8 A.M. on 11th April, the bridgehead was still held.

Captain Christie fortunately recovered from his wounds in the hands of the Germans, and for his gallant leadership and devotion to duty was awarded the D.S.O.

During the action at Vieille Chapelle the enemy was struggling to extend his hold on the Lestrem-Fosse-Locon road southwards. In this attempt heavy casualties were inflicted on him. On one occasion a large body of Germans marching in close order along the road was shattered by the artillery, while again and again machine-guns and Lewis guns took full advantage of splendid targets offered to them as the enemy's troops advanced to the attack.

Gradually, however, in spite of his losses, he forced a way between Zelobes and Vieille Chapelle. Here he isolated and cut off two platoons of the 6th Seaforth Highlanders guarding the western end of the Vieille Chapelle bridge, who continued to resist while completely surrounded in an attempt to force an exit from Vieille Chapelle for the 6th Gordon Highlanders and King Edward's Horse inside the village.

Having effected a lodgment between Vieille Chapelle and Zelobes, the enemy finally, after having suffered numerous casualties at the hands of the 6th Gordon Highlanders, forced his way into Zelobes, throwing the garrison back on Les Lobes.

As a result of these operations, the defending troops had become still more disorganised ; but though units were considerably intermingled, and the number of officers and N.C.O.'s still surviving had further diminished, the men remained disposed in such a manner that the Division continued to maintain an uninterrupted line of resistance.

At noon (11th April) the line was held as follows : from the Canal de la Lawe on the Divisional right boundary to north of Le Vert Lannot lay three companies of the 7th Argyll and Sutherland Highlanders, supported by the fourth company with a company of the 4th Gordon Highlanders. The line was then continued towards the northeast corner of La Tombe Willot by two companies of the 4th Gordons and 200 reinforcements of the 4th Seaforth Highlanders. The line then curved round to the north of La Tombe Willot, and was held for a distance of 600 yards by elements of the 5th and 6th Seaforth Highlanders, and of the 6th Gordon Highlanders, disposed in depth. The remainder of the reinforcements of the 4th Seaforth Highlanders held the line along the Le Cornet Malo-Croix Marmuse road. Two companies of the 8th Royal Scots then linked up the 4th Seaforth reinforcements to the 2/6 Warwicks, who were holding the line from the church at Paradis to a point 300 yards south of Le Bouzateux farm, held by elements of the 6th and 7th Black Watch and 7th Gordon Highlanders. On their left came the 5th D.C.L.I., holding the line as far northwards as the railway crossing west of Merville, while further elements of the 6th and 7th Black Watch and some of the 8th Royal Scots manned the railway on the left flank of the D.C.L.I. facing southwards.

The reserves were now reduced to one company of the 39th Machine Gun Battalion and the 404th Field Company, R.E., about Pacaut Wood, the remaining three companies of the 39th Machine Gun Battalion being already in position between Le Cornet Malo and Calonne.

It will thus be seen that though the line, as has been stated, was continuous, it can only be described as patchwork ; and it had become evident that no orders as regards a properly co-ordinated advance or retirement, which either the Divisional or brigade commanders might issue, were likely to be put into operation successfully. All that could be expected was that each unit would conform to the movement of the troops on its flanks, the success of this conformation being dependent on the leadership of the local commanders, who in many cases were junior officers if not junior N.C.O.'s.

The enemy continued his efforts during the afternoon, with the result that the line was forced back so as to run through Le Vert Lannot and La Tombe Willot. On the left, however, the fighting was not so severe, though the enemy succeeded in occupying the whole of Paradis.

Meanwhile a large number of men of all regiments who had become detached from their units had during the morning been collected at the headquarters of the 153rd Brigade. They were, however, entirely without officers, and almost entirely without N.C.O.'s. Volunteers were therefore called for from the 256th and 12th Australian Brigades of field artillery to officer these infantrymen. Of those that came forward Captain Rickard, M.C., and Lieutenant Seton, M.C., of the 12th Australians, and 2nd Lieutenants Inkson and Gordon of the 256th Brigade were selected to reorganise the men and to lead them forward into action. These four gunner officers, acting as platoon commanders, did admirable work under very difficult conditions. Having led their commands forward, they remained in action with them until the 13th inst. Throughout this period they kept their troops well under control, particularly during the series of withdrawals in the face of vastly superior forces in the rearguard action which took place on the 12th inst. They, indeed, all proved themselves highly capable infantry leaders.

In the first instance the men were formed into a reserve, and took up a position in rear of the line Pacaut-Bouzateux Farm, as further battalions of the 61st Division were now arriving with orders to take over all ground north of an east and west line through L'Epinette. At 4.30 P.M. the first of these battalions, the 5th Gordon Highlanders, late of the Highland Division, took up its position along the stream L'Ancienne Lys, with its left flank in contact with the 50th Division.

The situation now appeared to be improving: an additional reserve had been improvised; the reinforcing Division had substantially joined up with the 50th Division on the north; Givenchy on the south still held out owing to the magnificent resistance of the 55th Division, and the 154th Brigade was maintaining itself on the right flank in the same gallant and efficient manner as it had done three weeks earlier at Hermies and Beaumetz. Moreover, another Division, the 3rd, was moving up to support the 154th Brigade and 55th Division.

In these circumstances General Carter-Campbell decided to make a firmer line by withdrawing his foremost troops north of Bouzateux Farm on to the Paradis-Merville road, so as to join up satisfactorily with the line held by the 5th Gordon Highlanders.

In the course of these operations the fighting had necessitated further withdrawals by the artillery brigades, the 255th Brigade taking up positions in Riez-du-Vinage, the 256th Brigade in Carvin, and the Australians west of the river Clarence in Calonne.

During the night of the 11th-12th a further adjustment in the infantry took place, the 76th Brigade of the 3rd Division having arrived and relieved the 154th Brigade up to and including La Tombe Willot, leaving only a very small portion of the front line held by the 4th Seaforth reinforcements, under the command of General Buchanan.

The order of battle in the front line was now as follows: the 4th Seaforth reinforcements extended from La Tombe Willot half-way to Pacaut, the 2/6 Warwicks and 8th Royal Scots continued the line thence up to but excluding Bouzateux Farm. Elements of the 153rd Brigade next held the line along the Pacaut-Merville road just west of Bouzateux Farm. On the left lay the 5th D.C.L.I., who were in touch with the 5th Gordon Highlanders on the Ancienne Lys.

At dawn on the 12th a sudden and disastrous collapse occurred. The enemy launched an attack on the centre of the position, which came in the nature of a surprise. Patrols of the 2/6 Warwicks were covering the front, but they did not return with information that the enemy was advancing, doubtless having been cut off.

At 5.15 A.M. it was reported from an artillery O.P. at Pacaut that the enemy could be seen advancing. At the same time numbers of men were found falling back about

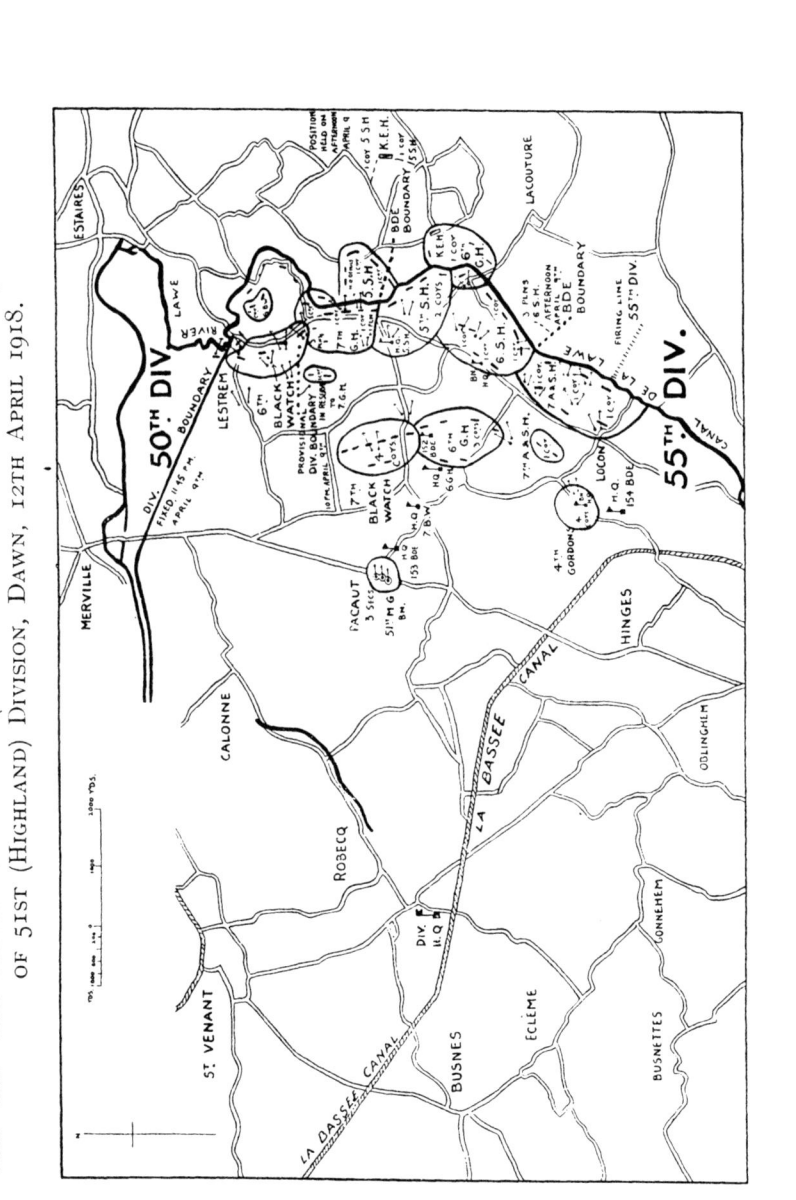

Map XI.—The German Offensive. (The Battle of the River Lawe.) Dispositions of 51st (Highland) Division, Dawn, 12th April 1918.

the headquarters of the 2/6 Warwicks on the west of Pacaut and at the headquarters of the 8th Royal Scots in the village, the officer commanding and the adjutant of the latter battalion already having been cut off.

Five minutes after this report had been received from the O.P. in Pacaut, close-range rifle and machine-gun fire were brought to bear on Riez-du-Vinage from the east, south, and south-west.

The enemy during this advance had all but surrounded the headquarters of the 152nd and 153rd Brigades on the eastern outskirts of the village. Colonel Dyson, Captain Wrathall, the brigade-major, and the remainder of the staff of the 153rd Brigade managed to extricate themselves and escape just as the leading German troops were entering the front of the cottage that had been used as brigade headquarters.

On the opposite side of the road the 152nd Brigade were not so fortunate, and just as they were preparing to leave the cottage they were occupying, the Germans closed in on it from all sides. Brigadier-General J. Dick-Cunynghame, Captains Berney-Fiklin and W. Drummond, the brigade-major and staff-captain, Lieutenants Cummings and Simpson, the signal and intelligence officers, and the whole of the headquarters personnel, with Colonel Fleming commanding the 255th Brigade, R.F.A., who was acting as artillery liaison officer to the brigade, fell into the hands of the enemy. They had delayed their attempt to escape from their headquarters by less than a minute after the 153rd Brigade, who had made good their escape, only to find the Germans entering their cottage.

Meanwhile the Divisional artillery was adding possibly the greatest chapters to its history. Gunners have few opportunities of engaging the enemy at close quarters, and their work is for the most part of a nature that precludes them from performing outstanding acts of valour that attract the public eye. This occasion, on which the enemy broke through the infantry and with little warning appeared in close proximity to portions of our gun line, was an exception of which they took full advantage.

In spite of the complete surprise, "A" and "B" Batteries of the 255th Brigade in the vicinity of Riez-du-Vinage managed to limber up and withdraw south-west across the canal, although they suffered severe casualties amongst their horses from machine-gun fire. "C" and "D" Batteries of the same brigade could not get their guns away in spite of many gallant attempts, as the teams were all knocked out by machine-gun fire; but they remained in action, keeping up a rapid rate of fire to cover the withdrawal of "A" and "B," and did not leave their guns until the enemy were almost amongst them. The headquarters of 255th Brigade just managed to escape with the loss of all its horses.

Farther north the 256th Brigade were in equal danger of falling into the enemy's hands. The officers of the 153rd Brigade headquarter staff, who themselves had only recently escaped from the enemy by a hair's-breadth, collected stragglers and formed a line to protect the withdrawal of the batteries. The gunners remained in action engaging targets at close range with direct observation though under rifle and machine-gun fire at some 500 yards' range. They finally withdrew in succession, the last battery, "D" 256, only clearing its position when the enemy was 300 yards from it on the left front. Sergeant V. Illidge was partly responsible for the successful withdrawal of this battery. He cut out several killed and wounded horses from the different teams, assisted in their hooking-in, and remained in the position until the last gun had left.

Lieutenant M'Farlane of the same battery, who was acting as liaison officer with the 6th Black Watch, was last seen emptying his revolver into the enemy at close quarters.

The 12th Australian Army Brigade, R.F.A., also found themselves in an awkward situation, heavy close-range rifle and machine-gun fire suddenly being opened on them from their left.

The limbers were brought up at the gallop just as the enemy opened on the position with his artillery, and in spite of the machine-gun and shell fire, the guns were got safely away through Robecq. The gunners with a few infantry stragglers provided their own covering parties, and with their battery Lewis guns checked the enemy's advance until the positions were successfully evacuated.

"A" and "B" Batteries, 255th Brigade, crossed the canal by the bridge due south of Riez-du-Vinage, closely followed by the enemy. Majors Davidson and Jack, the two battery commanders, however, each dropped the last of their guns within 300 yards of the bridge to cover the withdrawal of their remaining guns. Of these one gun covered a foot-bridge and the other a drawbridge.

The Germans were so close on the heels of the artillery that they were able to rush the drawbridge and establish themselves in a house on the west side of it. Major Jack, however, brought such effective shell-fire on to this house that the enemy fled from it and recrossed the canal, whereupon Major Fairlie, Lieutenant Mackay, and Driver Boyd took up rifles, occupied the bridgehead, and by their fire forced the enemy to retire down the road.

In the meantime Major Davidson with his gun was firing on enemy machine-guns which had been brought up close to the Canal, and by the accuracy of his fire effectually covered the withdrawal of two heavy batteries which were coming up out of action under heavy fire.

A description of this action, in which Major Davidson and Major Jack were mentioned by name, was included in the Commander-in-Chief's despatches dealing with the battle, Major Davidson being subsequently awarded a bar to the D.S.O. and Major Jack the D.S.O.

It would be difficult to overestimate the valuable part played by these two guns and the gallant conduct of all concerned in restoring a situation at so critical a stage. Undoubtedly had it not been for the prompt action of Davidson and Jack, the enemy would have succeeded in establishing himself on the southern bank of the La Bassée Canal.

The enemy, opening fanwise from his area of penetration, had been rapidly pressing his attack north, west, and southwards. Numerous attempts were made to improvise lines of defence, but in the absence of officers these all broke down until the infantry had withdrawn across the Clarence river, where they linked up with the 5th D.C.L.I. in front of Calonne. The line was then continued northwards along the Turbeaute and Ancienne Lys rivers.

Southwards, as has already been described, the enemy reached the northern bank of the La Bassée Canal.

The 154th Brigade farther eastwards had, however, formed a defensive flank, which prevented the enemy from extending his gains in this quarter. The 4th Seaforth reinforcements throughout these operations had held their ground about La Tombe Willot, the remnants of the 152nd Brigade were disposed facing north about La Vertbois Farm, extending from La Tombe Willot almost to Pacaut Wood. Here they joined part of the 8th Royal Scots and 404th Field Company in Pacaut Wood facing north. Meanwhile patrols of the 1st Gordon Highlanders, 3rd Division, were entering Pacaut Wood from the south.

The 7th Argyll and Sutherland Highlanders, who had been relieved and were just withdrawing from the line, took up the lines of the La Bassée Canal from Pacaut Wood to Robecq.

After the infantry had all been withdrawn behind some natural obstacle such as the canal or the streams on the left, in spite of the disorganisation that had resulted from the enemy's successful surprise and the depth of his advance, the line began to harden again.

The 154th Brigade were adequately safeguarding the canal, and were in touch with the 55th Division.

One battalion of the 61st Division was already moving forward to occupy the line of the Clarence river from the canal at Robecq to Carvin. This section of the line had at one time been seriously threatened, as the enemy had reached the outskirts of Robecq, thus somewhat precipitating the departure of Divisional headquarters to Busnes. He had, however, withdrawn, and Robecq was occupied by elements of the 189th Brigade, 61st Division, the 400th Field Company, R.E., and elements of the 404th Field Company, R.E., who were disposed on an extended front covering the eastern approaches to the village.

North of Carvin the 61st Division had one battalion already in position on a line running from that village to Baquerolles Farm, and a second battalion continuing the line towards Calonne.

North of Calonne remnants of the 5th D.C.L.I. and elements of the 153rd Brigade had withdrawn beyond the Lys canal, and were engaged during the remainder of the day in the fighting about Merville.

By 1 P.M. the three brigades of artillery were all established in new positions : the 256th Brigade on the Robecq-St Venant road, the 255th Brigade at L'Ecleme, and the

12th Australian Brigade at La Pierrière. While in these positions the artillery drew its ammunition from an army ammunition dump, in spite of the fact that one end of it had been set on fire and was blazing furiously.

It will thus be seen that General Carter-Campbell had been able to restore his battle line with the help of these additional battalions from the 61st Division in such a manner that the enemy was not likely to make further serious progress, at any rate until he could move a considerable number of his guns forward. Thus valuable time was secured in which troops could be reorganised, and which enabled other battalions of the 61st Division to arrive on the scene.

The line from La Tombe Willot to Pacaut was not seriously threatened during the morning, but throughout the afternoon the pressure against it steadily increased.

The 4th Seaforth reinforcements north of the Vertbois Farm were well in advance of the remainder of this line; the 4th Gordon Highlanders, who had been concentrated on the south side of the canal, were therefore ordered to join up the left flank of the Seaforth reinforcements with the canal by forming a line through Pacaut Wood.

While the 4th Gordon Highlanders were moving forward to carry out these orders, information was received that the 3rd Division, to shorten their frontage, were falling back on to the line Locon-La Bassée Canal, and that all troops were to conform to this movement.

This withdrawal was therefore begun; but the 4th Seaforth reinforcements, under the command of Major Jobson, either never received these orders or received them too late, and were left in the air by the troops on their flanks. The enemy, discovering their position, pressed round them on either flank, and Major Jobson realised that their only hope of escape was to cut their way out. In this attempt Major Jobson was wounded, and with the remainder of his party, being completely surrounded, was captured.

Those Seaforth reinforcements, who had not even joined their battalion, but had been employed as a separate unit, with four officers to weld it into shape, had stubbornly fought for many hours, and had maintained themselves on their ground in spite of strong attempts made by the enemy to drive them in. They remained fighting gamely to the end in an isolated position, cut off from all hopes of relief. Many of them were only boys who had just arrived in France for the first time, and the steadiness with which they conducted themselves in their first and last fight was worthy of the highest praise.

The remainder of the line gradually withdrew, but in good order, and it was not until 8.40 P.M. that the 4th Gordon Highlanders, who had moved forward to the vicinity of Le Cornet Malo and had fallen back fighting through Pacaut Wood, crossed with elements of the 152nd Infantry Brigade to the south side of the canal.

Meanwhile the defence of the La Bassée Canal was handed over to the Ist Corps, the 51st Division being ordered to cover the junction between the XIth and Ist Corps. A composite brigade was therefore formed under the command of Lieut.-Colonel A. Fleming, D.S.O., the C.R.E., known as Fleming's Force, which took up a line from the bridge over the canal south of Robecq, east of Robecq, to the hamlet of Les Amusoires. Fleming's Force, as it took over this line, was composed of the following :—

Echelons B (transport men, quartermasters' staffs, bands, &c.) and further reinforcements of the 154th Brigade.
One hundred officers and men, details of the 152nd Brigade.
Two hundred officers and men, details of the 153rd Brigade.
Nos. 1 and 2, special companies, R.E., 300 strong (gas projector companies).
Two companies, 11th Canadian Railway Construction Battalion, 250 strong.
One company, 51st Division M.G. Company.
One company, 39th Division M.G. Company.

Some further elements of the 152nd Brigade were collected in reserve at Hollanderie.

The 154th Brigade was ordered to withdraw to Busnes as soon as it was relieved by the 3rd Division.

By 3 A.M. on the 13th Colonel Fleming had organised his force into two sectors, the right being commanded by Major Campbell of the 6th Black Watch, and the left by Major Stein, 4th Gordon Highlanders.

THE GERMAN OFFENSIVE

The night of the 13th passed quietly, and was employed by Colonel Fleming in advancing his line by 700 yards and in reorganising his force. The railway companies and some elements of the Berkshire Regiment, who had become attached to the Division, were withdrawn. Their place in the line was taken by the 7th Gordon Highlanders, who had by this time been collected and reorganised. The remnants of the 152nd and 153rd Brigades were also collected and formed into a composite battalion under Lieut.-Colonel J. M. Scott, D.S.O., commanding the 5th Seaforth Highlanders.

On 14th April orders were issued for the 154th Brigade to relieve Fleming's Force during the coming evening. Shortly before this relief took place the 4th Division, which had recently arrived in the area, attacked northwards from the canal bank and established themselves on a line from the canal through Riez-du-Vinage to Carvin. Thus when at 2 A.M. the relief of Fleming's Force was completed, the actual firing line was for the most part well to the east of the line actually held by the 154th Brigade.

The situation then remained unchanged until the night of 23-24th April, when the 154th Brigade was withdrawn.

Throughout this engagement the 4th Seaforth Highlanders had been attached to the 55th Division, and had taken part in the obstinate and successful defence of the defensive flank which that Division had formed from Givenchy to Le Touret.

On the morning of the 9th April the 4th Seaforth Highlanders had been in billets at the Ferme du Roi near Bethune, in close proximity to the 55th Divisional front. In consequence, when the sudden break through the Portuguese lines occurred, they were placed under the orders of the 166th Infantry Brigade under the command of General Kentish.

Their first move was to the banks of the Canal de Lawe. Later, during the same day, it was discovered that a gap existed in the line held by the 166th Infantry Brigade, north of Le Touret. The battalion was therefore moved forward under cover of darkness and disposed so as to fill this gap, their headquarters being established at Les Faucons.

During the day (10th April) the enemy did not attack in force, but he made several local attempts to penetrate the line held by the 4th Seaforth Highlanders. On each occasion he was repulsed, and the position was maintained intact throughout.

On 11th April, about 11 A.M., the German attacked in force. The 4th Seaforth Highlanders resisted all his attempts to drive back their line. Later in the day, the battalion on their left was driven in. The Seaforths, however, formed a defensive flank, and in spite of numerous attempts made by the enemy to roll up their line, maintained themselves in their position and inflicted heavy losses on him. Subsequently the Northumberland Fusiliers, on the left of the 4th Seaforth Highlanders, delivered a counter-attack, which successfully restored the situation. The Seaforths assisted this attack by giving covering fire from the right flank, and inflicted serious losses on the enemy as he fell back in front of the Northumberland Fusiliers.

On the night of the 11th the 4th Seaforth Highlanders were relieved by the 1st Division, and took up a reserve position in rear of the stream south-west of Les Faucons. Here in the course of the fighting on 12th April they were attacked about 5 P.M., the enemy everywhere being completely repulsed. On the 13th they were relieved and moved back to billets at Oblingham.

The 4th Seaforth Highlanders had conducted themselves magnificently. They had been in action for five days, had been repeatedly attacked, but had not yielded a yard of ground to the enemy. General Kentish, in a telegram to the officer commanding, expressed his great appreciaton of the splendid resistance offered by the battalion when fighting under his command. General Jeudwine, commanding the 55th Division, also wired : " Please accept from all ranks 55th Division our hearty thanks for the willing co-operation of the 4th Seaforths. Their help and plucky fighting have been an invaluable aid to maintaining our line through a long period of strain."

The battle of the Lys was perhaps the most trying ordeal through which the Highland Division passed in the whole course of its service in France and Flanders.

It had just emerged from the operations round Bapaume, in which numbers of officers and irreplaceable N.C.O.'s had become casualties. It had received large numbers of reinforcements, mostly boys of eighteen and a half and nineteen years of age, with no previous experience of war. With its units incomplete in their organisation and under-officered, the Division moved forward to stem the tide after the Portuguese had been driven from their trenches. Information as regards the progress of the enemy's advance was scanty, so that he was encountered in unexpected places, with the result that in the initial stages of the attack a solid front was not opposed to the German advance until the enemy had reached the line of the river Lawe.

To increase the difficulties attending these operations, not only were the roads in the early stages of the fight so congested with the retiring Portuguese that forward movement, particularly for vehicles, became at times absolutely impracticable, but also the whole area was covered with civilians evacuating their homes, constantly under shell-fire, and at times under machine-gun fire. Indeed, the advance of the Germans had been so rapid, and the penetration made by them so deep, that in many cases fighting took place in farms and cottages still occupied by old men, women, and children. The sufferings of these poor people were deplorable; many were killed and wounded, as were also their beasts; others became involved in gas-shelling, and with no knowledge of anti-gas defence, were overcome by the poisonous fumes. Of the survivors, some fled from their houses as they stood, while others packed their household effects, surmounted by the inevitable box-mattress, on their waggons, and driving their beasts before them, congested every road and track in the area. Others, again, particularly the more elderly, overcome by the suddenness of the arrival of the German infantry, were stupefied, and could not be persuaded to take any action beyond sitting in their houses in a helpless state of collapse.

Later the capture of a complete brigade headquarters, in the course of a prolonged rearguard action, was itself sufficient to break down the organisation. The loss sustained by the Division in this unfortunate incident was a grave one. No better successor to General Pelham Burn could have been selected than General Dick-Cunynghame.

That he should have fallen into the hands of the enemy within a few days of having taken over command was a piece of cruel ill-fortune, felt as acutely by the brigade itself as by its commander. Moreover, in Captains Berney-Fiklin and Drummond, two most reliable staff officers had been lost to the Division; the latter was the embodiment of efficiency as a staff captain, and had held every rank in the British army from private soldier to captain.

In this battle the part played by the 55th Division on the right of the 51st was a memorable one. The Division, after all the troops on its left had given, formed a defensive flank and brought the German advance to a complete standstill, in spite of many violent attacks. The 51st was only able finally to hold up the German advance by the fact that its right was always thus secured.

On completion of the relief the 154th Brigade moved back to join the Division, which was resting in the Norrent-Fontes area.

On 16th April, General Sir H. S. Horne, K.C.B., K.C.M.G., commanding the First Army, sent the following message to General Carter-Campbell: "I must write you a line to tell you how highly I appreciate the splendid fight that you and the 51st (Highland) Division have put up, not only against very superior numbers, but under particularly trying circumstances. You have done wonders. I am proud to be a Scotsman at any time, but more than ever now. Tell all ranks I know how well the Division has done, and what splendid fighting qualities and determination they have displayed. It is this determination to 'stick it out' that makes all the difference, and will win this war."

General Harper wired his congratulations to the Division on its recent splendid fighting, and also General Lukin, commanding the 64th (Highland) Division.

The results of the battle of the Lys were far-reaching. The decision of the German Higher Command to exploit to the full the Portuguese debacle resulted in the using up of nearly the whole German reserve, and undoubtedly led towards their final collapse.

CHAPTER XVI.

WITH THE FRENCH IN CHAMPAGNE.

WHEN the Division was resting in the Norrent-Fontes area two new brigadiers were appointed to it, in place of Generals Dick-Cunynghame and Beckwith. The command of the 153rd Brigade was assumed by Lieut.-Colonel W. Green, D.S.O., Black Watch. Colonel Green at the time of his appointment was commanding the 9th Royal Scots, and thus was well known to the Division. He had been in command of this battalion when it had been transferred from the 51st to the 61st Division, and had proved himself a most capable battalion commander. It was, in fact, felt at the time of his departure that the Division was losing in Colonel Green one of the best infantry leaders that had served with it. It was therefore with the greatest satisfaction to all that news was received that he was rejoining his Division as commander of the 153rd Brigade.

On 16th April Brigadier-General E. I. de S. Thorpe, D.S.O., Bedfordshire Regiment, was appointed to the command of the 152nd Infantry Brigade. On 28th April he was, however, transferred to the command of another brigade, Colonel R. Laing, D.S.O., M.C., Seaforth Highlanders, being appointed in place of him.

Colonel Laing had not previously served with the Division, but he had been in close contact with it in the Arras fighting in 1917, in which he commanded his battalion in the 4th Division with considerable distinction.

On 3rd May the Division began moving to familiar areas north of Arras, the 153rd Brigade group moving to the Mont St Eloi-Neuville St Vaast area, the 152nd and 154th Brigades to Ecoivres-Bray areas, Divisional headquarters opening at Marœuil.

On the 6th and 7th May the 152nd and 153rd Brigades went into the line, relieving the 10th and 12th Brigades of the 4th Canadian Division in the sector stretching from Bailleul on the right to Willerval on the left, the front line trenches being situated at the foot of the eastern slopes of the Vimy Ridge.

The sector was well known to the older veterans of the Division, as it covered in its reserve area the greater part of the front held from March to July in 1916, and practically the whole of the front held in February and April 1917.

On the right of the Division were the 15th (Scottish) Division and on the left the 52nd (Lowland) Division, so that on this occasion the line from the river Scarpe on the south almost up to Lens on the north was held by Scottish troops.

The area occupied by the Division had been the scene of a great German attack on 28th March 1918. The 56th (London) Division had, however, offered a magnificent resistance, and apart from the loss of the foremost trenches held by their outposts had held their ground in spite of repeated attacks delivered by the Germans in great strength.

The actual line taken over by the 51st Division as the front line had before the attack been the reserve line, or, rather, the front line of the reserve system. The whole scheme of defence had therefore to be recast so as to transform this reserve system into an outpost system and to create a new reserve system in rear. There was not the same amount of new work required as had been the case in the sector astride the Bapaume-Cambrai road, since numerous trenches and dug-outs existed which could be incorporated into the new scheme. As, however, the Division was now primarily composed of boys, who were unable to carry out a daily task equal to that of the old trained soldiers, the work contemplated was more than sufficient to keep the Division fully occupied for many months.

In the new scheme of defence the system of holding a position by a series of trench lines was abandoned. The experience of the last two months had proved that the Germans were conducting their attacks in the main according to a stereotyped plan. This plan was to attack frontally with a great weight of artillery and trench-mortars on a narrow front, and thus blast open by an intense bombardment an area of penetration through which the attacking troops could pass and operate outwards against the flanks thus created. In this manner they had been able to roll up one trench line after another in a series of flank attacks.

To meet this form of advance a trench system was planned which consisted of a number of localities, sited checkerwise, each locality being capable of all-round defence. Thus if the enemy penetrated any portion of the defences, whichever way he turned he would be met by entrenched troops facing the direction of his advance.

The introduction of this system necessitated the laying out of a complete new system of defence, which, though existing trenches were largely utilised, entailed a vast amount of new work in the sector.

In carrying out this work much difficulty was at first encountered owing to the inexperience of the troops, and the fact that the bulk of them were not fully developed men. The Jocks, however, played up magnificently, almost surpassing their efforts in the early part of the year; and in a few weeks the defences, though not actually completed, contained the framework of a series of well-wired localities, in which the troops could have offered a stubborn resistance.

It was, in fact, evident from the manner in which the work was carried out that, in spite of the immense number of casualties sustained in the last two months, the traditions established in the Division for hard work were being well maintained by the new drafts.

On one occasion while this work was in progress, a party was working at night in front of Bailleul when a machine-gun opened, and a boy slid from the berm into the trench and lay on the duckboard groaning heavily. The platoon sergeant jumped down beside him and said, "What are ye groaning for, laddie?" "I've a bullet in the fleshy part of my leg," was the reply. "Fleshy part of the leg!" said the war-weary sergeant, with visions of a peaceful spell at home, "what the h——l are you complaining about?"

Throughout this period there were occasions on which the enemy's artillery was extremely active. High-velocity guns paid considerable attention to the back areas, particularly to Ecurie, Ecoivres, and Marœuil. On one occasion a shell from one of them landed in the machine-gun battalion camp at Ecurie, killing two men and wounding Major Clarke and Captain Biddulph, the second in command and adjutant respectively, and wounding seven other ranks.

The battery positions of the heavy artillery and the Concrete Road, a famous overland route made of concrete running from Roclincourt to the Arras-Lens Railway, received a daily ration of heavy shells.

The enemy also occasionally carried out intense bombardments with gas shells. On one particular occasion, the night 16-17th May, he fired three half-hour violent bursts of mustard-gas shell at intervals of three hours, causing casualties to 3 officers and 139 other ranks of the 7th Argyll and Sutherland Highlanders.

On 25th May over 800 shells were fired into the area near Thelus by 4·2, 5·9, and 8-inch howitzers without a single casualty being caused.

Shellings of this nature continued until 9th June, gas shells frequently being mixed with high explosive; but the dug-out system had been so rapidly improved under the directing energy of Colonel Fleming, the C.R.E., that only slight casualties were caused.

After 9th June, the hostile artillery slackened off considerably. High-velocity guns ceased to trouble the back areas, and the front trenches, except for occasional intense bursts, received little attention. On the 23rd the casualties in the entire Division for twenty-four hours had dropped to one man killed and two wounded.

On 10th June a new form of gas attack was delivered on the Divisional front, known as a "gas beam" attack. Forty truck-loads of cylinders were run up to the most advanced point on the light railway, which lay in front of Bailleul and just behind the support line.

These cylinders were arranged so that they could all be opened simultaneously by an electrical device. This was a marked improvement on the old system, in which each cylinder required four men to carry it up to the front line, and then had to be left in position until a wind of the right velocity was blowing in the required direction, in danger of being burst by shell-fire and flooding our own trenches with gas. In the case of the "gas beam" the train was not moved up to the position of discharge until the wind was suitable, so that the gas could be released immediately on arrival, and was thus stored in the trench area for the shortest possible time.

Prior to the discharge the front and support lines in the area liable to be affected by the gas were evacuated by their garrisons. The train carrying the cylinders was then moved into position without incident. A machine-gun bullet penetrated one of the cylinders, but the escape of gas was quickly stopped by the presence of mind of one of the gas personnel, who plugged the holes made in the cylinder with clay.

The discharge then took place, and as far as could be seen the "gas beam" rolled slowly over to the German lines, the wind at the time having dropped to about four miles an hour.

In the morning the Flying Corps observers reported that a broad belt of discoloured grass showed that the beam had travelled some 4000-5000 yards into the enemy's country towards Douai. What effect it had on the Germans is not known. No kind of alarms seem to have been given from the German front-line trenches. The German batteries in the area affected by the gas were, however, silent for several days.

When the troops returned to the front and support lines after the discharge, they found numbers of rats, moles, and beetles dead at the bottom of the trenches, while the brass shell-cases hung up as gas-gongs were coated with a deposit of verdigris about the depth of a half-crown piece, evident signs that the gas was a fairly powerful mixture.

During this period General Carter-Campbell had a heavy task to perform. Not only had a new system of defence to be planned and put into effect, but the Division itself required time and opportunity to recuperate. As the official despatch says: "All battalions were urgently in need of rest, and contained large numbers of young, partially trained, and wholly inexperienced recruits, and subordinate commanders had had little or no opportunity of becoming acquainted with their men."

To meet this contingency intensive training was carried out by the brigade and the battalions resting, in so far as the demands made upon them for working parties would allow. Divisional classes were formed, and every effort was made by commanders to turn their battalions into trained units in the shortest possible time.

The inexperience on the part of the men, and the successful way in which it was eliminated, is well illustrated by their efforts on patrol. Six to eight patrols were out in No Man's Land covering the Divisional front every night, but these were at first almost ineffective; not only did they hesitate to engage enemy patrols and were inclined to avoid them, but they allowed themselves to be outwitted by them. By 26th May the Division had lost one officer and three men missing without a single prisoner having been captured.

On 26th May an enemy patrol reached our lines, bombed a post, and wounded two men. This date was, however, the turning-point; the next night a similar attempt was made, but was defeated. The following night a sergeant of the 100th Grenadiers was captured, on 9th June a second N.C.O. was captured, and on the 12th a private. Finally, on 14th June, a patrol of one officer and four other ranks of the 6th Seaforth Highlanders waylaid an enemy patrol of seven men and captured it complete.

By the end of the tour in this sector, the men had become really good on patrol, completely dominated No Man's Land, and would immediately attack and disperse any patrol they encountered.

In other directions the training of young officers and men was no less successful, and, in spite of many obstacles, by the time the Division left the area in July it was able to remain in action in a great battle for eleven consecutive days and to add further to its laurels.

When it is considered that it had sustained 7480 casualties in the four weeks ending 15th April 1918, it will be appreciated how much those responsible for its efficiency are to be congratulated, particularly since between 24th April and 11th July the Division was only completely out of the line for ten consecutive days.

By 11th July 1918 the Division had been relieved in the Bailleul and Willerval sector by the 4th Canadians, and had begun its move to the Dieval-Monchy-Breton-Chelers area.

Shortly before this relief Lieut.-Colonel L. M. Dyson, who had commanded the 255th Brigade, R.F.A., for some years, very reluctantly gave up command of his brigade, ill-health and two severe wounds compelling him to do so. He may be said to represent the best type of modern gunner lieut.-colonel. Always willing, cheerful, and untiring, he was the best possible companion to the infantry brigade with which he worked. At the same time, he kept well abreast of modern developments in artillery. It is difficult to estimate the debt the Division owed to colonels like Dyson, Dawson, and Rorie.

This latest move was due to a request from Marshal Foch that four British Divisions might be transferred, two of them to areas south of the Somme, and two to positions astride that river, so as to ensure the connection between the French and British armies about Amiens, and to enable him to move four French Divisions farther east to his right flank.

On 13th July Sir Douglas Haig received a further request from Marshal Foch that these four British Divisions might be placed unreservedly at his disposal. This request was agreed to, and accordingly the 15th, 34th, 51st, and 62nd British Divisions were formed into the XXIInd Corps under the command of Lieut.-General Sir A. Godley, and were ordered to move down to the French front.

The entire Division moved to the new scene of operations by train, the intended destination being the Chalons-sur-Marne area. It was estimated that the journey *viâ* the southern outskirts of Paris would take thirty hours. The trains, of which thirty-four were employed, steamed off at intervals of one hour, the first leaving Bryas at 5 P.M. on 14th July, the last train, carrying the Divisional artillery, leaving Pernes at 3 A.M. on 16th July.

Before the first troops had reached their destination the Germans, on the morning of the 14th July, launched an offensive on a front of eighty kilometres east and south-west of Rheims, which carried them across the Marne, but which was finally held by the French, American, and Italian forces on this front. This attack was in the first instance checked east and north of Rheims, but as it was making progress westwards along the valley of the Marne towards Epernay and towards the Montagne de Rheims, the destination of the Division was altered, and on the evening of the 15th the first of the Divisional units were detraining in the Nogent-sur-Seine area.

As each unit arrived on the 16th it was moved by motor lorry towards the south bank of the Marne in the Epernay area, the manner in which this move was organised by the French being admirable and few delays occurring.

During the night of the 16-17th Divisional headquarters opened at Moussy, three miles south-west of Epernay. On the following day the enemy continued his advance north and south of the Marne, and had also further encroached on the Montagne de Rheims, his farthest point of penetration in the Epernay area being Boursault, a village four and a half miles north-west of Moussy on the other side of the forest of Epernay.

During the night of the 17th the 152nd, 153rd, and 154th Brigades established their headquarters at Le Mesnil, Pierry, and Chouilly respectively, the infantry battalions, now almost complete, being grouped in villages and woods about their brigade headquarters.

Regimental transport, field companies, and field ambulances, which were marching from their detraining stations, had not yet arrived in their brigade group area, the first being still many miles behind, while the Divisional artillery was still detraining during the day.

On 18th July Marshal Foch opened his counter-offensive on the western flank of the Rheims-Soissons salient, which, with a series of counter-attacks delivered south of the Marne, arrested the enemy's advance. While these operations were in progress, the Divisional artillery were on the march from their detraining station, Nogent-sur-Seine, and the bulk of the regimental transport, field ambulances, and field companies were arriving in their brigade group areas.

During the night 18-19th July the original plan of employing the Division south of the Marne was changed, and orders were received at 1 A.M. for it to move to the Forêt de la Montagne de Rheims. This move was carried out on the morning of the 19th, the troops crossing the Marne at Epernay and moving to the south-western fringe of the Forêt de la Montagne.

By 9 A.M. Divisional headquarters had been established

at Hautvillers, 152nd Brigade headquarters at Champillon, 153rd Brigade headquarters at Romery, and 154th Brigade in woods one mile north of Bellevue.

The Divisional artillery had also concentrated on the Moussy-Pierry area.

All these moves were carried out in a hilly country in days of intense heat, broken on the 18th by a violent thunderstorm, and proved extremely trying both to men and horses—to the former particularly after nine weeks of continual trench warfare. The Divisional artillery had covered eighty miles in three days by forced marches, and after the storm on the 18th had found the roads impassable in many places owing to trees which had been blown down in the storm and which had to be cleared before the batteries could pass on.

During the 19th heavy fighting went on throughout the day, in which the balance was in favour of the French, though German patrols had penetrated as far as Nanteuil le Fosse. As soon as night fell the Division continued its march and passed through the 14th and 120th French Divisions to positions in the valley of the Ardre and the Bois de Coutron, with orders to advance the following morning in conjunction with the 62nd Division and drive the enemy back.

The area in which the Division was to operate was on the western edge of the Montagne de Rheims, the great massif which the enemy had endeavoured to seize in order to turn the Rheims defences from the south and to dominate the Marne valley.

The sector allotted to the XXIInd British Corps covered a front of 8000 yards astride the Ardre river, a stream running northwards to the Vesle, and consisting of an open valley bottom with steep wooded slopes on either side. Both valleys and slopes were studded with villages and hamlets, which were for the most part intact, and afforded excellent cover.

The northern boundary of the 51st Division was the river Ardre, which at the point where the attack began was little more than a ditch.

The most formidable obstacle in the path of the Division was the dense wood, the Bois de Coutron, which stretched for 3500 yards from the jumping-off line in the direction of the attack. This wood was composed of a thick tangle of trees traversed by rides and country tracks, both laterally and from front to rear. On the slopes of the valley at the edge of this wood lay the hamlets of Espilly, Les Haies, and Nappes, which linked up the defenders in the wood with various *points d'appui* in the valley.

The valley itself was also admirably suited for concealed defences, consisting as it did of small woods, mills, banks, and sunken roads hidden by standing corn.

During the 19th the course of the fighting had been such that in the instructions received by the Division it was stated that the enemy appeared to be retiring on a wide front covered by rearguards.

The orders issued for the attack therefore provided for a deep advance into enemy territory, the final objective selected, the Brown line, being at its greatest distance nine and a half kilometres from the jumping-off line. The first objective, the Blue line, corresponded roughly with the old French front line, and was from four to six kilometres from the jumping-off line. As far as the Division was concerned, this line ran roughly north and south along the western edge of the Bois des Eclisses.

The troops formed up for the attack on a two-brigade front on a line stretching four kilometres as the crow flies, from the Ardre just west of Pourcy to a point in the Bois de Coutron one kilometre south-east of Paradis; the 154th Brigade on the right, the 153rd on the left, and the 152nd in reserve. The attack was to be continued on the right by the 62nd Division, and on the left by the 7th French Division.

Each attacking brigade advanced on a one-battalion front, the leading battalions employing their companies in line and keeping one in reserve. The objective allotted to the leading battalions was an intermediate objective known as the Green line, which ran from Chaumuzy to the north-western edge of the Bois de Coutron. The plan was that after the capture of the Green line, a second battalion on each brigade front should pass on to the capture of the Blue line, and the third battalion to the capture of the Brown.

The artillery covering the attack was placed in the hands of the C.R.A., and consisted, in addition to the

ON 27TH AND 28TH JULY 1918.

Divisional artillery, of two groups of French 155 mm. guns, and seven groups of 75's. It was arranged that the French artillery should cover the advance of the infantry up to the Green line, and that the Divisional artillery should then move forward and cover the remainder of the advance.

The artillery, and indeed all arms, were considerably hampered by the scanty supply of French maps. Those that were issued were difficult to read for British troops, and appeared very inaccurate when compared with those produced by the topographical section of the general staff. Indeed, it was not until the French maps were issued that it was appreciated what a valuable asset the accuracy of the British maps was, and it was found that whereas a barrage could be accurately fired from a British map, the French maps could not always be depended on to give satisfactory results.

At the time of the attack three enemy Divisions were in line opposite the 51st—the 103rd Hessian Division in the centre, the 123rd (Saxon) Division on the German right, and the 22nd (Sachsen Meiningen) Division on the German left, the two latter both overlapping the front attacked by the 51st. All three were classified by Intelligence as of average quality; but the 123rd had been badly cut up in the fighting of the previous days, and on the 20th units of the 50th Division had already begun to relieve it astride the Ardre.

The move to the jumping-off line through units of the 14th and 120th French Divisions was laborious and of long duration. The troops were considerably delayed by the congestion on the roads and tracks, and did not reach their positions until 4 A.M. The shortage of French guides considerably added to their difficulties. Moreover, touch was not obtained between the leading troops of the two attacking brigades until after the attack had begun.

So far, to the Jocks the move to Champagne had been a great adventure; the entrainment of the complete Division, the passing through the outskirts of Paris, the journey on the French lorries, as well as the arrival in a country of new and beautiful scenery, had all been of deep interest to them. Most of them for the first time saw the French army in the field, and no doubt realised, as most men do on the first occasion that they have dealings with an active French Division, what magnificent men they are, and what a false impression of them is obtained from the odd and rather bedraggled French soldiers that were occasionally seen on leave in the zone of the British armies.

Great adventure, indeed, it was. Not only had the Highland Division the privilege of taking part in the early phases of Marshal Foch's great counter-stroke which turned the German invasion of France into a hasty retirement, but it was to maintain itself for eleven days in the heat of sanguinary fighting without relief, and to advance its line over four and a quarter miles through a country heavy with dense woods and magnificently adapted by nature for stubborn defence, and in which an enemy only recently victorious was offering an heroic resistance.

At 8 A.M. the artillery barrage opened and the advance began, the 4th Seaforth Highlanders leading on the right, and the 6th Black Watch on the left. Nor had the battle long been in progress before it became evident that the enemy, so far from retiring on this portion of the front, was holding on to his position with great determination.

Immediately in front of the 154th Brigade lay a large and partially wooded hill of which the slopes on the enemy's side were dominated by Marfaux on the north bank of the Ardre and by the Bois de l'Aulnay. On its eastern side this hill sloped steeply to the river Ardre.

In front of the 153rd Brigade lay the dense Bois de Coutron, divided by a main ride running in the direction of the attack.

Both brigades captured the enemy outpost line with a total of 150 prisoners without meeting serious resistance.

The 4th Seaforth Highlanders then carried the hill in front of them, and were making their way down the slopes on the enemy's side when they came in view of Marfaux, the Bois de l'Aulnay and Espilly, and heavy machine-gun fire was opened on them, with the result that the advance was checked. The right company had by this time occupied Bullin Farm, and passed some 200 yards beyond it; the centre company had, however, mistaken Marfaux for its true objective, Chaumuzy, and had edged its way over towards that village, becoming intermingled with the right company. The left company had reached the sunken road running from Espilly to Bullin Farm. In this advance heavy fighting against machine-gun nests had taken place, and the barrage was in consequence irretrievably lost, so that for the present the attack could only be continued if the infantry could subdue Marfaux and the Bois de l'Aulnay on the right and Espilly in the centre with their own weapons. The battalion was, however, much disorganised, as the centre company had lost its direction, and the left company, in touch on neither of its flanks, was being badly enfiladed from Espilly.

The Seaforths, however, made repeated attempts to close with the enemy; but these were all held off by the great volume of the fire produced by the vast number of machine-guns that were encountered. Even men trying to make their way by creeping through the standing crops attracted so much fire that this method of advance had to be abandoned.

In this position two companies of the 4th Gordon Highlanders advanced to support the 4th Seaforth Highlanders along the valley of the Ardre, and two along a track leading to Espilly. The latter automatically filled the gap between the two brigades, and became heavily involved in the fighting as they approached the road known as Bullin road, running almost north and south across the position about 700 yards east of Espilly. Here, finding the enemy in strength lining the road, they immediately deployed and assaulted the position, and though they suffered serious losses, they made their way forward with the greatest gallantry. The enemy in face of these attacks finally broke, abandoned the line of the road, and fell back into some woods in rear of it.

Lieut.-Colonel Bickmore, D.S.O., commanding the 4th Gordon Highlanders, finding that all the officers in one company had become casualties, immediately took command of it, and, supported by the second company, personally led his troops against the enemy in the wood. Shortly after crossing the road the companies came under a burst of close-range machine-gun fire and rifle grenades, and the attack was shattered, Colonel Bickmore being mortally wounded at the head of his men.

The remnants of the two companies then withdrew and lined the road they had captured.

By 12 noon the 7th Argyll and Sutherland Highlanders were advancing in rear of the 4th Seaforth and 4th Gordon Highlanders. This battalion captured a machine-gun still in action in the right rear of the 4th Seaforth Highlanders, which had been causing them considerable trouble, and subsequently combined with the Seaforths in their attempts to free themselves from the machine-guns on their right front and centre.

In spite of many gallant attempts which were made during the continuous fighting throughout this day, the volume of enemy fire never abated, and no substantial advance could be made. An N.C.O. and a few men did, however, manage to enter the outskirts of Marfaux.

Though these battalions, in spite of the fact that they had become much intermixed and disorganised, never relaxed their efforts to get on and maintained a continuous pressure against the enemy, their gallantry was not rewarded by success.

The line thus remained as it stood for the remainder of the day, with the exception that the company in the sunken road was subjected to so much fire that it could not maintain itself in its isolated position, and withdrew first to behind the crest, subsequently to move forward and dig itself in in view of the enemy.

Meanwhile, on the left, the 153rd Brigade had experienced heavy fighting throughout the day in particularly trying and difficult circumstances.

After they had captured the outpost line this leading battalion, the 6th Black Watch, disappeared into the wood. At this point an unusual incident occurred, which greatly added to the confusion which must inevitably occur during an action fought in dense woods.

Shortly after the advance began the Germans opened a heavy barrage about the jumping-off line. In consequence, the 7th Black Watch and 7th Gordon Highlanders pressed forward close on the heels of the 6th Black Watch so as to get clear of the barraged area as quickly as possible.

There was, however, a gap in this barrage between the main drive and the south-western edge of the Bois de Coutron, which resulted in the bulk of the 7th Black Watch and 7th Gordon Highlanders being attracted into that area.

Meanwhile the 6th Black Watch were with great difficulty forcing their way through the wood. The enemy was, however, in considerable strength, particularly as regards machine-guns, and everywhere offered a stubborn resistance. The going in the wood was desperate, tangled undergrowth and the numerous trees making the physical effort of advancing very considerable. In addition, the country was so blind that it afforded the enemy every facility for ambushing the most advanced troops.

In these circumstances the keeping of direction became a matter of the greatest difficulty. Not only were the troops unable to see more than fifty yards or so in front of them, but also they were constantly led out of their true direction to deal with some hidden point of resistance which suddenly engaged them. In fact, the wood fighting became a question of isolated bodies of troops making their own way through the wood as best they could, platoons and even sections of the enemy completely detached and losing touch with their neighbours on both flanks.

On the right the 6th Black Watch fought their way successfully through the wood until they came under heavy fire from the vicinity of Espilly. This village proved itself to be the centre of a strongly-defended locality which, in spite of repeated attempts, could not be stormed by the infantry. By the time the leading troops came under fire from the Espilly defences, so much time had been spent in fighting in the wood that the barrage had passed on, so that the infantry were here also dependent on their own weapons alone to cover their forward movement.

On the left, as, owing to the density of the wood, it was impossible to see the position of neighbouring troops, the 6th Black Watch, the 7th Black Watch, and the 7th Gordon Highlanders all became involved in the fighting and became split up into numerous detached parties.

On the extreme left elements of all these battalions, led by Lieutenant M'Corquodale, 6th Black Watch, and accompanied by some French Senegalese troops, reached the north-western edge of the Bois de Courton, and even passed on to the southern edge of the Bois des Eclisses. They were, however, met with so heavy a fire in this advanced position, and were entirely unsupported on either flank, and so fell back to the edge of the Bois de Coutron.

The remainder of these battalions were for the most part held up by the western and south-western defences of the Espilly locality, though some of them fought their way well beyond the La Neuville-Les Haies road.

Subsequently the Senegalese troops on the left, finding that they were unsupported by the remainder of their battalion, and learning that Paradis was still in the hands of the enemy, fell back to the line held by the remainder of their unit. The foremost troops of the 153rd Brigade were thus left holding a narrow front well in advance of all neighbouring troops ; and as the enemy were threatening to cut them off from the rear, they were compelled to withdraw gradually to a line some 200 yards north of the La Neuville-Les Haies road.

The success of the 153rd Brigade was largely due to the gallantry and leadership of the commanding officer of the 7th Black Watch, Lieut.-Colonel J. C. Miller, M.C.

Colonel Miller, seeing that his attacking waves had lost direction owing to the gap in the enemy barrage, pushed forward with his intelligence officer, and passed through part of the heaviest of the barrage. He was thus able to direct a company from his rear wave to fill the gap. In passing through the barrage Colonel Miller lost his intelligence officer and both orderlies, and was himself blown over by shells on more than one occasion.

2nd Lieutenant J. B. Cable, 7th Black Watch, also showed fine qualities of leadership. After his company commander had become a casualty, he took over command of his company, and with his two leading platoons succeeded in capturing an enemy lieutenant and twenty-five prisoners. He then pushed forward and captured another twenty prisoners. Subsequently, finding that he was being fired on from his unprotected right flank and rear, he successfully withdrew his company. Later, hearing that troops on his right flank were advancing, he again led his platoons forward and captured several machine-gun nests.

As it was now evident that the three battalions of the 153rd Brigade were seriously intermingled, orders were issued to consolidate the line held, to obtain touch on the flanks, and to reorganise.

During the afternoon the French made a second attempt to capture Paradis and so cover our left; they were, however, unable to gain their objective.

At 6 P.M. the enemy, who had been reinforced, began to exert pressure. He had already delivered a small counter-attack against the right of the 154th Brigade at 4.30 P.M., which had been shattered by rifle and Lewis-gun fire, and he was now seriously threatening both flanks of the 153rd Brigade. As the battalions were considerably reduced in strength, and could ill spare the men required to protect their exposed flanks, they were withdrawn to the line of the road running from La Neuville to Les Haies.

The 6th Seaforth Highlanders were then placed at the disposal of the 153rd Brigade, and moved forward to fill the gap between the left of the brigade and the French, and also to take over the front line so that the three battalions of 153rd Brigade could reorganise.

At 6.30 P.M. an intense bombardment against the right of the Division broke out. As the enemy had launched a great premeditated attack on this front a few days previously, he naturally had a large number of guns available for this bombardment, and the shell-fire was therefore more than usually severe. This was followed by an attack delivered by two parties advancing from different directions and converging on the high ground on the right, about one hundred men altogether being employed. The parties advanced to within a few yards of the position held by the 7th Argyll and Sutherland Highlanders, when they were caught in enfilade fire.

The Germans winced for a moment under this burst of fire, whereupon an N.C.O. led his section forward and charged them, with the result that they immediately broke and fled in disorder down the hill.

During the day the artillery had begun to move forward, beginning about 9 A.M. By 11 A.M. the 256th Brigade were in action by Pourcy, and 255th Brigade in front of Nanteuil.

As the enemy was found to be resisting much more strongly than had been anticipated, and as counter-attacks appeared likely, the guns, except the forward sections, moved back to behind Nanteuil. The forward guns were left in close support of the infantry, in some cases 1200 yards from the enemy, and continued harassing him all night. These forward guns, as well as trench-mortars and machine-guns, had all been employed in attempting to subdue the hostile machine-gun nests in close support of the infantry. The first had proved themselves particularly useful; but as regards the trench-mortars and machine-guns, the mere physical labour of carrying the guns forward through the dense undergrowth made it impossible to get them into action with the foremost troops until late in the day. Even then, in the confusion that existed, one section of the 153rd Brigade Trench-Mortar Battery found itself unexpectedly in ground occupied by the enemy, and was dispersed by their fire.

During the day 8 officers and 360 other ranks were taken prisoners, 2 officers and 50 other ranks being taken from a single wired-in post in the Bois de Coutron. In addition, about thirty machine-guns and eight trench-mortars were captured, and a battery of 75's and many mitrailleuses that had been taken from the French were recovered.

In spite of the fact that a withdrawal had been anticipated, the resistance had been stubborn. This was due to the fact that during the day the enemy had withdrawn across the Marne at the southern end of the salient, and was covering this movement by a desperate defence of the flanks from Rheims to the Marne, on which the withdrawal was hinging.

During the night, while the relief by the 6th Seaforth Highlanders was taking place on the left brigade front, the enemy maintained his pressure, with the result that the line was again forced back about 1000 yards south of the Neuville-Les Haies road.

It was arranged that the 152nd Infantry Brigade should take over the 153rd Brigade front and carry out a second attack. The general plan was that the brigade should advance on a one-battalion front, the 5th Seaforth Highlanders leading, the 6th Gordon Highlanders next, and the 6th Seaforth Highlanders in the rear. Three objectives were selected for the attack, the first being the north-west edge of the Bois de Coutron, the second the southern slopes of the Bois des Eclisses, and the third the northern slopes.

The 153rd Brigade were to form such defensive flanks as became necessary during the progress of the attack, the 7th Gordon Highlanders on the right, and the 7th Black Watch on the left. On the right of the Highland Division the 62nd Division were to attack with a view to encircling the Marfaux locality from the north while the 9th French Division were attacking on the left, the village of Paradis being the particular stumbling-block in their path which they hoped to remove.

The artillery barrage fell, as had been planned, south of the Les Haies-La Neuville road ; but as the enemy had closely followed our troops during their last withdrawal, he had been able to establish many machine-gun posts close to the jumping-off line. The result was that the barrage fell behind the enemy's foremost troops, and the machine-guns of his outposts were untouched.

In consequence, the 6th Gordon Highlanders met with the stoutest opposition from the outset of the attack, a storm of bullets greeting them as soon as their advance began. Nevertheless, the troops on the right, with fine determination, brushed back all resistance until they had reached a point which was estimated to be about 200 yards from the north-west edge of the Bois de Coutron. Here the enemy were found to be holding a carefully-prepared line of resistance supported by numerous and well-sited machine-guns and trench-mortars.

In spite of many gallant attempts made by the battalion to carry this line, it held firm, the Germans defending themselves skilfully and courageously with rifles and hand-grenades. For an hour the 6th Gordon Highlanders tried to come to close grips with them, and drive them from their position, but without results.

Meanwhile the enemy displayed on his part the greatest initiative, making repeated attempts to filter through gaps in our front line and on the right flank, and ultimately became so threatening on the right rear of the 6th Gordon Highlanders that they were compelled to fall back on that flank to a position some 200 yards in advance of their jumping-off line.

On the left the advance was held up after the wood had been cleared for some 500 yards. Paradis had successfully withstood the repeated attempts of the French to storm it, so that the left flank of the Division's attack was again in the air. In consequence, the leading troops in this part of the battlefield also fell back on to the same line as the right flank had done, the 7th Black Watch forming a defensive flank to connect the left of the 6th Gordon Highlanders with the right of the French.

A company of the 5th Seaforth Highlanders was also sent forward to fill gaps which had occurred in the centre of the 6th Gordon Highlanders' line.

As had been the case on the previous day, the difficulties of the operation were greatly increased by the blindness of the country, it being almost impossible to locate exactly the positions and flanks of advanced parties in the wood.

However, by noon a continuous line had been formed joining the left of the 154th Brigade to the right of the French.

The troops were closely engaged throughout the day, and it became necessary to move forward companies from all three battalions of the 152nd Brigade to strengthen the line in places where it was becoming weakened. On the left the successful resistance of the Germans in Paradis had made it necessary to occupy a line which curved round the eastern side of that village some 300 yards from it, while on the right flank the 6th Seaforth Highlanders, after some fighting with enemy machine-guns, established themselves on a line facing north some 700 yards south of Espilly.

On the 154th Brigade front no particular incidents occurred. Strong patrols attempted to advance and make ground towards the enemy, but they found him everywhere in strength, and were unable to get forward. For a time the high ground on the extreme right was harassed by machine-guns. However, a Stokes mortar from the 154th Trench-Mortar Battery was brought into action against them, and after firing forty rounds silenced them. A patrol subsequently found twelve dead Germans in one machine-gun nest that had thus been dealt with.

So ended another day of severe fighting. The 152nd Brigade had taken over the whole of the front on the left, the 5th and 6th Seaforth Highlanders having been employed, either in strengthening the line held by the 6th

Gordon Highlanders, or in protecting their flanks, while the 153rd Brigade, which had been reorganised during the previous night, lay in close support to it.

In the day's operations eighty-one prisoners with a number of machine-guns and trench-mortars were captured. The forward guns of the Divisional artillery had been constantly in action, moving continually in close support to the attacking troops and making every effort to help the infantry forward. Their activities were, however, equally hampered by the blindness of the country.

On the following day no serious infantry action took place until 4 P.M. During the morning the 4th Gordon Highlanders, who had extended their left so as to take over the front as far as the main drive in the Bois de Coutron, attempted to make ground towards Espilly by means of strong patrols.

They, however, found the enemy as alert and as strong as ever, and could make no appreciable progress.

Early in the day it was arranged that the 7th Black Watch should operate during the afternoon with a view to establishing themselves in a position on the south-west edge of the Bois de Coutron, north of Paradis, from which they could cover with their fire an attack to be delivered by the French against that village.

To make this operation possible, it was necessary to advance the left of the line, so as to allow the 7th Black Watch to get into this position; the 6th Black Watch were therefore detailed to carry out an operation with this intention.

Accordingly at 4 P.M. the 6th Black Watch passed through the 6th Gordon Highlanders in the front line and attempted to dribble forward by individual rushes and establish a line behind which the 7th could reach their position on the flank of the French attack.

The enemy machine-gun nests in the wood, however, appeared to have been reinforced, for the volume of fire developed by them was such that the advancing parties were knocked out or driven back again and again. In spite of many determined efforts made by the 6th Black Watch, by five o'clock they had not been able to make any progress.

At this hour the French attack on Paradis was launched,

but it was immediately met with such an intense volume of machine-gun fire from the village that the troops, after having made their way forward with heavy losses for 100 yards, were compelled to dig themselves in.

Night thus fell with the position materially unchanged on the front of the 51st Division; the 62nd Division had, however, successfully attacked the enemy's lines on their right on the Bois du Petit Champ and cleared the wood.

It had now been decided that an attack should be delivered by the 152nd Brigade on the following day on the front of the 154th Brigade, the objective given being a line from the Bois de l'Aulnay inclusive to Espilly. Accordingly the hours of darkness were taken up with a complete rearrangement of the troops, battalions of the 152nd Brigade having to be relieved by the 153rd Brigade and transferred to the front of the 154th Brigade. These moves were successfully accomplished without incident, except for the fact that one company of the 6th Gordon Highlanders was relieved too late to take part in the initial attack. The firing line of the left was taken over by two companies of the 8th Royal Scots (Pioneers) who had been placed at the disposal of the 153rd Brigade, and by two companies of the 7th Black Watch.

The 152nd Brigade assembled for the attack with the 5th and 6th Seaforth Highlanders on the right and centre respectively, and with the 6th Gordon Highlanders on the left. On the left of the 6th Gordon Highlanders parties of the 7th Argyll and Sutherland Highlanders and 4th Gordon Highlanders were ordered to push through the Bois de Coutron to the west of Espilly, and sweep up the enemy in the western defences of the Espilly locality.

The barrage provided by the Divisional and French artillery was arranged to come down at zero 200 yards ahead of the forming-up line, and to advance 100 metres every five minutes. A barrage was also to be fired by the Divisional machine-gun battalion.

At 6.10 A.M. the barrage opened, but unfortunately on the left a considerable proportion of the shells fired by the French artillery fell short amongst the infantry with serious results. All the officers in one company of the 6th Gordon Highlanders became casualties before the advance was fairly launched. The 6th Seaforth Highlanders also suffered a number of casualties, while on the front of the 154th Brigade the 7th Argyll and Sutherland Highlanders suffered sufficiently to become seriously disorganised.

Partly on account of this error in the firing of the barrage, and partly on account of the great natural strength of Espilly, the attack progressed in ratio to the distance of the troops engaged from that village.

On the right the 5th Seaforth Highlanders had a brisk fight for half an hour, captured six machine-guns which attempted to bar their way, and were well up with the barrage when it passed on to the Bois de l'Aulnay. The 6th Seaforth Highlanders were also close to the barrage at the pause, but their left company were suffering severely from machine-gun fire both from front and flank, and the reserve company had to be pushed forward to help them.

Opposite Espilly the 6th Gordon Highlanders were working their way slowly towards the village under a heavy shelling, and being badly enfiladed by machine-gun fire. Farther to the left, the 4th Gordon Highlanders and the 7th Argyll and Sutherland Highlanders were heavily shelled, and were faced from the start by strong machine-gun posts which the barrage had failed to subdue, and so were unable to make ground.

On the other hand, the two companies of the 8th Royal Scots, pioneers though they were, were operating magnificently as infantry. By 7 A.M. they were well up with the barrage, and had captured two machine-guns; they finally fought their way unsupported on either flank for 500 yards into the Bois de Coutron.

When the barrage moved forward after the pause, the enemy in the Bois de l'Aulnay put up a poor fight, and by 8.30 A.M. the 5th Seaforth Highlanders and a company of the 6th Seaforth Highlanders had reached the northern edge of the wood. The 5th Seaforth Highlanders also formed a defensive flank on the eastern edge of the wood, as the enemy were still holding the ground on the opposite bank of the Ardre.

On the left a few men of the 6th Seaforth Highlanders reached the spur south-west of the Bois de l'Aulnay, but the bulk of them, with the 6th Gordon Highlanders, were checked in the sunken road running from the wood to Espilly. From here men of both battalions strove to cross the open and assault Espilly in face of a terrific fire. The open country was, however, so swept by rifles and machine-guns that every attempt broke down.

Farther to the left, though the 7th Argyll and Sutherland Highlanders and 4th Gordon Highlanders made similar efforts to get forward, the enemy pinned them to the ground by the intensity of his fire, and prevented them from making any headway.

Meanwhile, on the extreme left of the attack, the two platoons of the 8th Royal Scots, still unsupported on either flank, found themselves in a precarious position 500 yards in advance of the remainder of the line. They accordingly withdrew slowly with a bag of twenty-eight prisoners to their jumping-off line.

At 11 A.M. a fresh attack by two companies of the 7th Argyll and Sutherland Highlanders was carried out on the left of the 6th Gordon Highlanders.

These companies, in an advance which demanded great physical efforts from the men, carried the line forward through dense undergrowth for 400 yards, clearing up two enemy machine-gun posts. In this position a line was established with great difficulty.

From noon to dusk repeated efforts were made to reach Espilly, but the troops engaged were so scourged by machine-gun fire that every attempt broke down.

During the day contact was obtained with the foremost troops of the 62nd Division, which had also advanced their line.

At the end of the operation, the Bois de l'Aulnay was held. From its southern end the line followed the course of the sunken road towards Espilly to the point where it enters the Bois de Coutron east of that village. Here it joined up with the new position won by the 7th Argyll and Sutherland Highlanders in the wood, which for the most part was facing west, and thence to the original line as held in the morning.

In this operation the Divisional artillery suffered heavily. During the previous night several of the batteries had been subjected to a heavy gas bombardment, but in spite of it they continued to carry out a strong harassing-fire programme.

In this operation " A " and " C " Batteries, 256th

Brigade, then went forward to positions west of Nanteuil to support the infantry advance. Here they were subjected to intense bombardments, and suffered some casualties to personnel and horses, particularly from mustard gas.

Little occurred during the evening and night except that the 7th Argyll and Sutherland Highlanders, having located some enemy machine-gun nests by patrols, forced them back, and advanced their line by an additional 100 yards.

Meanwhile, immediately north of the Marne, the enemy was being hard pressed where his salient was becoming dangerously narrowed by the Franco-American advance northwards from Chateau Thierry.

The 24th passed without any major operation taking place.

It had been intended to carry out an attack on the Bois de Coutron on the 24th, with a view to gaining the line of the Haies-Neuville road ; but it was decided in the afternoon of the 23rd to postpone this operation until Espilly had fallen.

The 7th Argyll and Sutherland Highlanders therefore attempted to gain ground by means of strong patrols south and south-east of Espilly, with a view to forming the locality into a salient which would lend itself to attack. In this they were partially successful, and though the enemy's resistance was as strong as ever, they were able to establish posts, of which the most northerly was about 350 yards south-east of Espilly.

On the right the 152nd Brigade spent the day reorganising. The character of the fighting they had been engaged in is well illustrated by the fact that battalions were so reduced in numbers that the 5th Seaforth Highlanders were reorganised as two companies and the 6th as one. Each of these battalions, in exchange for some reinforcements that had arrived the night before, sent back to rest a hundred of its most exhausted men.

During the night the 153rd Brigade was relieved by the French 35th Regiment of the 14th Division, and encamped in woods near St Imoges.

Throughout the whole of these operations the enemy's defence had been supported by a considerable artillery. He had concentrated on this front a great number of batteries with which he had been supporting his attacks, and when the Division checked his advance these guns were still available to assist him in his defence.

He could therefore put down heavy barrages on back areas and across the approaches to the front, so that troops in process of relief and in moving to assembly positions were frequently caught in violent bursts of shell-fire. In addition, during the actual attacks, a heavy volume of fire was often directed against the area of the jumping-off line and on tactical features that had been captured.

This shell-fire and the countless machine-guns that barred the advance across the whole front had thus made the fighting of the last few days a severe ordeal, which must have reminded the veterans of High Wood and the chemical works, and which must have tried the young reinforcements highly. They, however, stood the test like men. To take the case of the 153rd Brigade as an illustration. This brigade had lost 30 per cent of its strength in casualties up to the time of its relief on the 24th, but was able after twenty-four hours' rest to conduct itself gallantly during a further four days of active operations in which it lost an additional 500 officers and men.

After the relief of the 153rd Brigade by the French, the southern boundary of the Divisional sector was found to run along the main drive in the Bois de Coutron and thence to Chantereine Farm on the south-west corner of the Bois des Eclisses, the 152nd Brigade remaining in position on the right, the 154th on the left.

No attack was made on the 25th or 26th, but strong patrols maintained continuous pressure against the enemy. As a result of successful enterprises by these patrols the line was in certain parts of the front sensibly advanced. On the right the 5th Seaforth Highlanders pushed out eight posts sixty yards clear of the Bois de l'Aulnay; they also reached the Moulin de Voipreux, and found it unoccupied. The 4th Seaforth Highlanders advanced their line by some 100 yards in the wood, though not without having some stiff fighting for their gains.

The 7th Argyll and Sutherland Highlanders were continuously engaged in the wood in trying to make headway, but the resistance they at all times encountered was such as to deny them any substantial progress.

WITH THE FRENCH IN CHAMPAGNE

After further fighting on the 26th, the 4th Seaforth Highlanders made good another fifty yards of ground. Both on this and the previous day there were occasions on which our troops suffered considerably from the enemy's artillery, which at times became intensely active both on his forward and back areas.

The 26th was, however, the last day on which the enemy stood his ground in Espilly and the Bois de Coutron. On the north banks of the Marne he had now been crushed into a small forward salient between Belval-sous-Chatillon on the east and the Forêt de Riz on the west; and while arrangements were being made to renew the attack on the Divisional front, he was perfecting his plans to evacuate his position before it was too late for him to disengage.

It had been intended to attack on the 26th, but it had been decided to give the troops, all of whom had now been engaged for several days, the benefit of twenty-four hours' rest—a rest which was unfortunately denied to most of them by deluges of rain which fell incessantly through the night.

The plan was to attack on a three-brigade front, 152nd being on the right, 187th Brigade (from the 62nd Division) in the centre, and the 153rd Brigade on the left, the 154th Brigade being withdrawn to the woods between Nanteuil and St Imoges. It would at first sight appear abnormal that a brigade from the 62nd Division should attack between two brigades of the 51st; but by this time the liaison with the 62nd Division, commanded by General Braithwaite, had become so complete that these dispositions caused no lack of cohesion in the attack.

A careful barrage programme was arranged, which allowed ample time for the 153rd Brigade to fight their way through the difficulties of the wood.

Two objectives were selected, the first being roughly the line Moulin de Voipreux-Neuville within the Divisional boundaries, the second being a line some 500-700 yards beyond this, including the village of Nappes.

At zero hour, 6 A.M. on 27th July, the artilleries of the 51st and 62nd Divisions, with the attached French batteries and twenty-four guns of the Divisional machine-gun batteries, opened the barrage.

The attack was met on the left by a light artillery

barrage, and on the right by a fairly heavy shelling of the banks of the river and the Bois de l'Aulnay, but no infantry action beyond some long-range machine-gun fire was encountered. The whole front, including the redoubtable Espilly, had been evacuated.

At 10 A.M. the final objective was reached on the right just in time for the troops to see the last of the enemy transport hurriedly leaving Chaumuzy.

By 10.40 A.M. it was apparent that a general retirement was taking place on the whole front, and mounted patrols were sent forward to get into touch with the German rearguard.

The attacking brigades were therefore ordered forward to the line from Chaumuzy to the north-west corner of the Bois de Coutron, and by 1 P.M. the whole Division—infantry, artillery, and machine-gunners disposed in depth, and well covered by strong infantry patrols as well as the cavalry—were on the move, while the sappers were at work repairing the communications.

The last fight in the much-hated Bois de Coutron and in Espilly had been fought, and those centres of resistance which had for so many hours appeared almost impregnable had at last fallen into our hands almost without a shot being fired.

It was with a sense of relief to all that it was found that the whole Division was advancing practically unmolested through an area on which a few hours previously the advance of even a section had been welcomed by a shower of machine-gun bullets. This sense of relief lost nothing from the fact that in the last two battles in which the Division had been engaged the whole Division had similarly been on the move, but in the wrong direction!

At 2 P.M. Chaumuzy was entered, and the artillery came into action near the north-east corner of the Bois de l'Aulnay, engaging the enemy who were reported by the mounted patrols to be falling back on the line of the road from Bligny to Chambrecy. At this time the German artillery from positions in rear of this road were becoming increasingly active on the Divisional front.

By 3 P.M. the battalions ordered to the line beyond Charmuzy were all in position, and patrols were sent forward to the old French trench line skirting the western edge of the Bois des Eclisses and curving round the Montagne de Bligny.

Later in the afternoon the mounted patrols definitely located the enemy on a line from Montagne de Bligny to the south of Chambrecy.

Orders were therefore issued at 4 P.M. that as soon as patrols had reported the wood clear brigades should advance and occupy the old French trench line as the main defensive line—that is to say, that the Division was to take up a position facing west. The Bligny-Chambrecy road was to become the Divisional right boundary, and Chantereine Farm the left. The 187th Infantry Brigade was to drop out of the Divisional line and come under orders of the 62nd Division.

At midnight, 27-28th, patrols reported the Bois des Eclisses clear, and the forward move began in a downpour of rain.

Meanwhile the enemy were retreating in the Rheims-Soissons salient, their line after passing the front of the French Division on our left running almost due west, the Marne being some five to eight miles south of it.

Throughout the night the troops were moving to their new positions, suffering no casualties except from occasional bursts of shell-fire.

By 11 A.M., 28th, the 62nd Division, which had attacked at dawn, had gained a footing on the Montagne de Bligny, while the 6th Seaforth Highlanders, in touch with them, had successfully occupied the old French trenches as far as La Garenne. In close support to them in the wood lay the 5th Seaforth Highlanders; while on their left, also in the French trenches, the 7th Gordon Highlanders connected the 6th Seaforth Highlanders' left with the right of the French. The latter were still advancing northwards, with patrols of the 153rd Brigade keeping in touch with them.

It was reported at 9.45 A.M. that the French had taken Chambrecy, and at 1 P.M. the 152nd Brigade was ordered to advance to the line Chambrecy-Michel Renaut Farm. It was, however, later discovered that the Germans were still occupying Chambrecy, and the movement could not be carried out.

It was then decided that the French should attack Ville

en Tardenois at 3 P.M., and that the 51st should co-operate. The 153rd Brigade was therefore ordered to advance to the high ground north of Chambrecy, with the French on its left and the 62nd Division on its right.

The artillery brigades moved forward to support this attack from positions about Chaumuzy. To reach this area they had to advance under direct observation for half a mile over open ground. The gunners, however, made their best pace, and as the shelling was erratic their losses were small.

"B" 255th Battery, commanded by Major F. C. Jack, D.S.O., M.C., were ordered to move to a position north of Chaumuzy. On arrival near the village, Major Jack found it and its approaches being subjected to a heavy bombardment by 5·9 howitzers. He therefore instructed his guns and limbers to gallop through the village at intervals of a minute, he himself galloping through with his orderly first. By this means his whole battery passed successfully through the village. It was a very gallant performance, and was much appreciated by the infantry.

The attack was launched by the French at 3 P.M., and failed under heavy machine-gun, rifle, and shell fire. The 7th Gordon Highlanders and 6th Black Watch, however, advanced at 4.20 P.M., and attacked across the valley towards Chambrecy and east of the village. Violent machine and shell fire was opened on the battalions soon after they left the trenches in the Bois des Eclisses; but in spite of their losses elements of the 7th Gordon Highlanders carried on, crossed the Bligny-Michel Renaut Farm road, and tried to make their way into the farm.

Similarly advanced parties of the 6th Black Watch passed through Chambrecy to the north-east and north-west of it.

By 6 P.M. the two battalions were held up on a line roughly from a point 500 yards south-west of Michel Renaut Farm to the north-east outskirts of Chambrecy. From here, unsupported on either flank and pounded by the German artillery and machine-gunners, they were compelled to withdraw, the 7th Gordon Highlanders to the old French trenches, while the 6th Black Watch finally established a line from the Bois des Eclisses to 200 yards south of Chambrecy.

WITH THE FRENCH IN CHAMPAGNE

During the night the 154th Brigade were ordered to take over the front; the 4th Seaforth Highlanders accordingly relieved on the right, with their right flank just south of the Montagne de Bligny, and the 4th Gordon Highlanders relieved the line recently established by the 6th Black Watch. The 7th Argyll and Sutherland Highlanders were in support on the Bois des Eclisses.

The 154th Brigade was instructed to keep in touch with any forward movement on the flanks, and to patrol actively with a view to preventing the enemy from withdrawing unobserved. Chambrecy at this time and during the following days remained in No Man's Land. It was visited constantly by patrols, but the heavy enemy machine-gun fire drawn by their visits forbade its occupation.

In these respects, apart from heavy enemy shelling, in which quantities of gas shells were employed, the 29th July passed uneventfully.

In the evening the Divisional front was extended so as to include the Montagne de Bligny. The 5th West Yorks, from whom this position was taken over, had at 7 P.M. attacked the enemy position on the western slopes of the hill. Though they had not been completely successful, they had made ground on the crest, the 7th Argyll and Sutherland Highlanders taking over this new position.

On 30th July the situation remained stationary, though constant pressure was maintained against the enemy by means of patrols, which at all times found him alert. "Constant pressure," which played so large a part in this and the following actions, is one of the most disagreeable features of battle. To attack, supported by artillery, with units attacking on either flank, produces its own attitude of mind which makes it tolerable; to sit in trenches on a quiet front had come in those strenuous years to be regarded as a holiday; to maintain "constant pressure" required a considerable display of courage in cold blood. It was a thing that might have to be maintained for many hours and perhaps for many days, as had been the case during the last ten days. It meant that any weakness on the part of the enemy had to be tested and exploited. How could his weak points be discovered? Only by gallant men working their way forward until they were shot at. His strength or weakness was in direct ratio to the number of bullets this forward movement provoked. The Division, when it had not been fighting actively, had maintained constant pressure for ten days. It was a cold-blooded operation which required resolute troops to perform it conscientiously and effectively.

The 7th Argyll and Sutherland Highlanders, situated on the bare and exposed crest of the Montagne de Bligny, had employed the night 29-30th in digging themselves in well. It was fortunate that they had done so, for during the day they had to withstand a systematic and heavy shelling; and at 8 P.M., after fifteen minutes intense bombardment, an attack was launched against them. They, however, stood their ground, and with rifles and Lewis guns shattered the fifty odd Germans who advanced against them from the west.

This was the last incident of note that occurred. During the day of the 30th preparations had been made for the relief of the Division by the 14th French Division. The 255th Brigade, R.F.A., was relieved at noon, and the 256th Brigade during the night. At dusk the relief of the 62nd Division also began, and the most advanced troops of the Highland Division were thus left with French battalions on either side of them.

Throughout the following day the 154th Brigade remained in position, active patrolling continuing till dusk, when the Brigade was relieved by the 14th Regiment, 14th French Division. Command of the sector passed to the G.O.C. 14th Division at 10 P.M.

When the Highland Division moved north again, it left behind it 38 officers and 417 other ranks who had fallen, the total casualties in killed, wounded, and missing being 173 officers and 3690 men. The total of 3863 represents probably the largest number of casualties that the Division ever sustained during a single period in the line.

It represents the losses that occurred in two attacks on a two-brigade front, three on a one-brigade front, and in constant minor attacks carried out by one or two battalions, and in maintaining constant pressure for the whole eleven days to prevent the enemy from disengaging and extricating himself unobserved from the increasingly awkward situation in which Marshal Foch's counter-stroke was placing him.

In these eleven days the youth in the Highland Division, many of whom were blooded for the first time in this battle, engaged six German Divisions, stemmed their advance, and hurled them back four and a half miles—days which were described in the following terms by General Berthelot, commanding the Fifth French Army.

"Order of the day No. 63 of the Fifth French Army (translation) :—

"Now that the XXIInd British Corps has orders to leave the Fifth (French) Army, the Army Commander expresses to all the thanks and admiration which the great deeds that it has just accomplished deserve.

"The very day of its arrival, feeling in honour bound to take part in the victorious counter-attack which had just stopped the enemy's furious onslaught on the Marne and had begun to hurl him back in disorder to the north, the XXIInd Corps, by forced marches and with minimum opportunity for reconnaissance, threw itself with ardour into the battle.

"By constant efforts, by harrying and driving back the enemy for ten successive days, it has made itself master of the valley of the Ardre, which it has so freely watered with its blood.

"Thanks to the heroic courage and to the proverbial tenacity of the British, the combined efforts of the brave Army Corps have not been in vain.

"Twenty-one officers and 1300 other ranks taken prisoners; 140 machine-guns and 40 guns captured from the enemy, four of whose Divisions have been successively broken and repulsed; the upper valley of the Ardre with its commanding heights to the north and south reconquered; such is the record of the British share in the operations of the Fifth Army.

"Highlanders under the orders of General Carter-Campbell, commanding the 51st Division; Yorkshire lads under the orders of General Braithwaite, commanding the 62nd Division; Australian and New Zealand mounted troops; all officers and men of the XXIInd Army Corps so ably commanded by Sir A. Godley, you have added a glorious page to your history.

" Marfaux, Chaumuzy, Montagne de Bligny—all those famous names will be written in letters of gold in the annals of your regiments.

" Your French comrades will always remember with emotion your splendid gallantry and your perfect fellowship in the fight.

BERTHELOT,
le General Commandant
la Vme Armée."

30th *July* 1918.

The Corps Commander, Lieut.-General Sir A. Godley, K.C.B., K.C.M.G., addressed the following messages to the Divisional Commander :—

" 21*st July*.—The Corps Commander wishes to convey to all ranks of your Division his appreciation of the great work that has been done by them during the past two days' fighting.

" The French Army Commander told him to-day that he was entirely satisfied with the result and the good bag of prisoners obtained in face of most obstinate resistance by picked troops of the enemy, who are under special orders to hold the front in order to allow for the safe retreat of the German troops beaten and driven back by the French across the Marne and on the Soissons front.

" Tactically, strategically, and politically the gallant fighting of your Division may have far-reaching results."

" 28*th July*.—Will you please convey to all ranks of your Division my hearty congratulations on the most successful result of their hard week's fighting.

" The valour and tenacity with which the troops have continuously engaged the enemy, and their endurance in face of exceptional difficulties of country and latterly of bad weather, have resulted in heavy losses to the Germans, and in their full retreat closely pursued by our victorious troops."

At the conclusion of these operations a special honour was conferred upon the 6th Black Watch—namely, that of being mentioned in the orders of the French army, " Cité à l'ordre d'Armée,' and of being decorated with the Legion of Honour.

WITH THE FRENCH IN CHAMPAGNE

The following is a translation of the Army Order :—

"The general officer commanding the Fifth (French) Army hereby specially mentions in orders the 6th Battalion Royal Highlanders. This battalion d'élite, under the brilliant command of Lieutenant-Colonel Francis Rowland Tarleton, has given splendid proof of its dash and fury in the course of several hard-fought battles between the 20th and 30th July 1918. After seven days of furious fighting, in spite of exhaustion and heavy losses caused by intense enemy machine-gun fire, it successfully stormed a wood splendidly fortified and stubbornly defended by the enemy.

GUILLAUMAT,
General Officer Commanding
Fifth (French) Army."

The Jocks entraining on their departure from the French zone were a memorable sight. They had exploited the resources of the country with great industry, and every man appeared to have a tin of bully beef in one hand and a bottle of champagne in the other.

CHAPTER XVII.

THE CAPTURE OF GREENLAND HILL.

ON 4th August 1918 Divisional headquarters opened at Villers Chatel, and the last of the trains conveying troops of the Division from Champagne began its journey. By this time the brigades had almost completed concentrating in the familiar country north-west of Arras—the 152nd Brigade at Caucourt, the 153rd Brigade at Chateau de la Haie, the 154th Brigade at Berles, and the Divisional artillery at Acq and Aubigny.

About this time Brigadier-General E. Segrave, D.S.O., H.L.I., who had been brigade-major to General Harper when commanding a brigade in the 6th Division, was appointed to the command of the 152nd Infantry Brigade. General Segrave had already gained a considerable reputation as a gallant battalion commander. His was one of the many happy appointments in the higher ranks of the Division.

The Division, now in G.H.Q. reserve, continued in this area until 14th August, when it returned to the command of the XVIIth Corps, and began to take over the line. Between 14th and 18th August the 154th Brigade relieved a brigade of the 52nd (Lowland) Division in the trenches east of Bailleul, of which many had been dug by the Jocks in May and June of the same year; the 153rd Brigade relieved a brigade of the 57th Division between that village of ill repute, Fampoux, and the right of the 154th Brigade, and the 152nd Brigade relieved a second brigade of the 57th Division in the Fampoux sector. At the same time the 170th Brigade, 57th Division, south of the Scarpe came under orders of the 51st Division, so that General Carter-Campbell was commanding a front of some 7600

THE CAPTURE OF GREENLAND HILL

yards extending from Tilloy les Moufflaines (exclusive) on the south to Bailleul (exclusive) on the north.

The Division had thus had less than ten clear days in which to rest, refit, and recuperate since its return from the second battle of the Marne, before it was again facing the enemy on what came to be an active front.

It was hoped that after its experiences and heavy losses in Champagne a longer period of rest would be vouchsafed to the troops. The days of rest in this period were, however, becoming fewer and fewer, and the whole of the British line was becoming agitated preparatory to uprooting itself and beginning its three months advance towards Germany. This uprooting, as far as the Highland Division was concerned, began gradually. It developed from the repeated testing of the enemy's lines, resulting in the occupation of portions of them, and finally culminating in the overrunning of the whole of the German front system, and in the capture of the main tactical features behind it —Greenland Hill and Hausa and Delbar Woods.

The results of this advance were far-reaching, for as long as Greenland Hill and the two woods on its southern slopes remained in enemy hands, they stood as a menace to any attack delivered south of the Scarpe; and the plan was to deliver the British counter-stroke in a few days' time, which was to extend from the south of the Scarpe down to the right of the British line.

Greenland Hill can be described as the point on which the great forward move to the Canal du Nord hinged.

It was fitting that the Highland Division should begin its final advance from the Arras country. Bailleul it had known in May 1916 from intelligence summaries as a place behind the long ridge in front of it, in which German reserve battalions rested, and through which they passed during their reliefs. Almost a year later, in April 1917, the big ridge was captured, and the Division saw Bailleul for the first time, and its patrols entered it. On relief it saw the 2nd Division occupy it unopposed. Again a year later it had occupied Bailleul itself and reconstructed its defences. Fampoux it knew in April 1917 as a village that shells were just beginning to destroy; it watched the hamlet change into a heap of brick dust, and learnt to avoid it like the plague. Farther to the right lay Roeux and the chemical works—"the comical works" that "made one windy even when it wasn't shelling," in which all units of the Division had experienced the bitterest infantry fighting and the most infernal shelling. In rear lay Greenland Hill, which in 1917 men of the 7th Gordon Highlanders had reached, but which the Division had never captured—the treacherous hill marked on the map on the wrong side of the railway. To the south of it lay those two woods, Hausa and Delbar, which throughout the fighting of April and May 1917 had looked down on the forward trenches, and from which the Germans saw every movement and signalled it to the gunners.

In these operations, which began eighteen days after the last troops came out of action in Champagne, the eastern outskirts of Fampoux were cleared. Greenland Hill, Roeux, the chemical works, Hausa and Delbar Woods, fell into our hands, and a firm line was established east of Plouvain.

At this time the enemy was reported to be carrying out a withdrawal opposite the line held by the Third and Fifth Armies. It appeared improbable that this withdrawal would extend as far north as the front of the 51st Division, but there were reasons for thinking that the enemy might have thinned out the troops in the forward zone with a view to avoiding casualties.

A vigorous policy was therefore adopted by General Carter-Campbell so as to obtain more information concerning the enemy's dispositions, and to take full advantage of any opportunity offered of gaining ground in order to deepen the British outpost zone in front of the main line of resistance.

On 17th August patrols found the enemy alert and holding the front line. On the 18th, however, they reported that he appeared to be holding his line lightly, while a prisoner captured by the Division on the right stated that the enemy was withdrawing the bulk of their front system garrison to the line Monchy-Pelves-Biache, leaving only weak outposts in position. It was therefore decided to advance and occupy the front line.

Accordingly the right brigade (170th) was ordered to test the enemy front line opposite to it and occupy it, the 152nd Brigade was ordered to clear the east end of

THE CAPTURE OF GREENLAND HILL

Fampoux, and the 153rd Brigade was given similar orders to the 170th Brigade.

In these operations the 170th Brigade made a successful advance. They found the enemy's front line unoccupied, and carried on for some 700 yards into a farther trench, in which they captured six prisoners.

On other parts of the front the enemy was found to be in strength; indeed, north of Fampoux he attempted a small raid with two parties, which, however, bore no result except that the German officer in charge of the raiders lost his life.

From the information obtained in these encounters, it was decided that the 170th Brigade should continue their advance, while north of the Scarpe a series of operations were planned in order to gain the enemy's outpost zone from the Scarpe as far north as the Arras-Gavrelle road.

It was hoped by this means to gain a good jumping-off line for an advance which the Division had now been ordered to carry out on the left of the Canadian Corps on 26th August.

In planning these operations the governing factor was the amount of artillery available, which, as regards field artillery, in no case exceeded four brigades. This precluded any attack from being carried out on a frontage wider than 1500 yards.

The first of these operations took place on the night 19-20th August. On the right the 170th Brigade advanced some 500 yards and occupied a trench from which they had driven a small party of Germans. However, at 9 A.M. on the 20th they were counter-attacked after a hurricane trench-mortar bombardment, and driven back into the trench from which they had started the operations. In this position they were bombarded all day, particularly by heavy trench-mortars. By 4.30 P.M. this bombardment had become intense, and was at that hour followed by a counter-attack. This attack was, however, shattered by artillery and rifle fire, and made no progress. The bombardment then reopened, and by 9 P.M., as the foremost troops of the 170th Brigade had been so badly harried all day, they were withdrawn by orders of the XVIIth Corps to their original front line.

North of the Scarpe a company of the 5th Seaforth

Highlanders attacked a sunken road running due north from Fampoux, at 4.30 A.M. on the 20th. They reached their objective, but were subjected to so much rifle-fire and bombing that they were driven back. However, at 8.30 A.M. they advanced again to the attack, and made good their objective. The 7th Gordon Highlanders of the 153rd Brigade on their left had also made an attempt to occupy the enemy's front line, but had been unsuccessful. At 5.30 P.M. the 5th Seaforth Highlanders were counter-attacked in the sunken road. They had, however, consolidated their new position well, and drove back the enemy with some loss.

On 21st August command of the Division passed to General Oldfield, General Carter-Campbell having gone home on leave. The General had gone home on the understanding that a fresh Division would undertake the coming attack in this sector. After his departure the Army Commander asked if the 51st would carry out the attack, as it was of the utmost importance to keep a fresh Division in reserve. General Oldfield in these circumstances agreed to undertake the offensive. Accordingly on 21st August an operation was carried out by the 6th Gordon Highlanders (152nd Brigade) with a view to occupying the country lying between the Fampoux-Fresnes and Fampoux-Gavrelle roads for some 500 yards from their junction. This operation, after a considerable amount of infantry fighting in which two companies were engaged, was successfully carried out, an officer, seven men, and three machine-guns being captured.

On the same day patrols from the 153rd Brigade reported that Pippin Trench and a trench running roughly parallel to the Fampoux-Gavrelle road on the west side of it was protected by a belt of wire in good condition.

It was therefore decided that an operation should be carried out to capture Pippin Trench and a support trench behind it east of the Fampoux-Gavrelle road called Zion Alley for a distance of 700 yards from the area recently occupied by the 6th Gordons.

These operations were ordered to be carried out on 24th August, so as to give the artillery time to cut the wire in front of Pippin Trench, and to enable two companies of the 7th Black Watch to practise the attack over a life-

THE CAPTURE OF GREENLAND HILL

size replica of the German trenches marked out with tracing-tapes behind the line.

On the 23rd August patrols reported that the artillery had cut five clear gaps through the wire in front of Pippin, and that the whole belt of wire was considerably damaged.

Orders were therefore issued for an attack to be carried out at 4.30 A.M. on 24th August. This operation was also successful. On the right the 7th Black Watch reached both their objectives according to the programme, but on the left a prolonged resistance, chiefly by rifle-fire and bombing, continued until 11 A.M. Even then a pocket of twenty Germans remained holding out in Hyderabad Redoubt, at the northern end of the support trench, until they were dislodged the following morning.

Hyderabad Redoubt had an evil reputation in 1917, and still retained it at this time. It was a group of headquarter dug-outs, situated so that their entrances were connected by a trench roughly in the shape of a triangle. It was perched on the summit of a crest which overlooked Arras and the neighbouring country on one side, and Plouvain and Biache St Vaast on the other. Its numerous dug-outs made it capable of prolonged resistance, while when it was captured it became a target for every gun in the neighbourhood.

On other points of the front Divisional patrols reported that the enemy showed no signs of vacating his positions without offering resistance, and it appeared that he had no intention of withdrawing north of the Scarpe, even though he was not holding his forward trench lines in great strength.

On 26th August a third operation took place. The trenches captured on the 25th continued northwards. The first line, known as Newton Trench, widened out to a distance of some 500 yards west of the Fampoux-Gavrelle road, the Support line, known as Hoary, Haggard, and Naval trenches, being just west of the road. The plan was to capture these two trenches to within 600 yards of Gavrelle, the depth of penetration ordered being 600 yards on the right to 900 yards on the left, the frontage attacked being some 1100 yards in breadth. The advance was undertaken by the 6th Black Watch operating on a two-company front, the 154th Brigade being ordered to form a defensive flank facing north as the attack progressed.

This attack should have been carried out at 5 A.M., covered by an artillery and machine-gun barrage, but before that hour an S.O.S. signal was fired on the new front occupied by the 7th Black Watch, as in the half-light parties of enemy infantry were seen moving in the open. As a result of this signal, our barrage and the enemy's came down almost simultaneously ; but no infantry action followed, the parties of the enemy seen being probably troops relieving his front-line posts.

In consequence of this artillery fire the attack was delayed until 6 A.M. At 8 A.M. all objectives had been gained and twenty-three prisoners captured.

These operations had now established the Division on a line running practically due north and south from the eastern outskirts of Fampoux to a point 600 yards south-west of Gavrelle. Four battalions—the 5th Seaforth Highlanders, 6th Gordon Highlanders, and 6th and 7th Black Watch—had been engaged, but had suffered comparatively small losses.

Thus the first of the objectives which the Division had set itself to attain—namely, to establish a firm and regular line from which it could initiate its attack in support of the left flank of the Canadian Corps—had been successfully realised by 25th August, one day before the major operations were due to begin.

While these actions were being fought great developments had taken place in the south. By the 25th August the Third and Fourth Armies had formed a salient of the German positions opposite Arras according to a prearranged plan, and had thus prepared the enemy's strong positions on Orange Hill and about Monchy le Preux for assault.

The intention was that the First Army, which prolonged the line on the left of the Third Army, should extend the attack northwards, and by driving eastwards from Arras, with their left covered by the Scarpe and Sensee rivers, turn the enemy's position on the Somme battlefield and cut his railway communications, which ran southwards across the front.

As has already been pointed out, the Scarpe in itself

THE CAPTURE OF GREENLAND HILL

could not sufficiently cover this advance as long as Greenland Hill lay in the hands of the enemy. It therefore fell to the lot of the 51st Division to capture this hill and make good the commanding ground on the north bank of the Scarpe, so as to free the Canadian Corps from molestation from that quarter.

It was arranged that the 51st should not attack in force, but should push forward along the Scarpe as the Canadian Divisions advanced and protect their flanks.

The front line held by the Canadians (who had by this time relieved the 170th Brigade, 57th Division, south of the Scarpe), running as it did roughly from Feuchy (inclusive) to Thilloy les Moufflaines (inclusive), lay considerably in rear of the line now held by the Highland Division. It was therefore arranged that the latter should not move until the Canadians had captured Orange Hill and the commanding village of Monchy le Preux. Both these positions were of great natural strength, particularly the latter, and afforded observation over a wide area of our lines, particularly to the north.

The plan of attack was that the Canadian advance should begin at 3 A.M. on 26th, and that as soon as it was reported that they had passed Monchy le Preux, the 152nd and the 153rd Brigades were to advance and occupy a line of trenches parallel with the Roeux-Gavrelle road at an average distance of 500 yards west of it. The depth of this advance would vary from some 500-700 yards.

At 8 A.M. 26th August, it was learnt that the Canadians had captured Monchy le Preux and were still going well. Orders were therefore issued for the advance of the 152nd and 153rd Brigades to begin at 10.30 A.M.

The operation was begun as arranged, the troops meeting with practically no opposition. By 11.30 A.M. the line was occupied by the 6th Gordon Highlanders on the right, and by the 6th and 7th Black Watch on the left, each on a two-company front.

As soon as this line was established, the 6th Gordon Highlanders pushed parties southwards to occupy a continuation of the captured trench line, which joined the Scarpe about 400 yards east of Roeux. By noon the Germans still gave no signs of making a stand, and parties of them could be seen on the road retiring towards Fresnes.

By 4 P.M. the 6th Gordon Highlanders had passed through Mount Pleasant Wood, and had occupied Roeux Station and the chemical works.

Meanwhile in the centre the 153rd Brigade had reached a trench some 400 yards east of the Gavrelle road running parallel to it, and had found it vacated.

The 154th Brigade on the left hand also occupied the enemy's front line, and by 5.30 P.M. were patrolling towards Gavrelle. It was anticipated, however, that the resistance might soon begin to stiffen, as reinforcements had been seen advancing towards Fresnes soon after noon, and more were reported to be detraining at Biache. The heavy artillery had accordingly taken the necessary action.

It had been the intention to establish a line on Greenland Hill and east of Hausa and Delbar Woods. As, however, the day was now well spent, this plan was modified, and an objective line was given running north and south from the railway on the western slopes of Greenland Hill.

This objective the 153rd Brigade attacked at 7 P.M. under a barrage, having formed up on the Roeux-Gavrelle road. Again only slight opposition was encountered, except on the right, where the 7th Gordon Highlanders were held off from their objective by German machine-gunners posted on the lips of a deep railway cutting.

Thus did history repeat itself, as on more than one occasion in the past machine-gunners posted on this same embankment, and probably firing from the same emplacements, had denied farther advance to the Highland Division. This embankment was a commanding place admirably suited for purposes of defence, which lent itself perfectly to the German genius for improvising strong points of resistance.

South of the railway the 6th Gordon Highlanders entered Roeux, and established a line east of the chemical works. This was the second occasion on which Roeux had fallen into the hands of the 152nd Brigade, and as was the case on the first occasion, it was entered practically without opposition, resulting in another "meatless day," as the Jocks described their first unopposed occupation of this village.

On the 154th Brigade front patrols were out north and south of Gavrelle, but the village had not yet been entered.

THE CAPTURE OF GREENLAND HILL

On the right of the Highland Division the 2nd Canadian Division were about 1000 yards west of Pelves, and on the left the 8th Division had occupied the enemy's front line.

During the night patrols of the 7th Argyll and Sutherland Highlanders passed through Gavrelle.

On the following day, 27th August, considerable advances were made, though an attempt to capture Greenland Hill failed.

At 10.30 A.M. the 153rd Brigade launched an attack under an artillery and machine-gun barrage, with the 7th Gordon Highlanders on the right and the 6th Black Watch on the left. The 7th Gordon Highlanders had set foot on Greenland Hill in 1917 under the gallant leadership of Lieutenant Still, but had been unable to maintain themselves there unsupported in their isolated position. On this occasion, too, the hill remained at the end of the day in German hands. Both the 7th Gordon Highlanders and the 6th Black Watch were at first reported to have gained their objectives, but it soon transpired that this was not the case, the German signal for " enemy attacking " having been mistaken for the British signal " objective gained."

The 7th Gordon Highlanders had succeeded in establishing a footing towards the summit of the western slopes of the hill; but the enemy dribbled strong reinforcements through the railway cutting, and into the trenches and sunken roads leading from it.

This cutting, already referred to as used extensively in the operations in April and May 1917, afforded a covered approach from Biache, from which troops could spread northwards, westwards, and southwards into the trenches and sunken roads on either side of the cutting. During operations, when the smoke and dust allowed, individuals could be seen moving forward or falling back along the cutting throughout the day; but, as a rule, the numbers doing so were so regulated that there were seldom sufficient to justify a large expenditure of artillery ammunition.

In this instance, after much fluctuating fighting, the enemy became so threatening on the flanks of the 7th Gordon Highlanders that they were compelled to withdraw from the position they had gained.

The 6th Black Watch, whose troops were not directly interfered with by the German reinforcements arriving through the cutting, reached a line just short of the summit of Greenland Hill before their advance was checked by machine-gun fire. In this position they maintained themselves for the remainder of the day.

On the flanks of the 153rd Brigade substantial advances were made by the 152nd and 154th Brigades.

Hearing that Greenland Hill had been captured, the 6th Seaforth Highlanders, extended on a wide front from the Scarpe to the railway, attacked from a line east of Roeux and the chemical works, with a line of trenches immediately west of Plouvain as their objective.

They pushed their advance for some 800-1000 yards, but then encountered strong resistance. Hausa and Delbar Woods, with their magnificent observation, were found to be well organised with machine-guns, which swept the glacis in front of them, as also was the large chalk-pit on the edge of the Roeux-Plouvain road just in front of the woods.

The advance was checked at this point, while on the left the enemy, again making use of the railway cutting, compelled the flank platoons to withdraw back into line with the 7th Gordon Highlanders north of the cutting.

The deepest advance made during the day was that of the 154th Brigade on the left. This Brigade, after many encounters between small patrols and small parties of the enemy, brushed aside all resistance and established a line in touch with the 6th Black Watch 500 yards east of Gavrelle, and linked up with the 8th Division on the outer flank.

In the afternoon three of our posts north of Gavrelle were rushed by the enemy, who attacked them under cover of the maze of trenches in which they were situated. Two of these were restored by the 7th Argyll and Sutherlanders, but the third was considered so particularly liable to this form of attack that no effort was made to retake it.

During the night 27-28th the 154th Brigade was relieved by the 8th Division, the Divisional front being thus considerably shortened.

Activity on the following day was confined largely to patrol actions on the front of the 152nd Brigade.

The position held by the 6th Seaforth Highlanders was

so dominated by Hausa and Delbar Woods and the chalk-pit, from which the enemy was continually harassing them with machine-gun fire, that attempts were made to work forward by patrols and make good the woods and quarry. These, however, all broke down in face of the volume of machine-gun fire, from which the openness of the country afforded no escape.

On the front of the 153rd Brigade the enemy made two attempts to rush posts, but in each case was successfully driven back.

During the evening of the 28th preparations were made for an attack on Greenland Hill to be carried out on the following morning.

Just south of Delbar Wood the Scarpe bends in a north-easterly direction, while the country between Plouvain and Biache is covered by wide pools and marshes. In consequence, the German positions about Hausa and Delbar Woods were enclosed on their southern and eastern sides by water.

In view of this, it was decided by General Oldfield to obviate the necessity of a direct attack on the woods, which was certain to be expensive in casualties, by manœuvring the enemy out of them. The plan was to strike from the north of the Divisional front towards Plouvain, and thus threaten the only communication by which the garrisons of the Hausa and Delbar Woods positions could extricate themselves.

The 154th Brigade were therefore ordered to advance against Greenland Hill on the whole Divisional front north of the railway and for 250 yards south of it.

Two objectives were selected: the first, a line which gave the attacking troops a position on the summit of the hill, and the second, a line about the Plouvain-Gavrelle road which gave them a firmer hold on it.

The 4th Gordon Highlanders (right) and the 7th Argyll and Sutherland (left) were detailed for the operation, each battalion detailing two companies for the capture of each objective.

To enable a more accurate barrage to be fired by the artillery, the troops were all withdrawn to a trench which had been the old British front line before the Germans had attacked in this sector earlier in the year. The barrage was arranged so as to come down on what had then been the German front line.

The attack was a complete success in every detail. The enemy posts on Greenland Hill put up a poor fight, in all about twenty prisoners being taken. At 10 A.M. the final objective was reached. Moreover, exactly as had been planned, the enemy south of the attack, seeing Highlanders on Greenland Hill, and advancing along the railway towards Plouvain, and knowing that they could only extricate themselves along the banks of the Scarpe, evacuated their positions, fearing lest that exit might also be closed to them.

The 152nd Brigade followed close on their heels, and captured 1 officer and 15 other ranks who had left their withdrawal too late. At 1 P.M. our artillery ceased shelling Hausa and Delbar Woods, and at 2.20 P.M. the 6th Seaforth Highlanders had reached their eastern edges.

Thus, like many other places that had for some time been a bitter thorn in the flesh, such as the Brown line at Arras in April, Flesquières in November 1917, and Espilly and the Bois de Coutron of more recent memory, the formidable Hausa and Delbar Woods ultimately fell undefended.

After occupying the woods, the 6th Seaforth Highlanders continued their advance and occupied a line of trenches about 1500 yards west of Plouvain, capturing another eight prisoners.

During the evening Greenland Hill was consolidated, machine-guns and artillery moving forward into close support of the infantry.

Thus ended a completely successful day, in which Greenland Hill, 1 officer, 52 other ranks, 10 machine-guns and 2 light trench-mortars were captured.

Early on the morning of the following day patrols were pushed forward with orders to get into touch with the enemy and establish posts in contact with him. The Germans were soon located holding a strongly-wired trench line in front of Biache and Fresnes, and were found to be active and alert. Some posts were accordingly established during the day in front of the new line.

In view of its great tactical importance, every effort was made to ensure the holding of Greenland Hill should a counter-attack be made to regain it.

South of the Scarpe the great advance was proceeding rapidly towards Cambrai, and as its left flank increased in depth, so did the importance of holding Greenland Hill increase.

The three field companies and the 8th Royal Scots were at once employed in giving effect to a scheme of defence that had been prepared.

This scheme embodied, in the first place, the defence of Greenland Hill against a frontal attack, a main line of resistance being constructed east of Hausa and Delbar Woods and Windmill Copse on the railway embankment. A defensive flank was also sited facing south along the river Scarpe, and a second defensive flank facing northwards designed to meet an attack developing through Gavrelle. Five companies of machine-guns were placed in the line and three held in reserve.

In these operations the Division, under the command of General Oldfield, the C.R.A., had fulfilled all the tasks allotted to it absolutely, with a total loss of 1145, including 4 officers and 182 other ranks killed and missing.

During the attacks against Greenland Hill the Division was placed under orders of Lieut.-General Sir A. W. Currie, K.C.B., K.C.M.G., commanding the Canadian Corps. On the return of the Division to the XXIInd Corps, on 30th August, General Oldfield received the following congratulatory message from General Currie:—

"Now that the gallant 51st Division is passing from my command, may I be permitted to say that I shall always remember with the greatest pride that for six stirring days you formed part of the Canadian Corps. I remember very well when the Division first came to France in May 1915, and that we took part together in the fighting at Festubert and Givenchy. Again we were associated in the memorable battle of Arras in April 1917, and now again we have kicked off side by side in an advance the results of which I have every reason to believe will be far-reaching. That your Division was able after the continuous fighting in which it has been engaged this year to take and keep the strong position of Greenland Hill, testifies in the strongest possible manner to the fact that

2 A

the fighting qualities of the 51st are second to none in all the Allied armies.

"On behalf of the Canadian Divisions I thank you most sincerely for the splendid help and support you have given to the main advance south of the river. I wish you all the best of luck always, and have every confidence that the splendid reputation that the Division now enjoys will ever be maintained."

Until 14th September, when the Division was relieved by the 49th Division, no events occurred which materially changed the tactical situation. The period was not, however, a quiet one. The enemy was at times extremely active with his guns, on occasions using quantities of mustard gas, the targets against which he chiefly vented his spleen being the railway cutting, Greenland Hill, and Fampoux.

Enemy aircraft were also unusually active in this area, particularly in bombing the troops in the line. On one occasion in particular, 4th September, aircraft were crossing over lines frequently throughout the night—singly, by twos, and in flights up to six in number—which heavily bombed the vicinity of Roeux, Fampoux, and the valley north of Fampoux.

Patrolling was maintained with the greatest energy, as it was anticipated that the success of the operations in the south in which Cambrai was becoming threatened might at any time lead the enemy to further withdrawals.

In consequence, encounters in No Man's Land were of frequent occurrence, in which considerable damage was inflicted on the enemy—not, however, without losses also being sustained by the Jocks. On one occasion a daylight patrol of the 6th Seaforth Highlanders, consisting of one officer and two other ranks, had a lively fight with an enemy post 200 yards from Biache power station. They killed two of the enemy and wounded several others, and then returned to our lines, all three having first been wounded.

On relief on 14th September the Division remained at rest and training until 24th September, when it again returned to the same sector, and remained in the line until 4th October, when it was again relieved by the 44th Division. This relief was not, however, carried out with the object of allowing the Division a period of rest, but for the purpose of its being moved to another portion of the front to take part again in active operations.

Probably, in common with many other Divisions, the men of the 51st had come to consider that they were doing more than their fair share of battle fighting. They had, indeed, been engaged in nine major operations in the period of seventeen months from April 1917 to August 1918.

The men thus felt entitled to covet the long periods of rest such as fell to the lot of some of the more fortunate Corps and Divisions, which occasionally were given five or six weeks' rest in which to regain their form after an operation.

They, however, comforted themselves by the thought that they were so continuously employed in the forefront of the battle because the Higher Command had learnt to rely on them to carry to a successful issue any task that was set them.

CHAPTER XVIII.

THE OPERATIONS TOWARDS VALENCIENNES.

On 5th October the Division began its move southwards, with orders to relieve the 3rd Canadian Division in the line north-west of Cambrai, and by the evening of 8th October was concentrated in the Queant-Inchy area. However, a rapidly-changing situation on the 8th necessitated an alteration in the plans. On that date an attack was delivered by the Third and Fourth British Armies, which was continued by the French on their right. Farther south on the same date French troops attacked east of the Meuse and in Champagne. This attack progressed for some three or four miles into the enemy's lines, with the result that his resistance temporarily gave way. During the night the Canadian Corps captured Ramillies and crossed the Scheldt Canal at Pont d'Aire, and entered Cambrai from the north. The following day the advance was continued. Cambrai was in our hands, and our troops established themselves on a line three miles east of the town.

Orders were therefore issued for the 51st Division to move to the Bourlon area, and to be placed under the command of the Canadian Corps. Accordingly on 10th October the 152nd Brigade moved to Bourlon village, 153rd Brigade to the area north-east of Bourlon, and 154th Brigade north of Fontaine Notre Dame, the village in which they had experienced such savage fighting in November 1917.

On 11th October orders were issued for the 51st Division to relieve the 2nd Canadian Division, which was attacking the village of Iwuy on the same day, the instructions being that the 51st was to take over from the 2nd Canadians on whatever line they had established themselves at the conclusion of the operations.

Prior to these moves an important change had taken place in the composition of the Division: the 6th Argyll and Sutherland Highlanders, who had been employed as pioneer battalion to the 5th Division ever since they had left the 51st in the Labyrinth in 1916, rejoined the Division as an infantry battalion. They were allotted to the 153rd Brigade in place of the 7th Gordon Highlanders, who, on account of the difficulty of finding further reinforcements, were transferred to the 152nd Brigade and amalgamated with the 6th Gordon Highlanders. This composite battalion was known as the 6/7 Gordon Highlanders.

In view of the coming relief, the 152nd and 154th Brigades moved forward during the morning into the 2nd Canadian Division area, the 153rd Brigade moved towards Tilloy and Essars, and the Divisional staff headquarters opened a report centre at the headquarters of the 2nd Canadian Division at Escadœuvres.

At 4 P.M. the 51st Division again came under the XXIInd Corps, and received orders that it would attack through the 2nd Canadian Division on the following day in conjunction with an attack to be delivered by the Corps on either flank.

The operations on which the Division was now to embark constituted a complete change from any in which it had previously taken part. Trench warfare, in which the enemy's defences can be largely definitely located, now belonged to the past. The scene of the fighting was for the future to be laid amidst large uplands, checkered with undestroyed villages, many of them still occupied by their civilian inhabitants, and with occasional woods and spinneys with living trees in full leaf. Continuous trenches no longer stretched across the battle front.

The country was, however, well adapted for the rearguard action which the enemy was fighting. On the western edge of the uplands he could adequately cover the eastern slopes of those facing him with comparatively few machine-guns, skilfully hidden in spinneys and sunken roads, in positions which dominated the open country over which the attacking troops must advance.

Moreover, two serious obstacles in the shape of rivers

completely crossed the Divisional front—namely, the river Selle and the river Ecaillon. These rivers, with soft treacherous beds and steep muddy sides, were not fordable. Further, their course ran through narrow steeply-sloped valleys, so that the high ground on the eastern banks afforded magnificent observation to machine-gunners and artillery observers of the western slopes of the valleys and of the crossings of the river.

To the north of the Divisional front ran the Canal de l'Escaut in a north-easterly direction until it passed Denain, where, in a short reach, it suddenly turned south-east and traversed almost half the Divisional front before it again bent north-eastwards and resumed its course.

Traversing the Divisional front obliquely from south-west to north-east ran the great Cambrai-Valenciennes road.

The country was for the most part not so enclosed as it was further south, where innumerable orchards, spinneys, and woods blinded the enemy's troops, and so compelled him either to fall back to more open country, or to employ strong rearguards to cover the ground and hold it. In this case each attack required delicate handling to prevent large numbers of men falling victims in an endeavour to close with a few marksmen on well-sited machine-gun nests.

To protect the infantry from this fate creeping barrages were arranged wherever possible, and even when this form of attack was not considered advisable or was impracticable, sections of field-guns and howitzers were invariably detailed, as far as the crossings of the river allowed, to accompany the infantry in close support. In fact, it will be seen that in this battle the co-operation between the artillery and infantry had reached an abnormally high standard, due to the gallantry, initiative, and efficiency of the junior officers and men.

In appreciating the true value of the success of the Highland Division in this, its last engagement, it must not be forgotten that since 21st March it had lost in major operations, apart from sickness and trench warfare, over a thousand officers and many thousands of men. Thus it was embarking on a form of warfare of which the bulk of its commanders had had no experience, and with its infantry composed for the most part of immature youths or men who had only recently joined the ranks of the infantry. Taking these facts into consideration, the repeated incidents of unusual daring and gallantry displayed in these operations will give clear proof of the great vitality of the Division. This was largely due to the manner in which its reinforcements, earnestly applying themselves to the upholding of its traditions, supported the commanders and more experienced comrades.

In the early hours of 12th October 1918, orders were received that the Division was to form up on a line roughly 1000 yards north-east of the village of Iwuy, and to attack with the object of capturing a line running from Avesnes le Sec inclusive along the Lieu St Amand road as far as Maison Blanche Farm, thence to the railway at Houdain, the breadth of line to be attacked being about 5000 yards.

The 49th Division was co-operating in this attack on the right, and a brigade of the 2nd Canadian Division was to operate on the left flank and clear the country between the railway and the Canal de l'Escaut.

Two brigades were detailed by the G.O.C. for the attack, the 152nd Brigade on the right and 154th Brigade on the left. The 152nd Brigade attacked on a two-battalion front, the leading battalions being the 5th Seaforth Highlanders and the 6/7 Gordon Highlanders, each on a two-company front. The 154th Brigade, however, employed only one battalion on the front line, the 4th Seaforth Highlanders, who formed up on a three-company front.

By 4.45 A.M. the attacking brigades had completed the relief of the 4th and 6th Canadian Infantry Brigades. The remainder of the morning was spent by the battalions in moving into position and completing their arrangements for the attack.

At 8 A.M. General Carter-Campbell took over command of the sector.

At 10 A.M. reports were received at Divisional headquarters that the enemy were withdrawing on the front of the 49th Division on the right, and that their brigades were moving forward without waiting for the artillery barrage. No reports could, however, be obtained on the Divisional front that the enemy had withdrawn there; it was in consequence decided that the attack should be carried out as originally planned.

Accordingly at 12 noon the infantry advanced, preceded by a creeping barrage fired by six brigades of field artillery. It, however, quickly transpired that the attack had coincided with an enemy withdrawal, and the prescribed objective was reached with little opposition. On the extreme right the 5th Seaforth Highlanders had some fighting in clearing Avesnes le Sec; while on the left, on crossing the spur facing Lieu St Amand, the 4th Seaforth Highlanders came under heavy fire from that village, but managed in spite of it to establish themselves on the forward slope.

By 1.30 P.M. the objective was gained on the whole Divisional front.

It had been previously arranged that if success attended these operations the 7th Argyll and Sutherland Highlanders, accompanied by a mobile 18-pounder section under the command of Lieutenant J. Gillespie of "A" Battery, 256th Brigade, should pass through the 4th Seaforth Highlanders and if possible occupy Lieu St Amand and the station at Pavé de Valenciennes, situated close to the junction of the railway and the Valenciennes-Cambrai road near Lieu St Amand.

Accordingly, as soon as the protective barrage that was covering the 4th Seaforth Highlanders had ceased, two companies of the 7th Argyll and Sutherland Highlanders continued the advance. Though at first under fairly heavy hostile artillery barrage, they moved rapidly forward until on a line about 150 yards from the southernmost houses of the village. Here, faced by the enemy, who appeared to have established a firm line all along the front, they came under a heavy burst of machine-gun fire which first checked their pace, and, finally, as the German machine-gunners began to get on to their targets, brought the general advance to a standstill.

The 18-pounder section at once came into action in the open, and silenced many of the machine-guns; but the guns hidden amongst the houses could not be located, and so could not be effectively bombarded. While searching for these guns, a German 8-inch howitzer battery got on to the 18-pounder section, and shelled it so effectively that it was forced to withdraw temporarily.

The 7th Argyll and Sutherland Highlanders, however, did not give up their attempts to reach the village, and each platoon endeavoured to work its way forward. One of them, from a point 200 yards from the south-west corner of the village, crawled forward between the furrows of a newly-ploughed field until within twenty-five yards of two machine-guns which were firing from behind a bank.

Unfortunately, just at the moment when the sections were about to rise and rush this post, a burst of enfilade machine-gun fire from the railway caught them. Swept by the bullets from this gun, they were unable to rise from the furrows, and movement forwards, rearwards, or to the flank became impossible. In this position they remained until an hour or so later. About 4 P.M. the men were able to dribble back to cover singly.

During this movement on the left, the information having been received at Divisional headquarters that all objectives had been gained, orders had therefore been issued for the attacking brigades to move forward to gain a line running from the river Selle just north of Haspres round Lieu St Amand to the railway. The 152nd Brigade on the right, however, found the resistance as strong as it had been in front of the 7th Argyll and Sutherland Highlanders, and no substantial alterations in the line took place.

It was therefore decided to subject Lieu St Amand to a heavy bombardment from 5 P.M. to 5.30 P.M., and then to advance strong patrols against the village, and if possible occupy it.

At that time many batteries were moving forward, and though the 18-pounder section attached to the infantry again did gallant work in the open, the officer commanding the company of the 7th Argyll and Sutherland Highlanders concerned decided that the attack was unlikely to be successful, and so cancelled the orders for the advance. One platoon, however, which did not receive its instructions in time, had already moved forward, and reached a line about 100 yards from the outskirts of the village. At this point they were swept by machine-gun fire from the houses; but, nevertheless, with a fine determination to reach their objective, the men rushed the village and disappeared amongst the buildings. Those of them who had successfully crossed the open in face of the hostile fire and reached the village were at once subjected to close-range fire from all sides. The survivors, however, hung on behind what cover they could obtain from walls and buildings, and managed to extricate themselves one by one when darkness came.

The performances of the two platoons of the 7th Argyll and Sutherland Highlanders, which each had tried to carry Lieu St Amand individually, were characterised by great gallantry and skill on the part of the men. They had not only advanced against considerable machine-gun opposition, but they had also, having found themselves cut off from immediate assistance and at close grips with an enemy considerably superior to them in numbers and fire power, successfully extricated themselves from serious predicaments.

The mobile section accompanying the Argylls had supported the infantry in these attacks magnificently. They had drawn considerable shell-fire when in action in the open, and had had one of their ammunition limbers set on fire, Lieutenant Gillespie himself extinguishing the flames.

By 6 P.M., a farther advance that evening appearing impracticable, orders were issued for a line to be consolidated roughly on the original objective given for the first attack.

At 9 P.M. orders were received from the Corps that pressure was to be exercised against the enemy's rearguards on the morrow by carrying out an attack with the object of gaining a line running from the railway east of the river Selle 1000 yards north of Haspres, east of Fleury and Noyelles, and thence running westwards to the railway north of Lieu St Amand.

October 13th turned out to be a day of heavy and costly fighting. It was evident from the outset that the enemy was making a determined stand south of Valenciennes, so as to secure the flanks of his withdrawals that were taking place in other parts of the front. Indeed, orders captured during the forthcoming operations showed that the troops had been instructed to hold the line of the river Selle at all costs. In consequence, he was holding his position with machine-guns in considerable strength.

Moreover, the protection afforded him by the river Selle and the Canal de l'Escaut enabled him to mass to the north-east a weight of artillery which he would not otherwise have dared to maintain in action in such close support to the infantry of his rearguard.

To increase his powers of resistance further, he also employed on this portion of the front a number of aeroplanes, which flew low over our attacking waves, and constantly bombed and machine-gunned the troops and batteries.

The enemy's determination to stand not having yet been disclosed at this time, it was decided to attempt to gain this objective by exploitation, and not to employ a creeping barrage. The 255th Brigade, R.F.A., was, however, detailed to follow the infantry in close support as a mobile brigade.

At 9 A.M. on the 18th the same four battalions as had been engaged on the 12th moved forward to the attack, two sections of machine-guns being sent forward with each leading battalion, as well as three light trench-mortars which accompanied them.

Prior to the attack, places which appeared suitable for enemy concentrations and nests of machine-guns had been heavily bombarded by the artillery.

Only on the right was any substantial progress made. On that flank the 5th Seaforth Highlanders, suffering heavy casualties from frontal and enfilade machine-gun fire, forced their way forward to a line 1000 yards north-east of Avesnes le Sec, where they were finally checked.

On their left the 6/7 Gordon Highlanders came under such a blast of machine-gun fire that they made practically no advance, and sustained over 300 casualties; the effect of this fire was so destructive that the four sections of machine-guns, in their efforts to beat it down, had three officers killed and six guns knocked out, while the teams of the light trench-mortars lost so heavily that the survivors were too few in number to work the guns, and so joined in the fighting as infantry.

Meanwhile the enemy had also opened an intense artillery barrage all along the line.

In order to help forward the infantry on this point of the field, 2nd Lieutenant P. H. Unwin from "A" Battery, 256th Brigade, R.F.A., brought his section into action at 800 yards' distance from the enemy, and immediately opened fire with great effect, driving back parties of infantry that were counter-attacking, and inflicting serious losses on them. 2nd Lieutenant Unwin remained in action in his exposed position throughout the day, and gave great moral assistance to the infantry.

On the left brigade front it was arranged that the 7th Argyll and Sutherland Highlanders on the left flank should move forward and capture Lieu St Amand before the 6th Seaforth Highlanders on the left centre moved forward to attack.

Two companies of the 7th Argyll and Sutherland Highlanders therefore went forward with the artillery bombarding the village; but as soon as the guns lifted off the southernmost houses, a white Very light was fired by the enemy, followed by an intense burst of machine-gun fire which swept the attacking waves.

As no covered approaches existed except on the right, all forward movement was at once paralysed, apart from that of one platoon on the extreme right flank. Here a certain amount of cover existed, and the men worked their way forward to within fifty yards of some enemy machine-guns, and maintained themselves there, unable to make further progress, as the country had again become open.

Attempts to rush forward were beaten down by hostile fire; and though one Lewis-gun team worked its way into position, and by excellent shooting knocked out a machine-gun team and inflicted casualties on parties seen in the village, no further progress was made.

The advance made by the 7th Argyll and Sutherland Highlanders had not carried the line sufficiently forward to enable the 4th Seaforth Highlanders to gain Maison Blanche in the centre, and by 11 A.M. most of the attacking waves were back on the jumping-off line, though seriously depleted in numbers.

On the right, however, parties of the 5th Seaforth Highlanders, with both their flanks in the air, were digging-in along the railway north of Avesnes le Sec, and held on in this position until 2 P.M. A party of an officer and twenty men protecting their right beat off several attempts to work round their flanks, covered the withdrawal of the troops on the railway, and remained in position until dusk, when they regained our lines.

The platoons of the 7th Argyll and Sutherland Highlanders, which had also been brought to a standstill, with both its flanks in the air, close against Lieu St Amand, similarly regained our lines at dusk, this being the third platoon of this battalion which had made a great endeavour to carry Lieu St Amand single-handed.

Neither of the Divisions on the flanks was able to make progress during this day, and it was clearly evident that the enemy had selected the line of the Haspres-Lieu St Amand road as his line of resistance for his rearguards.

No further attack was carried out until 19th October. As a result of operations in other parts of this line, everything pointed to an early withdrawal on the front south of Douai, which might possibly extend as far southwards as the front of the 51st Division. Extensive patrolling was therefore carried out during this period, but the enemy was always found in strength and alert, and numerous patrol encounters took place.

The artillery, who were well provided with good observation posts, carried out numerous bombardments against enemy movement, and selected strong places with satisfactory results. They, however, received in return a very considerable ration of shells from the German gunners, who were still in force, and harassed the forward areas and battery positions continuously, particularly with gas.

On the 17th October the enemy withdrawal south of Douai began, and on the 18th it had extended as far as the front occupied by the Canadians on the left flank of the 51st. The enemy was, however, still firmly in position along the Haspres-Lieu St Amand road.

These days of respite from active operations were employed by the R.E. in solving many problems. Water for the forward troops was located in damaged wells in Avesnes le Sec and Iwuy, which had to be repaired and tested.

A track for horse transport had to be made south of the village of Iwuy on account of the continuous bombardment of that village by the German artillery.

The enemy had also, with characteristic thoroughness, destroyed all the bridges on the railway from Cambrai to Denain, and had thus effectually interfered with lateral communications on this area. The 8th Royal Scots were therefore employed working continuously in conjunction with a field company of the 4th Division in removing the débris of the broken arches from the roads so as to reopen them for troops and transport.

An attack was now planned for the 20th October, the objectives given being the same as had been arranged for the attack on the 12th.

However, on the early morning of 19th October, favoured by a thick mist, the enemy withdrew on the Divisional front. At this time the 153rd Brigade had taken over the line on the left, while the 154th Brigade had, after three days' rest, relieved the 152nd Brigade on the right.

Until the mist lessened the enemy could not be actively followed, but patrols from both brigades came into contact with him shortly after dawn.

On the left of the Division the Canadians also reported that the enemy was withdrawing on their front, and that they were moving forward to seize the crossing on the left bank of the Canal de l'Escaut at Bouchain, north-west of Lieu St Amand.

The withdrawal on the front of the 51st Division was, however, slow, and by noon patrols had reported that the enemy was still in position both on the right front and in Lieu St Amand.

However, at 2.10 P.M., the enemy began to bombard the latter, and twenty minutes later patrols of the 6th Argyll and Sutherland Highlanders were in its streets.

Orders were then issued for the brigades to gain the line Fleury-Noyelles-Douchy, or, in other words, to seize the bridgeheads across the river Selle. The advance began on the greater part of the Divisional front at 3 P.M., covered by detachments of the Corps cyclists and infantry patrols. It was at once discovered that while the resistance on the left was almost negligible, the enemy was holding on to Haspres, and was making some effort to delay the advance on the right.

On the left progress became rapid. The two leading battalions, the 6th Argyll and Sutherland Highlanders and the 7th Black Watch, at first moved forward in extended order ; but later, as only stray groups of the enemy were encountered at this stage, a screen of scouts was sent forward, the companies following in artillery formation, and later by platoons in column of route. Simultaneously the artillery brigades advanced to positions in and about Avesnes le Sec and Lieu St Amand with mobile 18-pounder sections closely following the infantry battalions.

By 6 P.M. the woods east of Maison Blanche were cleared, and the troops were well east of Lieu St Amand. Before midnight Neuville sur l'Escaut, in which 1500 civilians were found, and Douchy, also full of civilians, were rushed. In the latter village a few riflemen had been left behind by the enemy to check the advance, but these fled as the leading troops approached.

On the right brigade front the 4th Gordon Highlanders advanced towards Fleury with two companies, the remaining two companies forming a defensive flank to protect the right, as Haspres was still held by the enemy.

As they approached Fleury they came under considerable artillery and machine-gun fire; but they pushed forward in spite of it, and reached the west banks of the river Selle. Here they found all bridges destroyed, so that the stream, some 20 feet wide, 5 feet deep, and with muddy banks and a soft bed, presented a serious obstacle. The advance therefore came to a standstill, while the troops collected material with which to improvise bridges.

On the left of the 4th Gordon Highlanders the 7th Argyll and Sutherland Highlanders had made rapid progress. They had, in fact, outrun their neighbouring battalions, and their three leading companies were in consequence compelled to form deep flanks as they advanced, while the fourth company moved in close support to them on their right flank.

By 7 P.M. they had reached Noyelles, which they found clear of the enemy, but, like Douchy and Neuville, occupied by numbers of civilians. They had dispersed a small party of Germans on the east bank of the river Selle, and though the bridge had been blown up, three companies had established themselves on the east bank of the river by 9.45 P.M. in touch with the 6th Argyll and Sutherland Highlanders. The 4th Seaforth Highlanders also advanced in rear of the 1/7 Argyll and Sutherland Highlanders towards Noyelles, while sections of the 400th and 404th Field Companies, R.E., were hastening forward with bridging material so as to prepare passages across the river for artillery at the earliest possible moment.

The situation of the troops at midnight 19-20th October was thus as described above, while on the right, though Saubroir had fallen, the enemy in Haspres were still gallantly holding out. On the left the 4th Canadian Division had reached Denain.

During the night the 404th Field Company, R.E., who had reconnoitred and selected a site for a bridge just north of Noyelles as soon as the infantry patrols had passed that village, moved forward with the pontoon and trestle waggons. Though they came under both rifle and machine-gun fire as they neared the village, the waggons reached the site successfully, and a bridge of two Weldon trestles was completed by 3.45 A.M. The construction of a bridge within eight hours of the infantry having reached the east bank of the river, within a few hundred yards of enemy riflemen and machine-gunners, was an exceptionally fine performance.

The advance continued throughout the night, but it was found that the enemy was making a stand roughly on the line of the road from Haspres through La Croix St Marie to Denain.

On the right the 4th Gordon Highlanders, by improvising rough bridges from beams, branches, and straw, crossed the river Selle south of Fleury, and at 6.45 A.M. on 20th October occupied the village. The enemy machine-gun teams had bolted from the eastern outskirts of the village as the troops approached.

The 4th Seaforth Highlanders then crossed the river at Noyelles over the bridge just completed by the R.E., and formed up on a two-company front east and south of the village on the left of the 4th Gordon Highlanders; and with the 7th Argyll and Sutherland Highlanders on their left, the Argylls and Seaforths then attempted to advance at 5 A.M.

Heavy machine-gun fire was, however, at once opened on the 4th Seaforth Highlanders, with such effect that they were unable to make material progress, and were compelled to dig in only slightly in advance of their forming-up line. In this position they tried to locate the enemy machine-guns so that they might deal with them and continue the advance.

The 7th Argyll and Sutherland Highlanders also found

that their patrols could not get forward on to the high ground north of Noyelles, and so discontinued their advance until arrangements could be made for artillery support.

Similarly on the left the two leading battalions were well across the river Selle at dawn, but were in their turn checked by machine-gun fire from the wood north-west of La Croix St Marie, and were also preparing to attack with artillery.

Considerable fighting occurred during the early part of the day. In the night two attacks carried out by the 4th Seaforth Highlanders and one by the 7th Argyll and Sutherland Highlanders ultimately, about 8 A.M., forced the enemy beyond the Haspres-La Croix St Marie road, machine-guns being captured at Maison Rouge. Beyond this point, however, the troops could make no headway against the volume of fire drawn by any attempt to move forward in the open.

On the left brigade front the artillery came into action at 9.30 A.M., when a concentrated fifteen minutes shoot was carried out against the woods and houses west of La Croix St Marie. The infantry line attacked, but failed to dislodge the enemy.

The shoot was then repeated for a second fifteen minutes, and the 6th Argyll and Sutherland Highlanders and 7th Black Watch again went forward, cleared the woods and houses, and quickly reached the La Croix St Marie-Denain road, touch being obtained in Denain with the 4th Canadians on the left.

The mobile section of "A" Battery, 256th Brigade, R.F.A., under the command of Lieutenant S. Simkins, attached to the 6th Argyll and Sutherland Highlanders, had materially assisted in this advance. Lieutenant Simkins, having been pointed out houses in which machine-guns were located, engaged them over open sights. Civilians who were taking shelter in the cellar of one of these houses afterwards told Lieutenant Simkins that the shooting was very accurate, and that the enemy machine-gunner in that house had left badly wounded.

In spite of the proximity of the enemy and the fighting going on in that neighbourhood, the 404th Field Company, R.E., erected a bridge at Fleury. Owing to the hostile fire they could not get their waggons forward until 11.30

A.M., but by 6.10 P.M. a bridge consisting of a pontoon and a trestle was completed and brought into use.

The 400th Field Company, R.E., had been ordered to bridge the river at Douchy, but they experienced similar difficulty in getting their waggons forward. They, however, found and repaired a partially-destroyed German bridge, and constructed a new bridge of two Weldon trestles south of the village. In each case the bridges were completed in time for the advance of the artillery.

At 12 noon the 153rd Brigade continued its advance and made rapid progress. The enemy on the extreme left, fearing that he might be driven against the now bridgeless Canal de l'Escaut, withdrew rapidly, the 7th Black Watch reaching the canal bank along their whole front by 5 P.M. They then detached two platoons to operate against the rear of the Germans resisting the 4th Canadians at Wavrechain, north of the canal, but they were held up through being unable to find a crossing.

The advance of the 6th Argyll and Sutherland Highlanders was slower, not so much on account of the German resistance to them frontally, but on account of the fire which came from the high ground on their right flank. However, by 10 P.M. they had established themselves on the canal bank from the rubber factory south of Prouvy westwards, capturing Haulchin and releasing 1500 French civilians. This advance was materially assisted by the Corps Cyclists, who patrolled the country well in front of the infantry, and enabled the latter to advance with few delays.

After dark, at 8 P.M., the 7th Argyll and Sutherland Highlanders resumed their advance, the 4th Seaforth Highlanders on the Divisional right at 10 P.M. This advance proceeded successfully, and by midnight the leading troops had reached the eastern edges of the Grand Bois and the Bois de l'Entrée, the line running thence north-westwards to the railway leading to Denain.

Throughout the night 20-21st October, which fortunately was light and clear, the advance continued. The 153rd Brigade had already reached the canal bank throughout their front, and had formed a defensive flank on their right along the railway line facing Thiant. The 7th Argyll and Sutherland Highlanders on the right of the 153rd

Brigade also made great progress. In the grey of the morning their first company entered Thiant. Here they encountered a burst of machine-gun fire, but by 9 A.M. they had beaten down all resistance, and had worked through the village as far as to the banks of the Ecaillon. They, however, found the enemy in strength on the eastern banks, and so took up positions in houses and hedgerows on the edge of the stream. At 10 A.M. 21st October they gained touch with the Canadians, who had entered Prouvy.

The 4th Seaforth Highlanders and the 11th Brigade, 4th Division, who were now up in line with them on the high ground overlooking Monchaux and the river Ecaillon, were now unable to make further progress towards the banks of the river, as they found the western sides of the river valley were very exposed and covered by the fire of the enemy holding strong natural positions in sunken roads.

During the day the field artillery moved into positions west of Thiant.

From this point onwards, as the villages in front of the line were occupied by French civilians, the Divisional commander decided only to use 18-pounder shrapnel against them. Similarly, for the same reason, gas was not employed against the villages. This was a great deprivation, as a large supply of the long awaited mustard gas had just arrived.

Naturally the Germans used gas in similar circumstances freely.

Meanwhile the bridges thrown across the Selle were only sufficient for field-guns and horsed transport. Arrangements had therefore to be made by the C.R.E., Lieut.-Colonel Napier-Clavering, to provide bridges which would enable the Corps heavy artillery and lorry traffic to keep pace with the advance, so that all weapons would be available to engage the enemy should he decide to stand on the east banks of the Ecaillon.

Reconnaissances were therefore carried out by the 400th and 404th Field Companies, R.E., at Douchy and Noyelles for sites for the construction of heavy bridges over the river Selle. In both places the enemy had destroyed the original brick bridges, totally removing the central pier and one abutment in each case. The Douchy gap measured

72 feet and that at Noyelles 88 feet. No long girders were available to bridge these gaps without piers, and the difficulty of securing foundations for the piers on the mass of brick débris in the river-bed had therefore to be overcome.

For the Douchy bridge standard girder spans of 16 feet by 18 feet were available, so that work was begun by the 400th Field Company, R.E., on the 20th. By 10.30 A.M. on the 23rd the bridge was completed for all traffic except heavy tanks, thus enabling the heavy artillery to cross the river in time to take part in the attack to be delivered on the 24th.

For the bridge at Noyelles only salved German materials were available, which had to be collected and brought to the site of the bridge by horse transport. Work was begun on the 21st, and the bridge was completed for heavy traffic on the 28th.

The result of the preceding operations had materially altered the dispositions of the Division. The 153rd Brigade had been pinched out of the front line, the 4th Seaforth Highlanders and the 7th Argyll and Sutherland Highlanders of the 154th Brigade occupying the whole of what was now the Divisional front, with the 4th Gordon Highlanders in support of them at Fleury. The 153rd Brigade was therefore concentrated at Haulchin and Douchy, while the 152nd Brigade moved forward to Douchy and Noyelles.

The 21st, 22nd, and 23rd October were passed in making preparations for forcing the passage of the river Ecaillon. At 11 A.M. on the 21st the enemy began to shell Thiant, and for the next three days the artillery and machine-gun fire against our positions on the west bank of the river continued briskly. Orders were issued to accept any opportunity offered of crossing the river, but in only one case was an attempt to carry out this order successful, and then only temporarily. The 7th Argyll and Sutherland Highlanders had made three such attempts at Thiant, and at the third a small party succeeded in crossing the river. They rushed a machine-gun post, but the alarm had been given, and a strong machine-gun and trench-mortar bombardment was opened by the enemy. In the face of this fire no support could be pushed across the river to help the Argylls, and they were therefore compelled to return, bringing the captured machine-gun with them.

On 22nd October the 4th Seaforth Highlanders successfully advanced, and occupied the sunken road running parallel with the Ecaillon west of Monchaux. Their patrols had previously reached the west bank of the river, but had drawn such a storm of fire from the east bank that they were unable to maintain themselves there.

While the troops were thus situated, it was decided to carry out an attack to force the passage of the Ecaillon on the 24th. On the evening of the 23rd, the 153rd Brigade, to whom this attack was to be entrusted, accordingly relieved the 154th Brigade in the line.

The objective allotted to the Division for this attack was the village of Maing and the high ground south-east of it, the 4th Division being ordered to attack simultaneously on the right with a similar objective. The frontage of the attack allotted to the Division was 3000 yards in breadth, and for the operation seven brigades of field artillery and one of heavy artillery were placed at the disposal of the Divisional commander.

Three intermediate objectives were selected, the first being the river Ecaillon including the eastern outskirts of Thiant, and for the 4th Division, Monchaux; the second objective was the western outskirts of Maing, while the railway running north and south between Maing and Famars was given as a line of exploitation for the operations if the attack was successful.

The artillery, as soon as it had got into its own position east of the Selle, had fired Chinese barrages over the enemy's front system on the 22nd and 23rd. These were most successful, the enemy becoming completely demoralised, vacating his rifle-pits and running from one place to another, undoubtedly suffering many casualties, as the number of stretcher parties seen at work after each barrage had lifted proved.

It was therefore hoped that when the real attack came the German infantry would be considerably shaken, although patrols up to this point had always found them in position and alert on the east bank.

Two companies of machine-guns were also detailed to fire a barrage, while a section of machine-guns and light trench-mortars accompanied each infantry battalion.

Further, two sections of machine-guns were placed in the

4th Canadian Division area amongst the houses on the north bank of the canal to enfilade the positions to be attacked.

As it was necessary for the infantry to cross the Ecaillon on a broad front to enable them to take full advantage of the barrage, a number of bridges of 15 and 20 feet span were made. These were fitted with petrol tins and cork floats, which would prevent them from sinking should any of them prove too short to span the river.

Demonstrations in the use of these bridges were given to officers and men at the river Selle at Noyelles, but no adequate inspection of the places where they were to be employed in the crossing of the Ecaillon could be made, owing to the vigilance of the enemy's patrols.

The two Black Watch battalions were detailed for this attack by the 153rd Brigade, and were disposed with the 6th battalion on the right on a two-company front, and the 7th battalion on the left on a one-company front.

At 4 A.M. on 24th October, supported by a great weight of artillery, this attack was launched. Each company carried with it eight bridges, each supported by two to four men. Several of these, however, were destroyed by shell-fire before they had arrived at the water's edge.

The Ecaillon was found to be swollen by recent rains, and south of Thiant to be about 20 feet wide, from 4 to 6 feet deep, with bed and sides of soft mud, and banks, often steep, from 3 to 6 feet high. A single line of wire entanglement, except at Thiant, ran along the east bank of the river, and also along the greater part of the western bank.

The right company of the 6th Black Watch, whose advance had to be carried out down a glacis dominated by the village of Monchaux, encountered strong opposition. In the first instance, only one platoon, No. 11, commanded by Lieutenant Walker, managed to cross the river. This platoon, on the left of its company frontage, found its bridge too short to span the river; it was therefore discarded, and Lieutenant Walker, with his sergeant and runner, under the fire of machine-guns, plunged into the water and swam across to the other side. They were then followed by the remainder of the platoon, whom they helped to drag ashore as they struggled across the river, swimming and wading, in their heavy kits.

The next platoon on their right found themselves in a zone of machine-gun bullets, and in ten minutes only a corporal and six men were surviving. Nevertheless, the corporal crossed the stream alone, but had to return, and then crawled back with his six men to the assembly position.

The platoon in rear then renewed the attempt, but after suffering many casualties on a glacis destitute of cover, had also to withdraw.

The second platoon on the left—that is, the one in rear of No. 11—placed their bridge in position across the wreckage of an old German bridge and scrambled across.

Meanwhile the commander of No. 11 platoon and the company commander, realising that the machine-guns holding up the advance of the platoons on the right were located in Monchaux, turned their men right-handed, entered the village, and set upon the machine-gunners with their rifles and destroyed them. The two platoons that had already failed to cross then ran down to the river banks, and assisted by some men on the east bank, who threw out a stout ladder towards them, managed to cross the river. Three Lewis guns were then put out at once north-east of Monchaux to pin the enemy into that village while No. 11 platoon was dealing with the enemy in it. Monchaux was finally cleared, 68 prisoners and 9 machine-guns being captured there. Touch was also established in the village with men of the Hampshire Regiment, 4th Division.

The left-hand company of the 6th Black Watch, not being involved in the close-range machine-gun fire from Monchaux, and meeting no direct fire, quickly threw their bridges across the river, and were at once in possession of their first objective.

The company of the 6th Black Watch on the left crossed after many adventurous incidents by six bridges, placed across the river between the northern and southern outskirts of Thiant. Three of these had been quietly placed in position across the river before zero hour, and were crossed without difficulty when the barrage opened. The fixing of the remaining bridges, however, presented several difficulties. In one case, when the bridges were too short, one was used as a ladder down to the water, and a second was attached to it and to débris on the other side. Another party crossed by a hand-rail and girder remaining on a destroyed bridge. Another bridge, which was found to be too short, was floated across the river and lashed by a wire to a tree, each man having to leap from the bridge on to the beach on the opposite bank.

Crossings were made by a section at a time. In each case the foremost man as he reached the bank rushed into the nearest house to deal with the enemy there. Throughout, the crossing was effected under fairly lively machine-gun and trench-mortar fire.

The second objective was attacked by two companies on the right and one on the left of the same battalions. The advance was met by heavy shelling and considerable machine-gun fire. The progress was slow, and it was not before 8 A.M. that the objective was reached. The 7th Black Watch had for some time been held up by machine-guns in the Chateau des Pres, but they brought their Lewis guns into action, successfully countered the guns, and rushed the chateau. Farther on, in the outskirts of the village, they captured a German trench-mortar, which they turned on the enemy with good effect.

Heavy fighting ensued in the attack on Maing. The troops operating south of the village, one of the companies of the 6th Black Watch which had forced the passage of the Ecaillon, found it impossible to advance owing to the severity of the fire from the south-east corner of the village and from the sunken roads in front of them.

On the left, where two companies entered the village of Maing, close fighting went on for many hours in the streets and amongst the houses. Mobile 18-pounders, two reserve sections of machine-guns and the German trench-mortars already referred to, were all employed in the effort to secure the village. It was not, however, until 3 P.M. that the bulk of Maing was captured, the line then running round the eastern outskirts of the village to the cemetery, and thence along the sunken road running south-eastwards. The chateau at the eastern corner still remained in the enemy's hands.

Meanwhile the Divisional engineers had made every effort to bridge the Ecaillon for the passage of artillery. A section of the 404th Field Company had moved to the river-banks early in the morning to build foot-bridges for infantry; the remainder of the company also came up with bridging material, but owing to the heavy hostile barrage fire which greeted the attack, they were unable for some time to get their waggons forward. By 9 A.M., however, the reconnaissances of the bridge sites had been completed, and between 9 and 10 A.M., in spite of heavy shell-fire, the waggons moved forward. The first bridge just north of Thiant was completed by 10.30 A.M., and the second at the southern edge of the village by 11.45 A.M. The 400th Field Company completed a third bridge just south of the village. The first was completed in sufficient time to allow the mobile sections of the field artillery to be in action in close support of the infantry by 11 A.M.

A reconnaissance for a site for a heavy bridge at Thiant capable of carrying lorry traffic was made during the morning of the attack, and the abutments and foundations of the pier of a bridge destroyed by the Germans were found to be sound.

In spite of a considerable amount of shell-fire, work was carried on in preparing this site. The material for the bridge could not, however, be dumped at the site until the débris of the railway bridge over the Denain-Thiant road which had been blown up had been cleared away. The 8th Royal Scots had begun working continuously on the removal of this débris on 23rd October. In the course of the morning of the 24th they had cleared a path for horse-drawn vehicles, which greatly assisted the artillery moving forward, and by 3 P.M. of 25th October a passage was ready for lorry traffic. Shortly after this hour the lorries carrying the material for the heavy bridge reached Thiant, and by 7.50 A.M. on 26th October the bridge was ready for all traffic, including heavy tanks.

On the conclusion of this day's fighting the following message was received by the G.O.C. from the Corps Commander, Lieut.-General Sir A. J. Godley :—

" Will you please accept for yourself and convey to all concerned very heartiest congratulations and thanks for the excellent and successful attack made by the Division to-day. The gallantry and steadiness of the 153rd Infantry Brigade were most marked, the artillery barrage was all that could be desired, and the work on this and previous days in bridging the river under heavy shell-fire and difficult circumstances was beyond all praise."

October 25th was a day of heavy fighting, in which the enemy sustained serious losses. The Canadians were facing Valenciennes from the west bank of the canal, and the Highland Division and the 4th Division were ordered to continue the pressure on the east bank of the canal. The objective given for this attack was the high ground east of the railway east of Maing, and it was also hoped that it might be possible to gain Famars and Mont Houy by exploitation.

Of these objectives Mont Houy was an outstanding hillock north of Famars 88·1 metres in height, from which practically all the ground from the Ecaillon to the foot of the hillock could be observed. It thus commanded the approaches to Valenciennes from the south.

For this attack the Divisional front was divided into two sectors, the 152nd Infantry Brigade relieving the 6th Black Watch on the right, the 153rd Brigade relieving the 7th Black Watch on the left. The 152nd Brigade employed two battalions, the 6/7 Gordon Highlanders on the right and the 6th Seaforth Highlanders on the left in the front line of the attack, and the 153rd Brigade one, the 6th Argyll and Sutherland Highlanders.

So that the attack might be launched behind a regular barrage, all troops were withdrawn behind a line running through the centre of Maing village.

At 7 A.M. the advance began and at once made rapid progress. Two companies of the 6/7 Gordon Highlanders reached the railway embankment without difficulty; the two remaining companies passed through them and established themselves by 11 A.M. on the high ground at Caumont Farm and Grand Mont—not, however, without some brisk fighting with machine-gun posts. The 6th Seaforth Highlanders met with some stiff resistance on the railway, where they rushed a machine-gun post and captured an officer and twelve men. They met further opposition on Rouge Mont, but were equally successful in dealing with it. From this point, however, they came in contact with a strong enemy line west of Famars, which checked all their further efforts to advance.

On the left the 6th Argyll and Sutherland Highlanders on their right flank reached their objective by 8.30 A.M., but on the left they met determined resistance opposite La Fontenelle and at the houses alongside the canal opposite Trith-St Leger. It was not until they had successfully employed their light trench-mortars that on this part of the field they reached their objective at noon.

In this action, a section of 4·5 howitzers (under the command of Lieutenant D. L. MacMasters, M.C.) was employed as a mobile section for the first time, and did excellent work.

It engaged machine-guns in La Fontenelle and Poirier Farm with direct observation, and made such accurate shooting that the enemy ran in a panic in all directions.

On the attainment of these objectives, the fighting did not abate. All along the front our troops were in close contact with the enemy holding his line in strength. Our line then ran from the northern Divisional boundary along the railway down to the point where it crosses the Maing-Famars road, and then bulged forward in a loop to enclose Rouge Mont, Grand Mont, and Caumont.

Enemy machine-guns at fairly close range throughout the day kept up continual bursts of fire, which made any movement a matter of great difficulty, while low-flying aeroplanes constantly machine-gunned the troops in their new positions. The shelling was also very heavy, particularly along the railway, where, owing to the large proportion of gas used, masks had to be worn almost continuously.

At 4 P.M. the enemy opened a hurricane bombardment of our lines, and shortly afterwards launched a counter-attack. The S.O.S. was fired, and the artillery protective barrage came down. Observing officers reported that this was most effective, and that the enemy, who was counter-attacking in large numbers from the village of Famars, was well caught in the barrage and suffered seriously.

He was, however, in spite of his losses in the barrage, able to push back the line of the 6/7 Gordon Highlanders in the loop, and compel them gradually to give way until they were able to take up a firm stand along the railway.

The conformation of our line now enabled him to press the 6th Seaforth Highlanders on both flanks. They opposed his advance resolutely, inflicting further serious losses on him with rifle and Lewis-gun fire, until their ammunition, of which a quantity had been expended in combating low-flying aeroplanes, began to run short. They then fell back fighting by stages to the railway.

On the left, where the 6th Argyll and Sutherland Highlanders had taken up their position west of the railway, the attack was stopped before it reached our lines. In this action two sections of machine-guns distributed along the railway caught the enemy in their fire just as the artillery had done, and also took a heavy toll of them. The mobile section of 18-pounders attached to the 6/7 Gordon Highlanders also seized many opportunities of cutting up enemy parties crossing over the high ground west of Famars.

Considering the amount of fire in which it became involved, this counter-attack was a gallant performance on the part of a retiring enemy, and proved that the *morale* of his troops was, at any rate in some units, still high.

At 6 P.M. the enemy delivered a second counter-attack, this time with its weight against the 6th Argyll and Sutherland Highlanders. The Argylls, who had knocked out the first attack against their lines with rifle-fire, on this occasion adopted another method. As the enemy approached, they sprang from their shell-holes and charged down the hill against the approaching enemy with such vigour that those attackers who survived the onslaught fled from the field. The net result was that the Argylls carried their line forward for 500 yards, and established themselves in a line of trenches which, running east of the railway on the left, crossed it 100-200 yards south-west of La Fontenelle Wood. In this brilliant action they captured seventy-four unwounded prisoners, a trench-mortar, and several machine-guns. After this treatment the enemy had no further stomach for counter-attacks, but he vented his spleen by maintaining a heavy bombardment of our whole line with his artillery and machine-guns, which he maintained throughout the night.

October 26th was another day of savage fighting, the enemy resisting stubbornly, and being aggressive with his artillery and in counter-attacks.

Orders were issued for the advance to be resumed in

OPERATIONS TOWARDS VALENCIENNES

conjunction with the 4th Division, the objectives of the 51st being Famars and Mont Houy.

For this attack the 152nd Brigade employed the 6/7 Gordon Highlanders on the right and the 4th Gordon Highlanders (attached) on the left, while the 153rd Brigade employed the 6th Black Watch. The artillery fired a creeping barrage, and a company of machine-guns was again placed across the canal at Trith-St Leger in positions in enfilade, in which it had many opportunities of engaging good targets with machine-gun fire.

The attack was launched at 10 A.M., and on the right both battalions made good progress. Caumont and Betterave Farm were soon in the hands of the leading companies of the 6/7 Gordon Highlanders, and these joined with the 4th Gordon Highlanders on the left in surrounding Rouge Mont Copse and accounting for its entire garrison. The rear two companies then passed through them, and also reached the objective allotted to them, a line south of Famars facing the Rhonelle river.

The two leading companies of the 4th Gordon Highlanders were no less successful. They forced their way by short rushes to the high ground south of Famars, having rounded up a number of machine-guns *en route*. The two following companies then passed through them and entered Famars village. Here, after a series of struggles with machine-gun posts and some street fighting, the village was cleared and posts established east of it by 11.30 A.M.

On the left the 6th Black Watch carried out their advance successfully, though subjected to considerable artillery and machine-gun fire. By 11.30 A.M. the two leading companies had made their way close up to Mont Houy. The two rear companies then passed through them, the one to attack the hill, and the other to continue the advance beyond La Poirier Station. These troops were assisted by one of the machine-guns on the north side of the river, which, seeing some infantry held up by an enemy machine-gun, fired a burst into the gun, scattered the survivors of the detachment, and enabled the infantry to capture it.

On Mont Houy there was prolonged rather close fighting, but the company, now much depleted by losses from machine-gun and shell-fire, gradually overcame the Germans, and eventually forced its way to the summit of the hill and held on there. The left company got to within about 200 yards of La Poirier Station, when machine-gun fire from houses on the canal bank which caught them in the left flank brought their advance to a standstill.

Throughout the afternoon fighting continued in the neighbourhood of Mont Houy, where the situation was very obscure. Finally, after the protective barrage had stopped, the enemy dribbled round the flanks of the position, and by 5 P.M. the remnants of the 6th Black Watch were almost surrounded, and compelled to extricate themselves, falling back to a line between Famars and La Fontenelle.

When the situation had become clear, orders were issued that at dusk the 6/7 Gordon Highlanders, with artillery support, should advance to secure a bridgehead over the Rhonelle river at Aulnoy, while the 6th Black Watch, with one company of the 6th Argyll and Sutherland Highlanders, were ordered to push forward beyond Mont Houy.

At the same time the enemy decided to counter-attack with a view to regaining Famars. It thus happened that while the troops were moving forward to give effect to these orders, the enemy put down a tremendous gas-shell and high-explosive bombardment, which stretched in depth from our foremost trenches to Maing. This bombardment led up to a counter-attack, which succeeded in forcing the 4th and 6/7 Gordon Highlanders out of Famars. They were, however, immediately reorganised at the south end of the village and led forward again. They forced their way back through the village, drove out the enemy, and restored the line.

Meanwhile, on the left, owing to the darkness and the fact that the bombardment had cut all communications, the advance of the 6th Black Watch and 6th Argyll and Sutherland Highlanders was rendered very difficult. However, in spite of this, it was attempted ; but the machine-gun fire was so severe that it offered no prospect of success, and was in consequence abandoned.

Patrols of the 6/7 Gordon Highlanders then advanced, but they found Aulnoy strongly held, and it was therefore decided that for the present no further advance should be contemplated.

During the day 2 officers and 172 other ranks were captured, and many machine-guns. On the right the 4th Division were now established on the line Betterave Farm-Artres.

At the conclusion of the day's fighting the following message was received by the G.O.C. from the Corps Commander :—

" The Corps Commander wishes to compliment the Division on their continued success of yesterday and to-day, and would be glad if you would convey his special congratulations to the 1/6 Argyll and Sutherland Highlanders on their fine repulse of yesterday's counter-attack."

October 27th, though no attack on a large scale was planned, turned out a day of fighting almost as strenuous as that of the last three days, the enemy becoming active and aggressive.

It had been decided that the 154th Brigade should take over the front during the night 26-27th October; but the situation had fluctuated and remained so obscure that this relief was not carried out. Certain reliefs, however, did take place.

The 4th Seaforth Highlanders took over from the 6th Black Watch, the front-line reliefs having to be carried out by the incomers and outgoers dribbling in and out singly, owing to the lightness of the morning. The operation was, however, successfully completed by 9 A.M. On the right one company of the 7th Argyll and Sutherland Highlanders went into the line north of Famars, the remaining three companies holding the line of the railway, while the 6/7 and 4th Gordon Highlanders remained in position under the command of the B.G.C. 154th Brigade.

Famars was now to change hands for a fourth and fifth time. During the morning the enemy continued to shell it heavily, and after an intense bombardment attacked at 10.30 A.M. The 4th Gordon Highlanders were gradually pressed back, and the enemy established posts in the village. A counter-attack was therefore immediately organised. At 12.30 P.M. parties were put out round the flanks, and when these had worked their way forward, the counter-attack companies advanced through the village. The enemy fought stubbornly amongst the houses; but after he had suffered many casualties at the hands of the 4th Gordon Highlanders in heavy street fighting, his resistance collapsed, and the line was again restored east of Famars.

No further infantry action followed, though the enemy continued to shell our front positions viciously, employing large quantities of gas.

In the afternoon, as much movement had been observed in Mont Houy by the artillery observers, a series of five Chinese barrages were fired across it. A mobile section of 4·5 howitzers also did good work, and materially assisted the infantry. 2nd Lieutenant W. Baines, who was in command, established an observation post in Famars, and from it silenced a forward section of German field-guns that were harassing our infantry, and also engaged much enemy movement.

From this point the importance of the capture of Mont Houy increased, as an attack on a wider front south of Valenciennes was now being planned which necessitated the move of the artillery supporting this attack into the valley south of Maing, which was in full view of the summit of Mont Houy. It was of great importance, therefore, to deny to the enemy the use of the hill for purposes of observation.

In view of this attack further readjustments had taken place. The 5th and 6th Seaforth Highlanders had taken over the line on the right and the 4th Seaforth Highlanders on the left. The latter were ordered to carry out an attack against Mont Houy on the morning of 28th October, the 7th Argyll and Sutherland Highlanders being detailed to link up the new line reached with the right brigade front, and to support the attack and exploit it should it be successful.

The final objective was a line from the cross-roads west of Aulnoy to a point 400 yards north of La Poirier Station.

All four companies of the 4th Seaforth Highlanders were launched in this attack at 5.15 A.M., covered by a barrage fired by the artillery, by a machine-gun company on the east bank of the canal, and by machine-guns firing from the railway.

The Seaforths advanced with three companies leading, supported by two sections of machine-guns, and followed by the fourth company 150 yards in rear of the centre.

The right company worked along Mont Houy Wood, two platoons going to the right and two to the left. The Germans were in the wood in strength, but after some hard fighting fifty prisoners were captured and a line established through the wood.

The centre company advanced with great gallantry in the face of heavy shell and machine-gun fire, which was inflicting considerable casualties on them. They captured some forty prisoners defending a quarry at the north-west corner of the wood, and finally reached their objective— a trench north-west of Chemin Vert—after all its ranks had fallen with the exception of twelve men. The effort to reach their objective shown by these twelve survivors after having been shelled and machine-gunned during an advance of 1500 yards shows what a spirit of determination animated the men even after a fortnight's continuous fighting.

The support company at once sent two platoons to reinforce the twelve men, and two platoons to the cemetery east of Aulnoy. The former successfully reached their objective, and captured those Germans that were not killed in the assault. The latter reached the cross-roads, but, owing to the number of houses in the vicinity in which machine-guns were mounted, they were pinned to the ground and surrounded. Their comrades on their left were too closely engaged to render them any help, and it is assumed that they were all either killed or captured.

The company on the left, divided into two waves, reached a line about 400 yards north of La Poirier Station before being held up by machine-gun fire from La Targette. In this advance the first wave captured four machine-guns and the second wave ten, and cleared numerous factories along the canal bank occupied by parties of the enemy.

At 8 A.M., then, the whole of the 4th Seaforth Highlanders were on or close to their objectives, had captured many machine-guns and prisoners, and killed a number of the enemy. They had, however, experienced heavy fighting, and were weakened by serious losses, and had one half-company surrounded and isolated. Parties of the enemy were also still left in Mont Houy Wood.

The situation, however, remained obscure, and as the runners from the most advanced troops had to traverse areas swept by machine-gun bullets, few of them survived to deliver their messages. It was therefore not known in what serious straits the 4th Seaforth Highlanders were. Gradually the enemy dribbled his men in between the posts and began threatening them on their flanks and forcing them back. Machine-guns also were active against them from parts of Mont Houy that had not been entirely cleared.

The 4th Seaforth Highlanders were now too weak to maintain themselves in this situation against the increasing numbers of the enemy, and they were thus gradually forced back, still fighting, to a line running a little north of La Poirier Station, and west and south of Mont Houy Wood, to the junction with the 7th Argyll and Sutherland Highlanders north-west of Famars.

During these operations a company of the 7th Argyll and Sutherland Highlanders that had been waiting in readiness to move forward for exploitation had advanced on its own initiative to the support of the 4th Seaforth Highlanders left, while a second company, having been sent forward to strengthen the centre, found the troops establishing the line just described at about 12 noon and joined them.

In view of the situation, the 6th Argyll and Sutherland Highlanders, who were on the march to rest billets at Lieu St Amand, were turned back to Maing and placed at the disposal of the 154th Brigade.

Fighting went on all day, but there was no substantial alteration in the line. The action had so far resulted in the infantry establishing themselves so close to Mont Houy that it could no longer be used as an observation post, so that the objectives had in some degree been obtained.

At 4 P.M. the artillery fire again became intense along the whole forward area. This was followed by what the enemy intended for a counter-attack. The German infantry had, however, apparently experienced all the fighting that they could endure for one day, and few of them left their trenches. Those that did were easily dispersed with machine-gun and Lewis-gun fire.

During this day's fighting 117 unwounded prisoners were taken.

On the 28th orders had been issued for the relief of the left brigade by the 4th Canadian Division, and of the right

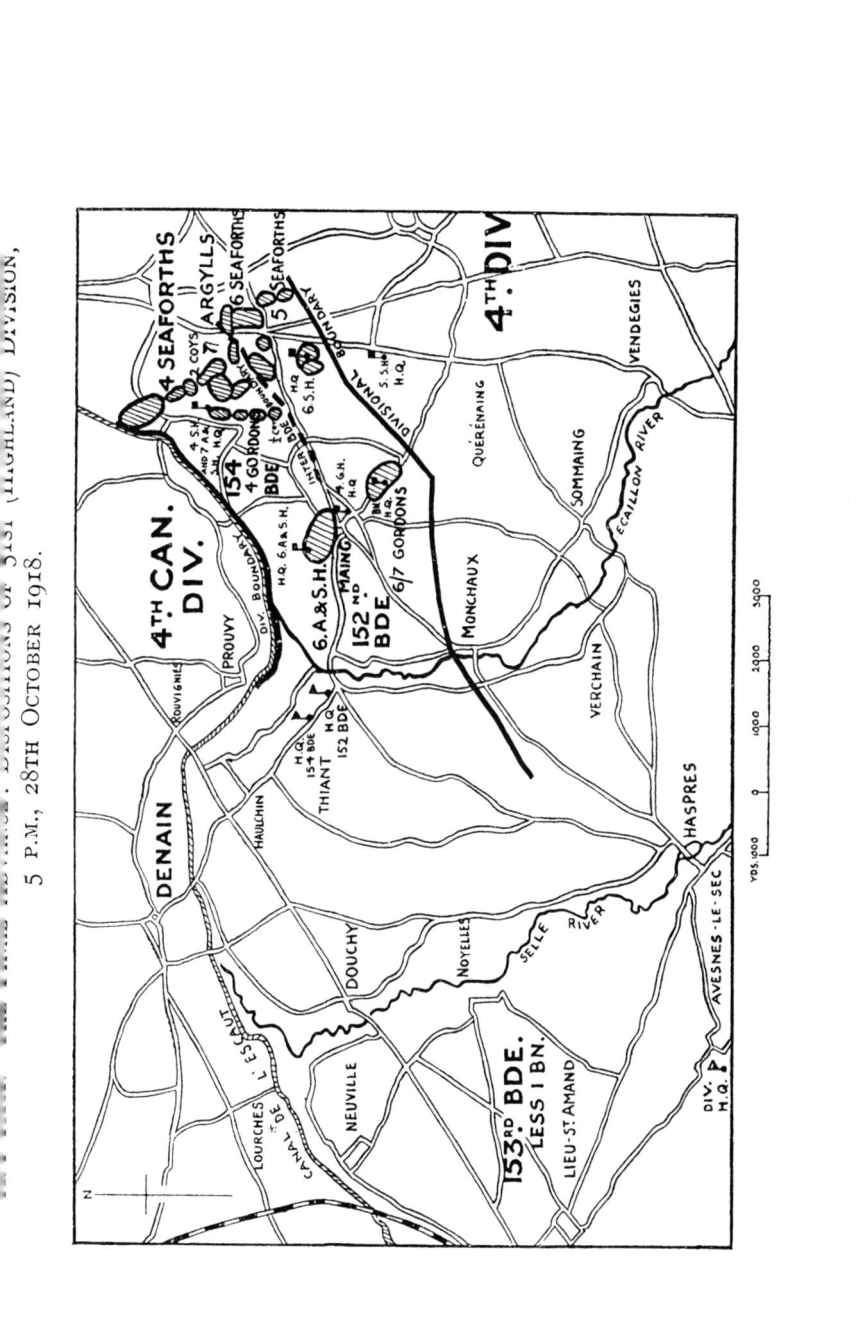

THE FIFTH ARMY: POSITIONS OF 51ST (HIGHLAND) DIVISION,
5 P.M., 28TH OCTOBER 1918.

brigade by the 49th Division. This arrangement had been made to allow the Canadians, whose general line faced Valenciennes from the west, also to attack the town from the south. Only the relief of the 49th Division was, however, carried out, as the situation about Mont Houy was still considered too obscure for adequate arrangements to be made. The relief of the left sector was therefore postponed for twenty-four hours. The troops about Mont Houy were, however, greatly reduced in fighting strength, and were exhausted; the 6th Argyll and Sutherland Highlanders therefore relieved the 4th Seaforth Highlanders and the two companies of the 7th Argyll and Sutherland Highlanders who had joined with them in consolidating the line. One company of the 7th Argyll and Sutherland Highlanders remained in the front line north of Famars.

On 29th October the line of the 6th Argyll and Sutherland Highlanders, who had already successfully dealt with several counter-attacks, was twice tested by the enemy. The night 28-29th had passed quietly, the 6th Argyll and Sutherland Highlanders putting the enemy's inactivity to good use by establishing a post on the southern edge of Mont Houy.

At 6.30 A.M. the enemy attacked on the left, but chiefly on account of the fire which took him in enfilade from the recently established post the attack broke down in front of our lines.

At 4 P.M., after another heavy artillery bombardment, the enemy again attacked, about 250 of his infantry debouching from Mont Houy Wood. The Argylls and machine-gunners, however, stood their ground, and had smothered the attack with their fire before it reached our lines, the new post again giving effective aid.

Meanwhile the G.O.C. 49th Division had taken over command of the Divisional front at 10 A.M.

At 9 P.M., 29th October, the 6th and 7th Argylls, the last of the infantry of the Highland Division to hold the battle front in France, were relieved by the 10th Canadian Infantry Brigade. The Divisional artillery, however, remained in the line, and continued the battle for Valenciennes.

In these operations the Division advanced its line ten miles, captured 661 unwounded prisoners, 164 machine-guns, 4 trench-mortars, 3 minnenwerfers, and 6 anti-tank rifles.

Though the enemy's military power was fast crumpling, the armistice occurring twelve days after the relief of the Division, the resistance encountered, particularly as regards artillery, was at times very formidable. On four occasions attacks were delivered on a two-brigade front, and twice on a one-brigade front, a heavy burden of fighting to be borne in nineteen days by nine battalions of infantry. The casualties were not light, amounting as they did to 112 officers and 2723 other ranks, some battalions suffering particularly heavily, such as the 5th Seaforth Highlanders (14 officers and 409 other ranks), the 6th Seaforth Highlanders (13 officers and 283 other ranks), the 6/7 Gordon Highlanders (16 officers and 425 other ranks), the 7th Argyll and Sutherland Highlanders (8 officers and 294 other ranks), while the 4th Seaforth Highlanders and the 4th Gordon Highlanders lost 13 and 14 officers respectively. Fortunately the numbers of killed and missing—21 officers and 292 men killed, and 6 officers and 184 men missing—were not so proportionately high as had been the case in some of the previous operations.

In few battles did the various arms of the service co-operate more successfully in face of such great difficulties.

The support given by the artillery to the infantry and machine-gunners contributed largely to the success of the advance, inflicted considerable casualties on the enemy, and materially reduced our losses by its effectiveness. This support was largely made possible by the work of the R.E., who, in spite of all the attempts made by the German gunners to hinder their work, completed their bridges in the minimum of time, and so allowed the gunners to keep in close support of the infantry.

As regards the infantry, these battles were a succession of gallant acts and heroism. The 7th Argylls at Lieu St Amand, and again at Thiant, the charge of the 6th Argylls, the forcing of the Ecaillon by the Black Watch battalions, take one back to a war of romance, such as the long days of stationary warfare and stereotyped trench-to-trench attacks had led one to forget. There must, however, always exist a natural feeling of sorrow for the loss of those officers and men who, in many cases after months of continuous

OPERATIONS TOWARDS VALENCIENNES

fighting, gave their lives within a few days of the close of the war, particularly perhaps for those men of the 4th Seaforth Highlanders who pressed on to the farthest point reached by the infantry of the Highland Division in the Great War, and fell at Aulnoy cemetery.

The work of the R.A.M.C. in battle, since it is usually performed during the times when the thoughts of all are naturally turned to the foremost infantry, does not always take its fair place in the public eye. On this occasion it was carried out in face of great difficulties, due to the abnormal conditions. Nevertheless, it reached the same standards which the R.A.M.C. had set for itself in the varying circumstances that had arisen during the retirements in March and April and in the advance in Champagne.

In the first place, the demolition of cross-roads by mines and the blocking of routes by the blowing up of railway arches and bridges rendered the evacuation of casualties a difficult matter. Ford ambulances were, however, employed immediately any route was sufficiently cleared to give them passage. They proved invaluable, as owing to their lightness they could cross fields, pick their way through shell-holes in the roads, climb banks, or be man-handled through soft cut-up ground.

They could therefore in most cases be run up to regimental aid-posts, and in consequence a large amount of their work was done under heavy shell-fire. In the village of Iwuy one Ford was hit twice by shell-fire, one orderly being killed and the M.O. wounded. On both occasions the driver, Private Highmore, D.C.M., M.M., M.T., R.A.S.C., attached 1/2 Highland Field Ambulance, managed temporarily to repair his car under shell-fire and safely evacuate the cases entrusted to him.

During this advance a problem entirely new to the Division arose. The civil population was present in large numbers in the area of active operations, either in process of being evacuated from their homes or of returning from the back areas to villages recently released from the enemy. About one-half of these people were ill, largely owing to exhaustion, exposure, and long-continued under-feeding while in enemy hands. A large proportion of them were tubercular; for instance, in the village of Haulchin, with a population of 1500, over 90 cases of tubercular disease, many of them in an advanced stage, were treated, and this was by no means the total.

Medical attendance of the sick was organised through the field ambulances and M.O.'s of units; in Neuville sur l'Escaut alone over 200 cases were visited in three hours.

Soup kitchens and centres of distribution of bones were installed and handed over to the French authorities in eleven different villages, and it is estimated that over 5000 civilians were supplied with nourishing food, in addition to the rations and medical comforts issued.

On 30th October 3760 rations were issued to the inhabitants of Douchy, Haulchin, Noyelles, Neuville, and Famars.

Thirty-five cases of civilians suffering either from gunshot wounds or gas were also evacuated, most of them from Famars.

The French authorities and the people themselves expressed the greatest appreciation of the work carried out on their behalf by the Division, and especially by the R.A.M.C.

In all the reoccupied areas the sanitation was in a deplorable condition. In view of the enemy's boasted efficiency in this respect, this was probably intentional on his part. The conditions were made worse by the amount of refuse which had to be cleared out of the houses. Owing to the mildness of the weather, these conditions produced a plague of flies. Moreover, incineration, the usual safeguard against them, was seriously handicapped by the fact that it could only be carried out with the greatest caution owing to the number of loose bombs, hand-grenades, and booby traps in general that had been left behind by the enemy. For instance, in Iwuy a bomb had been placed inside a mattress that had been intentionally fouled, with the result that when it was burnt the bomb exploded, wounding two men.

At Douchy a refuse-pit full of dry refuse, inviting incineration, was found on examination to have the bottom layer lined with hand-grenades.

Throughout the operations two parties, each of an officer and ten men of the 172nd Tunnelling Company, were employed in making a systematic search for mines and traps, and a large number of them were found and removed.

The work carried out by the 51st Divisional Ammunition Column in these operations was enormous. They organised and controlled six different ammunition dumps. Throughout they assisted the batteries in the supply of ammunition to the gun line, and at the same time salved and brought forward all ammunition left behind in old gun positions and rear dumps. They also collected the empty cartridge-cases from the vacated gun positions, and thousands of these were salved, boxed, and returned to railhead.

During the operations the D.A.C. handled 229,162 rounds of 18-pounder and 73,000 rounds of 4·5 howitzer ammunition.

The work of the signal company was also heavier than it had been in any other offensive operation. They not only had to compete with an advance of ten miles, but also with the following number of changes in the location of the various headquarters :—

Divisional headquarters with Divisional artillery headquarters	2
152nd Brigade headquarters	6
153rd Brigade headquarters	9
154th Brigade headquarters	5

The fact that Signals were able to maintain an efficient service throughout these operations was largely due to the energy and skill of the officer commanding the 51st Divisional Signal Company, Major J. Muirhead, D.S.O., M.C.

In short, probably no previous operation had demanded a greater or more prolonged effort on the part of all arms and branches of the service than this, the last fight of the Highland Division.

CHAPTER XIX.

CONCLUSION.

THE Divisional artillery came out of action in the neighbourhood of Famars on 2nd November, but returned to the line on 6th November under orders of the C.R.A. 56th Division. They remained attached to the advancing Divisions until the declaration of the armistice at 11 A.M. on 11th November, within forty-eight hours of the second anniversary of the battle of Beaumont Hamel.

With the armistice ends the real history of the Highland Division, and it is well to leave the story of the gradual fading away of the Division during the period of demobilisation untold. Suffice it to say that the last commander who finally hauled down the Divisional flag was Brigadier-General L. Oldfield, C.B., C.M.G., D.S.O., the C.R.A., who had joined the Division on July 1916, and had served longer with it than any other of its Brigadiers.

The last of the battalions that had served with the Division left in Belgium or France was the 8th Argyll and Sutherland Highlanders, who remained at Charleroi under the command of Major Andrew Lockie. Attached to this battalion were a number of non-demobilisable Jocks from many different battalions, and it in consequence came to be known as the 8th Argyll and some other Highlanders.

No history of the Highland Division would be complete without a word spoken about both the incomparable Jock and his adversary the Boche.

That the Boche was such a magnificent fighter reflects more to the credit of the Highland Division probably than any other factor. The picture of the Boche as a fat, crop-eared, spectacled, middle-aged gentleman, holding up his hands and crying " Kamerad," was a libellous portrait of him that appeared almost daily in the illustrated press, and sickened the men who had to fight him.

The German was, in fact, a magnificent worker in trenches, a rifle-shot full of initiative, a machine-gunner whose courage did not fail him up to the last days of the war, an accurate gunner, a skilful and at times very aggressive airman, an infantryman capable of great skill and initiative in his attacks, of prolonged resistance in the defence, and of occasional bursts of great enterprise in raiding.

That the Jocks should have defeated him in every department of the game from 13th November 1916 until 29th October 1918 would not have been so praiseworthy a feat were the military qualities of the Germans less.

As regards the Jock, the men of the Highland Division, while Scotland had men to give, were difficult to equal. Of splendid physique, and with their fine characteristic open countenances, they compared favourably in appearance with the Guards Division.

At Arras in 1916, as one walked round the vast hollow square of Highland soldiers within which the Divisional band of 100 pipers used to play, one felt that one would never be privileged to see the manhood of a nation better expressed, or a nation that could provide a better exhibition of manhood.

Here were men from all those various callings which by their nature tend to give men physical strength—miners, fishermen, farm-servants, gillies, stalkers, all in their prime of life. Later, particularly in 1918, when the Highlands had nothing further to give but her boys, the physique and general appearance of the Division naturally deteriorated. However, though called upon to shoulder a man's burden before their physical development was complete, these same boys, in Champagne and in the last phases of the war, showed that they had at least inherited the spirit of their fathers and elder brothers.

The past records of the Highland regiments had afforded ample proof that the Highlander was well endowed by nature for any form of warfare that he had taken part in prior to the Great War. From the time that they were raised there has hardly been a battle of first importance in which some act of gallantry on the part of one or other of the kilted regiments has not become proverbial. But experience had already proved that this war was not one in which the *arme blanche, élan,* and physical courage, unassisted by considerable tactical skill and the power of prolonged endurance of nerve-shattering things, could hope for success.

Modern conditions of war have, however, only added lustre to the reputation of the Highlander as a fighting man. The Jock soon learned to temper his natural courage and dash with skill and intelligence. He regarded the war not as a sport, but as a business. He took his training seriously, and in consequence was easily trained. In battle his great virtue was that he did not " see red " or lose his head, but coolly and intelligently put into practice what he had learnt in his training. The men had thus the necessary aptitude to be moulded by their commanders into a highly-perfected fighting machine.

According to their own statements, the Germans feared the Highland Division more than any other Division on the Western Front. This was not because it was the most savage, for the Jock was a clean fighter, if anything overkind, but because, after the evil days of High Wood, the Division never knew failure.

One of the great factors on which the reputation of the 51st Division rested was its intense *esprit de division,* which continuously increased as success followed success. No matter in what arm of the service he might be, the Jock was proud of the 51st. As a result, the various arms were all animated by the common ideal of enhancing the reputation of their Division.

This feeling dominated the whole Division from its commanders down to the cook in the Divisional soup kitchen, and the old warrior, some sixty years of age, who drove the Foden disinfector.

Proud of their Division and proud of their record, the *morale* of the Jocks was always maintained at a high pitch throughout the war, with perhaps the exception of the period after the two heavy German attacks with the consequent enormous losses in March and April 1918.

During this period the Division was so decimated and so exhausted that a fear existed that it might never regain its old fighting efficiency. However, a quiet tour of trench life on the familiar Vimy Ridge soon dispelled this fear, and the Division was able to give as good an account of itself as ever when fighting alongside the French in Champagne in the following July and August.

In billets the Jock was as good a soldier as he was in the field; crime, apart from the most minor offences, was almost non-existent. The periods of rest, which were seldom long, were ungrudgingly devoted to restoring uniform and equipment to an almost pre-war standard of smartness and to training for further encounters.

The inhabitants of France and Belgium had a deep affection for *les Écossais* and the 51st. This, no doubt, was in a measure due to the Highland dress, but more particularly to the natural courtesy and kindly disposition of the Jocks.

It will always remain a mystery how the Jock understood the patois of the natives, and how the natives understood the mixture of broad Scots and bad French which the Jock employed. The fact remained that their disabilities in respect of language apparently placed little restriction on their intimacy with one another.

For many years to come the inhabitants of the erstwhile British lines in France and Belgium will regard the 51st (Highland) Division not only with admiration for their fighting qualities, but also with deep affection for that gallant gentleman, the Jock.